Access Your Online Resources

Don't miss out on the Online Resources included with your purchase!

Your purchase of this product unlocks access to our Online Resources page. Elevate your study experience with our **interactive practice test interface**, along with all of the additional resources that we couldn't include in this book.

Flip to the Online Resources section at the end of this book to find the link and a QR code to get started!

Mometrix
TEST PREPARATION

Mometrix
TEST PREPARATION

TABE® 13 and 14 Study Guide

3 Full-Length Practice Tests

TABE® Exam Prep Secrets Book with Step-by-Step Video Tutorials

Includes Detailed Answer Explanations

Written and edited by Matthew Bowling

Printed in the United States of America

This paper meets the requirements of ANSI/NISO Z39.48-1992 (Permanence of Paper).

Mometrix offers volume discount pricing to institutions. For more information or a price quote, please contact our sales department at sales@mometrix.com or 888-248-1219.

ISBN 13: 978-1-5167-2803-9
ISBN 10: 1-5167-2803-3

Dear Future Exam Success Story

First of all, **THANK YOU** for purchasing Mometrix study materials!

Second, congratulations! You are one of the few determined test-takers who are committed to doing whatever it takes to excel on your exam. **You have come to the right place.** We developed these study materials with one goal in mind: to deliver you the information you need in a format that's concise and easy to use.

In addition to optimizing your guide for the content of the test, we've outlined our recommended steps for breaking down the preparation process into small, attainable goals so you can make sure you stay on track.

We've also analyzed the entire test-taking process, identifying the most common pitfalls and showing how you can overcome them and be ready for any curveball the test throws you.

Standardized testing is one of the biggest obstacles on your road to success, which only increases the importance of doing well in the high-pressure, high-stakes environment of test day. Your results on this test could have a significant impact on your future, and this guide provides the information and practical advice to help you achieve your full potential on test day.

Your success is our success

We would love to hear from you! If you would like to share the story of your exam success or if you have any questions or comments in regard to our products, please contact us at **800-673-8175** or **support@mometrix.com**.

Thanks again for your business and we wish you continued success!

Sincerely,
The Mometrix Test Preparation Team

Need more help? Check out our flashcards at:
https://mometrixflashcards.com/TABE

TABLE OF CONTENTS

Introduction

Thank you for purchasing this resource! You have made the choice to prepare yourself for a test that could have a huge impact on your future, and this guide is designed to help you be fully ready for test day. Obviously, it's important to have a solid understanding of the test material, but you also need to be prepared for the unique environment and stressors of the test, so that you can perform to the best of your abilities.

For this purpose, the first section that appears in this guide is the **Secret Keys**. We've devoted countless hours to meticulously researching what works and what doesn't, and we've boiled down our findings to the five most impactful steps you can take to improve your performance on the test. We start at the beginning with study planning and move through the preparation process, all the way to the testing strategies that will help you get the most out of what you know when you're finally sitting in front of the test.

We recommend that you start preparing for your test as far in advance as possible. However, if you've bought this guide as a last-minute study resource and only have a few days before your test, we recommend that you skip over the first two Secret Keys since they address a long-term study plan.

If you struggle with **test anxiety**, we strongly encourage you to check out our recommendations for how you can overcome it. Test anxiety is a formidable foe, but it can be beaten, and we want to make sure you have the tools you need to defeat it.

Review Video Directory

As you work your way through this guide, you will see numerous review video links interspersed with the written content. If you would like to access all of these review videos in one place, click on the video directory link found on the online resources page: **mometrix.com/resources719/tabe1314**

Secret Key #1 – Plan Big, Study Small

There's a lot riding on your performance. If you want to ace this test, you're going to need to keep your skills sharp and the material fresh in your mind. You need a plan that lets you review everything you need to know while still fitting in your schedule. We'll break this strategy down into three categories.

Information Organization

Start with the information you already have: the official test outline. From this, you can make a complete list of all the concepts you need to cover before the test. Organize these concepts into groups that can be studied together, and create a list of any related vocabulary you need to learn so you can brush up on any difficult terms. You'll want to keep this vocabulary list handy once you actually start studying since you may need to add to it along the way.

Time Management

Once you have your set of study concepts, decide how to spread them out over the time you have left before the test. Break your study plan into small, clear goals so you have a manageable task for each day and know exactly what you're doing. Then just focus on one small step at a time. When you manage your time this way, you don't need to spend hours at a time studying. Studying a small block of content for a short period each day helps you retain information better and avoid stressing over how much you have left to do. You can relax knowing that you have a plan to cover everything in time. In order for this strategy to be effective though, you have to start studying early and stick to your schedule. Avoid the exhaustion and futility that comes from last-minute cramming!

Study Environment

The environment you study in has a big impact on your learning. Studying in a coffee shop, while probably more enjoyable, is not likely to be as fruitful as studying in a quiet room. It's important to keep distractions to a minimum. You're only planning to study for a short block of time, so make the most of it. Don't pause to check your phone or get up to find a snack. It's also important to **avoid multitasking**. Research has consistently shown that multitasking will make your studying dramatically less effective. Your study area should also be comfortable and well-lit so you don't have the distraction of straining your eyes or sitting on an uncomfortable chair.

The time of day you study is also important. You want to be rested and alert. Don't wait until just before bedtime. Study when you'll be most likely to comprehend and remember. Even better, if you know what time of day your test will be, set that time aside for study. That way your brain will be used to working on that subject at that specific time and you'll have a better chance of recalling information.

Finally, it can be helpful to team up with others who are studying for the same test. Your actual studying should be done in as isolated an environment as possible, but the work of organizing the information and setting up the study plan can be divided up. In between study sessions, you can discuss with your teammates the concepts that you're all studying and quiz each other on the details. Just be sure that your teammates are as serious about the test as you are. If you find that your study time is being replaced with social time, you might need to find a new team.

Secret Key #2 – Make Your Studying Count

You're devoting a lot of time and effort to preparing for this test, so you want to be absolutely certain it will pay off. This means doing more than just reading the content and hoping you can remember it on test day. It's important to make every minute of study count. There are two main areas you can focus on to make your studying count.

Retention

It doesn't matter how much time you study if you can't remember the material. You need to make sure you are retaining the concepts. To check your retention of the information you're learning, try recalling it at later times with minimal prompting. Try carrying around flashcards and glance at one or two from time to time or ask a friend who's also studying for the test to quiz you.

To enhance your retention, look for ways to put the information into practice so that you can apply it rather than simply recalling it. If you're using the information in practical ways, it will be much easier to remember. Similarly, it helps to solidify a concept in your mind if you're not only reading it to yourself but also explaining it to someone else. Ask a friend to let you teach them about a concept you're a little shaky on (or speak aloud to an imaginary audience if necessary). As you try to summarize, define, give examples, and answer your friend's questions, you'll understand the concepts better and they will stay with you longer. Finally, step back for a big picture view and ask yourself how each piece of information fits with the whole subject. When you link the different concepts together and see them working together as a whole, it's easier to remember the individual components.

Finally, practice showing your work on any multi-step problems, even if you're just studying. Writing out each step you take to solve a problem will help solidify the process in your mind, and you'll be more likely to remember it during the test.

Modality

Modality simply refers to the means or method by which you study. Choosing a study modality that fits your own individual learning style is crucial. No two people learn best in exactly the same way, so it's important to know your strengths and use them to your advantage.

For example, if you learn best by visualization, focus on visualizing a concept in your mind and draw an image or a diagram. Try color-coding your notes, illustrating them, or creating symbols that will trigger your mind to recall a learned concept. If you learn best by hearing or discussing information, find a study partner who learns the same way or read aloud to yourself. Think about how to put the information in your own words. Imagine that you are giving a lecture on the topic and record yourself so you can listen to it later.

For any learning style, flashcards can be helpful. Organize the information so you can take advantage of spare moments to review. Underline key words or phrases. Use different colors for different categories. Mnemonic devices (such as creating a short list in which every item starts with the same letter) can also help with retention. Find what works best for you and use it to store the information in your mind most effectively and easily.

Secret Key #3 – Practice the Right Way

Your success on test day depends not only on how many hours you put into preparing, but also on whether you prepared the right way. It's good to check along the way to see if your studying is paying off. One of the most effective ways to do this is by taking practice tests to evaluate your progress. Practice tests are useful because they show exactly where you need to improve. Every time you take a practice test, pay special attention to these three groups of questions:

- The questions you got wrong
- The questions you had to guess on, even if you guessed right
- The questions you found difficult or slow to work through

This will show you exactly what your weak areas are, and where you need to devote more study time. Ask yourself why each of these questions gave you trouble. Was it because you didn't understand the material? Was it because you didn't remember the vocabulary? Do you need more repetitions on this type of question to build speed and confidence? Dig into those questions and figure out how you can strengthen your weak areas as you go back to review the material.

Additionally, many practice tests have a section explaining the answer choices. It can be tempting to read the explanation and think that you now have a good understanding of the concept. However, an explanation likely only covers part of the question's broader context. Even if the explanation makes perfect sense, **go back and investigate** every concept related to the question until you're positive you have a thorough understanding.

As you go along, keep in mind that the practice test is just that: practice. Memorizing these questions and answers will not be very helpful on the actual test because it is unlikely to have any of the same exact questions. If you only know the right answers to the sample questions, you won't be prepared for the real thing. **Study the concepts** until you understand them fully, and then you'll be able to answer any question that shows up on the test.

It's important to wait on the practice tests until you're ready. If you take a test on your first day of study, you may be overwhelmed by the amount of material covered and how much you need to learn. Work up to it gradually.

On test day, you'll need to be prepared for answering questions, managing your time, and using the test-taking strategies you've learned. It's a lot to balance, like a mental marathon that will have a big impact on your future. Like training for a marathon, you'll need to start slowly and work your way up. When test day arrives, you'll be ready.

Start with the strategies you've read in the first two Secret Keys—plan your course and study in the way that works best for you. If you have time, consider using multiple study resources to get different approaches to the same concepts. It can be helpful to see difficult concepts from more than one angle. Then find a good source for practice tests. Many times, the test website will suggest potential study resources or provide sample tests.

Practice Test Strategy

If you're able to find at least three practice tests, we recommend this strategy:

Untimed and Open-Book Practice

Take the first test with no time constraints and with your notes and study guide handy. Take your time and focus on applying the strategies you've learned.

Timed and Open-Book Practice

Take the second practice test open-book as well, but set a timer and practice pacing yourself to finish in time.

Timed and Closed-Book Practice

Take any other practice tests as if it were test day. Set a timer and put away your study materials. Sit at a table or desk in a quiet room, imagine yourself at the testing center, and answer questions as quickly and accurately as possible.

Keep repeating timed and closed-book tests on a regular basis until you run out of practice tests or it's time for the actual test. Your mind will be ready for the schedule and stress of test day, and you'll be able to focus on recalling the material you've learned.

Secret Key #4 – Pace Yourself

Once you're fully prepared for the material on the test, your biggest challenge on test day will be managing your time. Just knowing that the clock is ticking can make you panic even if you have plenty of time left. Work on pacing yourself so you can build confidence against the time constraints of the exam. Pacing is a difficult skill to master, especially in a high-pressure environment, so **practice is vital**.

Set time expectations for your pace based on how much time is available. For example, if a section has 60 questions and the time limit is 30 minutes, you know you have to average 30 seconds or less per question in order to answer them all. Although 30 seconds is the hard limit, set 25 seconds per question as your goal, so you reserve extra time to spend on harder questions. When you budget extra time for the harder questions, you no longer have any reason to stress when those questions take longer to answer.

Don't let this time expectation distract you from working through the test at a calm, steady pace, but keep it in mind so you don't spend too much time on any one question. Recognize that taking extra time on one question you don't understand may keep you from answering two that you do understand later in the test. If your time limit for a question is up and you're still not sure of the answer, mark it and move on, and come back to it later if the time and the test format allow. If the testing format doesn't allow you to return to earlier questions, just make an educated guess; then put it out of your mind and move on.

On the easier questions, be careful not to rush. It may seem wise to hurry through them so you have more time for the challenging ones, but it's not worth missing one if you know the concept and just didn't take the time to read the question fully. Work efficiently but make sure you understand the question and have looked at all of the answer choices, since more than one may seem right at first.

Even if you're paying attention to the time, you may find yourself a little behind at some point. You should speed up to get back on track, but do so wisely. Don't panic; just take a few seconds less on each question until you're caught up. Don't guess without thinking, but do look through the answer choices and eliminate any you know are wrong. If you can get down to two choices, it is often worthwhile to guess from those. Once you've chosen an answer, move on and don't dwell on any that you skipped or had to hurry through. If a question was taking too long, chances are it was one of the harder ones, so you weren't as likely to get it right anyway.

On the other hand, if you find yourself getting ahead of schedule, it may be beneficial to slow down a little. The more quickly you work, the more likely you are to make a careless mistake that will affect your score. You've budgeted time for each question, so don't be afraid to spend that time. Practice an efficient but careful pace to get the most out of the time you have.

Secret Key #5 – Have a Plan for Guessing

When you're taking the test, you may find yourself stuck on a question. Some of the answer choices seem better than others, but you don't see the one answer choice that is obviously correct. What do you do?

The scenario described above is very common, yet most test takers have not effectively prepared for it. Developing and practicing a plan for guessing may be one of the single most effective uses of your time as you get ready for the exam.

In developing your plan for guessing, there are three questions to address:

- When should you start the guessing process?
- How should you narrow down the choices?
- Which answer should you choose?

When to Start the Guessing Process

Unless your plan for guessing is to select C every time (which, despite its merits, is not what we recommend), you need to leave yourself enough time to apply your answer elimination strategies. Since you have a limited amount of time for each question, that means that if you're going to give yourself the best shot at guessing correctly, you have to decide quickly whether or not you will guess.

Of course, the best-case scenario is that you don't have to guess at all, so first, see if you can answer the question based on your knowledge of the subject and basic reasoning skills. Focus on the key words in the question and try to jog your memory of related topics. Give yourself a chance to bring the knowledge to mind, but once you realize that you don't have (or you can't access) the knowledge you need to answer the question, it's time to start the guessing process.

It's almost always better to start the guessing process too early than too late. It only takes a few seconds to remember something and answer the question from knowledge. Carefully eliminating wrong answer choices takes longer. Plus, going through the process of eliminating answer choices can actually help jog your memory.

Summary: Start the guessing process as soon as you decide that you can't answer the question based on your knowledge.

How to Narrow Down the Choices

The next chapter in this book (**Test-Taking Strategies**) includes a wide range of strategies for how to approach questions and how to look for answer choices to eliminate. You will definitely want to read those carefully, practice them, and figure out which ones work best for you. Here though, we're going to address a mindset rather than a particular strategy.

Your odds of guessing an answer correctly depend on how many options you are choosing from.

Number of options left	5	4	3	2	1
Odds of guessing correctly	20%	25%	33%	50%	100%

You can see from this chart just how valuable it is to be able to eliminate incorrect answers and make an educated guess, but there are two things that many test takers do that cause them to miss out on the benefits of guessing:

- Accidentally eliminating the correct answer
- Selecting an answer based on an impression

We'll look at the first one here, and the second one in the next section.

To avoid accidentally eliminating the correct answer, we recommend a thought exercise called **the $5 challenge**. In this challenge, you only eliminate an answer choice from contention if you are willing to bet $5 on it being wrong. Why $5? Five dollars is a small but not insignificant amount of money. It's an amount you could afford to lose but wouldn't want to throw away. And while losing $5 once might not hurt too much, doing it twenty times will set you back $100. In the same way, each small decision you make—eliminating a choice here, guessing on a question there—won't by itself impact your score very much, but when you put them all together, they can make a big difference. By holding each answer choice elimination decision to a higher standard, you can reduce the risk of accidentally eliminating the correct answer.

The $5 challenge can also be applied in a positive sense: If you are willing to bet $5 that an answer choice *is* correct, go ahead and mark it as correct.

Summary: Only eliminate an answer choice if you are willing to bet $5 that it is wrong.

Which Answer to Choose

You're taking the test. You've run into a hard question and decided you'll have to guess. You've eliminated all the answer choices you're willing to bet $5 on. Now you have to pick an answer. Why do we even need to talk about this? Why can't you just pick whichever one you feel like when the time comes?

The answer to these questions is that if you don't come into the test with a plan, you'll rely on your impression to select an answer choice, and if you do that, you risk falling into a trap. The test writers know that everyone who takes their test will be guessing on some of the questions, so they intentionally write wrong answer choices to seem plausible. You still have to pick an answer though, and if the wrong answer choices are designed to look right, how can you ever be sure that you're not falling for their trap? The best solution we've found to this dilemma is to take the decision out of your hands entirely. Here is the process we recommend:

Once you've eliminated any choices that you are confident (willing to bet $5) are wrong, select the first remaining choice as your answer.

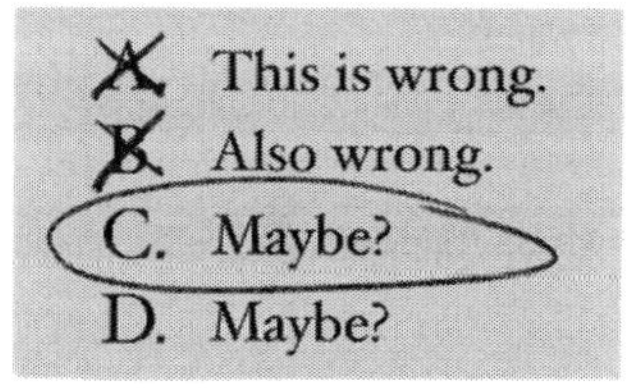

Whether you choose to select the first remaining choice, the second, or the last, the important thing is that you use some preselected standard. Using this approach guarantees that you will not be enticed into selecting an answer choice that looks right, because you are not basing your decision on how the answer choices look.

This is not meant to make you question your knowledge. Instead, it is to help you recognize the difference between your knowledge and your impressions. There's a huge difference between thinking an answer is right because of what you know, and thinking an answer is right because it looks or sounds like it should be right.

Summary: To ensure that your selection is appropriately random, make a predetermined selection from among all answer choices you have not eliminated.

Test-Taking Strategies

This section contains a list of test-taking strategies that you may find helpful as you work through the test. By taking what you know and applying logical thought, you can maximize your chances of answering any question correctly!

It is very important to realize that every question is different and every person is different: no single strategy will work on every question, and no single strategy will work for every person. That's why we've included all of them here, so you can try them out and determine which ones work best for different types of questions and which ones work best for you.

Question Strategies

✓ Read Carefully

Read the question and the answer choices carefully. Don't miss the question because you misread the terms. You have plenty of time to read each question thoroughly and make sure you understand what is being asked. Yet a happy medium must be attained, so don't waste too much time. You must read carefully and efficiently.

✓ Contextual Clues

Look for contextual clues. If the question includes a word you are not familiar with, look at the immediate context for some indication of what the word might mean. Contextual clues can often give you all the information you need to decipher the meaning of an unfamiliar word. Even if you can't determine the meaning, you may be able to narrow down the possibilities enough to make a solid guess at the answer to the question.

✓ Prefixes

If you're having trouble with a word in the question or answer choices, try dissecting it. Take advantage of every clue that the word might include. Prefixes can be a huge help. Usually, they allow you to determine a basic meaning. *Pre-* means before, *post-* means after, *pro-* is positive, *de-* is negative. From prefixes, you can get an idea of the general meaning of the word and try to put it into context.

✓ Hedge Words

Watch out for critical hedge words, such as *likely, may, can, often, almost, mostly, usually, generally, rarely,* and *sometimes.* Question writers insert these hedge phrases to cover every possibility. Often an answer choice will be wrong simply because it leaves no room for exception. Be on guard for answer choices that have definitive words such as *exactly* and *always.*

✓ Switchback Words

Stay alert for *switchbacks.* These are the words and phrases frequently used to alert you to shifts in thought. The most common switchback words are *but, although,* and *however.* Others include *nevertheless, on the other hand, even though, while, in spite of, despite,* and *regardless of.* Switchback words are important to catch because they can change the direction of the question or an answer choice.

✓ Face Value

When in doubt, use common sense. Accept the situation in the problem at face value. Don't read too much into it. These problems will not require you to make wild assumptions. If you have to go beyond creativity and warp time or space in order to have an answer choice fit the question, then you should move on and consider the other answer choices. These are normal problems rooted in reality. The applicable relationship or explanation may not be readily apparent, but it is there for you to figure out. Use your common sense to interpret anything that isn't clear.

Answer Choice Strategies

⊘ Answer Selection

The most thorough way to pick an answer choice is to identify and eliminate wrong answers until only one is left, then confirm it is the correct answer. Sometimes an answer choice may immediately seem right, but be careful. The test writers will usually put more than one reasonable answer choice on each question, so take a second to read all of them and make sure that the other choices are not equally obvious. As long as you have time left, it is better to read every answer choice than to pick the first one that looks right without checking the others.

⊘ Answer Choice Families

An answer choice family consists of two (in rare cases, three) answer choices that are very similar in construction and cannot all be true at the same time. If you see two answer choices that are direct opposites or parallels, one of them is usually the correct answer. For instance, if one answer choice says that quantity *x* increases and another either says that quantity *x* decreases (opposite) or says that quantity *y* increases (parallel), then those answer choices would fall into the same family. An answer choice that doesn't match the construction of the answer choice family is more likely to be incorrect. Most questions will not have answer choice families, but when they do appear, you should be prepared to recognize them.

⊘ Eliminate Answers

Eliminate answer choices as soon as you realize they are wrong, but make sure you consider all possibilities. If you are eliminating answer choices and realize that the last one you are left with is also wrong, don't panic. Start over and consider each choice again. There may be something you missed the first time that you will realize on the second pass.

⊘ Avoid Fact Traps

Don't be distracted by an answer choice that is factually true but doesn't answer the question. You are looking for the choice that answers the question. Stay focused on what the question is asking for so you don't accidentally pick an answer that is true but incorrect. Always go back to the question and make sure the answer choice you've selected actually answers the question and is not merely a true statement.

⊘ Extreme Statements

In general, you should avoid answers that put forth extreme actions as standard practice or proclaim controversial ideas as established fact. An answer choice that states the "process should be used in certain situations, if..." is much more likely to be correct than one that states the "process should be discontinued completely." The first is a calm rational statement and doesn't even make a definitive, uncompromising stance, using a hedge word *if* to provide wiggle room, whereas the second choice is far more extreme.

⊘ Benchmark

As you read through the answer choices and you come across one that seems to answer the question well, mentally select that answer choice. This is not your final answer, but it's the one that will help you evaluate the other answer choices. The one that you selected is your benchmark or standard for judging each of the other answer choices. Every other answer choice must be compared to your benchmark. That choice is correct until proven otherwise by another answer choice beating it. If you find a better answer, then that one becomes your new benchmark. Once you've decided that no other choice answers the question as well as your benchmark, you have your final answer.

⊘ Predict the Answer

Before you even start looking at the answer choices, it is often best to try to predict the answer. When you come up with the answer on your own, it is easier to avoid distractions and traps because you will know exactly what to look for. The right answer choice is unlikely to be word-for-word what you came up with, but it should be a close match. Even if you are confident that you have the right answer, you should still take the time to read each option before moving on.

General Strategies

⊘ Tough Questions

If you are stumped on a problem or it appears too hard or too difficult, don't waste time. Move on! Remember though, if you can quickly check for obviously incorrect answer choices, your chances of guessing correctly are greatly improved. Before you completely give up, at least try to knock out a couple of possible answers. Eliminate what you can and then guess at the remaining answer choices before moving on.

⊘ Check Your Work

Since you will probably not know every term listed and the answer to every question, it is important that you get credit for the ones that you do know. Don't miss any questions through careless mistakes. If at all possible, try to take a second to look back over your answer selection and make sure you've selected the correct answer choice and haven't made a costly careless mistake (such as marking an answer choice that you didn't mean to mark). This quick double check should more than pay for itself in caught mistakes for the time it costs.

⊘ Pace Yourself

It's easy to be overwhelmed when you're looking at a page full of questions; your mind is confused and full of random thoughts, and the clock is ticking down faster than you would like. Calm down and maintain the pace that you have set for yourself. Especially as you get down to the last few minutes of the test, don't let the small numbers on the clock make you panic. As long as you are on track by monitoring your pace, you are guaranteed to have time for each question.

⊘ Don't Rush

It is very easy to make errors when you are in a hurry. Maintaining a fast pace in answering questions is pointless if it makes you miss questions that you would have gotten right otherwise. Test writers like to include distracting information and wrong answers that seem right. Taking a little extra time to avoid careless mistakes can make all the difference in your test score. Find a pace that allows you to be confident in the answers that you select.

⊘ Keep Moving

Panicking will not help you pass the test, so do your best to stay calm and keep moving. Taking deep breaths and going through the answer elimination steps you practiced can help to break through a stress barrier and keep your pace.

Final Notes

The combination of a solid foundation of content knowledge and the confidence that comes from practicing your plan for applying that knowledge is the key to maximizing your performance on test day. As your foundation of content knowledge is built up and strengthened, you'll find that the strategies included in this chapter become more and more effective in helping you quickly sift through the distractions and traps of the test to isolate the correct answer.

Now that you're preparing to move forward into the test content chapters of this book, be sure to keep your goal in mind. As you read, think about how you will be able to apply this information on the test. If you've already seen sample questions for the test and you have an idea of the question format and style, try to come up with questions of your own that you can answer based on what you're reading. This will give you valuable practice applying your knowledge in the same ways you can expect to on test day.

Good luck and good studying!

Three-Week TABE Study Plan

On the next few pages, we've provided an optional study plan to help you use this study guide to its fullest potential over the course of three weeks. If you have six weeks available and want to spread it out more, spend two weeks on each section of the plan.

Below is a quick summary of the subjects covered in each week of the plan.

- Week 1: Reading
- Week 2: Language
- Week 3: Mathematics

Please note that not all subjects will take the same amount of time to work through.

Two full-length practice tests are included in this study guide. We recommend saving any additional tests until after you've completed the study plan. Take these practice tests without any reference materials a day or two before the real thing as practice runs to get you in the mode of answering questions at a good pace.

Week 1: Reading

Instructional Content

First, read carefully through the Reading chapters in this book, checking off your progress as you go:

- ❑ Informational Texts
- ❑ Persuasive Techniques
- ❑ Arguments and Logical Errors
- ❑ Figurative Language
- ❑ Reading Comprehension
- ❑ Interactions with Texts

As you read, do the following:

- Highlight any sections, terms, or concepts you think are important
- Draw an asterisk (*) next to any areas you are struggling with
- Watch the review videos to gain more understanding of a particular topic
- Take notes in your notebook or in the margins of this book

After you've read through everything, go back and review any sections that you highlighted or that you drew an asterisk next to, referencing your notes along the way.

Practice Test #1

Now that you've read over the instructional content, it's time to take a practice test. Complete the Reading Practice Questions section of Practice Test #1. Take this test with **no time constraints**, and feel free to reference the applicable sections of this guide as you go. Once you've finished, check your answers against the provided answer key. For any questions you answered incorrectly, review the answer rationale, and then **go back and review** the applicable sections of the book. The goal in this stage is to understand why you answered the question incorrectly, and make sure that the next time you see a similar question, you will get it right.

Practice Test #2

Next, take the Reading Practice Questions section of Practice Test #2. This time, give yourself **100 minutes** (the amount of time you will have on the real TABE) to complete all of the questions. You should again feel free to reference the guide and your notes, but be mindful of the clock. If you run out of time before you finish all of the questions, mark where you were when time expired, but go ahead and finish taking the practice test. Once you've finished, check your answers against the provided answer key and as before, review the answer rationale for any that you answered incorrectly and go back and review the associated instructional content. Your goal is still to increase understanding of the content but also to get used to the time constraints you will face on the test.

Week 2: Language

Instructional Content

First, read carefully through the Language chapters in this book, checking off your progress as you go:

❑ Foundations of Grammar
❑ Agreement and Sentence Structure
❑ Punctuation
❑ Common Usage Mistakes
❑ The Writing Process
❑ Outlining and Organizing Ideas
❑ Style and Form
❑ Modes of Writing
❑ Vocabulary and Word Relationships

As you read, do the following:

- Highlight any sections, terms, or concepts you think are important
- Draw an asterisk (*) next to any areas you are struggling with
- Watch the review videos to gain more understanding of a particular topic
- Take notes in your notebook or in the margins of this book

After you've read through everything, go back and review any sections that you highlighted or that you drew an asterisk next to, referencing your notes along the way.

Practice Test #1

Now that you've read over the instructional content, it's time to take a practice test. Complete the Language Practice Questions section of Practice Test #1. Take this test with **no time constraints**, and feel free to reference the applicable sections of this guide as you go. Once you've finished, check your answers against the provided answer key. For any questions you answered incorrectly, review the answer rationale, and then **go back and review** the applicable sections of the book. The goal in this stage is to understand why you answered the question incorrectly, and make sure that the next time you see a similar question, you will get it right.

Practice Test #2

Next, take the Language Practice Questions section of Practice Test #2. This time, give yourself **50 minutes** (the amount of time you will have on the real TABE) to complete all of the questions. You should again feel free to reference the guide and your notes, but be mindful of the clock. If you run out of time before you finish all of the questions, mark where you were when time expired, but go ahead and finish taking the practice test. Once you've finished, check your answers against the provided answer key, and as before, review the answer rationale for any that you answered incorrectly and then go back and review the associated instructional content. Your goal is still to increase understanding of the content but also to get used to the time constraints you will face on the test.

Week 3: Mathematics Test

Instructional Content

First, read carefully through the Mathematics chapters in this book, checking off your progress as you go:

- ❑ Numbers and Operations
- ❑ Factoring
- ❑ Rational Numbers
- ❑ Proportions and Ratios
- ❑ Expressions and Equations
- ❑ Inequalities
- ❑ Systems of Equations
- ❑ Polynomial Algebra
- ❑ Quadratics
- ❑ Basic and Advanced Functions
- ❑ Measurement Principles
- ❑ Units of Measurement
- ❑ Lines, Planes, and Angles
- ❑ Transformations
- ❑ Two- and Three- Dimensional Shapes
- ❑ Triangles and Trigonometry
- ❑ Probability
- ❑ Statistics and Statistical Analysis
- ❑ Displaying Information

As you read, do the following:

- Highlight any sections, terms, or concepts you think are important
- Draw an asterisk (*) next to any areas you are struggling with
- Watch the review videos to gain more understanding of a particular topic
- Take notes in your notebook or in the margins of this book

After you've read through everything, go back and review any sections that you highlighted or that you drew an asterisk next to, referencing your notes along the way.

Practice Test #1

Now that you've read over the instructional content, it's time to take a practice test. Complete the Mathematics Practice Questions section of Practice Test #1. Take this test with **no time constraints**, and feel free to reference the applicable sections of this guide as you go. Once you've finished, check your answers against the provided answer key. For any questions you answered incorrectly, review the answer rationale, and then **go back and review** the applicable sections of the book. The goal in this stage is to understand why you answered the question incorrectly, and make sure that the next time you see a similar question, you will get it right.

Practice Test #2

Next, take the Mathematics Practice Questions section of Practice Test #2. This time, give yourself **60 minutes** (the amount of time you will have on the real TABE) to complete all of the questions. You should again feel free to reference the guide and your notes, but be mindful of the clock. If you run out of time before you finish all of the questions, mark where you were when time expired, but go ahead and finish taking the practice test. Once you've finished, check your answers against the provided answer key, and as before, review the answer rationale for any that you answered incorrectly and then go back and review the associated instructional content. Your goal is still to increase understanding of the content but also to get used to the time constraints you will face on the test.

Reading

Key Ideas and Details

Main Ideas and Supporting Details

Identifying Topics and Main Ideas

One of the most important skills in reading comprehension is the identification of **topics** and **main ideas**. There is a subtle difference between these two features. The topic is the subject of a text (i.e., what the text is all about). The main idea, on the other hand, is the most important point being made by the author. The topic is usually expressed in a few words at the most while the main idea often needs a full sentence to be completely defined. As an example, a short passage might be written on the topic of penguins, and the main idea could be written as *Penguins are different from other birds in many ways.* In most nonfiction writing, the topic and the main idea will be **stated directly** and often appear in a sentence at the very beginning or end of the text. When being tested on an understanding of the author's topic, you may be able to skim the passage for the general idea by reading only the first sentence of each paragraph. A body paragraph's first sentence is often—but not always—the main **topic sentence** which gives you a summary of the content in the paragraph.

However, there are cases in which the reader must figure out an **unstated** topic or main idea. In these instances, you must read every sentence of the text and try to come up with an overarching idea that is supported by each of those sentences.

Note: The main idea should not be confused with the thesis statement. While the main idea gives a brief, general summary of a text, the thesis statement provides a **specific perspective** on an issue that the author supports with evidence.

Review Video: Topics and Main Ideas
Visit mometrix.com/academy and enter code: 407801

Supporting Details

Supporting details are smaller pieces of evidence that provide backing for the main point. In order to show that a main idea is correct or valid, an author must add details that prove their point. All texts contain details, but they are only classified as supporting details when they serve to reinforce some larger point. Supporting details are most commonly found in informative and persuasive texts. In some cases, they will be clearly indicated with terms like *for example* or *for instance*, or they will be enumerated with terms like *first, second,* and *last.* However, you need to be prepared for texts that do not contain those indicators. As a reader, you should consider whether the author's supporting details really back up his or her main point. Details can be factual and correct, yet they may not be **relevant** to the author's point. Conversely, details can be relevant, but be ineffective because they are based on opinion or assertions that cannot be proven.

Review Video: Supporting Details
Visit mometrix.com/academy and enter code: 396297

Author's Purpose

Author's Purpose

Usually, identifying the author's **purpose** is easier than identifying his or her **position**. In most cases, the author has no interest in hiding his or her purpose. A text that is meant to entertain, for instance, should be written to please the reader. Most narratives, or stories, are written to entertain, though they may also inform or persuade. Informative texts are easy to identify, while the most difficult purpose of a text to identify is persuasion because the author has an interest in making this purpose hard to detect. When a reader discovers that the author is trying to persuade, he or she should be skeptical of the argument. For this reason, persuasive texts often try to establish an entertaining tone and hope to amuse the reader into agreement. On the other hand, an informative tone may be implemented to create an appearance of authority and objectivity.

An author's purpose is evident often in the **organization** of the text (e.g., section headings in bold font points to an informative text). However, you may not have such organization available to you in your exam. Instead, if the author makes his or her main idea clear from the beginning, then the likely purpose of the text is to **inform**. If the author begins by making a claim and provides various arguments to support that claim, then the purpose is probably to **persuade**. If the author tells a story or wants to gain the reader's attention more than to push a particular point or deliver information, then his or her purpose is most likely to **entertain**. As a reader, you must judge authors on how well they accomplish their purpose. In other words, you need to consider the type of passage (e.g., technical, persuasive, etc.) that the author has written and if the author has followed the requirements of the passage type.

Review Video: Understanding the Author's Intent
Visit mometrix.com/academy and enter code: 511819

Informational Texts

An **informational text** is written to educate and enlighten readers. Informational texts are almost always nonfiction and are rarely structured as a story. The intention of an informational text is to deliver information in the most comprehensible way. So, look for the structure of the text to be very clear. In an informational text, the thesis statement is one or two sentences that normally appears at the end of the first paragraph. The author may use some colorful language, but he or she is likely to put more emphasis on clarity and precision. Informational essays do not typically appeal to the emotions. They often contain facts and figures and rarely include the opinion of the author; however, readers should remain aware of the possibility for bias as those facts are presented. Sometimes a persuasive essay can resemble an informative essay, especially if the author maintains an even tone and presents his or her views as if they were established fact.

Review Video: Informational Text
Visit mometrix.com/academy and enter code: 924964

Persuasive Writing

In a persuasive essay, the author is attempting to change the reader's mind or **convince** him or her of something that he or she did not believe previously. There are several identifying characteristics of **persuasive writing**. One is **opinion presented as fact**. When authors attempt to persuade readers, they often present their opinions as if they were fact. Readers must be on guard for statements that sound factual but which cannot be subjected to research, observation, or experiment. Another characteristic of persuasive writing is **emotional language**. An author will often try to play on the emotions of readers by appealing to their sympathy or sense of morality. When an author uses colorful or evocative language with the intent of arousing the reader's passions, then the author may be attempting to persuade. Finally, in many cases, a persuasive text will give an **unfair explanation of opposing positions**, if these positions are mentioned at all.

Entertaining Texts

The success or failure of an author's intent to **entertain** is determined by those who read the author's work. Entertaining texts may be either fiction or nonfiction, and they may describe real or imagined people, places, and events. Entertaining texts are often narratives or poems. A text that is written to entertain is likely to contain **colorful language** that engages the imagination and the emotions. Such writing often features a great deal of figurative language, which typically enlivens the subject matter with images and analogies.

Though an entertaining text is not usually written to persuade or inform, authors may accomplish both of these tasks in their work. An entertaining text may *appeal to the reader's emotions* and cause him or her to think differently about a particular subject. In any case, entertaining texts tend to showcase the personality of the author more than other types of writing.

Descriptive Text

In a sense, almost all writing is descriptive, insofar as an author seeks to describe events, ideas, or people to the reader. Some texts, however, are primarily concerned with **description**. A descriptive text focuses on a particular subject and attempts to depict the subject in a way that will be clear to readers. Descriptive texts contain many adjectives and adverbs (i.e., words that give shades of meaning and create a more detailed mental picture for the reader). A descriptive text fails when it is unclear to the reader. A descriptive text will certainly be informative and may be persuasive and entertaining as well.

Review Video: Descriptive Texts
Visit mometrix.com/academy and enter code: 174903

Expression of Feelings

When an author intends to **express feelings**, he or she may use **expressive and bold language**. An author may write with emotion for any number of reasons. Sometimes, authors will express feelings because they are describing a personal situation of great pain or happiness. In other situations, authors will attempt to persuade the reader and will use emotion to stir up the passions. This kind of expression is easy to identify when the writer uses phrases like *I felt* and *I sense*. However, readers may find that the author will simply describe feelings without introducing them. As a reader, you must know the importance of recognizing when an author is expressing emotion and not to become overwhelmed by sympathy or passion. Readers should maintain some **detachment** so that they can still evaluate the strength of the author's argument or the quality of the writing.

Review Video: Emotional Language in Literature
Visit mometrix.com/academy and enter code: 759390

Expository Passage

An **expository** passage aims to **inform** and enlighten readers. Expository passages are nonfiction and usually center around a simple, easily defined topic. Since the goal of exposition is to teach, such a passage should be as clear as possible. Often, an expository passage contains helpful organizing words, like *first, next, for example,* and *therefore*. These words keep the reader **oriented** in the text. Although expository passages do not need to feature colorful language and artful writing, they are often more effective with these features. For a reader, the challenge of expository passages is to maintain steady attention. Expository passages are not always about subjects that will naturally interest a reader, so the writer is often more concerned with **clarity** and **comprehensibility** than with engaging the reader. By reading actively, you can ensure a good habit of focus when reading an expository passage.

Review Video: Expository Passages
Visit mometrix.com/academy and enter code: 256515

Narrative Passage

A **narrative** passage is a story that can be fiction or nonfiction. However, there are a few elements that a text must have in order to be classified as a narrative. First, the text must have a **plot** (i.e., a series of events). Narratives often proceed in a clear sequence, but this is not a requirement. If the narrative is good, then these events will be interesting to readers. Second, a narrative has **characters**. These characters could be people, animals, or even inanimate objects—so long as they participate in the plot. Third, a narrative passage often contains **figurative language** which is meant to stimulate the imagination of readers by making comparisons and observations. For instance, a *metaphor*, a common piece of figurative language, is a description of one thing in terms of another. *The moon was a frosty snowball* is an example of a metaphor. In the literal sense this is obviously untrue, but the comparison suggests a certain mood for the reader.

Technical Passage

A **technical** passage is written to *describe* a complex object or process. Technical writing is common in medical and technological fields, in which complex ideas of mathematics, science, and engineering need to be explained *simply* and *clearly*. To ease comprehension, a technical passage usually proceeds in a very logical order. Technical passages often have clear headings and subheadings, which are used to keep the reader oriented in the text. Additionally, you will find that these passages divide sections up with numbers or letters. Many technical passages look more like an outline than a piece of prose. The amount of **jargon** or difficult vocabulary will vary in a technical passage depending on the intended audience. As much as possible, technical passages try to avoid language that the reader will have to research in order to understand the message, yet readers will find that jargon cannot always be avoided.

> **Review Video: Technical Passages**
> Visit mometrix.com/academy and enter code: 478923

Common Organizations of Texts

Organization of the Text

The way a text is organized can help readers understand the author's intent and his or her conclusions. There are various ways to organize a text, and each one has a purpose and use. Usually, authors will organize information logically in a passage so the reader can follow and locate the information within the text. However, since not all passages are written with the same logical structure, you need to be familiar with several different types of passage structure.

> **Review Video: Sequence of Events in a Story**
> Visit mometrix.com/academy and enter code: 807512

Chronological

When using **chronological** order, the author presents information in the order that it happened. For example, biographies are typically written in chronological order. The subject's birth and childhood are presented first, followed by their adult life, and lastly the events leading up to the person's death.

Cause and Effect

One of the most common text structures is **cause and effect**. A **cause** is an act or event that makes something happen, and an **effect** is the thing that happens as a result of the cause. A cause-and-effect relationship is not always explicit, but there are some terms in English that signal causes, such as *since*, *because*, and *due to*. Furthermore, terms that signal effects include *consequently, therefore, this leads to*. As an example, consider the sentence *Because the sky was clear, Ron did not bring an umbrella*. The cause is the clear sky, and the effect is that Ron did not bring an umbrella. However, readers may find that sometimes the cause-and-effect relationship will not be clearly noted. For instance, the sentence *He was late and missed the meeting* does not contain any signaling words, but the sentence still contains a cause (he was late) and an effect (he missed the meeting).

> **Review Video: Cause and Effect**
> Visit mometrix.com/academy and enter code: 868099

Review Video: Rhetorical Strategy of Cause and Effect Analysis
Visit mometrix.com/academy and enter code: 725944

Multiple Effects

Be aware of the possibility for a single cause to have **multiple effects.** (e.g., *Single cause*: Because you left your homework on the table, your dog engulfed the assignment. *Multiple effects*: As a result, you receive a failing grade, your parents do not allow you to go out with your friends, you miss out on the new movie, and one of your classmates spoils it for you before you have another chance to watch it).

Multiple Causes

Also, there is the possibility for a single effect to have **multiple causes.** (e.g., *Single effect*: Alan has a fever. *Multiple causes*: An unexpected cold front came through the area, and Alan forgot to take his multi-vitamin to avoid getting sick.) Additionally, an effect can in turn be the cause of another effect, in what is known as a cause-and-effect chain. (e.g., As a result of her disdain for procrastination, Lynn prepared for her exam. This led to her passing her test with high marks. Hence, her resume was accepted and her application was approved.)

Cause and Effect in Persuasive Essays

Persuasive essays, in which an author tries to make a convincing argument and change the minds of readers, usually include cause-and-effect relationships. However, these relationships should not always be taken at face value. Frequently, an author will assume a cause or take an effect for granted. To read a persuasive essay effectively, readers need to judge the cause-and-effect relationships that the author is presenting. For instance, imagine an author wrote the following: *The parking deck has been unprofitable because people would prefer to ride their bikes.* The relationship is clear: the cause is that people prefer to ride their bikes, and the effect is that the parking deck has been unprofitable. However, readers should consider whether this argument is conclusive. Perhaps there are other reasons for the failure of the parking deck: a down economy, excessive fees, etc. Too often, authors present causal relationships as if they are fact rather than opinion. Readers should be on the alert for these dubious claims.

Problem-Solution

Some nonfiction texts are organized to **present a problem** followed by a solution. For this type of text, the problem is often explained before the solution is offered. In some cases, as when the problem is well known, the solution may be introduced briefly at the beginning. Other passages may focus on the solution, and the problem will be referenced only occasionally. Some texts will outline multiple solutions to a problem, leaving readers to choose among them. If the author has an interest or an allegiance to one solution, he or she may fail to mention or describe accurately some of the other solutions. Readers should be careful of the author's agenda when reading a problem-solution text. Only by understanding the author's perspective and interests can one develop a proper judgment of the proposed solution.

Compare and Contrast

Many texts follow the **compare-and-contrast** model in which the similarities and differences between two ideas or things are explored. Analysis of the similarities between ideas is called **comparison**. In an ideal comparison, the author places ideas or things in an equivalent structure, i.e., the author presents the ideas in the same way. If an author wants to show the similarities between cricket and baseball, then he or she may do so by summarizing the equipment and rules for each game. Be mindful of the similarities as they appear in the passage and take note of any differences that are mentioned. Often, these small differences will only reinforce the more general similarity.

Review Video: Compare and Contrast
Visit mometrix.com/academy and enter code: 798319

Thinking critically about ideas and conclusions can seem like a daunting task. One way to ease this task is to understand the basic elements of ideas and writing techniques. Looking at the ways different ideas relate to each other can be a good way for readers to begin their analysis. For instance, sometimes authors will write about two ideas that are in opposition to each other. Or, one author will provide his or her ideas on a topic, and another author may respond in opposition. The analysis of these opposing ideas is known as **contrast**. Contrast is often marred by the author's obvious partiality to one of the ideas. A discerning reader will be put off by an author who does not engage in a fair fight. In an analysis of opposing ideas, both ideas should be presented in clear and reasonable terms. If the author does prefer a side, you need to read carefully to determine the areas where the author shows or avoids this preference. In an analysis of opposing ideas, you should proceed through the passage by marking the major differences point by point with an eye that is looking for an explanation of each side's view. For instance, in an analysis of capitalism and communism, there is an importance in outlining each side's view on labor, markets, prices, personal responsibility, etc. Additionally, as you read through the passages, you should note whether the opposing views present each side in a similar manner.

SEQUENCE

Readers must be able to identify a text's **sequence**, or the order in which things happen. Often, when the sequence is very important to the author, the text is indicated with signal words like *first*, *then*, *next*, and *last*. However, a sequence can be merely implied and must be noted by the reader. Consider the sentence *He walked through the garden and gave water and fertilizer to the plants*. Clearly, the man did not walk through the garden before he collected water and fertilizer for the plants. So, the implied sequence is that he first collected water, then he collected fertilizer, next he walked through the garden, and last he gave water or fertilizer as necessary to the plants. Texts do not always proceed in an orderly sequence from first to last. Sometimes they begin at the end and start over at the beginning. As a reader, you can enhance your understanding of the passage by taking brief notes to clarify the sequence.

Review Video: Sequence
Visit mometrix.com/academy and enter code: 489027

MAKING AND EVALUATING PREDICTIONS

MAKING PREDICTIONS

When we read literature, **making predictions** about what will happen in the writing reinforces our purpose for reading and prepares us mentally. A **prediction** is a guess about what will happen next. Readers constantly make predictions based on what they have read and what they already know. We can make predictions before we begin reading and during our reading. Consider the following sentence: *Staring at the computer screen in shock, Kim blindly reached over for the brimming glass of water on the shelf to her side.* The sentence suggests that Kim is distracted, and that she is not looking at the glass that she is going to pick up. So, a reader might predict that Kim is going to knock over the glass. Of course, not every prediction will be accurate: perhaps Kim will pick the glass up cleanly. Nevertheless, the author has certainly created the expectation that the water might be spilled.

As we read on, we can test the accuracy of our predictions, revise them in light of additional reading, and confirm or refute our predictions. Predictions are always subject to revision as the reader acquires more information. A reader can make predictions by observing the title and illustrations; noting the structure, characters, and subject; drawing on existing knowledge relative to the subject; and asking "why" and "who" questions. Connecting reading to what we already know enables us to learn new information and construct meaning. For example, before third-graders read a book about Johnny Appleseed, they may start a KWL chart—a list of what they *Know*, what they *Want* to know or learn, and what they have *Learned* after reading.

Activating existing background knowledge and thinking about the text before reading improves comprehension.

Review Video: Predictive Reading
Visit mometrix.com/academy and enter code: 437248

Test-taking tip: To respond to questions requiring future predictions, your answers should be based on evidence of past or present behavior and events.

EVALUATING PREDICTIONS

When making predictions, readers should be able to explain how they developed their prediction. One way readers can defend their thought process is by citing textual evidence. Textual evidence to evaluate reader predictions about literature includes specific synopses of the work, paraphrases of the work or parts of it, and direct quotations from the work. These references to the text must support the prediction by indicating, clearly or unclearly, what will happen later in the story. A text may provide these indications through literary devices such as foreshadowing. Foreshadowing is anything in a text that gives the reader a hint about what is to come by emphasizing the likelihood of an event or development. Foreshadowing can occur through descriptions, exposition, and dialogue. Foreshadowing in dialogue usually occurs when a character gives a warning or expresses a strong feeling that a certain event will occur. Foreshadowing can also occur through irony. However, unlike other forms of foreshadowing, the events that seem the most likely are the opposite of what actually happens. Instances of foreshadowing and irony can be summarized, paraphrased, or quoted to defend a reader's prediction.

Review Video: Textual Evidence for Predictions
Visit mometrix.com/academy and enter code: 261070

MAKING INFERENCES AND DRAWING CONCLUSIONS

Inferences are logical conclusions that readers make based on their observations and previous knowledge. An inference is based on both what is found in a passage or a story and what is known from personal experience. For instance, a story may say that a character is frightened and can hear howling in the distance. Based on both what is in the text and personal knowledge, it is a logical conclusion that the character is frightened because he hears the sound of wolves. A good inference is supported by the information in a passage.

IMPLICIT AND EXPLICIT INFORMATION

By inferring, readers construct meanings from text that are personally relevant. By combining their own schemas or concepts and their background information pertinent to the text with what they read, readers interpret it according to both what the author has conveyed and their own unique perspectives. Inferences are different from **explicit information**, which is clearly stated in a passage. Authors do not always explicitly spell out every meaning in what they write; many meanings are implicit. Through inference, readers can comprehend implied meanings in the text, and also derive personal significance from it, making the text meaningful and memorable to them. Inference is a natural process in everyday life. When readers infer, they can draw conclusions about what the author is saying, predict what may reasonably follow, amend these predictions as they continue to read, interpret the import of themes, and analyze the characters' feelings and motivations through their actions.

EXAMPLE OF DRAWING CONCLUSIONS FROM INFERENCES

Read the excerpt and decide why Jana finally relaxed.

> Jana loved her job, but the work was very demanding. She had trouble relaxing. She called a friend, but she still thought about work. She ordered a pizza, but eating it did not help. Then, her kitten jumped on her lap and began to purr. Jana leaned back and began to hum a little tune. She felt better.

Reading

You can draw the conclusion that Jana relaxed because her kitten jumped on her lap. The kitten purred, and Jana leaned back and hummed a tune. Then she felt better. The excerpt does not explicitly say that this is the reason why she was able to relax. The text leaves the matter unclear, but the reader can infer or make a "best guess" that this is the reason she is relaxing. This is a logical conclusion based on the information in the passage. It is the best conclusion a reader can make based on the information he or she has read. Inferences are based on the information in a passage, but they are not directly stated in the passage.

Test-taking tip: While being tested on your ability to make correct inferences, you must look for **contextual clues**. An answer can be true, but not the best or most correct answer. The contextual clues will help you find the answer that is the **best answer** out of the given choices. Be careful in your reading to understand the context in which a phrase is stated. When asked for the implied meaning of a statement made in the passage, you should immediately locate the statement and read the **context** in which the statement was made. Also, look for an answer choice that has a similar phrase to the statement in question.

Review Video: Inference
Visit mometrix.com/academy and enter code: 379203

Review Video: How to Support a Conclusion
Visit mometrix.com/academy and enter code: 281653

Reading Comprehension and Connecting with Texts

Comparing Two Stories

When presented with two different stories, there will be **similarities** and **differences** between the two. A reader needs to make a list, or other graphic organizer, of the points presented in each story. Once the reader has written down the main point and supporting points for each story, the two sets of ideas can be compared. The reader can then present each idea and show how it is the same or different in the other story. This is called **comparing and contrasting ideas**.

The reader can compare ideas by stating, for example: "In Story 1, the author believes that humankind will one day land on Mars, whereas in Story 2, the author believes that Mars is too far away for humans to ever step foot on." Note that the two viewpoints are different in each story that the reader is comparing. A reader may state that: "Both stories discussed the likelihood of humankind landing on Mars." This statement shows how the viewpoint presented in both stories is based on the same topic, rather than how each viewpoint is different. The reader will complete a comparison of two stories with a conclusion.

Review Video: How to Compare and Contrast
Visit mometrix.com/academy and enter code: 833765

Outlining a Passage

As an aid to drawing conclusions, **outlining** the information contained in the passage should be a familiar skill to readers. An effective outline will reveal the structure of the passage and will lead to solid conclusions. An effective outline will have a title that refers to the basic subject of the text, though the title does not need to restate the main idea. In most outlines, the main idea will be the first major section. Each major idea in the passage will be established as the head of a category. For instance, the most common outline format calls for the main ideas of the passage to be indicated with Roman numerals. In an effective outline of this kind, each of the main ideas will be represented by a Roman numeral and none of the Roman numerals will designate minor details or secondary ideas. Moreover, all supporting ideas and details should be placed in the appropriate place on the outline. An outline does not need to include every detail listed in the text, but it should feature all of those that are central to the argument or message. Each of these details should be listed under the corresponding main idea.

Review Video: Outlining as an Aid to Drawing Conclusions
Visit mometrix.com/academy and enter code: 584445

Using Graphic Organizers

Ideas from a text can also be organized using **graphic organizers**. A graphic organizer is a way to simplify information and take key points from the text. A graphic organizer such as a timeline may have an event listed for a corresponding date on the timeline, while an outline may have an event listed under a key point that occurs in the text. Each reader needs to create the type of graphic organizer that works the best for him or her in terms of being able to recall information from a story. Examples include a spider-map, which takes a main idea from the story and places it in a bubble with supporting points branching off the main idea. An outline is useful for diagramming the main and supporting points of the entire story, and a Venn diagram compares and contrasts characteristics of two or more ideas.

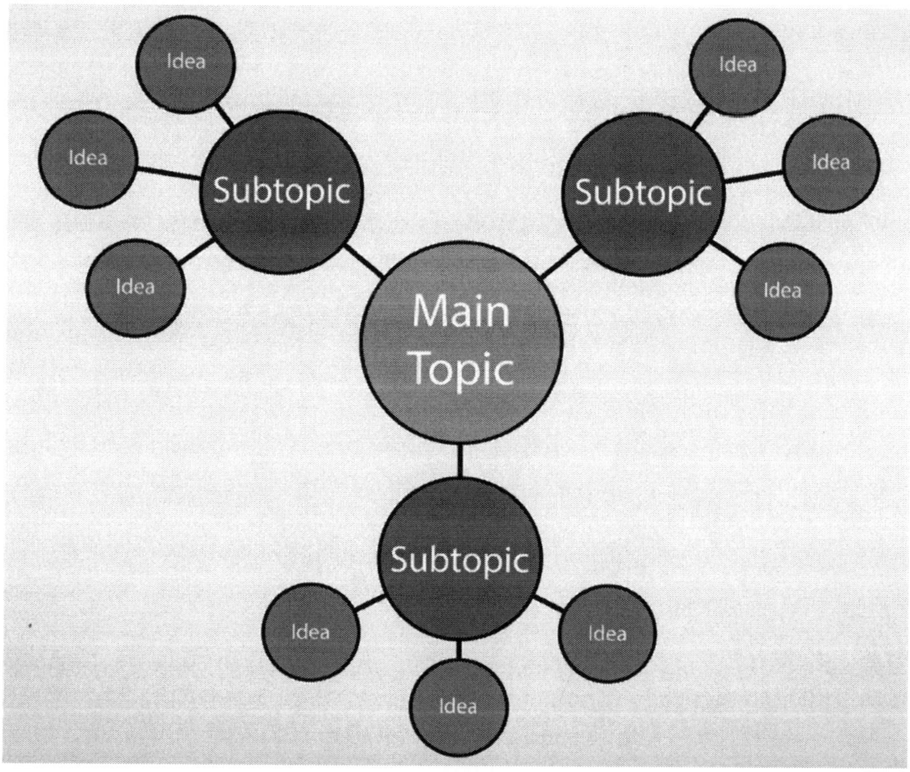

Review Video: Graphic Organizers
Visit mometrix.com/academy and enter code: 665513

Making Logical Conclusions about a Passage

A reader should always be drawing conclusions from the text. Sometimes conclusions are **implied** from written information, and other times the information is **stated directly** within the passage. One should always aim to draw conclusions from information stated within a passage, rather than to draw them from mere implications. At times an author may provide some information and then describe a counterargument. Readers should be alert for direct statements that are subsequently rejected or weakened by the author. Furthermore, you should always read through the entire passage before drawing conclusions. Many readers are trained to expect the author's conclusions at either the beginning or the end of the passage, but many texts do not adhere to this format.

Drawing conclusions from information implied within a passage requires confidence on the part of the reader. **Implications** are things that the author does not state directly, but readers can assume based on what the author does say. Consider the following passage: *I stepped outside and opened my umbrella. By the time I got to work, the cuffs of my pants were soaked.* The author never states that it is raining, but this fact is clearly implied. Conclusions based on implication must be well supported by the text. In order to draw a solid conclusion, readers should have **multiple pieces of evidence**. If readers have only one piece, they must be assured that there is no other possible explanation than their conclusion. A good reader will be able to draw many conclusions from information implied by the text, which will be a great help on the exam.

Drawing Conclusions

A common type of inference that a reader has to make is **drawing a conclusion**. The reader makes this conclusion based on the information provided within a text. Certain facts are included to help a reader come to a specific conclusion. For example, a story may open with a man trudging through the snow on a cold winter day, dragging a sled behind him. The reader can logically **infer** from the setting of the story that the man is wearing heavy winter clothes in order to stay warm. Information is implied based on the setting of a story, which is why **setting** is an important element of the text. If the same man in the example was trudging down a beach on a hot summer day, dragging a surf board behind him, the reader would assume that the man is not wearing heavy clothes. The reader makes inferences based on their own experiences and the information presented to them in the story.

Test-taking tip: When asked to identify a conclusion that may be drawn, look for critical "hedge" phrases, such as *likely*, *may*, *can*, and *will often*, among many others. When you are being tested on this knowledge, remember the question that writers insert into these hedge phrases to cover every possibility. Often an answer will be wrong simply because there is no room for exception. Extreme positive or negative answers (such as always or never) are usually not correct. When answering these questions, the reader **should not** use any outside knowledge that is not gathered directly or reasonably inferred from the passage. Correct answers can be derived straight from the passage.

Example

Read the following sentence from *Little Women* by Louisa May Alcott and draw a conclusion based upon the information presented:

> *You know the reason Mother proposed not having any presents this Christmas was because it is going to be a hard winter for everyone; and she thinks we ought not to spend money for pleasure, when our men are suffering so in the army.*

Based on the information in the sentence, the reader can conclude, or **infer**, that the men are away at war while the women are still at home. The pronoun *our* gives a clue to the reader that the character is speaking about men she knows. In addition, the reader can assume that the character is speaking to a brother or sister, since the term "Mother" is used by the character while speaking to another person. The reader can also come to the conclusion that the characters celebrate Christmas, since it is mentioned in the **context** of the sentence. In the sentence, the mother is presented as an unselfish character who is opinionated and thinks about the wellbeing of other people.

Summarizing

A helpful tool is the ability to **summarize** the information that you have read in a paragraph or passage format. This process is similar to creating an effective outline. First, a summary should accurately define the main idea of the passage, though the summary does not need to explain this main idea in exhaustive detail. The summary should continue by laying out the most important supporting details or arguments from the passage. All of the significant supporting details should be included, and none of the details included should be irrelevant or insignificant. Also, the summary should accurately report all of these details. Too often, the desire for brevity in a summary leads to the sacrifice of clarity or accuracy. Summaries are often difficult to read because they omit all of the graceful language, digressions, and asides that distinguish great writing. However, an effective summary should communicate the same overall message as the original text.

Review Video: Summarizing Text
Visit mometrix.com/academy and enter code: 172903

Paraphrasing

Paraphrasing is another method that the reader can use to aid in comprehension. When paraphrasing, one puts what they have read into their own words by rephrasing what the author has written, or one "translates" all of what the author shared into their own words by including as many details as they can.

Evaluating a Passage

It is important to understand the logical conclusion of the ideas presented in an informational text. **Identifying a logical conclusion** can help you determine whether you agree with the writer or not. Coming to this conclusion is much like making an inference: the approach requires you to combine the information given by the text with what you already know and make a logical conclusion. If the author intended for the reader to draw a certain conclusion, then you can expect the author's argumentation and detail to be leading in that direction.

One way to approach the task of drawing conclusions is to make brief **notes** of all the points made by the author. When the notes are arranged on paper, they may clarify the logical conclusion. Another way to approach conclusions is to consider whether the reasoning of the author raises any pertinent questions. Sometimes you will be able to draw several conclusions from a passage. On occasion these will be conclusions that were never imagined by the author. Therefore, be aware that these conclusions must be **supported directly by the text**.

Evaluation of Summaries

A summary of a literary passage is a condensation in the reader's own words of the passage's main points. Several guidelines can be used in evaluating a summary. The summary should be complete yet concise. It should be accurate, balanced, fair, neutral, and objective, excluding the reader's own opinions or reactions. It should reflect in similar proportion how much each point summarized was covered in the original passage. Summary writers should include tags of attribution, like "Macaulay argues that" to reference the original author whose ideas are represented in the summary. Summary writers should not overuse quotations; they should only quote central concepts or phrases they cannot precisely convey in words other than those of the original author. Another aspect of evaluating a summary is considering whether it can stand alone as a coherent, unified composition. In addition, evaluation of a summary should include whether its writer has cited the original source of the passage they have summarized so that readers can find it.

Making Connections to Enhance Comprehension

Reading involves thinking. For good comprehension, readers make **text-to-self**, **text-to-text**, and **text-to-world connections**. Making connections helps readers understand text better and predict what might occur next based on what they already know, such as how characters in the story feel or what happened in another text. Text-to-self connections with the reader's life and experiences make literature more personally relevant and meaningful to readers. Readers can make connections before, during, and after reading—including whenever the text reminds them of something similar they have encountered in life or other texts. The genre, setting, characters, plot elements, literary structure and devices, and themes an author uses allow a reader to make connections to other works of literature or to people and events in their own lives. Venn diagrams and other graphic organizers help visualize connections. Readers can also make double-entry notes: key content, ideas, events, words, and quotations on one side, and the connections with these on the other.

Craft and Structure

Reading Informational Texts

Language Use

Literal and Figurative Language

As in fictional literature, informational text also uses both **literal language**, which means just what it says, and **figurative language**, which imparts more than literal meaning. For example, an informational text author might use a simile or direct comparison, such as writing that a racehorse "ran like the wind." Informational text authors also use metaphors or implied comparisons, such as "the cloud of the Great Depression." Imagery may also appear in informational texts to increase the reader's understanding of ideas and concepts discussed in the text.

> **Review Video: Figurative Language**
> Visit mometrix.com/academy and enter code: 584902

Explicit and Implicit Information

When informational text states something explicitly, the reader is told by the author exactly what is meant, which can include the author's interpretation or perspective of events. For example, a professor writes, "I have seen students go into an absolute panic just because they weren't able to complete the exam in the time they were allotted." This explicitly tells the reader that the students were afraid, and by using the words "just because," the writer indicates their fear was exaggerated out of proportion relative to what happened. However, another professor writes, "I have had students come to me, their faces drained of all color, saying 'We weren't able to finish the exam.'" This is an example of implicit meaning: the second writer did not state explicitly that the students were panicked. Instead, he wrote a description of their faces being "drained of all color." From this description, the reader can infer that the students were so frightened that their faces paled.

> **Review Video: Explicit and Implicit Information**
> Visit mometrix.com/academy and enter code: 735771

Making Inferences About Informational Text

With informational text, reader comprehension depends not only on recalling important statements and details, but also on reader inferences based on examples and details. Readers add information from the text to what they already know to draw inferences about the text. These inferences help the readers to fill in the information that the text does not explicitly state, enabling them to understand the text better. When reading a nonfictional autobiography or biography, for example, the most appropriate inferences might concern the events in the book, the actions of the subject of the autobiography or biography, and the message the author means to convey. When reading a nonfictional expository (informational) text, the reader would best draw inferences about problems and their solutions, and causes and their effects. When reading a nonfictional persuasive text, the reader will want to infer ideas supporting the author's message and intent.

Structures or Organizational Patterns in Informational Texts

Informational text can be **descriptive**, appealing to the five senses and answering the questions what, who, when, where, and why. Another method of structuring informational text is sequence and order. **Chronological** texts relate events in the sequence that they occurred, from start to finish, while how-to texts organize information into a series of instructions in the sequence in which the steps should be followed. **Comparison-contrast** structures of informational text describe various ideas to their readers by pointing out how things or ideas are similar and how they are different. **Cause and effect** structures of informational text describe events that occurred and identify the causes or reasons that those events occurred. **Problem and solution** structures of informational texts introduce and describe problems and offer one or more solutions for each problem described.

Determining an Informational Author's Purpose

Informational authors' purposes are why they write texts. Readers must determine authors' motivations and goals. Readers gain greater insight into a text by considering the author's motivation. This develops critical reading skills. Readers perceive writing as a person's voice, not simply printed words. Uncovering author motivations and purposes empowers readers to know what to expect from the text, read for relevant details, evaluate authors and their work critically, and respond effectively to the motivations and persuasions of the text. The main idea of a text is what the reader is supposed to understand from reading it; the purpose of the text is why the author has written it and what the author wants readers to do with its information. Authors state some purposes clearly, while other purposes may be unstated but equally significant. When stated purposes contradict other parts of a text, the author may have a hidden agenda. Readers can better evaluate a text's effectiveness, whether they agree or disagree with it, and why they agree or disagree through identifying unstated author purposes.

Identifying Author's Point of View or Purpose

In some informational texts, readers find it easy to identify the author's point of view and purpose, such as when the author explicitly states his or her position and reason for writing. But other texts are more difficult, either because of the content or because the authors give neutral or balanced viewpoints. This is particularly true in scientific texts, in which authors may state the purpose of their research in the report, but never state their point of view except by interpreting evidence or data.

To analyze text and identify point of view or purpose, readers should ask themselves the following four questions:

1. With what main point or idea does this author want to persuade readers to agree?
2. How does this author's word choice affect the way that readers consider this subject?
3. How do this author's choices of examples and facts affect the way that readers consider this subject?
4. What is it that this author wants to accomplish by writing this text?

Review Video: Understanding the Author's Intent
Visit mometrix.com/academy and enter code: 511819

Review Video: Author's Position
Visit mometrix.com/academy and enter code: 827954

Evaluating Arguments Made by Informational Text Writers

When evaluating an informational text, the first step is to identify the argument's conclusion. Then identify the author's premises that support the conclusion. Try to paraphrase premises for clarification and make the conclusion and premises fit. List all premises first, sequentially numbered, then finish with the conclusion. Identify any premises or assumptions not stated by the author but required for the stated premises to support the conclusion. Read word assumptions sympathetically, as the author might. Evaluate whether premises reasonably support the conclusion. For inductive reasoning, the reader should ask if the premises are true, if they support the conclusion, and if so, how strongly. For deductive reasoning, the reader should ask if the argument is valid or invalid. If all premises are true, then the argument is valid unless the conclusion can be false. If it can, then the argument is invalid. An invalid argument can be made valid through alterations such as the addition of needed premises.

Use of Rhetoric in Informational Texts

There are many ways authors can support their claims, arguments, beliefs, ideas, and reasons for writing in informational texts. For example, authors can appeal to readers' sense of **logic** by communicating their reasoning through a carefully sequenced series of logical steps to help "prove" the points made. Authors can appeal to readers' **emotions** by using descriptions and words that evoke feelings of sympathy, sadness, anger, righteous indignation, hope, happiness, or any other emotion to reinforce what they express and share with their audience. Authors may appeal to the **moral** or **ethical values** of readers by using words and descriptions that can convince readers that something is right or wrong. By relating personal anecdotes, authors can supply readers with more accessible, realistic examples of points they make, as well as appealing to their emotions. They can provide supporting evidence by reporting case studies. They can also illustrate their points by making analogies to which readers can better relate.

TECHNICAL LANGUAGE

TECHNICAL LANGUAGE

Technical language is more impersonal than literary and vernacular language. Passive voice makes the tone impersonal. For example, instead of writing, "We found this a central component of protein metabolism," scientists write, "This was found a central component of protein metabolism." While science professors have traditionally instructed students to avoid active voice because it leads to first-person ("I" and "we") usage, science editors today find passive voice dull and weak. Many journal articles combine both. Tone in technical science writing should be detached, concise, and professional. While one may normally write, "This chemical has to be available for proteins to be digested," professionals write technically, "The presence of this chemical is required for the enzyme to break the covalent bonds of proteins." The use of technical language appeals to both technical and non-technical audiences by displaying the author or speaker's understanding of the subject and suggesting their credibility regarding the message they are communicating.

TECHNICAL MATERIAL FOR NON-TECHNICAL READERS

Writing about **technical subjects** for **non-technical readers** differs from writing for colleagues because authors place more importance on delivering a critical message than on imparting the maximum technical content possible. Technical authors also must assume that non-technical audiences do not have the expertise to comprehend extremely scientific or technical messages, concepts, and terminology. They must resist the temptation to impress audiences with their scientific knowledge and expertise and remember that their primary purpose is to communicate a message that non-technical readers will understand, feel, and respond to. Non-technical and technical styles include similarities. Both should formally cite any references or other authors' work utilized in the text. Both must follow intellectual property and copyright regulations. This includes the author's protecting his or her own rights, or a public domain statement, as he or she chooses.

Review Video: Technical Passages
Visit mometrix.com/academy and enter code: 478923

NON-TECHNICAL AUDIENCES

Writers of technical or scientific material may need to write for many non-technical audiences. Some readers have no technical or scientific background, and those who do may not be in the same field as the authors. Government and corporate policymakers and budget managers need technical information they can understand for decision-making. Citizens affected by technology or science are a different audience. Non-governmental organizations can encompass many of the preceding groups. Elementary and secondary school programs also need non-technical language for presenting technical subject matter. Additionally, technical authors will need to use non-technical language when collecting consumer responses to surveys, presenting scientific or para-scientific material to the public, writing about the history of science, and writing about science and technology in developing countries.

USE OF EVERYDAY LANGUAGE

Authors of technical information sometimes must write using non-technical language that readers outside their disciplinary fields can comprehend. They should use not only non-technical terms, but also normal, everyday language to accommodate readers whose native language is different than the language the text is written in. For example, instead of writing that "eustatic changes like thermal expansion are causing hazardous conditions in the littoral zone," an author would do better to write that "a rising sea level is threatening the coast." When technical terms cannot be avoided, authors should also define or explain them using non-technical language. Although authors must cite references and acknowledge their use of others' work, they should avoid the kinds of references or citations that they would use in scientific journals—unless they reinforce author messages. They should not use endnotes, footnotes, or any other complicated referential techniques because non-technical journal publishers usually do not accept them. Including high-resolution illustrations, photos, maps, or satellite images and incorporating multimedia into digital publications will enhance non-technical writing about technical subjects. Technical authors may publish using non-technical language in e-journals, trade journals, specialty newsletters, and daily newspapers.

Types of Technical Writing

Types of Printed Communication

Memo

A memo (short for *memorandum*) is a common form of written communication. There is a standard format for these documents. It is typical for there to be a **heading** at the top indicating the author, date, and recipient. In some cases, this heading will also include the author's title and the name of his or her institution. Below this information will be the **body** of the memo. These documents are typically written by and for members of the same organization. They usually contain a plan of action, a request for information on a specific topic, or a response to such a request. Memos are considered to be official documents, so they are usually written in a **formal** style. Many memos are organized with numbers or bullet points, which make it easier for the reader to identify key ideas.

Posted Announcement

People post **announcements** for all sorts of occasions. Many people are familiar with notices for lost pets, yard sales, and landscaping services. In order to be effective, these announcements need to *contain all of the information* the reader requires to act on the message. For instance, a lost pet announcement needs to include a good description of the animal and a contact number for the owner. A yard sale notice should include the address, date, and hours of the sale, as well as a brief description of the products that will be available there. When composing an announcement, it is important to consider the perspective of the **audience**—what will they need to know in order to respond to the message? Although a posted announcement can have color and decoration to attract the eye of the passerby, it must also convey the necessary information clearly.

Classified Advertisement

Classified advertisements, or **ads**, are used to sell or buy goods, to attract business, to make romantic connections, and to do countless other things. They are an inexpensive, and sometimes free, way to make a brief **pitch**. Classified ads used to be found only in newspapers or special advertising circulars, but there are now online listings as well. The style of these ads has remained basically the same. An ad usually begins with a word or phrase indicating what is being **sold** or **sought**. Then, the listing will give a brief **description** of the product or service. Because space is limited and costly in newspapers, classified ads there will often contain abbreviations for common attributes. For instance, two common abbreviations are *bk* for *black*, and *obo* for *or best offer*. Classified ads will then usually conclude by listing the **price** (or the amount the seeker is willing to pay), followed by **contact information** like a telephone number or email address.

Scale Readings of Standard Measurement Instruments

The scales used on **standard measurement instruments** are fairly easy to read with a little practice. Take the **ruler** as an example. A typical ruler has different units along each long edge. One side measures inches, and the other measures centimeters. The units are specified close to the zero reading for the ruler. Note that the ruler does not begin measuring from its outermost edge. The zero reading is a black line a tiny distance inside of the edge. On the inches side, each inch is indicated with a long black line and a number. Each half-inch is noted with a slightly shorter line. Quarter-inches are noted with still shorter lines, eighth-inches are noted with even shorter lines, and sixteenth-inches are noted with the shortest lines of all. On the centimeter side, the second-largest black lines indicate half-centimeters, and the smaller lines indicate tenths of centimeters, otherwise known as millimeters.

Visual Information in Informational Texts

Charts, Graphs, and Visuals

Tables

Tables are presented in a standard format so they will be easy to read and understand. A title is at the top, a short phrase indicating the information the table or graph intends to convey. The title of a table could be something like "Median Income for Various Education Levels" or "Price of Milk Compared to Demand." A table is composed of information laid out in vertical columns and horizontal rows. Typically, each column will have a label. If "Median Income for Various Education Levels" was placed in a table format, the two columns could be labeled "Education Level" and "Median Annual Salary." Each location on the table is called a cell, which holds a piece of information. Cells are defined by their column and row (e.g., second column, fifth row).

Median Annual Salary for Various Education Levels

Education Level	Median Annual Salary
Associate degree	$52,260
Bachelor's degree	$74,464
Master's degree	$86,372
Professional degree	$108,160
Doctoral degree	$108,316

Graphs

Like a table, a graph typically has a title at the top. This title may simply state the identities of the two axes: e.g., "Income vs. Education." However, the title may also be something more descriptive, like "A comparison of average income with level of education." In any case, bar and line graphs are laid out along two perpendicular lines, or axes. The vertical axis is called the *y*-axis, and the horizontal axis is called the *x*-axis. It is typical for the *x*-axis to be the independent variable and the *y*-axis to be the dependent variable. The independent variable is the one manipulated by the researcher or creator of the graph. In the above example, the independent variable would be "education level," since the maker of the graph will define these values (associate degree, bachelor's degree, master's degree, etc.). The dependent value is not controlled by the researcher.

When selecting a graph format, it is important to consider the intention and the structure of the presentation. A bar graph is appropriate for displaying the relations between a series of distinct quantities that are on the same scale. For instance, if one wanted to display the amount of money spent on groceries during the months of a year, a bar graph would be appropriate. The vertical axis would represent values of money, and the horizontal axis would identify each month. A line graph also requires data expressed in common units, but it is better for demonstrating the general trend in that data. If the grocery expenses were plotted on a line graph instead of a bar graph, there would be more emphasis on whether the amount of money spent rose or fell over the course of the year. Whereas a bar graph is good for showing the relationships between the different values plotted, the line graph is good for showing whether the values tended to increase, decrease, or remain stable.

Pie Chart

A pie chart, also known as a circle graph, is useful for depicting how a single unit or category is divided. The standard pie chart is a circle with designated wedges. Each wedge is **proportional** in size to a part of the whole. For instance, consider Shawna, a student at City College, who uses a pie chart to represent her budget. If she spends half of her money on rent, then the pie chart will represent that amount with a line through the center of the pie. If she spends a quarter of her money on food, there will be a line extending from the edge of the circle to the center at a right angle to the line depicting rent. This illustration would make it clear that the student spends twice the amount of money on rent as she does on food.

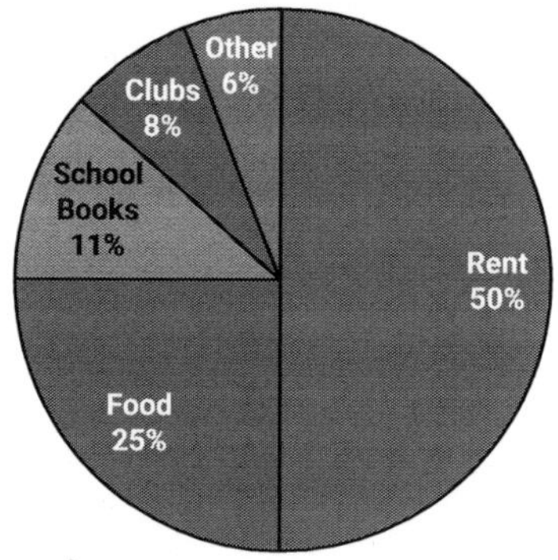

A pie chart is effective at showing how a single entity is divided into parts. They are not effective at demonstrating the relationships between parts of different wholes. For example, an unhelpful use of a pie chart would be to compare the respective amounts of state and federal spending devoted to infrastructure since these values are only meaningful in the context of the entire budget.

Bar Graph

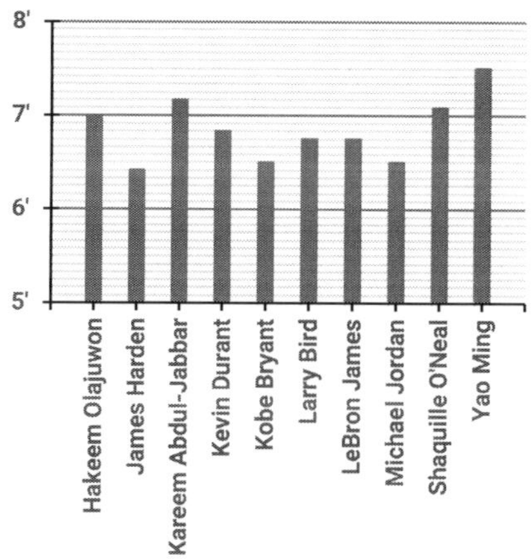

The bar graph is one of the most common visual representations of information. **Bar graphs** are used to illustrate sets of numerical **data**. The graph has a vertical axis (along which numbers are listed) and a horizontal axis (along which categories, words, or some other indicators are placed). One example of a bar graph is a depiction of the respective heights of famous basketball players: the vertical axis would contain numbers ranging from five to eight feet, and the horizontal axis would contain the names of the players. The length of the bar above the player's name would illustrate his height, and the top of the bar would stop perpendicular to the height listed along the left side. In this representation, one would see that Yao Ming is taller than Michael Jordan because Yao's bar would be higher.

Line Graph

A line graph is a type of graph that is typically used for measuring trends over time. The graph is set up along a vertical and a horizontal **axis**. The variables being measured are listed along the left side and the bottom side of the axes. Points are then plotted along the graph as they correspond with their values for each variable. For instance, consider a line graph measuring a person's income for each month of the year. If the person earned $1500 in January, there should be a point directly above January (perpendicular to the horizontal axis) and directly to the right of $1500 (perpendicular to the vertical axis). Once all of the lines are plotted, they are connected with a line from left to right. This line provides a nice visual illustration of the general **trends** of the data, if they exist. For instance, using the earlier example, if the line sloped up, then one would see that the person's income had increased over the course of the year.

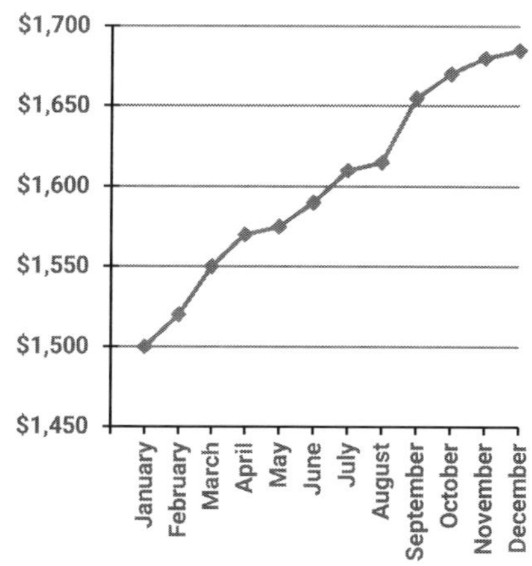

Pictographs

A **pictograph** is a graph, generally in the horizontal orientation, that uses pictures or symbols to represent the data. Each pictograph must have a key that defines the picture or symbol and gives the quantity each picture or symbol represents. Pictures or symbols on a pictograph are not always shown as whole elements. In this case, the fraction of the picture or symbol shown represents the same fraction of the quantity a whole picture or symbol stands for.

Review Video: Pictographs
Visit mometrix.com/academy and enter code: 147860

Plot and Story Structure

Plot and Story Structure

The **plot** includes the events that happen in a story and the order in which they are told to the reader. There are several types of plot structures, as stories can be told in many ways. The most common plot structure is the chronological plot, which presents the events to the reader in the same order they occur for the characters in the story. Chronological plots usually have five main parts, the **exposition**, **rising action**, the **climax**, **falling action**, and the **resolution**. This type of plot structure guides the reader through the story's events as the characters experience them and is the easiest structure to understand and identify. While this is the most common plot structure, many stories are nonlinear, which means the plot does not sequence events in the same order the characters experience them. Such stories might include elements like flashbacks that cause the story to be nonlinear.

Review Video: How to Make a Story Map
Visit mometrix.com/academy and enter code: 261719

Exposition

The **exposition** is at the beginning of the story and generally takes place before the rising action begins. The purpose of the exposition is to give the reader context for the story, which the author may do by introducing one or more characters, describing the setting or world, or explaining the events leading up to the point where the story begins. The exposition may still include events that contribute to the plot, but the **rising action** and main conflict of the story are not part of the exposition. Some narratives skip the exposition and begin the story with the beginning of the rising action, which causes the reader to learn the context as the story intensifies.

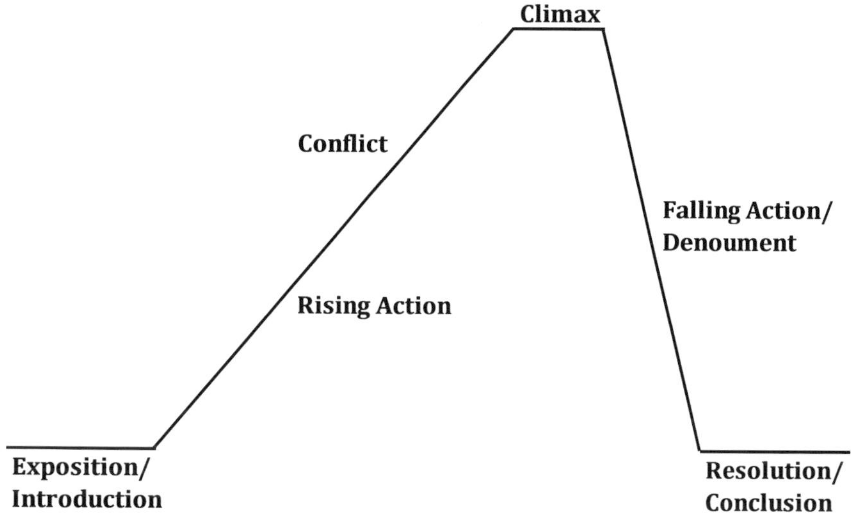

Review Video: Plot Line
Visit mometrix.com/academy and enter code: 944011

CONFLICT

A **conflict** is a problem to be solved. Literary plots typically include one conflict or more. Characters' attempts to resolve conflicts drive the narrative's forward movement. **Conflict resolution** is often the protagonist's primary occupation. Physical conflicts like exploring, wars, and escapes tend to make plots most suspenseful and exciting. Emotional, mental, or moral conflicts tend to make stories more personally gratifying or rewarding for many audiences. Conflicts can be external or internal. A major type of internal conflict is some inner personal battle, or **man versus self**. Major types of external conflicts include **man versus nature**, **man versus man**, and **man versus society**. Readers can identify conflicts in literary plots by identifying the protagonist and antagonist and asking why they conflict, what events develop the conflict, where the climax occurs, and how they identify with the characters.

Read the following paragraph and discuss the type of conflict present:

> Timothy was shocked out of sleep by the appearance of a bear just outside his tent. After panicking for a moment, he remembered some advice he had read in preparation for this trip: he should make noise so the bear would not be startled. As Timothy started to hum and sing, the bear wandered away.

There are three main types of conflict in literature: **man versus man**, **man versus nature**, and **man versus self**. This paragraph is an example of man versus nature. Timothy is in conflict with the bear. Even though no physical conflict like an attack exists, Timothy is pitted against the bear. Timothy uses his knowledge to "defeat" the bear and keep himself safe. The solution to the conflict is that Timothy makes noise, the bear wanders away, and Timothy is safe.

Review Video: Conflict
Visit mometrix.com/academy and enter code: 559550

Review Video: Determining Relationships in a Story
Visit mometrix.com/academy and enter code: 929925

Rising Action

The **rising action** is the part of the story where conflict **intensifies**. The rising action begins with an event that prompts the main conflict of the story. This may also be called the **inciting incident**. The main conflict generally occurs between the protagonist and an antagonist, but this is not the only type of conflict that may occur in a narrative. After this event, the protagonist works to resolve the main conflict by preparing for an altercation, pursuing a goal, fleeing an antagonist, or doing some other action that will end the conflict. The rising action is composed of several additional events that increase the story's tension. Most often, other developments will occur alongside the growth of the main conflict, such as character development or the development of minor conflicts. The rising action ends with the **climax**, which is the point of highest tension in the story.

Climax

The **climax** is the event in the narrative that marks the height of the story's conflict or tension. The event that takes place at the story's climax will end the rising action and bring about the results of the main conflict. If the conflict was between a good protagonist and an evil antagonist, the climax may be a final battle between the two characters. If the conflict is an adventurer looking for heavily guarded treasure, the climax may be the adventurer's encounter with the final obstacle that protects the treasure. The climax may be made of multiple scenes, but can usually be summarized as one event. Once the conflict and climax are complete, the **falling action** begins.

Falling Action

The **falling action** shows what happens in the story between the climax and the resolution. The falling action often composes a much smaller portion of the story than the rising action does. While the climax includes the end of the main conflict, the falling action may show the results of any minor conflicts in the story. For example, if the protagonist encountered a troll on the way to find some treasure, and the troll demanded the protagonist share the treasure after retrieving it, the falling action would include the protagonist returning to share the treasure with the troll. Similarly, any unexplained major events are usually made clear during the falling action. Once all significant elements of the story are resolved or addressed, the story's resolution will occur. The **resolution** is the end of the story, which shows the final result of the plot's events and shows what life is like for the main characters once they are no longer experiencing the story's conflicts.

Resolution

The way the conflict is **resolved** depends on the type of conflict. The plot of any book starts with the lead up to the conflict, then the conflict itself, and finally the solution, or **resolution**, to the conflict. In **man versus man** conflicts, the conflict is often resolved by two parties coming to some sort of agreement or by one party triumphing over the other party. In **man versus nature** conflicts, the conflict is often resolved by man coming to some realization about some aspect of nature. In **man versus self** conflicts, the conflict is often resolved by the character growing or coming to an understanding about part of himself.

Theme

A **theme** is a central idea demonstrated by a passage. Often, a theme is a lesson or moral contained in the text, but it does not have to be. It also is a unifying idea that is used throughout the text; it can take the form of a common setting, idea, symbol, design, or recurring event. A passage can have two or more themes that convey its overall idea. The theme or themes of a passage are often based on **universal themes**. They can frequently be expressed using well-known sayings about life, society, or human nature, such as "Hard work pays off" or "Good triumphs over evil." Themes are not usually stated **explicitly**. The reader must figure them out by carefully reading the passage. Themes are created through descriptive language or events in the plot. The events of a story help shape the themes of a passage.

EXAMPLE

Explain why "if you care about something, you need to take care of it" accurately describes the theme of the following excerpt.

> Luca collected baseball cards, but he wasn't very careful with them. He left them around the house. His dog liked to chew. One day, Luca and his friend Bart were looking at his collection. Then they went outside. When Luca got home, he saw his dog chewing on his cards. They were ruined.

This excerpt tells the story of a boy who is careless with his baseball cards and leaves them lying around. His dog ends up chewing them and ruining them. The lesson is that if you care about something, you need to take care of it. This is the theme, or point, of the story. Some stories have more than one theme, but this is not really true of this excerpt. The reader needs to figure out the theme based on what happens in the story. Sometimes, as in the case of fables, the theme is stated directly in the text. However, this is not usually the case.

Review Video: Themes in Literature
Visit mometrix.com/academy and enter code: 732074

CHARACTER DEVELOPMENT AND DIALOGUE

CHARACTER DEVELOPMENT

When depicting characters or figures in a written text, authors generally use actions, dialogue, and descriptions as characterization techniques. Characterization can occur in both fiction and nonfiction and is used to show a character or figure's personality, demeanor, and thoughts. This helps create a more engaging experience for the reader by providing a more concrete picture of a character or figure's tendencies and features. Characterizations also gives authors the opportunity to integrate elements such as dialects, activities, attire, and attitudes into their writing.

To understand the meaning of a story, it is vital to understand the characters as the author describes them. We can look for contradictions in what a character thinks, says, and does. We can notice whether the author's observations about a character differ from what other characters in the story say about that character. A character may be dynamic, meaning they change significantly during the story, or static, meaning they remain the same from beginning to end. Characters may be two-dimensional, not fully developed, or may be well developed with characteristics that stand out vividly. Characters may also symbolize universal properties. Additionally, readers can compare and contrast characters to analyze how each one developed.

A well-known example of character development can be found in Charles Dickens's *Great Expectations*. The novel's main character, Pip, is introduced as a young boy, and he is depicted as innocent, kind, and humble. However, as Pip grows up and is confronted with the social hierarchy of Victorian England, he becomes arrogant and rejects his loved ones in pursuit of his own social advancement. Once he achieves his social goals, he realizes the merits of his former lifestyle, and lives with the wisdom he gained in both environments and life stages. Dickens shows Pip's ever-changing character through his interactions with others and his inner thoughts, which evolve as his personal values and personality shift.

DIALOGUE

Effectively written dialogue serves at least one, but usually several, purposes. It advances the story and moves the plot, develops the characters, sheds light on the work's theme or meaning, and can, often subtly, account for the passage of time not otherwise indicated. It can alter the direction that the plot is taking, typically by introducing some new conflict or changing existing ones. **Dialogue** can establish a work's narrative voice and the characters' voices and set the tone of the story or of particular characters. When fictional characters display enlightenment or realization, dialogue can give readers an understanding of what those characters have discovered and how. Dialogue can illuminate the motivations and wishes of the story's characters. By using consistent thoughts and syntax, dialogue can support character development. Skillfully created, it can also represent real-life speech rhythms in written form. Via conflicts and ensuing action, dialogue also provides drama.

Dialogue in Fiction

In fictional works, effectively written dialogue does more than just break up or interrupt sections of narrative. While **dialogue** may supply exposition for readers, it must nonetheless be believable. Dialogue should be dynamic, not static, and it should not resemble regular prose. Authors should not use dialogue to write clever similes or metaphors, or to inject their own opinions. Nor should they use dialogue at all when narrative would be better. Most importantly, dialogue should not slow the plot movement. Dialogue must seem natural, which means careful construction of phrases rather than actually duplicating natural speech, which does not necessarily translate well to the written word. Finally, all dialogue must be pertinent to the story, rather than just added conversation.

Integration of Knowledge and Ideas

Critical Reading Skills

Opinions, Facts, and Fallacies

Critical thinking skills are mastered through understanding various types of writing and the different purposes authors can have for writing different passages. Every author writes for a purpose. When you understand their purpose and how they accomplish their goal, you will be able to analyze their writing and determine whether or not you agree with their conclusions.

Readers must always be aware of the difference between fact and opinion. A **fact** can be subjected to analysis and proven to be true. An **opinion**, on the other hand, is the author's personal thoughts or feelings and may not be altered by research or evidence. If the author writes that the distance from New York City to Boston is about two hundred miles, then he or she is stating a fact. If the author writes that New York City is too crowded, then he or she is giving an opinion because there is no objective standard for overpopulation. Opinions are often supported by facts. For instance, an author might use a comparison between the population density of New York City and that of other major American cities as evidence of an overcrowded population. An opinion supported by facts tends to be more convincing. On the other hand, when authors support their opinions with other opinions, readers should employ critical thinking and approach the argument with skepticism.

Review Video: Distinguishing Fact and Opinion
Visit mometrix.com/academy and enter code: 870899

Reliable Sources

When you read an argumentative passage, you need to be sure that facts are presented to the reader from **reliable sources**. An opinion is what the author thinks about a given topic. An opinion is not common knowledge or proven by expert sources, instead the information is the personal beliefs and thoughts of the author. To distinguish between fact and opinion, a reader needs to consider the type of source that is presenting information, the information that backs-up a claim, and the author's motivation to have a certain point-of-view on a given topic. For example, if a panel of scientists has conducted multiple studies on the effectiveness of taking a certain vitamin, then the results are more likely to be factual than those of a company that is selling a vitamin and simply claims that taking the vitamin can produce positive effects. The company is motivated to sell their product, and the scientists are using the scientific method to prove a theory. Remember, if you find sentences that contain phrases such as "I think...", then the statement is an opinion.

Biases

In their attempts to persuade, writers often make mistakes in their thought processes and writing choices. These processes and choices are important to understand so you can make an informed decision about the author's credibility. Every author has a point of view, but authors demonstrate a **bias** when they ignore reasonable counterarguments or distort opposing viewpoints. A bias is evident whenever the author's claims are presented in a way that is unfair or inaccurate. Bias can be intentional or unintentional, but readers should be skeptical of the author's argument in either case. Remember that a biased author may still be correct. However, the author will be correct in spite of, not because of, his or her bias.

A **stereotype** is a bias applied specifically to a group of people or a place. Stereotyping is considered to be particularly abhorrent because it promotes negative, misleading generalizations about people. Readers should be very cautious of authors who use stereotypes in their writing. These faulty assumptions typically reveal the author's ignorance and lack of curiosity.

> **Review Video: Bias and Stereotype**
> Visit mometrix.com/academy and enter code: 644829

PERSUASION AND RHETORIC

PERSUASIVE TECHNIQUES

To **appeal using reason**, writers present logical arguments, such as using "If... then... because" statements. To **appeal to emotions**, authors may ask readers how they would feel about something or to put themselves in another's place, present their argument as one that will make the audience feel good, or tell readers how they should feel. To **appeal to character**, **morality**, or **ethics**, authors present their points to readers as the right or most moral choices. Authors cite expert opinions to show readers that someone very knowledgeable about the subject or viewpoint agrees with the author's claims. **Testimonials**, usually via anecdotes or quotations regarding the author's subject, help build the audience's trust in an author's message through positive support from ordinary people. **Bandwagon appeals** claim that everybody else agrees with the author's argument and persuade readers to conform and agree, also. Authors **appeal to greed** by presenting their choice as cheaper, free, or more valuable for less cost. They **appeal to laziness** by presenting their views as more convenient, easy, or relaxing. Authors also anticipate potential objections and argue against them before audiences think of them, thereby depicting those objections as weak.

Authors can use **comparisons** like analogies, similes, and metaphors to persuade audiences. For example, a writer might represent excessive expenses as "hemorrhaging" money, which the author's recommended solution will stop. Authors can use negative word connotations to make some choices unappealing to readers, and positive word connotations to make others more appealing. Using **humor** can relax readers and garner their agreement. However, writers must take care: ridiculing opponents can be a successful strategy for appealing to readers who already agree with the author, but can backfire by angering other readers. **Rhetorical questions** need no answer, but create effect that can force agreement, such as asking the question, "Wouldn't you rather be paid more than less?" **Generalizations** persuade readers by being impossible to disagree with. Writers can easily make generalizations that appear to support their viewpoints, like saying, "We all want peace, not war" regarding more specific political arguments. **Transfer** and **association** persuade by example: if advertisements show attractive actors enjoying their products, audiences imagine they will experience the same. **Repetition** can also sometimes effectively persuade audiences.

> **Review Video: Using Rhetorical Strategies for Persuasion**
> Visit mometrix.com/academy and enter code: 302658

CLASSICAL AUTHOR APPEALS

In his *On Rhetoric,* ancient Greek philosopher Aristotle defined three basic types of appeal used in writing, which he called *pathos*, *ethos*, and *logos*. ***Pathos*** means suffering or experience and refers to appeals to the emotions (the English word *pathetic* comes from this root). Writing that is meant to entertain audiences, by making them either happy, as with comedy, or sad, as with tragedy, uses *pathos*. Aristotle's *Poetics* states that evoking the emotions of terror and pity is one of the criteria for writing tragedy. ***Ethos*** means character and connotes ideology (the English word *ethics* comes from this root). Writing that appeals to credibility, based on academic, professional, or personal merit, uses *ethos*. ***Logos*** means "I say" and refers to a plea, opinion, expectation, word or speech, account, opinion, or reason (the English word *logic* comes from this root.) Aristotle used it to mean persuasion that appeals to the audience through reasoning and logic to influence their opinions.

Rhetorical Devices

- An **anecdote** is a brief story authors may relate to their argument, which can illustrate their points in a more real and relatable way.
- **Aphorisms** concisely state common beliefs and may rhyme. For example, Benjamin Franklin's "Early to bed and early to rise / Makes a man healthy, wealthy, and wise" is an aphorism.
- **Allusions** refer to literary or historical figures to impart symbolism to a thing or person and to create reader resonance. In John Steinbeck's *Of Mice and Men,* protagonist George's last name is Milton. This alludes to John Milton, who wrote *Paradise Lost,* and symbolizes George's eventual loss of his dream.
- **Satire** exaggerates, ridicules, or pokes fun at human flaws or ideas, as in the works of Jonathan Swift and Mark Twain.
- A **parody** is a form of satire that imitates another work to ridicule its topic or style.
- A **paradox** is a statement that is true despite appearing contradictory.
- **Hyperbole** is overstatement using exaggerated language.
- An **oxymoron** combines seeming contradictions, such as "deafening silence."
- **Analogies** compare two things that share common elements.
- **Similes** (stated comparisons using the words *like* or *as*) and **metaphors** (stated comparisons that do not use *like* or *as*) are considered forms of analogy.
- When using logic to reason with audiences, **syllogism** refers either to deductive reasoning or a deceptive, very sophisticated, or subtle argument.
- **Deductive reasoning** moves from general to specific, **inductive reasoning** from specific to general.
- **Diction** is author word choice that establishes tone and effect.
- **Understatement** achieves effects like contrast or irony by downplaying or describing something more subtly than warranted.
- **Chiasmus** uses parallel clauses, the second reversing the order of the first. Examples include T. S. Eliot's "Has the Church failed mankind, or has mankind failed the Church?" and John F. Kennedy's "Ask not what your country can do for you; ask what you can do for your country."
- **Anaphora** regularly repeats a word or phrase at the beginnings of consecutive clauses or phrases to add emphasis to an idea. A classic example of anaphora was Winston Churchill's emphasis of determination: "[W]e shall fight on the beaches, we shall fight on the landing grounds, we shall fight in the fields and in the streets, we shall fight in the hills; we shall never surrender..."

Reading Argumentative Writing

Author's Argument in Argumentative Writing

In argumentative writing, the argument is a belief, position, or opinion that the author wants to convince readers to believe as well. For the first step, readers should identify the **issue**. Some issues are controversial, meaning people disagree about them. Gun control, foreign policy, and the death penalty are all controversial issues. The next step is to determine the **author's position** on the issue. That position or viewpoint constitutes the author's argument. Readers should then identify the **author's assumptions**: things he or she accepts, believes, or takes for granted without needing proof. Inaccurate or illogical assumptions produce flawed arguments and can mislead readers. Readers should identify what kinds of **supporting evidence** the author offers, such as research results, personal observations or experiences, case studies, facts, examples, expert testimony and opinions, and comparisons. Readers should decide how relevant this support is to the argument.

Review Video: Argumentative Writing
Visit mometrix.com/academy and enter code: 561544

Evaluating an Author's Argument

The first three reader steps to **evaluate an author's argument** are to identify the **author's assumptions**, identify the **supporting evidence**, and decide **whether the evidence is relevant**. For example, if an author is not an expert on a particular topic, then that author's personal experience or opinion might not be relevant. The fourth step is to assess the **author's objectivity**. For example, consider whether the author introduces clear, understandable supporting evidence and facts to support the argument. The fifth step is evaluating whether the author's **argument is complete**. When authors give sufficient support for their arguments and also anticipate and respond effectively to opposing arguments or objections to their points, their arguments are complete. However, some authors omit information that could detract from their arguments. If instead they stated this information and refuted it, it would strengthen their arguments. The sixth step in evaluating an author's argumentative writing is to assess whether the **argument is valid**. Providing clear, logical reasoning makes an author's argument valid. Readers should ask themselves whether the author's points follow a sequence that makes sense, and whether each point leads to the next. The seventh step is to determine whether the author's **argument is credible**, meaning that it is convincing and believable. Arguments that are not valid are not credible, so step seven depends on step six. Readers should be mindful of their own biases as they evaluate and should not expect authors to conclusively prove their arguments, but rather to provide effective support and reason.

Evaluating an Author's Method of Appeal

To evaluate the effectiveness of an appeal, it is important to consider the author's purpose for writing. Any appeals an author uses in their argument must be relevant to the argument's goal. For example, a writer that argues for the reclassification of Pluto, but primarily uses appeals to emotion, will not have an effective argument. This writer should focus on using appeals to logic and support their argument with provable facts. While most arguments should include appeals to logic, emotion, and credibility, some arguments only call for one or two of these types of appeal. Evidence can support an appeal, but the evidence must be relevant to truly strengthen the appeal's effectiveness. If the writer arguing for Pluto's reclassification uses the reasons for Jupiter's classification as evidence, their argument would be weak. This information may seem relevant because it is related to the classification of planets. However, this classification is highly dependent on the size of the celestial object, and Jupiter is significantly bigger than Pluto. This use of evidence is illogical and does not support the appeal. Even when appropriate evidence and appeals are used, appeals and arguments lose their effectiveness when they create logical fallacies.

Evidence

The term **text evidence** refers to information that supports a main point or minor points and can help lead the reader to a conclusion about the text's credibility. Information used as text evidence is precise, descriptive, and factual. A main point is often followed by supporting details that provide evidence to back up a claim. For example, a passage may include the claim that winter occurs during opposite months in the Northern and Southern hemispheres. Text evidence for this claim may include examples of countries where winter occurs in opposite months. Stating that the tilt of the Earth as it rotates around the sun causes winter to occur at different times in separate hemispheres is another example of text evidence. Text evidence can come from common knowledge, but it is also valuable to include text evidence from credible, relevant outside sources.

Review Video: Textual Evidence
Visit mometrix.com/academy and enter code: 486236

Evidence that supports the thesis and additional arguments needs to be provided. Most arguments must be supported by facts or statistics. A fact is something that is known with certainty, has been verified by several independent individuals, and can be proven to be true. In addition to facts, examples and illustrations can support an argument by adding an emotional component. With this component, you persuade readers in ways that facts and statistics cannot. The emotional component is effective when used alongside objective information that can be confirmed.

Credibility

The text used to support an argument can be the argument's downfall if the text is not credible. A text is **credible**, or believable, when its author is knowledgeable and objective, or unbiased. The author's motivations for writing the text play a critical role in determining the credibility of the text and must be evaluated when assessing that credibility. Reports written about the ozone layer by an environmental scientist and a hairdresser will have a different level of credibility.

> **Review Video: Author Credibility**
> Visit mometrix.com/academy and enter code: 827257

Appeal to Emotion

Sometimes, authors will appeal to the reader's emotion in an attempt to persuade or to distract the reader from the weakness of the argument. For instance, the author may try to inspire the pity of the reader by delivering a heart-rending story. An author also might use the bandwagon approach, in which he suggests that his opinion is correct because it is held by the majority. Some authors resort to name-calling, in which insults and harsh words are delivered to the opponent in an attempt to distract. In advertising, a common appeal is the celebrity testimonial, in which a famous person endorses a product. Of course, the fact that a famous person likes something should not really mean anything to the reader. These and other emotional appeals are usually evidence of poor reasoning and a weak argument.

> **Review Video: Emotional Language in Literature**
> Visit mometrix.com/academy and enter code: 759390

Counter Arguments

When authors give both sides to the argument, they build trust with their readers. As a reader, you should start with an undecided or neutral position. If an author presents only his or her side to the argument, then they are not exhibiting credibility and are weakening their argument.

Building common ground with readers can be effective for persuading neutral, skeptical, or opposed readers. Sharing values with undecided readers can allow people to switch positions without giving up what they feel is important. People who may oppose a position need to feel that they can change their minds without betraying who they are as a person. This appeal to having an open mind can be a powerful tool in arguing a position without antagonizing other views. Objections can be countered on a point-by-point basis or in a summary paragraph. Be mindful of how an author points out flaws in counter arguments. If they are unfair to the other side of the argument, then you should lose trust with the author.

Vocabulary Acquisition and Use

Using Context to Determine Meaning

Context Clues

Readers of all levels will encounter words that they have either never seen or have encountered only on a limited basis. The best way to define a word in **context** is to look for nearby words that can assist in revealing the meaning of the word. For instance, unfamiliar nouns are often accompanied by examples that provide a definition. Consider the following sentence: *Dave arrived at the party in hilarious garb: a leopard-print shirt, buckskin trousers, and bright green sneakers.* If a reader was unfamiliar with the meaning of garb, he or she could read the examples (i.e., a leopard-print shirt, buckskin trousers, and bright green sneakers) and quickly determine that the word means *clothing*. Examples will not always be this obvious. Consider this sentence: *Parsley, lemon, and flowers were just a few of the items he used as garnishes.* Here, the word *garnishes* is exemplified by parsley, lemon, and flowers. Readers who have eaten in a variety of restaurants will probably be able to identify a garnish as something used to decorate a plate.

Review Video: Reading Comprehension: Using Context Clues
Visit mometrix.com/academy and enter code: 613660

Using Contrast in Context Clues

In addition to looking at the context of a passage, readers can use contrast to define an unfamiliar word in context. In many sentences, the author will not describe the unfamiliar word directly; instead, he or she will describe the opposite of the unfamiliar word. Thus, you are provided with some information that will bring you closer to defining the word. Consider the following example: *Despite his intelligence, Hector's low brow and bad posture made him look obtuse.* The author writes that Hector's appearance does not convey intelligence. Therefore, *obtuse* must mean unintelligent. Here is another example: *Despite the horrible weather, we were beatific about our trip to Alaska*. The word *despite* indicates that the speaker's feelings were at odds with the weather. Since the weather is described as *horrible*, then *beatific* must mean something positive.

Substitution to Find Meaning

In some cases, there will be very few contextual clues to help a reader define the meaning of an unfamiliar word. When this happens, one strategy that readers may employ is **substitution**. A good reader will brainstorm some possible synonyms for the given word, and he or she will substitute these words into the sentence. If the sentence and the surrounding passage continue to make sense, then the substitution has revealed at least some information about the unfamiliar word. Consider the sentence: *Frank's admonition rang in her ears as she climbed the mountain.* A reader unfamiliar with *admonition* might come up with some substitutions like *vow, promise, advice, complaint*, or *compliment*. All of these words make general sense of the sentence, though their meanings are diverse. However, this process has suggested that an admonition is some sort of message. The substitution strategy is rarely able to pinpoint a precise definition, but this process can be effective as a last resort.

Occasionally, you will be able to define an unfamiliar word by looking at the descriptive words in the context. Consider the following sentence: *Fred dragged the recalcitrant boy kicking and screaming up the stairs.* The words *dragged, kicking*, and *screaming* all suggest that the boy does not want to go up the stairs. The reader may assume that *recalcitrant* means something like unwilling or protesting. In this example, an unfamiliar adjective was identified.

Additionally, using description to define an unfamiliar noun is a common practice compared to unfamiliar adjectives, as in this sentence: *Don's wrinkled frown and constantly shaking fist identified him as a curmudgeon of the first order.* Don is described as having a *wrinkled frown and constantly shaking fist*, suggesting that a *curmudgeon* must be a grumpy person. Contrasts do not always provide detailed information about the unfamiliar word, but they at least give the reader some clues.

Words with Multiple Meanings

When a word has more than one meaning, readers can have difficulty determining how the word is being used in a given sentence. For instance, the verb *cleave*, can mean either *join* or *separate*. When readers come upon this word, they will have to select the definition that makes the most sense. Consider the following sentence: *Hermione's knife cleaved the bread cleanly*. Since a knife cannot join bread together, the word must indicate separation. A slightly more difficult example would be the sentence: *The birds cleaved to one another as they flew from the oak tree.* Immediately, the presence of the words *to one another* should suggest that in this sentence *cleave* is being used to mean *join*. Discovering the intent of a word with multiple meanings requires the same tricks as defining an unknown word: look for contextual clues and evaluate the substituted words.

Context Clues to Help Determine Meanings of Words

If readers simply bypass unknown words, they can reach unclear conclusions about what they read. However, looking for the definition of every unfamiliar word in the dictionary can slow their reading progress. Moreover, the dictionary may list multiple definitions for a word, so readers must search the word's context for meaning. Hence context is important to new vocabulary regardless of reader methods. Four types of context clues are examples, definitions, descriptive words, and opposites. Authors may use a certain word, and then follow it with several different examples of what it describes. Sometimes authors actually supply a definition of a word they use, which is especially true in informational and technical texts. Authors may use descriptive words that elaborate upon a vocabulary word they just used. Authors may also use opposites with negation that help define meaning.

Examples and Definitions

An author may use a word and then give examples that illustrate its meaning. Consider this text: "Teachers who do not know how to use sign language can help students who are deaf or hard of hearing understand certain instructions by using gestures instead, like pointing their fingers to indicate which direction to look or go; holding up a hand, palm outward, to indicate stopping; holding the hands flat, palms up, curling a finger toward oneself in a beckoning motion to indicate 'come here'; or curling all fingers toward oneself repeatedly to indicate 'come on', 'more', or 'continue.'" The author of this text has used the word "gestures" and then followed it with examples, so a reader unfamiliar with the word could deduce from the examples that "gestures" means "hand motions." Readers can find examples by looking for signal words "for example," "for instance," "like," "such as," and "e.g."

While readers sometimes have to look for definitions of unfamiliar words in a dictionary or do some work to determine a word's meaning from its surrounding context, at other times an author may make it easier for readers by defining certain words. For example, an author may write, "The company did not have sufficient capital, that is, available money, to continue operations." The author defined "capital" as "available money," and heralded the definition with the phrase "that is." Another way that authors supply word definitions is with appositives. Rather than being introduced by a signal phrase like "that is," "namely," or "meaning," an appositive comes after the vocabulary word it defines and is enclosed within two commas. For example, an author may write, "The Indians introduced the Pilgrims to pemmican, cakes they made of lean meat dried and mixed with fat, which proved greatly beneficial to keep settlers from starving while trapping." In this example, the appositive phrase following "pemmican" and preceding "which" defines the word "pemmican."

Descriptions

When readers encounter a word they do not recognize in a text, the author may expand on that word to illustrate it better. While the author may do this to make the prose more picturesque and vivid, the reader can also take advantage of this description to provide context clues to the meaning of the unfamiliar word. For example, an author may write, "The man sitting next to me on the airplane was obese. His shirt stretched across his vast expanse of flesh, strained almost to bursting." The descriptive second sentence elaborates on and helps to define the previous sentence's word "obese" to mean extremely fat. A reader unfamiliar with the word "repugnant" can decipher its meaning through an author's accompanying description: "The way the child grimaced and shuddered as he swallowed the medicine showed that its taste was particularly repugnant."

Opposites

Text authors sometimes introduce a contrasting or opposing idea before or after a concept they present. They may do this to emphasize or heighten the idea they present by contrasting it with something that is the reverse. However, readers can also use these context clues to understand familiar words. For example, an author may write, "Our conversation was not cheery. We sat and talked very solemnly about his experience and a number of similar events." The reader who is not familiar with the word "solemnly" can deduce by the author's preceding use of "not cheery" that "solemn" means the opposite of cheery or happy, so it must mean serious or sad. Or if someone writes, "Don't condemn his entire project because you couldn't find anything good to say about it," readers unfamiliar with "condemn" can understand from the sentence structure that it means the opposite of saying anything good, so it must mean reject, dismiss, or disapprove. "Entire" adds another context clue, meaning total or complete rejection.

Syntax to Determine Part of Speech and Meanings of Words

Syntax refers to sentence structure and word order. Suppose that a reader encounters an unfamiliar word when reading a text. To illustrate, consider an invented word like "splunch." If this word is used in a sentence like "Please splunch that ball to me," the reader can assume from syntactic context that "splunch" is a verb. We would not use a noun, adjective, adverb, or preposition with the object "that ball," and the prepositional phrase "to me" further indicates "splunch" represents an action. However, in the sentence, "Please hand that splunch to me," the reader can assume that "splunch" is a noun. Demonstrative adjectives like "that" modify nouns. Also, we hand someone some*thing*—a thing being a noun; we do not hand someone a verb, adjective, or adverb. Some sentences contain further clues. For example, from the sentence, "The princess wore the glittering splunch on her head," the reader can deduce that it is a crown, tiara, or something similar from the syntactic context, without knowing the word.

Syntax to Indicate Different Meanings of Similar Sentences

The syntax, or structure, of a sentence affords grammatical cues that aid readers in comprehending the meanings of words, phrases, and sentences in the texts that they read. Seemingly minor differences in how the words or phrases in a sentence are ordered can make major differences in meaning. For example, two sentences can use exactly the same words but have different meanings based on the word order:

- "The man with a broken arm sat in a chair."
- "The man sat in a chair with a broken arm."

While both sentences indicate that a man sat in a chair, differing syntax indicates whether the man's or chair's arm was broken.

Review Video: Syntax Visit mometrix.com/academy and enter code: 242280

Determining Meaning of Phrases and Paragraphs

Like unknown words, the meanings of phrases, paragraphs, and entire works can also be difficult to discern. Each of these can be better understood with added context. However, for larger groups of words, more context is needed. Unclear phrases are similar to unclear words, and the same methods can be used to understand their meaning. However, it is also important to consider how the individual words in the phrase work together. Paragraphs are a bit more complicated. Just as words must be compared to other words in a sentence, paragraphs must be compared to other paragraphs in a composition or a section.

Determining Meaning in Various Types of Compositions

To understand the meaning of an entire composition, the type of composition must be considered. **Expository writing** is generally organized so that each paragraph focuses on explaining one idea, or part of an idea, and its relevance. **Persuasive writing** uses paragraphs for different purposes to organize the parts of the argument. **Unclear paragraphs** must be read in the context of the paragraphs around them for their meaning to be fully understood. The meaning of full texts can also be unclear at times. The purpose of composition is also important for understanding the meaning of a text. To quickly understand the broad meaning of a text, look to the introductory and concluding paragraphs. Fictional texts are different. Some fictional works have implicit meanings, but some do not. The target audience must be considered for understanding texts that do have an implicit meaning, as most children's fiction will clearly state any lessons or morals. For other fiction, the application of literary theories and criticism may be helpful for understanding the text.

RESOURCES FOR DETERMINING WORD MEANING AND USAGE

While these strategies are useful for determining the meaning of unknown words and phrases, sometimes additional resources are needed to properly use the terms in different contexts. Some words have multiple definitions, and some words are inappropriate in particular contexts or modes of writing. The following tools are helpful for understanding all meanings and proper uses for words and phrases.

- **Dictionaries** provide the meaning of a multitude of words in a language. Many dictionaries include additional information about each word, such as its etymology, its synonyms, or variations of the word.
- **Glossaries** are similar to dictionaries, as they provide the meanings of a variety of terms. However, while dictionaries typically feature an extensive list of words and comprise an entire publication, glossaries are often included at the end of a text and only include terms and definitions that are relevant to the text they follow.
- **Spell Checkers** are used to detect spelling errors in typed text. Some spell checkers may also detect the misuse of plural or singular nouns, verb tenses, or capitalization. While spell checkers are a helpful tool, they are not always reliable or attuned to the author's intent, so it is important to review the spell checker's suggestions before accepting them.
- **Style Manuals** are guidelines on the preferred punctuation, format, and grammar usage according to different fields or organizations. For example, the Associated Press Stylebook is a style guide often used for media writing. The guidelines within a style guide are not always applicable across different contexts and usages, as the guidelines often cover grammatical or formatting situations that are not objectively correct or incorrect.

Chapter Quiz

Ready to see how well you retained what you just read? Scan the QR code to go directly to the chapter quiz interface for this study guide. If you're using a computer, simply visit the online resources page at **mometrix.com/resources719/tabe1314** and click the Chapter Quizzes link.

Language

Knowledge of Language and Vocabulary

Word Roots and Prefixes and Suffixes

Affixes

Affixes in the English language are morphemes that are added to words to create related but different words. Derivational affixes form new words based on and related to the original words. For example, the affix *–ness* added to the end of the adjective *happy* forms the noun *happiness.* Inflectional affixes form different grammatical versions of words. For example, the plural affix *–s* changes the singular noun *book* to the plural noun *books*, and the past tense affix *–ed* changes the present tense verb *look* to the past tense *looked.* Prefixes are affixes placed in front of words. For example, *heat* means to make hot; *preheat* means to heat in advance. Suffixes are affixes placed at the ends of words. The *happiness* example above contains the suffix *–ness.* Circumfixes add parts both before and after words, such as how *light* becomes *enlighten* with the prefix *en-* and the suffix *–en.* Interfixes create compound words via central affixes: *speed* and *meter* become *speedometer* via the interfix *–o–*.

> **Review Video: Affixes**
> Visit mometrix.com/academy and enter code: 782422

Word Roots, Prefixes, and Suffixes to Help Determine Meanings of Words

Many English words were formed from combining multiple sources. For example, the Latin *habēre* means "to have," and the prefixes *in-* and *im-* mean a lack or prevention of something, as in *insufficient* and *imperfect.* Latin combined *in-* with *habēre* to form *inhibēre,* whose past participle was *inhibitus.* This is the origin of the English word *inhibit,* meaning to prevent from having. Hence by knowing the meanings of both the prefix and the root, one can decipher the word meaning. In Greek, the root *enkephalo-* refers to the brain. Many medical terms are based on this root, such as encephalitis and hydrocephalus. Understanding the prefix and suffix meanings (*-itis* means inflammation; *hydro-* means water) allows a person to deduce that encephalitis refers to brain inflammation and hydrocephalus refers to water (or other fluid) in the brain.

> **Review Video: Root Words in English**
> Visit mometrix.com/academy and enter code: 896380
>
> **Review Video: Determining Word Meanings**
> Visit mometrix.com/academy and enter code: 894894

Prefixes

Knowing common prefixes is helpful for all readers as they try to determining meanings or definitions of unfamiliar words. For example, a common word used when cooking is *preheat.* Knowing that *pre-* means in advance can also inform them that *presume* means to assume in advance, that *prejudice* means advance judgment, and that this understanding can be applied to many other words beginning with *pre-.* Knowing that the prefix *dis-* indicates opposition informs the meanings of words like *disbar, disagree, disestablish,* and many more. Knowing *dys-* means bad, impaired, abnormal, or difficult informs *dyslogistic, dysfunctional, dysphagia,* and *dysplasia.*

Suffixes

In English, certain suffixes generally indicate both that a word is a noun, and that the noun represents a state of being or quality. For example, *-ness* is commonly used to change an adjective into its noun form, as with *happy* and *happiness, nice* and *niceness,* and so on. The suffix *–tion* is commonly used to transform a verb into its noun form, as with *converse* and *conversation or move* and *motion*. Thus, if readers are unfamiliar with the second form of a word, knowing the meaning of the transforming suffix can help them determine meaning.

PREFIXES FOR NUMBERS

Prefix	Definition	Examples
bi-	two	bisect, biennial
mono-	one, single	monogamy, monologue
poly-	many	polymorphous, polygamous
semi-	half, partly	semicircle, semicolon
uni-	one	uniform, unity

PREFIXES FOR TIME, DIRECTION, AND SPACE

Prefix	Definition	Examples
a-	in, on, of, up, to	abed, afoot
ab-	from, away, off	abdicate, abjure
ad-	to, toward	advance, adventure
ante-	before, previous	antecedent, antedate
anti-	against, opposing	antipathy, antidote
cata-	down, away, thoroughly	catastrophe, cataclysm
circum-	around	circumspect, circumference
com-	with, together, very	commotion, complicate
contra-	against, opposing	contradict, contravene
de-	from	depart
dia-	through, across, apart	diameter, diagnose
dis-	away, off, down, not	dissent, disappear
epi-	upon	epilogue
ex-	out	extract, excerpt
hypo-	under, beneath	hypodermic, hypothesis
inter-	among, between	intercede, interrupt
intra-	within	intramural, intrastate
ob-	against, opposing	objection
per-	through	perceive, permit
peri-	around	periscope, perimeter
post-	after, following	postpone, postscript
pre-	before, previous	prevent, preclude
pro-	forward, in place of	propel, pronoun
retro-	back, backward	retrospect, retrograde
sub-	under, beneath	subjugate, substitute
super-	above, extra	supersede, supernumerary
trans-	across, beyond, over	transact, transport
ultra-	beyond, excessively	ultramodern, ultrasonic

NEGATIVE PREFIXES

Prefix	Definition	Examples
a-	without, lacking	atheist, agnostic
in-	not, opposing	incapable, ineligible
non-	not	nonentity, nonsense
un-	not, reverse of	unhappy, unlock

EXTRA PREFIXES

Prefix	Definition	Examples
for-	away, off, from	forget, forswear

Prefix	Definition	Examples
fore-	previous	foretell, forefathers
homo-	same, equal	homogenized, homonym
hyper-	excessive, over	hypercritical, hypertension
in-	in, into	intrude, invade
mal-	bad, poorly, not	malfunction, malpractice
mis-	bad, poorly, not	misspell, misfire
neo-	new	Neolithic, neoconservative
omni-	all, everywhere	omniscient, omnivore
ortho-	right, straight	orthogonal, orthodox
over-	above	overbearing, oversight
pan-	all, entire	panorama, pandemonium
para-	beside, beyond	parallel, paradox
re-	backward, again	revoke, recur
sym-	with, together	sympathy, symphony

Below is a list of common suffixes and their meanings:

ADJECTIVE SUFFIXES

Suffix	Definition	Examples
-able (-ible)	capable of being	toler*able*, ed*ible*
-esque	in the style of, like	picturesque, grotesque
-ful	filled with, marked by	thankful, zestful
-ific	make, cause	terrific, beatific
-ish	suggesting, like	churlish, childish
-less	lacking, without	hopeless, countless
-ous	marked by, given to	religious, riotous

NOUN SUFFIXES

Suffix	Definition	Examples
-acy	state, condition	accuracy, privacy
-ance	act, condition, fact	acceptance, vigilance
-ard	one that does excessively	drunkard, sluggard
-ation	action, state, result	occupation, starvation
-dom	state, rank, condition	serfdom, wisdom
-er (-or)	office, action	teach*er*, elevat*or*, hon*or*
-ess	feminine	waitress, duchess
-hood	state, condition	manhood, statehood
-ion	action, result, state	union, fusion
-ism	act, manner, doctrine	barbarism, socialism
-ist	worker, follower	monopolist, socialist
-ity (-ty)	state, quality, condition	acid*ity*, civil*ity*, twen*ty*
-ment	result, action	Refreshment
-ness	quality, state	greatness, tallness
-ship	position	internship, statesmanship
-sion (-tion)	state, result	revi*sion*, expedi*tion*
-th	act, state, quality	warmth, width
-tude	quality, state, result	magnitude, fortitude

Verb Suffixes

Suffix	Definition	Examples
-ate	having, showing	separate, desolate
-en	cause to be, become	deepen, strengthen
-fy	make, cause to have	glorify, fortify
-ize	cause to be, treat with	sterilize, mechanize

Nuance and Word Meanings

Synonyms and Antonyms

When you understand how words relate to each other, you will discover more in a passage. This is explained by understanding **synonyms** (e.g., words that mean the same thing) and **antonyms** (e.g., words that mean the opposite of one another). As an example, *dry* and *arid* are synonyms, and *dry* and *wet* are antonyms.

There are many pairs of words in English that can be considered synonyms, despite having slightly different definitions. For instance, the words *friendly* and *collegial* can both be used to describe a warm interpersonal relationship, and one would be correct to call them synonyms. However, *collegial* (kin to *colleague*) is often used in reference to professional or academic relationships, and *friendly* has no such connotation.

If the difference between the two words is too great, then they should not be called synonyms. *Hot* and *warm* are not synonyms because their meanings are too distinct. A good way to determine whether two words are synonyms is to substitute one word for the other word and verify that the meaning of the sentence has not changed. Substituting *warm* for *hot* in a sentence would convey a different meaning. Although warm and hot may seem close in meaning, warm generally means that the temperature is moderate, and hot generally means that the temperature is excessively high.

Antonyms are words with opposite meanings. *Light* and *dark*, *up* and *down*, *right* and *left*, *good* and *bad*: these are all sets of antonyms. Be careful to distinguish between antonyms and pairs of words that are simply different. *Black* and *gray*, for instance, are not antonyms because gray is not the opposite of black. *Black* and *white*, on the other hand, are antonyms.

Not every word has an antonym. For instance, many nouns do not. What would be the antonym of *chair*? During your exam, the questions related to antonyms are more likely to concern adjectives. You will recall that adjectives are words that describe a noun. Some common adjectives include *purple*, *fast*, *skinny*, and *sweet*. From those four adjectives, *purple* is the item that lacks a group of obvious antonyms.

Review Video: Synonyms and Antonyms
Visit mometrix.com/academy and enter code: 105612

Denotative vs. Connotative Meaning

The **denotative** meaning of a word is the literal meaning. The **connotative** meaning goes beyond the denotative meaning to include the emotional reaction that a word may invoke. The connotative meaning often takes the denotative meaning a step further due to associations the reader makes with the denotative meaning. Readers can differentiate between the denotative and connotative meanings by first recognizing how authors use each meaning. Most non-fiction, for example, is fact-based and authors do not use flowery, figurative language. The reader can assume that the writer is using the denotative meaning of words. In fiction, the author may use the connotative meaning. Readers can determine whether the author is using the denotative or connotative meaning of a word by implementing context clues.

Review Video: Connotation and Denotation
Visit mometrix.com/academy and enter code: 310092

Nuances of Word Meaning

A word's denotation is simply its objective dictionary definition. However, its connotation refers to the subjective associations, often emotional, that specific words evoke in listeners and readers. Two or more words can have the same dictionary meaning, but very different connotations. Writers use diction (word choice) to convey various nuances of thought and emotion by selecting synonyms for other words that best communicate the associations they want to trigger for readers. For example, a car engine is naturally greasy; in this sense, "greasy" is a neutral term. But when a person's smile, appearance, or clothing is described as "greasy," it has a negative connotation. Some words have even gained additional or different meanings over time. For example, *awful* used to be used to describe things that evoked a sense of awe. When *awful* is separated into its root word, awe, and suffix, -ful, it can be understood to mean "full of awe." However, the word is now commonly used to describe things that evoke repulsion, terror, or another intense, negative reaction.

Review Video: Word Usage in Sentences
Visit mometrix.com/academy and enter code: 197863

Conventions of Standard English

Parts of Speech

Nouns

A noun is a person, place, thing, or idea. The two main types of nouns are **common** and **proper** nouns. Nouns can also be categorized as abstract (i.e., general) or concrete (i.e., specific).

Common Nouns

Common nouns are generic names for people, places, and things. Common nouns are not usually capitalized.

Examples of common nouns:

People: boy, girl, worker, manager

Places: school, bank, library, home

Things: dog, cat, truck, car

Review Video: Nouns
Visit mometrix.com/academy and enter code: 344028

Proper Nouns

Proper nouns name specific people, places, or things. All proper nouns are capitalized.

Examples of proper nouns:

People: Abraham Lincoln, George Washington, Martin Luther King, Jr.

Places: Los Angeles, California; New York; Asia

Things: Statue of Liberty, Earth, Lincoln Memorial

Note: Some nouns can be either common or proper depending on their use. For example, when referring to the planet that we live on, *Earth* is a proper noun and is capitalized. When referring to the dirt, rocks, or land on our planet, *earth* is a common noun and is not capitalized.

General and Specific Nouns

General nouns are the names of conditions or ideas. **Specific nouns** name people, places, and things that are understood by using your senses.

General nouns:

Condition: beauty, strength

Idea: truth, peace

Specific nouns:

People: baby, friend, father

Places: town, park, city hall

Things: rainbow, cough, apple, silk, gasoline

Collective Nouns

Collective nouns are the names for a group of people, places, or things that may act as a whole. The following are examples of collective nouns: *class, company, dozen, group, herd, team,* and *public*. Collective nouns usually require an article, which denotes the noun as being a single unit. For instance, a choir is a group of singers. Even though there are many singers in a choir, the word choir is grammatically treated as a single unit. If we refer to the members of the group, and not the group itself, it is no longer a collective noun.

Incorrect: The *choir are* going to compete nationally this year.

Correct: The *choir is* going to compete nationally this year.

Incorrect: The *members* of the choir *is* competing nationally this year.

Correct: The *members* of the choir *are* competing nationally this year.

Pronouns

Pronouns are words that are used to stand in for nouns. A pronoun may be classified as personal, intensive, relative, interrogative, demonstrative, indefinite, and reciprocal.

Personal: *Nominative* is the case for nouns and pronouns that are the subject of a sentence. *Objective* is the case for nouns and pronouns that are an object in a sentence. *Possessive* is the case for nouns and pronouns that show possession or ownership.

Singular

	Nominative	Objective	Possessive
First Person	I	me	my, mine
Second Person	you	you	your, yours
Third Person	he, she, it	him, her, it	his, her, hers, its

Plural

	Nominative	Objective	Possessive
First Person	we	us	our, ours
Second Person	you	you	your, yours
Third Person	they	them	their, theirs

Intensive: I myself, you yourself, he himself, she herself, the (thing) itself, we ourselves, you yourselves, they themselves

Relative: which, who, whom, whose

Interrogative: what, which, who, whom, whose

Demonstrative: this, that, these, those

Indefinite: all, any, each, everyone, either/neither, one, some, several

Reciprocal: each other, one another

> **Review Video: Nouns and Pronouns**
> Visit mometrix.com/academy and enter code: 312073

VERBS

A verb is a word or group of words that indicates action or being. In other words, the verb shows something's action or state of being or the action that has been done to something. If you want to write a sentence, then you need a verb. Without a verb, you have no sentence.

TRANSITIVE AND INTRANSITIVE VERBS

A **transitive verb** is a verb whose action indicates a receiver. **Intransitive verbs** do not indicate a receiver of an action. In other words, the action of the verb does not point to an object.

Transitive: He drives a car. | She feeds the dog.

Intransitive: He runs every day. | She voted in the last election.

A dictionary will tell you whether a verb is transitive or intransitive. Some verbs can be transitive or intransitive.

ACTION VERBS AND LINKING VERBS

Action verbs show what the subject is doing. In other words, an action verb shows action. Unlike most types of words, a single action verb, in the right context, can be an entire sentence. **Linking verbs** link the subject of a sentence to a noun or pronoun, or they link a subject with an adjective. You always need a verb if you want a complete sentence. However, linking verbs on their own cannot be a complete sentence.

Common linking verbs include *appear, be, become, feel, grow, look, seem, smell, sound,* and *taste*. However, any verb that shows a condition and connects to a noun, pronoun, or adjective that describes the subject of a sentence is a linking verb.

Action: He sings. | Run! | Go! | I talk with him every day. | She reads.

Linking:

Incorrect: I am.

Correct: I am John. | The roses smell lovely. | I feel tired.

Note: Some verbs are followed by words that look like prepositions, but they are a part of the verb and a part of the verb's meaning. These are known as phrasal verbs, and examples include *call off*, *look up*, and *drop off*.

> **Review Video: Action Verbs and Linking Verbs**
> Visit mometrix.com/academy and enter code: 743142

VOICE

Transitive verbs may be in active voice or passive voice. The difference between active voice and passive voice is whether the subject is acting or being acted upon. When the subject of the sentence is doing the action, the verb is in **active voice**. When the subject is being acted upon, the verb is in **passive voice**.

Active: Jon drew the picture. (The subject *Jon* is doing the action of *drawing a picture*.)

Passive: The picture is drawn by Jon. (The subject *picture* is receiving the action from Jon.)

VERB TENSES

Verb **tense** is a property of a verb that indicates when the action being described takes place (past, present, or future) and whether or not the action is completed (simple or perfect). Describing an action taking place in the present (*I talk*) requires a different verb tense than describing an action that took place in the past (*I talked*). Some verb tenses require an auxiliary (helping) verb. These helping verbs include *am, are, is* | *have, has, had* | *was, were, will* (or *shall*).

Present: I talk	Present perfect: I have talked
Past: I talked	Past perfect: I had talked
Future: I will talk	Future perfect: I will have talked

Present: The action is happening at the current time.

Example: He *walks* to the store every morning.

To show that something is happening right now, use the progressive present tense: I *am walking*.

Past: The action happened in the past.

Example: She *walked* to the store an hour ago.

Future: The action will happen later.

Example: I *will walk* to the store tomorrow.

Present perfect: The action started in the past and continues into the present or took place previously at an unspecified time.

Example: I *have walked* to the store three times today.

Past perfect: The action was completed at some point in the past. This tense is usually used to describe an action that was completed before some other reference time or event.

Example: I *had eaten* already before they arrived.

Future perfect: The action will be completed before some point in the future. This tense may be used to describe an action that has already begun or has yet to begin.

Example: The project *will have been completed* by the deadline.

Review Video: Present Perfect, Past Perfect, and Future Perfect Verb Tenses
Visit mometrix.com/academy and enter code: 269472

CONJUGATING VERBS

When you need to change the form of a verb, you are **conjugating** a verb. The key forms of a verb are present tense (sing/sings), past tense (sang), present participle (singing), and past participle (sung). By combining these forms with helping verbs, you can make almost any verb tense. The following table demonstrates some of the different ways to conjugate a verb:

Tense	First Person	Second Person	Third Person Singular	Third Person Plural
Simple Present	I sing	You sing	He, she, it sings	They sing
Simple Past	I sang	You sang	He, she, it sang	They sang
Simple Future	I will sing	You will sing	He, she, it will sing	They will sing
Present Progressive	I am singing	You are singing	He, she, it is singing	They are singing
Past Progressive	I was singing	You were singing	He, she, it was singing	They were singing
Present Perfect	I have sung	You have sung	He, she, it has sung	They have sung
Past Perfect	I had sung	You had sung	He, she, it had sung	They had sung

MOOD

There are three **moods** in English: the indicative, the imperative, and the subjunctive.

The **indicative mood** is used for facts, opinions, and questions.

Fact: You can do this.

Opinion: I think that you can do this.

Question: Do you know that you can do this?

The **imperative** is used for orders or requests.

Order: You are going to do this!

Request: Will you do this for me?

The **subjunctive mood** is for wishes and statements that go against fact.

Wish: I wish that I were famous.

Statement against fact: If I were you, I would do this. (This goes against fact because I am not you. You have the chance to do this, and I do not have the chance.)

ADJECTIVES

An **adjective** is a word that is used to modify a noun or pronoun. An adjective answers a question: *Which one? What kind?* or *How many?* Usually, adjectives come before the words that they modify, but they may also come after a linking verb.

> Which one? The *third* suit is my favorite.
>
> What kind? This suit is *navy blue.*
>
> How many? I am going to buy *four* pairs of socks to match the suit.

Review Video: Descriptive Text
Visit mometrix.com/academy and enter code: 174903

ARTICLES

Articles are adjectives that are used to distinguish nouns as definite or indefinite. *A*, *an*, and *the* are the only articles. **Definite** nouns are preceded by *the* and indicate a specific person, place, thing, or idea. **Indefinite** nouns are preceded by *a* or *an* and do not indicate a specific person, place, thing, or idea.

Note: *An* comes before words that start with a vowel sound. For example, "Are you going to get an **u**mbrella?"

> **Definite**: I lost *the* bottle that belongs to me.
>
> **Indefinite**: Does anyone have *a* bottle to share?

Review Video: Function of Articles in a Sentence
Visit mometrix.com/academy and enter code: 449383

COMPARISON WITH ADJECTIVES

Some adjectives are relative and other adjectives are absolute. Adjectives that are **relative** can show the comparison between things. **Absolute** adjectives can also show comparison, but they do so in a different way. Let's say that you are reading two books. You think that one book is perfect, and the other book is not exactly perfect. It is not possible for one book to be more perfect than the other. Either you think that the book is perfect, or you think that the book is imperfect. In this case, perfect and imperfect are absolute adjectives.

Relative adjectives will show the different **degrees** of something or someone to something else or someone else. The three degrees of adjectives include positive, comparative, and superlative.

The **positive** degree is the normal form of an adjective.

> Example: This work is *difficult.* | She is *smart.*

The **comparative** degree compares one person or thing to another person or thing.

> Example: This work is *more difficult* than your work. | She is *smarter* than me.

The **superlative** degree compares more than two people or things.

> Example: This is the *most difficult* work of my life. | She is the *smartest* lady in school.

Review Video: Adjectives
Visit mometrix.com/academy and enter code: 470154

ADVERBS

An **adverb** is a word that is used to **modify** a verb, an adjective, or another adverb. Usually, adverbs answer one of these questions: *When? Where? How?* and *Why?* The negatives *not* and *never* are considered adverbs. Adverbs that modify adjectives or other adverbs **strengthen** or **weaken** the words that they modify.

Examples:

He walks *quickly* through the crowd.

The water flows *smoothly* on the rocks.

Note: Adverbs are usually indicated by the morpheme *-ly*, which has been added to the root word. For instance, *quick* can be made into an adverb by adding *-ly* to construct *quickly*. Some words that end in *-ly* do not follow this rule and can behave as other parts of speech. Examples of adjectives ending in *-ly* include: *early, friendly, holy, lonely, silly*, and *ugly*. To know if a word that ends in *-ly* is an adjective or adverb, check your dictionary. Also, while many adverbs end in *-ly*, you need to remember that not all adverbs end in *-ly*.

Examples:

He is *never* angry.

You are *too* irresponsible to travel alone.

Review Video: Adverbs
Visit mometrix.com/academy and enter code: 713951

Review Video: Adverbs that Modify Adjectives
Visit mometrix.com/academy and enter code: 122570

COMPARISON WITH ADVERBS

The rules for comparing adverbs are the same as the rules for adjectives.

The **positive** degree is the standard form of an adverb.

Example: He arrives *soon.* | She speaks *softly* to her friends.

The **comparative** degree compares one person or thing to another person or thing.

Example: He arrives *sooner* than Sarah. | She speaks *more softly* than him.

The **superlative** degree compares more than two people or things.

Example: He arrives *soonest* of the group. | She speaks the *most softly* of any of her friends.

Prepositions

A **preposition** is a word placed before a noun or pronoun that shows the relationship between that noun or pronoun and another word in the sentence.

Common prepositions:

about	before	during	on	under
after	beneath	for	over	until
against	between	from	past	up
among	beyond	in	through	with
around	by	of	to	within
at	down	off	toward	without

Examples:

The napkin is *in* the drawer.

The Earth rotates *around* the Sun.

The needle is *beneath* the haystack.

Can you find "me" *among* the words?

Review Video: Prepositions
Visit mometrix.com/academy and enter code: 946763

Conjunctions

Conjunctions join words, phrases, or clauses and they show the connection between the joined pieces. **Coordinating conjunctions** connect equal parts of sentences. **Correlative conjunctions** show the connection between pairs. **Subordinating conjunctions** join subordinate (i.e., dependent) clauses with independent clauses.

Coordinating Conjunctions

The **coordinating conjunctions** include: *and, but, yet, or, nor, for,* and *so*

Examples:

The rock was small, *but* it was heavy.

She drove in the night, *and* he drove in the day.

Correlative Conjunctions

The **correlative conjunctions** are: *either...or* | *neither...nor* | *not only...but also*

Examples:

Either you are coming *or* you are staying.

He *not only* ran three miles *but also* swam 200 yards.

Review Video: Coordinating and Correlative Conjunctions
Visit mometrix.com/academy and enter code: 390329

Review Video: Adverb Equal Comparisons
Visit mometrix.com/academy and enter code: 231291

Subordinating Conjunctions

Common **subordinating conjunctions** include:

after	since	whenever
although	so that	where
because	unless	wherever
before	until	whether
in order that	when	while

Examples:

I am hungry *because* I did not eat breakfast.

He went home *when* everyone left.

Review Video: Subordinating Conjunctions
Visit mometrix.com/academy and enter code: 958913

Interjections

Interjections are words of exclamation (i.e., audible expressions of great feeling) that are used alone or as a part of a sentence. Often, they are used at the beginning of a sentence for an introduction. Sometimes, they can be used in the middle of a sentence to show a change in thought or attitude.

Common Interjections: Hey! | Oh, | Ouch! | Please! | Wow!

Agreement and Sentence Structure

Subjects and Predicates

Subjects

The **subject** of a sentence names who or what the sentence is about. The subject may be directly stated in a sentence, or the subject may be the implied *you*. The **complete subject** includes the simple subject and all of its modifiers. To find the complete subject, ask *Who* or *What* and insert the verb to complete the question. The answer, including any modifiers (adjectives, prepositional phrases, etc.), is the complete subject. To find the **simple subject**, remove all of the modifiers in the complete subject. Being able to locate the subject of a sentence helps with many problems, such as those involving sentence fragments and subject-verb agreement.

Examples:

simple subject

The small, red car is the one that he wants for Christmas.

complete subject

simple subject

The young artist is coming over for dinner.

complete subject

Review Video: Subjects in English
Visit mometrix.com/academy and enter code: 444771

In **imperative** sentences, the verb's subject is understood (e.g., [You] Run to the store), but is not actually present in the sentence. Normally, the subject comes before the verb. However, the subject comes after the verb in sentences that begin with *There are* or *There was.*

Direct:

John knows the way to the park.	Who knows the way to the park?	John
The cookies need ten more minutes.	What needs ten minutes?	The cookies
By five o'clock, Bill will need to leave.	Who needs to leave?	Bill
There are five letters on the table for him.	What is on the table?	Five letters
There were coffee and doughnuts in the house.	What was in the house?	Coffee and doughnuts

Implied:

Go to the post office for me.	Who is going to the post office?	You
Come and sit with me, please?	Who needs to come and sit?	You

Predicates

In a sentence, you always have a predicate and a subject. The subject tells who or what the sentence is about, and the **predicate** explains or describes the subject. The predicate includes the verb or verb phrase and any direct or indirect objects of the verb, as well as any words or phrases modifying these.

Think about the sentence *He sings*. In this sentence, we have a subject (He) and a predicate (sings). This is all that is needed for a sentence to be complete. Most sentences contain more information, but if this is all the information that you are given, then you have a complete sentence.

Now, let's look at another sentence: *John and Jane sing on Tuesday nights at the dance hall.*

subject: John and Jane | predicate: sing on Tuesday nights at the dance hall.

Review Video: Complete Predicate
Visit mometrix.com/academy and enter code: 293942

SUBJECT-VERB AGREEMENT

Verbs must **agree** with their subjects in number and in person. To agree in number, singular subjects need singular verbs and plural subjects need plural verbs. A **singular** noun refers to **one** person, place, or thing. A **plural** noun refers to **more than one** person, place, or thing. To agree in person, the correct verb form must be chosen to match the first, second, or third person subject. The present tense ending *-s* or *-es* is used on a verb if its subject is third person singular; otherwise, the verb's ending is not modified.

Review Video: Subject-Verb Agreement
Visit mometrix.com/academy and enter code: 479190

NUMBER AGREEMENT EXAMPLES:

Single Subject and Verb: Dan (singular subject) calls (singular verb) home.

Dan is one person. So, the singular verb *calls* is needed.

Plural Subject and Verb: Dan and Bob (plural subject) call (plural verb) home.

More than one person needs the plural verb *call*.

PERSON AGREEMENT EXAMPLES:

First Person: I *am* walking.

Second Person: You *are* walking.

Third Person: He *is* walking.

COMPLICATIONS WITH SUBJECT-VERB AGREEMENT

WORDS BETWEEN SUBJECT AND VERB

Words that come between the simple subject and the verb have no bearing on subject-verb agreement.

Examples:

The joy (singular subject) of my life returns (singular verb) home tonight.

The phrase *of my life* does not influence the verb *returns*.

Language

singular subject / singular verb

The question that still remains unanswered is "Who are you?"

Don't let the phrase "*that still remains*..." trouble you. The subject *question* goes with *is.*

Compound Subjects

A compound subject is formed when two or more nouns joined by *and*, *or*, or *nor* jointly act as the subject of the sentence.

Joined by And

When a compound subject is joined by *and*, it is treated as a plural subject and requires a plural verb.

Examples:

plural subject / plural verb

You and Jon are invited to come to my house.

plural subject / plural verb

The pencil and paper belong to me.

Joined by Or/Nor

For a compound subject joined by *or* or *nor*, the verb must agree in number with the part of the subject that is closest to the verb (italicized in the examples below).

Examples:

subject / verb

Today or tomorrow is the day.

subject / verb

Stan or Phil wants to read the book.

subject / verb

Neither the pen nor the book is on the desk.

subject / verb

Either the blanket or pillows arrive this afternoon.

Indefinite Pronouns as Subject

An indefinite pronoun is a pronoun that does not refer to a specific noun. Some indefinite pronouns function as only singular, some function as only plural, and some can function as either singular or plural depending on how they are used.

Always Singular

Pronouns such as *each*, *either*, *everybody*, *anybody*, *somebody*, and *nobody* are always singular.

Examples:

singular subject / singular verb

Each of the runners has a different bib number.

singular verb / singular subject

Is either of you ready for the game?

Note: The words *each* and *either* can also be used as adjectives (e.g., *each* person is unique). When one of these adjectives modifies the subject of a sentence, it is always a singular subject.

> singular subject / singular verb
>
> Everybody grows a day older every day.

> singular subject / singular verb
>
> Anybody is welcome to bring a tent.

ALWAYS PLURAL

Pronouns such as *both*, *several*, and *many* are always plural.

Examples:

> plural subject / plural verb
>
> Both of the siblings were too tired to argue.

> plural subject / plural verb
>
> Many have tried, but none have succeeded.

DEPEND ON CONTEXT

Pronouns such as *some*, *any*, *all*, *none*, *more*, and *most* can be either singular or plural depending on what they are representing in the context of the sentence.

Examples:

> singular subject / singular verb
>
> All of my dog's food was still there in his bowl.

> plural subject / plural verb
>
> By the end of the night, all of my guests were already excited about coming to my next party.

OTHER CASES INVOLVING PLURAL OR IRREGULAR FORM

Some nouns are **singular in meaning but plural in form**: news, mathematics, physics, and economics.

> The *news is* coming on now.
>
> *Mathematics is* my favorite class.

Some nouns are plural in form and meaning, and have **no singular equivalent**: scissors and pants.

> Do these *pants come* with a shirt?
>
> The *scissors are* for my project.

Mathematical operations are **irregular** in their construction, but are normally considered to be **singular in meaning**.

> *One plus one is* two.
>
> *Three times three is* nine.

Note: Look to your **dictionary** for help when you aren't sure whether a noun with a plural form has a singular or plural meaning.

COMPLEMENTS

A complement is a noun, pronoun, or adjective that is used to give more information about the subject or object in the sentence.

DIRECT OBJECTS

A direct object is a noun or pronoun that tells who or what **receives** the action of the verb. A sentence will only include a direct object if the verb is a transitive verb. If the verb is an intransitive verb or a linking verb, there will be no direct object. When you are looking for a direct object, find the verb and ask *who* or *what.*

Examples:

> I took *the blanket.*
>
> Jane read *books.*

INDIRECT OBJECTS

An indirect object is a noun or pronoun that indicates what or whom the action had an **influence** on. If there is an indirect object in a sentence, then there will also be a direct object. When you are looking for the indirect object, find the verb and ask *to/for whom or what.*

Examples:

> We taught the old dog (indirect object) a new trick (direct object).
>
> I gave them (indirect object) a math lesson (direct object).

Review Video: Direct and Indirect Objects
Visit mometrix.com/academy and enter code: 817385

PREDICATE NOMINATIVES AND PREDICATE ADJECTIVES

As we looked at previously, verbs may be classified as either action verbs or linking verbs. A linking verb is so named because it links the subject to words in the predicate that describe or define the subject. These words are called predicate nominatives (if nouns or pronouns) or predicate adjectives (if adjectives).

Examples:

> My father (subject) is a lawyer (predicate nominative).
>
> Your mother (subject) is patient (predicate adjective).

PRONOUN USAGE

The **antecedent** is the noun that has been replaced by a pronoun. A pronoun and its antecedent **agree** when they have the same number (singular or plural) and gender (male, female, or neutral).

Examples:

antecedent / pronoun

Singular agreement: John came into town, and he played for us.

antecedent / pronoun

Plural agreement: John and Rick came into town, and they played for us.

To determine which is the correct pronoun to use in a compound subject or object, try each pronoun **alone** in place of the compound in the sentence. Your knowledge of pronouns will tell you which one is correct.

Example:

Bob and (I, me) will be going.

Test: (1) *I will be going* or (2) *Me will be going*. The second choice cannot be correct because *me* cannot be used as the subject of a sentence. Instead, *me* is used as an object.

Answer: Bob and I will be going.

When a pronoun is used with a noun immediately following (as in "we boys"), try the sentence **without the added noun**.

Example:

(We/Us) boys played football last year.

Test: (1) *We played football last year* or (2) *Us played football last year*. Again, the second choice cannot be correct because *us* cannot be used as a subject of a sentence. Instead, *us* is used as an object.

Answer: We boys played football last year.

Review Video: Pronoun Usage
Visit mometrix.com/academy and enter code: 666500

Review Video: Pronoun-Antecedent Agreement
Visit mometrix.com/academy and enter code: 919704

A pronoun should point clearly to the **antecedent**. Here is how a pronoun reference can be unhelpful if it is puzzling or not directly stated.

antecedent / pronoun

Unhelpful: Ron and Jim went to the store, and he bought soda.

Who bought soda? Ron or Jim?

antecedent / pronoun

Helpful: Jim went to the store, and he bought soda.

The sentence is clear. Jim bought the soda.

Some pronouns change their form by their placement in a sentence. A pronoun that is a **subject** in a sentence comes in the **subjective case**. Pronouns that serve as **objects** appear in the **objective case**. Finally, the pronouns that are used as **possessives** appear in the **possessive case**.

Examples:

Subjective case: *He* is coming to the show.

The pronoun *He* is the subject of the sentence.

Objective case: Josh drove *him* to the airport.

The pronoun *him* is the object of the sentence.

Possessive case: The flowers are *mine*.

The pronoun *mine* shows ownership of the flowers.

The word *who* is a subjective-case pronoun that can be used as a **subject**. The word *whom* is an objective-case pronoun that can be used as an **object**. The words *who* and *whom* are common in subordinate clauses or in questions.

Examples:

subject verb
He knows who wants to come.

object verb
He knows the man whom we want at the party.

Clauses

A clause is a group of words that contains both a subject and a predicate (verb). There are two types of clauses: independent and dependent. An **independent clause** contains a complete thought, while a **dependent (or subordinate) clause** does not. A dependent clause includes a subject and a verb, and may also contain objects or complements, but it cannot stand as a complete thought without being joined to an independent clause. Dependent clauses function within sentences as adjectives, adverbs, or nouns.

Example:

independent clause | dependent clause
I am running because I want to stay in shape.

The clause *I am running* is an independent clause: it has a subject and a verb, and it gives a complete thought. The clause *because I want to stay in shape* is a dependent clause: it has a subject and a verb, but it does not express a complete thought. It adds detail to the independent clause to which it is attached.

Review Video: Clauses
Visit mometrix.com/academy and enter code: 940170

Review Video: Independent and Dependent Clauses
Visit mometrix.com/academy and enter code: 556903

Types of Dependent Clauses

Adjective Clauses

An **adjective clause** is a dependent clause that modifies a noun or a pronoun. Adjective clauses begin with a relative pronoun (*who, whose, whom, which,* and *that*) or a relative adverb (*where, when,* and *why*).

Also, adjective clauses usually come immediately after the noun that the clause needs to explain or rename. This is done to ensure that it is clear which noun or pronoun the clause is modifying.

Examples:

I learned the reason (independent clause) why I won the award (adjective clause).

This is the place (independent clause) where I started my first job (adjective clause).

An adjective clause can be an essential or nonessential clause. An essential clause is very important to the sentence. **Essential clauses** explain or define a person or thing. **Nonessential clauses** give more information about a person or thing but are not necessary to define them. Nonessential clauses are set off with commas while essential clauses are not.

Examples:

A person who works hard at first (essential clause) can often rest later in life.

Neil Armstrong, who walked on the moon (nonessential clause), is my hero.

Review Video: Adjective Clauses and Phrases
Visit mometrix.com/academy and enter code: 520888

Adverb Clauses

An **adverb clause** is a dependent clause that modifies a verb, adjective, or adverb. In sentences with multiple dependent clauses, adverb clauses are usually placed immediately before or after the independent clause. An adverb clause is introduced with words such as *after, although, as, before, because, if, since, so, unless, when, where*, and *while.*

Examples:

When you walked outside (adverb clause), I called the manager.

I will go with you unless you want to stay (adverb clause).

Noun Clauses

A **noun clause** is a dependent clause that can be used as a subject, object, or complement. Noun clauses begin with words such as *how, that, what, whether, which, who,* and *why*. These words can also come with an adjective clause. Unless the noun clause is being used as the subject of the sentence, it should come after the verb of the independent clause.

Examples:

noun clause
The real mystery is how you avoided serious injury.

noun clause
What you learn from each other depends on your honesty with others.

Subordination

When two related ideas are not of equal importance, the ideal way to combine them is to make the more important idea an independent clause and the less important idea a dependent or subordinate clause. This is called **subordination**.

Example:

Separate ideas: The team had a perfect regular season. The team lost the championship.

Subordinated: Despite having a perfect regular season, *the team lost the championship.*

Phrases

A phrase is a group of words that functions as a single part of speech, usually a noun, adjective, or adverb. A **phrase** is not a complete thought and does not contain a subject and predicate, but it adds detail or explanation to a sentence, or renames something within the sentence.

Prepositional Phrases

One of the most common types of phrases is the prepositional phrase. A **prepositional phrase** begins with a preposition and ends with a noun or pronoun that is the object of the preposition. Normally, the prepositional phrase functions as an **adjective** or an **adverb** within the sentence.

Examples:

prepositional phrase
The picnic is on the blanket.

prepositional phrase
I am sick with a fever today.

prepositional phrase
Among the many flowers, John found a four-leaf clover.

Verbal Phrases

A **verbal** is a word or phrase that is formed from a verb but does not function as a verb. Depending on its particular form, it may be used as a noun, adjective, or adverb. A verbal does **not** replace a verb in a sentence.

Examples:

verb
Correct: Walk a mile daily.

This is a complete sentence with the implied subject *you.*

verbal

Incorrect: To walk a mile.

This is not a sentence since there is no functional verb.

There are three types of verbal: **participles**, **gerunds**, and **infinitives**. Each type of verbal has a corresponding **phrase** that consists of the verbal itself along with any complements or modifiers.

PARTICIPLES

A **participle** is a type of verbal that always functions as an adjective. The present participle always ends with -*ing*. Past participles end with *-d, -ed, -n,* or *-t*. Participles are combined with helping verbs to form certain verb tenses, but a participle by itself cannot function as a verb.

Examples: dance (verb) | dancing (present participle) | danced (past participle)

Participial phrases most often come right before or right after the noun or pronoun that they modify.

Examples:

Shipwrecked on an island (participial phrase), the boys started to fish for food.

Having been seated for five hours (participial phrase), we got out of the car to stretch our legs.

Praised for their work (participial phrase), the group accepted the first-place trophy.

GERUNDS

A **gerund** is a type of verbal that always functions as a **noun**. Like present participles, gerunds always end with *-ing*, but they can be easily distinguished from participles by the part of speech they represent (participles always function as adjectives). Since a gerund or gerund phrase always functions as a noun, it can be used as the subject of a sentence, the predicate nominative, or the object of a verb or preposition.

Examples:

We want to be known for teaching (gerund) the poor (teaching the poor: object of preposition).

Coaching (gerund) this team (Coaching this team: subject) is the best job of my life.

We like practicing (gerund) our songs (practicing our songs: object of verb) in the basement.

INFINITIVES

An **infinitive** is a type of verbal that can function as a noun, an adjective, or an adverb. An infinitive is made of the word *to* and the basic form of the verb. As with all other types of verbal phrases, an infinitive phrase includes the verbal itself and all of its complements or modifiers.

Examples:

infinitive
To join the team is my goal in life.
noun

infinitive
The animals have enough food to eat for the night.
adjective

infinitive
People lift weights to exercise their muscles.
adverb

Review Video: Verbals
Visit mometrix.com/academy and enter code: 915480

Appositive Phrases

An **appositive** is a word or phrase that is used to explain or rename nouns or pronouns. Noun phrases, gerund phrases, and infinitive phrases can all be used as appositives.

Examples:

appositive
Terriers, hunters at heart, have been dressed up to look like lap dogs.

The noun phrase *hunters at heart* renames the noun *terriers.*

appositive
His plan, to save and invest his money, was proven as a safe approach.

The infinitive phrase explains what the plan is.

Appositive phrases can be **essential** or **nonessential**. An appositive phrase is essential if the person, place, or thing being described or renamed is too general for its meaning to be understood without the appositive.

Examples:

essential
Two of America's Founding Fathers, George Washington and Thomas Jefferson, served as presidents.

nonessential
George Washington and Thomas Jefferson, two Founding Fathers, served as presidents.

Absolute Phrases

An absolute phrase is a phrase that consists of **a noun followed by a participle**. An absolute phrase provides **context** to what is being described in the sentence, but it does not modify or explain any particular word; it is essentially independent.

Examples:

The alarm ringing, he pushed the snooze button.
(noun: The alarm; participle: ringing; absolute phrase: The alarm ringing)

The music paused, she continued to dance through the crowd.
(noun: The music; participle: paused; absolute phrase: The music paused)

PARALLELISM

When multiple items or ideas are presented in a sentence in series, such as in a list, the items or ideas must be stated in grammatically equivalent ways. For example, if two ideas are listed in parallel and the first is stated in gerund form, the second cannot be stated in infinitive form. (e.g., *I enjoy reading and to study*. [incorrect]) An infinitive and a gerund are not grammatically equivalent. Instead, you should write *I enjoy reading and studying* OR *I like to read and to study*. In lists of more than two, all items must be parallel.

Example:

> **Incorrect**: He stopped at the office, grocery store, and the pharmacy before heading home.
>
> The first and third items in the list of places include the article *the*, so the second item needs it as well.
>
> **Correct**: He stopped at the office, *the* grocery store, and the pharmacy before heading home.

Example:

> **Incorrect**: While vacationing in Europe, she went biking, skiing, and climbed mountains.
>
> The first and second items in the list are gerunds, so the third item must be as well.
>
> **Correct**: While vacationing in Europe, she went biking, skiing, and *mountain climbing*.

Review Video: Parallel Sentence Construction
Visit mometrix.com/academy and enter code: 831988

SENTENCE PURPOSE

There are four types of sentences: declarative, imperative, interrogative, and exclamatory.

A **declarative** sentence states a fact and ends with a period.

> *The football game starts at seven o'clock.*

An **imperative** sentence tells someone to do something and generally ends with a period. An urgent command might end with an exclamation point instead.

> *Don't forget to buy your ticket.*

An **interrogative** sentence asks a question and ends with a question mark.

> *Are you going to the game on Friday?*

An **exclamatory** sentence shows strong emotion and ends with an exclamation point.

> *I can't believe we won the game!*

Language

SENTENCE STRUCTURE

Sentences are classified by structure based on the type and number of clauses present. The four classifications of sentence structure are the following:

Simple: A simple sentence has one independent clause with no dependent clauses. A simple sentence may have **compound elements** (i.e., compound subject or verb).

Examples:

single subject | single verb

Judy watered the lawn.

compound subject | single verb

Judy and Alan watered the lawn.

single subject | compound verb | compound verb

Judy watered the lawn and pulled weeds.

compound subject | compound verb | compound verb

Judy and Alan watered the lawn and pulled weeds.

Compound: A compound sentence has two or more independent clauses with no dependent clauses. Usually, the independent clauses are joined with a comma and a coordinating conjunction or with a semicolon.

Examples:

independent clause | independent clause

The time has come, and we are ready.

independent clause | independent clause

I woke up at dawn; the sun was just coming up.

Complex: A complex sentence has one independent clause and at least one dependent clause. Punctuation depends on whether the dependent (subordinate) clause comes before or after the independent (or main) clause. If the subordinate clause comes first, it needs to be set apart with a comma.

Examples:

dependent clause | independent clause

Although he had the flu, Harry went to work.

independent clause | dependent clause

Marcia got married after she finished college.

Compound-Complex: A compound-complex sentence has at least two independent clauses and at least one dependent clause.

Examples:

John is my friend (independent clause) who went to India, (dependent clause) and he brought back souvenirs. (independent clause)

You may not realize this, (independent clause) but we heard the music (independent clause) that you played last night. (dependent clause)

Review Video: Sentence Structure
Visit mometrix.com/academy and enter code: 700478

Sentence variety is important to consider when writing an essay or speech. A variety of sentence lengths and types creates rhythm, makes a passage more engaging, and gives writers an opportunity to demonstrate their writing style. Writing that uses the same length or type of sentence without variation can be boring or difficult to read. To evaluate a passage for effective sentence variety, it is helpful to note whether the passage contains diverse sentence structures and lengths. It is also important to pay attention to the way each sentence starts and avoid beginning with the same words or phrases.

SENTENCE FRAGMENTS

Recall that a group of words must contain at least one **independent clause** in order to be considered a sentence. If it doesn't contain even one independent clause, it is called a **sentence fragment**.

The appropriate process for **repairing** a sentence fragment depends on what type of fragment it is. If the fragment is a dependent clause, it can sometimes be as simple as removing a subordinating word (e.g., when, because, if) from the beginning of the fragment. Alternatively, a dependent clause can be incorporated into a closely related neighboring sentence. If the fragment is missing some required part, like a subject or a verb, the fix might be as simple as adding the missing part.

Examples:

Fragment: Because he wanted to sail the Mediterranean.

Removed subordinating word: He wanted to sail the Mediterranean.

Combined with another sentence: Because he wanted to sail the Mediterranean, he booked a Greek island cruise.

RUN-ON SENTENCES

Run-on sentences consist of multiple independent clauses that have not been joined together properly. Run-on sentences can be corrected in several different ways:

Join clauses properly: This can be done with a comma and coordinating conjunction, with a semicolon, or with a colon or dash if the second clause is explaining something in the first.

Example:

Incorrect: I went on the trip, we visited lots of castles.

Corrected: I went on the trip, and we visited lots of castles.

Split into separate sentences: This correction is most effective when the independent clauses are very long or when they are not closely related.

Example:

> **Incorrect**: The drive to New York takes ten hours, my uncle lives in Boston.
>
> **Corrected**: The drive to New York takes ten hours. My uncle lives in Boston.

Make one clause dependent: This is the easiest way to make the sentence correct and more interesting at the same time. It's often as simple as adding a subordinating word between the two clauses or before the first clause.

Example:

> **Incorrect**: I finally made it to the store and I bought some eggs.
>
> **Corrected**: When I finally made it to the store, I bought some eggs.

Reduce to one clause with a compound verb: If both clauses have the same subject, remove the subject from the second clause, and you now have just one clause with a compound verb.

Example:

> **Incorrect**: The drive to New York takes ten hours, it makes me very tired.
>
> **Corrected**: The drive to New York takes ten hours and makes me very tired.

Note: While these are the simplest ways to correct a run-on sentence, often the best way is to completely reorganize the thoughts in the sentence and rewrite it.

Review Video: Fragments and Run-on Sentences
Visit mometrix.com/academy and enter code: 541989

Dangling and Misplaced Modifiers

Dangling Modifiers

A dangling modifier is a dependent clause or verbal phrase that does not have a clear logical connection to a word in the sentence.

Example:

> **Incorrect**: Reading each magazine article [dangling modifier], the stories caught my attention.
>
> The word *stories* cannot be modified by *Reading each magazine article*. People can read, but stories cannot read. Therefore, the subject of the sentence must be a person.
>
> **Corrected**: Reading each magazine article [gerund phrase], I was entertained by the stories.

Example:

dangling modifier

Incorrect: Ever since childhood, my grandparents have visited me for Christmas.

The speaker in this sentence can't have been visited by her grandparents when *they* were children, since she wouldn't have been born yet. Either the modifier should be clarified or the sentence should be rearranged to specify whose childhood is being referenced.

dependent clause

Clarified: Ever since I was a child, my grandparents have visited for Christmas.

adverb phrase

Rearranged: Ever since childhood, I have enjoyed my grandparents visiting for Christmas.

Misplaced Modifiers

Because modifiers are grammatically versatile, they can be put in many different places within the structure of a sentence. The danger of this versatility is that a modifier can accidentally be placed where it is modifying the wrong word or where it is not clear which word it is modifying.

Example:

modifier

Incorrect: She read the book to a crowd that was filled with beautiful pictures.

The book was filled with beautiful pictures, not the crowd.

modifier

Corrected: She read the book that was filled with beautiful pictures to a crowd.

Example:

modifier

Ambiguous: Derek saw a bus nearly hit a man on his way to work.

Was Derek on his way to work or was the other man?

modifier

Derek: On his way to work, Derek saw a bus nearly hit a man.

modifier

The other man: Derek saw a bus nearly hit a man who was on his way to work.

Split Infinitives

A split infinitive occurs when a modifying word comes between the word *to* and the verb that pairs with *to*.

> Example: To *clearly* explain vs. *To explain* clearly | To *softly* sing vs. *To sing* softly

Though considered improper by some, split infinitives may provide better clarity and simplicity in some cases than the alternatives. As such, avoiding them should not be considered a universal rule.

Double Negatives

Standard English allows **two negatives** only when a **positive** meaning is intended. (e.g., The team was *not displeased* with their performance.) Double negatives to emphasize negation are not used in standard English.

Negative modifiers (e.g., never, no, and not) should not be paired with other negative modifiers or negative words (e.g., none, nobody, nothing, or neither). The modifiers *hardly, barely*, and *scarcely* are also considered negatives in standard English, so they should not be used with other negatives.

Punctuation

End Punctuation

Periods

Use a period to end all sentences except direct questions and exclamations. Periods are also used for abbreviations.

> Examples: 3 p.m. | 2 a.m. | Mr. Jones | Mrs. Stevens | Dr. Smith | Bill, Jr. | Pennsylvania Ave.

Note: An abbreviation is a shortened form of a word or phrase.

Question Marks

Question marks should be used following a **direct question**. A polite request can be followed by a period instead of a question mark.

> **Direct Question**: What is for lunch today? | How are you? | Why is that the answer?
>
> **Polite Requests**: Can you please send me the item tomorrow. | Will you please walk with me on the track.

Review Video: Question Marks
Visit mometrix.com/academy and enter code: 118471

Exclamation Marks

Exclamation marks are used after a word group or sentence that shows much feeling or has special importance. Exclamation marks should not be overused. They are saved for proper **exclamatory interjections**.

> Example: We're going to the finals! | You have a beautiful car! | "That's crazy!" she yelled.

Review Video: Exclamation Points
Visit mometrix.com/academy and enter code: 199367

COMMAS

The comma is a punctuation mark that can help you understand connections in a sentence. Not every sentence needs a comma. However, if a sentence needs a comma, you need to put it in the right place. A comma in the wrong place (or an absent comma) will make a sentence's meaning unclear.

These are some of the rules for commas:

Use Case	Example
Before a **coordinating conjunction** joining independent clauses	Bob caught three fish, and I caught two fish.
After an **introductory phrase**	After the final out, we went to a restaurant to celebrate.
After an **adverbial clause**	Studying the stars, I was awed by the beauty of the sky.
Between **items in a series**	I will bring the turkey, the pie, and the coffee.
For **interjections**	Wow, you know how to play this game.
After ***yes*** **and** ***no*** **responses**	No, I cannot come tomorrow.
Separate **nonessential modifiers**	John Frank, who coaches the team, was promoted today.
Separate **nonessential appositives**	Thomas Edison, an American inventor, was born in Ohio.
Separate **nouns of direct address**	You, John, are my only hope in this moment.
Separate **interrogative tags**	This is the last time, correct?
Separate **contrasts**	You are my friend, not my enemy.
Writing **dates**	July 4, 1776, is an important date to remember.
Writing **addresses**	He is meeting me at 456 Delaware Avenue, Washington, D.C., tomorrow morning.
Writing **geographical names**	Paris, France, is my favorite city.
Writing **titles**	John Smith, PhD, will be visiting your class today.
Separate **expressions like** ***he said***	"You can start," she said, "with an apology."

A comma is also used **between coordinate adjectives** not joined with *and*. However, not all adjectives are coordinate (i.e., equal or parallel). To determine if your adjectives are coordinate, try connecting them with *and* or reversing their order. If it still sounds right, they are coordinate.

Incorrect: The kind, brown dog followed me home.

Correct: The kind, loyal dog followed me home.

Review Video: When to Use a Comma
Visit mometrix.com/academy and enter code: 786797

Semicolons

The semicolon is used to join closely related independent clauses without the need for a coordinating conjunction. Semicolons are also used in place of commas to separate list elements that have internal commas. Some rules for semicolons include:

Use Case	Example
Between closely connected independent clauses **not connected with a coordinating conjunction**	You are right; we should go with your plan.
Between independent clauses **linked with a transitional word**	I think that we can agree on this; however, I am not sure about my friends.
Between items in a **series that has internal punctuation**	I have visited New York, New York; Augusta, Maine; and Baltimore, Maryland.

Review Video: How to Use Semicolons
Visit mometrix.com/academy and enter code: 370605

Colons

The colon is used to call attention to the words that follow it. When used in a sentence, a colon should only come at the **end** of a **complete sentence**. The rules for colons are as follows:

Use Case	Example
After an independent clause to **make a list**	I want to learn many languages: Spanish, German, and Italian.
For **explanations**	There is one thing that stands out on your resume: responsibility.
To give a **quote**	He started with an idea: "We are able to do more than we imagine."
After the **greeting in a formal letter**	To Whom It May Concern:
Show **hours and minutes**	It is 3:14 p.m.
Separate a **title and subtitle**	The essay is titled "America: A Short Introduction to a Modern Country."

Review Video: Using Colons
Visit mometrix.com/academy and enter code: 868673

Parentheses

Parentheses are used for additional information. Also, they can be used to put labels for letters or numbers in a series. Parentheses should not be used very often. If they are overused, parentheses can be a distraction instead of a help.

Examples:

Extra Information: The rattlesnake (see Image 2) is a dangerous snake of North and South America.

Series: Include in the email (1) your name, (2) your address, and (3) your question for the author.

Review Video: Parentheses
Visit mometrix.com/academy and enter code: 947743

QUOTATION MARKS

Use quotation marks to close off **direct quotations** of a person's spoken or written words. Do not use quotation marks around indirect quotations. An indirect quotation gives someone's message without using the person's exact words. Use **single quotation marks** to close off a quotation inside a quotation.

Direct Quote: Nancy said, "I am waiting for Henry to arrive."

Indirect Quote: Henry said that he is going to be late to the meeting.

Quote inside a Quote: The teacher asked, "Has everyone read 'The Gift of the Magi'?"

Quotation marks should be used around the titles of **short works**: newspaper and magazine articles, poems, short stories, songs, television episodes, radio programs, and subdivisions of books or websites.

Examples:

"Rip Van Winkle" (short story by Washington Irving)

"O Captain! My Captain!" (poem by Walt Whitman)

Although it is not standard usage, quotation marks are sometimes used to highlight **irony** or the use of words to mean something other than their dictionary definition. This type of usage should be employed sparingly, if at all.

Examples:

The boss warned Frank that he was walking on "thin ice."	Frank is not walking on real ice. Instead, he is being warned to avoid mistakes.
The teacher thanked the young man for his "honesty."	The quotation marks around *honesty* show that the teacher does not believe the young man's explanation.

Review Video: Quotation Marks
Visit mometrix.com/academy and enter code: 884918

Periods and commas are put **inside** quotation marks. Colons and semicolons are put **outside** the quotation marks. Question marks and exclamation points are placed inside quotation marks when they are part of a quote. When the question or exclamation mark goes with the whole sentence, the mark is left outside of the quotation marks.

Examples:

Period and comma	We read "The Gift of the Magi," "The Skylight Room," and "The Cactus."
Semicolon	They watched "The Nutcracker"; then, they went home.
Exclamation mark that is a part of a quote	The crowd cheered, "Victory!"
Question mark that goes with the whole sentence	Is your favorite short story "The Tell-Tale Heart"?

APOSTROPHES

An apostrophe is used to show **possession** or the **deletion of letters in contractions**. An apostrophe is not needed with the possessive pronouns *his, hers, its, ours, theirs, whose*, and *yours*.

Singular Nouns: David's car | a book's theme | my brother's board game

Plural Nouns that end with -*s*: the scissors' handle | boys' basketball

Plural Nouns that end without -*s*: Men's department | the people's adventure

> **Review Video: When to Use an Apostrophe**
> Visit mometrix.com/academy and enter code: 213068
>
> **Review Video: Punctuation Errors in Possessive Pronouns**
> Visit mometrix.com/academy and enter code: 221438

HYPHENS

Hyphens are used to **separate compound words**. Use hyphens in the following cases:

Use Case	Example
Compound numbers from 21 to 99 when written out in words	This team needs twenty-five points to win the game.
Written-out fractions that are used as adjectives	The recipe says that we need a three-fourths cup of butter.
Compound adjectives that come before a noun	The well-fed dog took a nap.
Unusual compound words that would be hard to read or easily confused with other words	This is the best anti-itch cream on the market.

Note: This is not a complete set of the rules for hyphens. A dictionary is the best tool for knowing if a compound word needs a hyphen.

> **Review Video: Hyphens**
> Visit mometrix.com/academy and enter code: 981632

DASHES

Dashes are used to show a **break** or a **change in thought** in a sentence or to act as parentheses in a sentence. When typing, use two hyphens to make a dash. Do not put a space before or after the dash. The following are the functions of dashes:

Use Case	Example
Set off parenthetical statements or an **appositive with internal punctuation**	The three trees—oak, pine, and magnolia—are coming on a truck tomorrow.
Show a **break or change in tone or thought**	The first question—how silly of me—does not have a correct answer.

ELLIPSIS MARKS

The ellipsis mark has **three** periods (...) to show when **words have been removed** from a quotation. If a **full sentence or more** is removed from a quoted passage, you need to use **four** periods to show the removed text and the end punctuation mark. The ellipsis mark should not be used at the beginning of a quotation. The ellipsis mark should also not be used at the end of a quotation unless some words have been deleted from the end of the final quoted sentence.

Example:

"Then he picked up the groceries...paid for them...later he went home."

Brackets

There are two main reasons to use brackets:

Use Case	Example
Placing **parentheses inside of parentheses**	The hero of this story, Paul Revere (a silversmith and industrialist [see Ch. 4]), rode through towns of Massachusetts to warn of advancing British troops.
Adding **clarification or detail to a quotation** that is not part of the quotation	The father explained, "My children are planning to attend my alma mater [State University]."

Review Video: Brackets
Visit mometrix.com/academy and enter code: 727546

Common Usage Mistakes

Commonly Confused Words

Which, That, and Who

The words *which*, *that*, and *who* can act as **relative pronouns** to help clarify or describe a noun.

Which is used for things only.

Example: Andrew's car, *which is old and rusty,* broke down last week.

That is used for people or things. *That* is usually informal when used to describe people.

Example: Is this the only book *that Louis L'Amour wrote?*

Example: Is Louis L'Amour the author *that wrote Western novels?*

Who is used for people or for animals that have an identity or personality.

Example: Mozart was the composer *who wrote those operas.*

Example: John's dog, *who is called Max,* is large and fierce.

Then and Than

Then is an adverb that indicates sequence or order:

Example: I'm going to run to the library and then come home.

Than is special-purpose word used only for comparisons:

Example: Susie likes chips more than candy.

Saw and Seen

Saw is the past-tense form of *see.*

Example: I saw a turtle on my walk this morning.

Seen is the past participle of *see.*

Example: I have seen this movie before.

Affect and Effect

There are two main reasons that *affect* and *effect* are so often confused: 1) both words can be used as either a noun or a verb, and 2) unlike most homophones, their usage and meanings are closely related to each other. Here is a quick rundown of the four usage options:

Affect (n): feeling, emotion, or mood that is displayed

Example: The patient had a flat *affect.* (i.e., his face showed little or no emotion)

Affect (v): to alter, to change, to influence

Example: The sunshine *affects* the plant's growth.

Effect (n): a result, a consequence

Example: What *effect* will this weather have on our schedule?

Effect (v): to bring about, to cause to be

Example: These new rules will *effect* order in the office.

The noun form of *affect* is rarely used outside of technical medical descriptions, so if a noun form is needed on the test, you can safely select *effect.* The verb form of *effect* is not as rare as the noun form of *affect,* but it's still not all that likely to show up on your test. If you need a verb and you can't decide which to use based on the definitions, choosing *affect* is your best bet.

Homophones

Homophones are words that sound alike (or similar) but have different **spellings** and **definitions**. A homophone is a type of **homonym**, which is a pair or group of words that are pronounced or spelled the same, but do not mean the same thing.

To, Too, and Two

To can be an adverb or a preposition for showing direction, purpose, and relationship. See your dictionary for the many other ways to use *to* in a sentence.

Examples: I went to the store. | I want to go with you.

Too is an adverb that means *also, as well, very,* or *in excess.*

Examples: I can walk a mile too. | You have eaten too much.

Two is a number.

Example: You have two minutes left.

There, Their, and They're

There can be an adjective, adverb, or pronoun. Often, *there* is used to show a place or to start a sentence.

Examples: I went there yesterday. | There is something in his pocket.

Their is a pronoun that is used to show ownership.

Examples: He is their father. | This is their fourth apology this week.

They're is a contraction of *they are.*

Example: Did you know that they're in town?

Knew and New

Knew is the past tense of *know*.

Example: I knew the answer.

New is an adjective that means something is current, has not been used, or is modern.

Example: This is my new phone.

Its and It's

Its is a pronoun that shows ownership.

Example: The guitar is in its case.

It's is a contraction of *it is.*

Example: It's an honor and a privilege to meet you.

Note: The *h* in honor is silent, so *honor* starts with the vowel sound *o*, which must have the article *an*.

Your and You're

Your is a pronoun that shows ownership.

Example: This is your moment to shine.

You're is a contraction of *you are.*

Example: Yes, you're correct.

Homographs

Homographs are words that share the same spelling, but have different meanings and sometimes different pronunciations. To figure out which meaning is being used, you should be looking for context clues. The context clues give hints to the meaning of the word. For example, the word *spot* has many meanings. It can mean "a place" or "a stain or blot." In the sentence "After my lunch, I saw a spot on my shirt," the word *spot* means "a stain or blot." The context clues of "After my lunch" and "on my shirt" guide you to this decision. A homograph is another type of homonym.

Bank

(noun): an establishment where money is held for savings or lending

(verb): to collect or pile up

Content

(noun): the topics that will be addressed within a book

(adjective): pleased or satisfied

(verb): to make someone pleased or satisfied

Fine

(noun): an amount of money that acts a penalty for an offense

(adjective): very small or thin

(adverb): in an acceptable way

(verb): to make someone pay money as a punishment

Incense

(noun): a material that is burned in religious settings and makes a pleasant aroma

(verb): to frustrate or anger

Lead

(noun): the first or highest position

(noun): a heavy metallic element

(verb): to direct a person or group of followers

(adjective): containing lead

Object

(noun): a lifeless item that can be held and observed

(verb): to disagree

Produce

(noun): fruits and vegetables

(verb): to make or create something

Refuse

(noun): garbage or debris that has been thrown away

(verb): to not allow

Subject

(noun): an area of study

(verb): to force or subdue

Tear

(noun): a fluid secreted by the eyes

(verb): to separate or pull apart

Commonly Misused Words and Phrases

A Lot

The phrase *a lot* should always be written as two words; never as *alot.*

Correct: That's a lot of chocolate!

Incorrect: He does that alot.

Can

The word *can* is used to describe things that are possible occurrences; the word *may* is used to described things that are allowed to happen.

Correct: May I have another piece of pie?

Correct: I can lift three of these bags of mulch at a time.

Incorrect: Mom said we can stay up thirty minutes later tonight.

Could Have

The phrase *could of* is often incorrectly substituted for the phrase *could have*. Similarly, *could of, may of,* and *might of* are sometimes used in place of the correct phrases *could have, may have*, and *might have.*

Correct: If I had known, I would have helped out.

Incorrect: Well, that could of gone much worse than it did.

Myself

The word *myself* is a reflexive pronoun, often incorrectly used in place of *I* or *me.*

Correct: He let me do it myself.

Incorrect: The job was given to Dave and myself.

Off

The phrase *off of* is a redundant expression that should be avoided. In most cases, it can be corrected simply by removing *of.*

Correct: My dog chased the squirrel off its perch on the fence.

Incorrect: He finally moved his plate off of the table.

Supposed To

The phrase *suppose to* is sometimes used incorrectly in place of the phrase *supposed to.*

Correct: I was supposed to go to the store this afternoon.

Incorrect: When are we suppose to get our grades?

Try To

The phrase *try and* is often used in informal writing and conversation to replace the correct phrase *try to.*

Correct: It's a good policy to try to satisfy every customer who walks in the door.

Incorrect: Don't try and do too much.

Text Types and Purposes

The Writing Process

Prewriting

The **prewriting stage** is the part of the process in which the writer focuses on **generating ideas** and developing a broad plan for what he or she wants to accomplish. **Brainstorming** is the process of thinking about a topic and writing down every thought that comes to mind. Brainstorming may also take the form of asking questions that need to be answered by the composition. **Free writing** has a similar goal of writing about a topic in a continuous flow for a short span of time (e.g., 2 to 3 minutes). The goal of these exercises is not to produce high-quality, polished thoughts, but to generate leads to follow when the more structured writing happens later in the process. In research writing, the prewriting stage may also include doing a literature review and **collecting information** to use as evidence in arguments later on. When collecting information, it is important to take clear notes of where an idea was originally found so it can be cited later on. Another key aspect of the prewriting process is **planning phase**. This entails deciding on the overall topic, purpose, tone, and general organization for the rest of the composition. The planning process may involve using aids like outlines, Venn diagrams, flowcharts, and other visual models to help collect and organize information. The planning process does not set the whole composition in stone, but it does help structure the ideas to be written in the drafting phase.

Drafting

The **drafting stage** of the writing process involves taking the plan for the composition and filling out all of the main ideas for the composition. Some writers prefer to start by writing the introduction and write their whole composition from start to finish, while others may prefer writing the main body paragraphs first and then coming back to the introduction and conclusion. In any case, the drafting process is a first attempt at writing the whole composition from start to finish. A writer may succeed in communicating what he or she wants in the first draft, but it often takes writing **several drafts** before the ideas and arguments take their final form. By the end of the drafting stage, the composition should be close to its final organization with its arguments clearly identified, but it will still need organizational, grammatical, and formatting improvements to be called complete.

Revising

The **revision stage** is when the writer reads back through his or her work and looks for big-picture issues that affect **clarity** and **cohesion**. These can include organizational issues or flaws in logical flow. Writers should look back through their work to find any assertions or arguments that may be misplaced or lacking in support. They should look also through their work to find any information that does not contribute to the main idea or goal of the composition. Beginning writers may find it difficult to clearly communicate more than two or three main points in their arguments. If this is the case, these writers should eliminate information that detracts from those main points. In this stage, clarity is often more important than comprehensiveness.

Editing/Proofreading

The **editing or proofreading stage** is focused specifically on improving the grammar and punctuation of the composition. The writer should read each paragraph closely and slowly to identify and fix any grammatical, spelling, or punctuation errors. Some of the worst offenders include subject-verb agreement in complex sentences, changes in tense throughout the document, and changes in perspective (first, second, or third person) or tone (professional, casual, opinionated, etc.). When writing at home, it is often helpful to have a friend or family member look for errors as well. Finally, this phase involves looking for very small errors, so multiple passes should be taken to catch as many problems as possible. One good rule of thumb is to keep reading through the whole document until a full read-through can be accomplished without finding any more errors.

PUBLISHING

The **publishing stage** refers to putting the document into its final format and delivering it to the audience. This involves formatting the document for presentation. In research writing, the final document may need to conform to a specific publishing standard, such as MLA or APA. In literal publishing, this would also take the form of presenting the document to the final audience, which may involve physical printing or digital publication. Note that once a composition has been published, it is often difficult to change or retract. Before reaching the publishing stage, the writer should have looped through the drafting, revision, and editing process a few times to ensure the writer says exactly what he or she wants before putting it before the final audience.

RECURSIVE WRITING PROCESS

However you approach writing, you may find comfort in knowing that the revision process can occur in any order. The **recursive writing process** is not as difficult as the phrase may make it seem. Simply put, the recursive writing process means that you may need to revisit steps after completing other steps. It also implies that the steps are not required to take place in any certain order. Indeed, you may find that planning, drafting, and revising can all take place at about the same time. The writing process involves moving back and forth between planning, drafting, and revising, followed by more planning, more drafting, and more revising until the writing is satisfactory.

Review Video: Recursive Writing Process
Visit mometrix.com/academy and enter code: 951611

OUTLINING AND ORGANIZING IDEAS

ESSAYS

Essays usually focus on one topic, subject, or goal. There are several types of essays, including informative, persuasive, and narrative. An essay's structure and level of formality depend on the type of essay and its goal. While narrative essays typically do not include outside sources, other types of essays often require some research and the integration of primary and secondary sources.

The basic format of an essay typically has three major parts: the introduction, the body, and the conclusion. The body is further divided into the writer's main points. Short and simple essays may have three main points, while essays covering broader ranges and going into more depth can have almost any number of main points, depending on length.

An essay's introduction should answer three questions:

1. What is the **subject** of the essay?
   If a student writes an essay about a book, the answer would include the title and author of the book and any additional information needed—such as the subject or argument of the book.
2. How does the essay **address** the subject?
   To answer this, the writer identifies the essay's organization by briefly summarizing main points and the evidence supporting them.
3. What will the essay **prove**?
   This is the thesis statement, usually the opening paragraph's last sentence, clearly stating the writer's message.

The body elaborates on all the main points related to the thesis, introducing one main point at a time, and includes supporting evidence with each main point. Each body paragraph should state the point in a topic sentence, which is usually the first sentence in the paragraph. The paragraph should then explain the point's meaning, support it with quotations or other evidence, and then explain how this point and the evidence are related to the thesis. The writer should then repeat this procedure in a new paragraph for each additional main point.

The conclusion reiterates the content of the introduction, including the thesis, to remind the reader of the essay's main argument or subject. The essay writer may also summarize the highlights of the argument or description contained in the body of the essay, following the same sequence originally used in the body. For example, a conclusion might look like: Point 1 + Point 2 + Point 3 = Thesis, or Point 1 → Point 2 → Point 3 → Thesis Proof. Good organization makes essays easier for writers to compose and provides a guide for readers to follow. Well-organized essays hold attention better and are more likely to get readers to accept their theses as valid.

Main Ideas, Supporting Details, and Outlining a Topic

A writer often begins the first paragraph of a paper by stating the **main idea** or point, also known as the **topic sentence**. The rest of the paragraph supplies particular details that develop and support the main point. One way to visualize the relationship between the main point and supporting information is by considering a table: the tabletop is the main point, and each of the table's legs is a supporting detail or group of details. Both professional authors and students can benefit from planning their writing by first making an outline of the topic. Outlines facilitate quick identification of the main point and supporting details without having to wade through the additional language that will exist in the fully developed essay, article, or paper. Outlining can also help readers to analyze a piece of existing writing for the same reason. The outline first summarizes the main idea in one sentence. Then, below that, it summarizes the supporting details in a numbered list. Writing the paper then consists of filling in the outline with detail, writing a paragraph for each supporting point, and adding an introduction and conclusion.

Introduction

The purpose of the introduction is to capture the reader's attention and announce the essay's main idea. Normally, the introduction contains 50-80 words, or 3-5 sentences. An introduction can begin with an interesting quote, a question, or a strong opinion—something that will **engage** the reader's interest and prompt them to keep reading. If you are writing your essay to a specific prompt, your introduction should include a **restatement or summarization** of the prompt so that the reader will have some context for your essay. Finally, your introduction should briefly state your **thesis or main idea**: the primary thing you hope to communicate to the reader through your essay. Don't try to include all of the details and nuances of your thesis, or all of your reasons for it, in the introduction. That's what the rest of the essay is for!

Review Video: Introduction
Visit mometrix.com/academy and enter code: 961328

Thesis Statement

The thesis is the main idea of the essay. A temporary thesis, or working thesis, should be established early in the writing process because it will serve to keep the writer focused as ideas develop. This temporary thesis is subject to change as you continue to write.

The temporary thesis has two parts: a **topic** (i.e., the focus of your essay based on the prompt) and a **comment**. The comment makes an important point about the topic. A temporary thesis should be interesting and specific. Also, you need to limit the topic to a manageable scope. These three questions are useful tools to measure the effectiveness of any temporary thesis:

- Does the focus of my essay have enough interest to hold an audience?
- Is the focus of my essay specific enough to generate interest?
- Is the focus of my essay manageable for the time limit? Too broad? Too narrow?

The thesis should be a generalization rather than a fact because the thesis prepares readers for facts and details that support the thesis. The process of bringing the thesis into sharp focus may help in outlining major sections of the work. Once the thesis and introduction are complete, you can address the body of the work.

Review Video: Thesis Statements
Visit mometrix.com/academy and enter code: 691033

SUPPORTING THE THESIS

Throughout your essay, the thesis should be **explained clearly and supported** adequately by additional arguments. The thesis sentence needs to contain a clear statement of the purpose of your essay and a comment about the thesis. With the thesis statement, you have an opportunity to state what is noteworthy of this particular treatment of the prompt. Each sentence and paragraph should build on and support the thesis.

When you respond to the prompt, use parts of the passage to support your argument or defend your position. Using supporting evidence from the passage strengths your argument because readers can see your attention to the entire passage and your response to the details and facts within the passage. You can use facts, details, statistics, and direct quotations from the passage to uphold your position. Be sure to point out which information comes from the original passage and base your argument around that evidence.

BODY

In an essay's introduction, the writer establishes the thesis and may indicate how the rest of the piece will be structured. In the body of the piece, the writer **elaborates** upon, **illustrates**, and **explains** the **thesis statement**. How writers arrange supporting details and their choices of paragraph types are development techniques. Writers may give examples of the concept introduced in the thesis statement. If the subject includes a cause-and-effect relationship, the author may explain its causality. A writer will explain or analyze the main idea of the piece throughout the body, often by presenting arguments for the veracity or credibility of the thesis statement. Writers may use development to define or clarify ambiguous terms. Paragraphs within the body may be organized using natural sequences, like space and time. Writers may employ **inductive reasoning**, using multiple details to establish a generalization or causal relationship, or **deductive reasoning**, proving a generalized hypothesis or proposition through a specific example or case.

Review Video: Drafting Body Paragraphs
Visit mometrix.com/academy and enter code: 724590

PARAGRAPHS

After the introduction of a passage, a series of body paragraphs will carry a message through to the conclusion. Each paragraph should be **unified around a main point**. Normally, a good topic sentence summarizes the paragraph's main point. A topic sentence is a general sentence that gives an introduction to the paragraph.

The sentences that follow support the topic sentence. However, though it is usually the first sentence, the topic sentence can come as the final sentence to the paragraph if the earlier sentences give a clear explanation of the paragraph's topic. This allows the topic sentence to function as a concluding sentence. Overall, the paragraphs need to stay true to the main point. This means that any unnecessary sentences that do not advance the main point should be removed.

The main point of a paragraph requires adequate development (i.e., a substantial paragraph that covers the main point). A paragraph of two or three sentences does not cover a main point. This is especially true when the main point of the paragraph gives strong support to the argument of the thesis. An occasional short paragraph is fine as a transitional device. However, a well-developed argument will have paragraphs with more than a few sentences.

METHODS OF DEVELOPING PARAGRAPHS

Common methods of adding substance to paragraphs include examples, illustrations, analogies, and cause and effect.

- **Examples** are supporting details to the main idea of a paragraph or a passage. When authors write about something that their audience may not understand, they can provide an example to show their point. When authors write about something that is not easily accepted, they can give examples to prove their point.
- **Illustrations** are extended examples that require several sentences. Well-selected illustrations can be a great way for authors to develop a point that may not be familiar to their audience.
- **Analogies** make comparisons between items that appear to have nothing in common. Analogies are employed by writers to provoke fresh thoughts about a subject. These comparisons may be used to explain the unfamiliar, to clarify an abstract point, or to argue a point. Although analogies are effective literary devices, they should be used carefully in arguments. Two things may be alike in some respects but completely different in others.
- **Cause and effect** is an excellent device to explain the connection between an action or situation and a particular result. One way that authors can use cause and effect is to state the effect in the topic sentence of a paragraph and add the causes in the body of the paragraph. This method can give an author's paragraphs structure, which always strengthens writing.

TYPES OF PARAGRAPHS

- A **paragraph of narration** tells a story or a part of a story. Normally, the sentences are arranged in chronological order (i.e., the order that the events happened). However, flashbacks (i.e., an anecdote from an earlier time) can be included.
- A **descriptive paragraph** makes a verbal portrait of a person, place, or thing. When specific details are used that appeal to one or more of the senses (i.e., sight, sound, smell, taste, and touch), authors give readers a sense of being present in the moment.
- A **process paragraph** is related to time order (i.e., First, you open the bottle. Second, you pour the liquid, etc.). Usually, this describes a process or teaches readers how to perform a process.
- **Comparing two things** draws attention to their similarities and indicates a number of differences. When authors contrast, they focus only on differences. Both comparing and contrasting may be done point-by-point, noting both the similarities and differences of each point, or in sequential paragraphs, where you discuss all the similarities and then all the differences, or vice versa.

BREAKING TEXT INTO PARAGRAPHS

For most forms of writing, you will need to use multiple paragraphs. As such, determining when to start a new paragraph is very important. Reasons for starting a new paragraph include:

- To mark off the introduction and concluding paragraphs
- To signal a shift to a new idea or topic
- To indicate an important shift in time or place
- To explain a point in additional detail
- To highlight a comparison, contrast, or cause and effect relationship

PARAGRAPH LENGTH

Most readers find that their comfort level for a paragraph is between 100 and 200 words. Shorter paragraphs cause too much starting and stopping and give a choppy effect. Paragraphs that are too long often test the attention span of readers. Two notable exceptions to this rule exist. In scientific or scholarly papers, longer paragraphs suggest seriousness and depth. In journalistic writing, constraints are placed on paragraph size by the narrow columns in a newspaper format.

The first and last paragraphs of a text will usually be the introduction and conclusion. These special-purpose paragraphs are likely to be shorter than paragraphs in the body of the work. Paragraphs in the body of the essay follow the subject's outline (e.g., one paragraph per point in short essays and a group of paragraphs per point in longer works). Some ideas require more development than others, so it is good for a writer to remain flexible. A paragraph of excessive length may be divided, and shorter ones may be combined.

Conclusion

Two important principles to consider when writing a conclusion are strength and closure. A strong conclusion gives the reader a sense that the author's main points are meaningful and important, and that the supporting facts and arguments are convincing, solid, and well developed. When a conclusion achieves closure, it gives the impression that the writer has stated all necessary information and points and completed the work, rather than simply stopping after a specified length. Some things to avoid when writing concluding paragraphs include:

- Introducing a completely new idea
- Beginning with obvious or unoriginal phrases like "In conclusion" or "To summarize"
- Apologizing for one's opinions or writing
- Repeating the thesis word for word rather than rephrasing it
- Believing that the conclusion must always summarize the piece

Coherence in Writing

Coherent Paragraphs

A smooth flow of sentences and paragraphs without gaps, shifts, or bumps will lead to paragraph **coherence**. Ties between old and new information can be smoothed using several methods:

- **Linking ideas clearly**, from the topic sentence to the body of the paragraph, is essential for a smooth transition. The topic sentence states the main point, and this should be followed by specific details, examples, and illustrations that support the topic sentence. The support may be direct or indirect. In **indirect support**, the illustrations and examples may support a sentence that in turn supports the topic directly.
- The **repetition of key words** adds coherence to a paragraph. To avoid dull language, variations of the key words may be used.
- **Parallel structures** are often used within sentences to emphasize the similarity of ideas and connect sentences giving similar information.
- Maintaining a **consistent verb tense** throughout the paragraph helps. Shifting tenses affects the smooth flow of words and can disrupt the coherence of the paragraph.

Review Video: How to Write a Good Paragraph
Visit mometrix.com/academy and enter code: 682127

Sequence Words and Phrases

When a paragraph opens with the topic sentence, the second sentence may begin with a phrase like *first of all*, introducing the first supporting detail or example. The writer may introduce the second supporting item with words or phrases like *also*, *in addition*, and *besides*. The writer might introduce succeeding pieces of support with wording like, *another thing*, *moreover*, *furthermore*, or *not only that, but*. The writer may introduce the last piece of support with *lastly*, *finally*, or *last but not least*. Writers get off the point by presenting off-target items not supporting the main point. For example, a main point *my dog is not smart* is supported by the statement, *he's six years old and still doesn't answer to his name*. But *he cries when I leave for school* is not supportive, as it does not indicate lack of intelligence. Writers stay on point by presenting only supportive statements that are directly relevant to and illustrative of their main point.

Review Video: Sequence
Visit mometrix.com/academy and enter code: 489027

Transitions

Transitions between sentences and paragraphs guide readers from idea to idea and indicate relationships between sentences and paragraphs. Writers should be judicious in their use of transitions, inserting them sparingly. They should also be selected to fit the author's purpose—transitions can indicate time, comparison, and conclusion, among other purposes. Tone is also important to consider when using transitional phrases, varying the tone for different audiences. For example, in a scholarly essay, *in summary* would be preferable to the more informal *in short*.

When working with transitional words and phrases, writers usually find a natural flow that indicates when a transition is needed. In reading a draft of the text, it should become apparent where the flow is disrupted. At this point, the writer can add transitional elements during the revision process. Revising can also afford an opportunity to delete transitional devices that seem heavy handed or unnecessary.

Review Video: Transitions in Writing
Visit mometrix.com/academy and enter code: 233246

Types of Transitional Words

Time	afterward, immediately, earlier, meanwhile, recently, lately, now, since, soon, when, then, until, before, etc.
Sequence	too, first, second, further, moreover, also, again, and, next, still, besides, finally
Comparison	similarly, in the same way, likewise, also, again, once more
Contrasting	but, although, despite, however, instead, nevertheless, on the one hand... on the other hand, regardless, yet, in contrast
Cause and Effect	because, consequently, thus, therefore, then, to this end, since, so, as a result, if... then, accordingly
Examples	for example, for instance, such as, to illustrate, indeed, in fact, specifically
Place	near, far, here, there, to the left/right, next to, above, below, beyond, opposite, beside
Concession	granted that, naturally, of course, it may appear, although it is true that
Repetition, Summary, or Conclusion	as mentioned earlier, as noted, in other words, in short, on the whole, to summarize, therefore, as a result, to conclude, in conclusion
Addition	and, also, furthermore, moreover
Generalization	in broad terms, broadly speaking, in general

Review Video: Transition Words
Visit mometrix.com/academy and enter code: 707563

Review Video: How to Effectively Connect Sentences
Visit mometrix.com/academy and enter code: 948325

Writing Style and Form

Writing Style and Linguistic Form

Linguistic form encodes the literal meanings of words and sentences. It comes from the phonological, morphological, syntactic, and semantic parts of a language. **Writing style** consists of different ways of encoding the meaning and indicating figurative and stylistic meanings. An author's writing style can also be referred to as his or her **voice**.

Writers' stylistic choices accomplish three basic effects on their audiences:

- They **communicate meanings** beyond linguistically dictated meanings,
- They communicate the **author's attitude**, such as persuasive or argumentative effects accomplished through style, and
- They communicate or **express feelings**.

Within style, component areas include:

- Narrative structure
- Viewpoint
- Focus
- Sound patterns
- Meter and rhythm
- Lexical and syntactic repetition and parallelism
- Writing genre
- Representational, realistic, and mimetic effects
- Representation of thought and speech
- Meta-representation (representing representation)
- Irony
- Metaphor and other indirect meanings
- Representation and use of historical and dialectal variations
- Gender-specific and other group-specific speech styles, both real and fictitious
- Analysis of the processes for inferring meaning from writing

TONE

Tone may be defined as the writer's **attitude** toward the topic, and to the audience. This attitude is reflected in the language used in the writing. The tone of a work should be **appropriate to the topic** and to the intended audience. While it may be fine to use slang or jargon in some pieces, other texts should not contain such terms. Tone can range from humorous to serious and any level in between. It may be more or less formal, depending on the purpose of the writing and its intended audience. All these nuances in tone can flavor the entire writing and should be kept in mind as the work evolves.

Review Video: Style, Tone, and Mood
Visit mometrix.com/academy and enter code: 416961

WORD SELECTION

A writer's choice of words is a signature of their style. Careful thought about the use of words can improve a piece of writing. A passage can be an exciting piece to read when attention is given to the use of vivid or specific nouns rather than general ones.

Example:

General: His kindness will never be forgotten.

Specific: His thoughtful gifts and bear hugs will never be forgotten.

ACTIVE AND PASSIVE LANGUAGE

Attention should also be given to the kind of verbs that are used in sentences. Active verbs (e.g., run, swim) are about an action. Whenever possible, an **active verb should replace a linking verb** to provide clear examples for arguments and to strengthen a passage overall. When using an active verb, one should be sure that the verb is used in the active voice instead of the passive voice. Verbs are in the active voice when the subject is the one doing the action. A verb is in the passive voice when the subject is the recipient of an action.

Example:

> Passive: The winners were called to the stage by the judges.
>
> Active: The judges called the winners to the stage.

Review Video: Word Usage In Sentences
Visit mometrix.com/academy and enter code: 197863

CONCISENESS

Conciseness is writing that communicates a message in the fewest words possible. Writing concisely is valuable because short, uncluttered messages allow the reader to understand the author's message more easily and efficiently. Planning is important in writing concise messages. If you have in mind what you need to write beforehand, it will be easier to make a message short and to the point. Do not state the obvious.

Revising is also important. After the message is written, make sure you have effective, pithy sentences that efficiently get your point across. When reviewing the information, imagine a conversation taking place, and concise writing will likely result.

APPROPRIATE KINDS OF WRITING FOR DIFFERENT TASKS, PURPOSES, AND AUDIENCES

When preparing to write a composition, consider the audience and purpose to choose the best type of writing. Four common types of writing are persuasive, expository, and narrative. **Persuasive**, or argumentative writing, is used to convince the audience to take action or agree with the author's claims. **Expository** writing is meant to inform the audience of the author's observations or research on a topic. **Narrative** writing is used to tell the audience a story and often allows more room for creativity. **Descriptive** writing is when a writer provides a substantial amount of detail to the reader so he or she can visualize the topic. While task, purpose, and audience inform a writer's mode of writing, these factors also impact elements such as tone, vocabulary, and formality.

For example, students who are writing to persuade their parents to grant them some additional privilege, such as permission for a more independent activity, should use more sophisticated vocabulary and diction that sounds more mature and serious to appeal to the parental audience. However, students who are writing for younger children should use simpler vocabulary and sentence structure, as well as choose words that are more vivid and entertaining. They should treat their topics more lightly, and include humor when appropriate. Students who are writing for their classmates may use language that is more informal, as well as age-appropriate.

Review Video: Writing Purpose and Audience
Visit mometrix.com/academy and enter code: 146627

FORMALITY IN WRITING

LEVEL OF FORMALITY

The relationship between writer and reader is important in choosing a **level of formality** as most writing requires some degree of formality. **Formal writing** is for addressing a superior in a school or work environment. Business letters, textbooks, and newspapers use a moderate to high level of formality. **Informal writing** is appropriate for private letters, personal emails, and business correspondence between close associates.

For your exam, you will want to be aware of informal and formal writing. One way that this can be accomplished is to watch for shifts in point of view in the essay. For example, unless writers are using a personal example, they will rarely refer to themselves (e.g., "*I* think that *my* point is very clear.") to avoid being informal when they need to be formal.

Also, be mindful of an author who addresses his or her audience **directly** in their writing (e.g., "Readers, *like you*, will understand this argument.") as this can be a sign of informal writing. Good writers understand the need to be consistent with their level of formality. Shifts in levels of formality or point of view can confuse readers and cause them to discount the message.

Clichés

Clichés are phrases that have been **overused** to the point that the phrase has no importance or has lost the original meaning. These phrases have no originality and add very little to a passage. Therefore, most writers will avoid the use of clichés. Another option is to make changes to a cliché so that it is not predictable and empty of meaning.

Examples:

> When life gives you lemons, make lemonade.
>
> Every cloud has a silver lining.

Jargon

Jargon is **specialized vocabulary** that is used among members of a certain trade or profession. Since jargon is understood by only a small audience, writers will use jargon in passages that will only be read by a specialized audience. For example, medical jargon should be used in a medical journal but not in a New York Times article. Jargon includes exaggerated language that tries to impress rather than inform. Sentences filled with jargon are not precise and are difficult to understand.

Examples:

> "He is going to *toenail* these frames for us." (Toenail is construction jargon for nailing at an angle.)
>
> "They brought in a *kip* of material today." (Kip refers to 1000 pounds in architecture and engineering.)

Slang

Slang is an **informal** and sometimes private language that is understood by some individuals. Slang terms have some usefulness, but they can have a small audience. So, most formal writing will not include this kind of language.

Examples:

> "Yes, the event was a blast!" (In this sentence, *blast* means that the event was a great experience.)
>
> "That attempt was an epic fail." (By *epic fail*, the speaker means that his or her attempt was not a success.)

Colloquialism

A colloquialism is a word or phrase that is found in informal writing. Unlike slang, **colloquial language** will be familiar to a greater range of people. However, colloquialisms are still considered inappropriate for formal writing. Colloquial language can include some slang, but these are limited to contractions for the most part.

Examples:

> "Can *y'all* come back another time?" (Y'all is a contraction of "you all.")
>
> "Will you stop him from building this *castle in the air*?" (A "castle in the air" is an improbable or unlikely event.)

Academic Language

In educational settings, students are often expected to use academic language in their schoolwork. Academic language is also commonly found in dissertations and theses, texts published by academic journals, and other forms of academic research. Academic language conventions may vary between fields, but general academic language is free of slang, regional terminology, and noticeable grammatical errors. Specific terms may also be used in academic language, and it is important to understand their proper usage. A writer's command of academic language impacts their ability to communicate in an academic or professional context. While it is acceptable to use colloquialisms, slang, improper grammar, or other forms of informal speech in social settings or at home, it is inappropriate to practice non-academic language in academic contexts.

Common Types of Writing

Autobiographical Narratives

Autobiographical narratives are narratives written by an author about an event or period in their life. Autobiographical narratives are written from one person's perspective, in first person, and often include the author's thoughts and feelings alongside their description of the event or period. Structure, style, or theme varies between different autobiographical narratives, since each narrative is personal and specific to its author and his or her experience.

Reflective Essay

A less common type of essay is the reflective essay. **Reflective essays** allow the author to reflect, or think back, on an experience and analyze what they recall. They should consider what they learned from the experience, what they could have done differently, what would have helped them during the experience, or anything else that they have realized from looking back on the experience. Reflection essays incorporate both objective reflection on one's own actions and subjective explanation of thoughts and feelings. These essays can be written for a number of experiences in a formal or informal context.

Journals and Diaries

A **journal** is a personal account of events, experiences, feelings, and thoughts. Many people write journals to express their feelings and thoughts or to help them process experiences they have had. Since journals are **private documents** not meant to be shared with others, writers may not be concerned with grammar, spelling, or other mechanics. However, authors may write journals that they expect or hope to publish someday; in this case, they not only express their thoughts and feelings and process their experiences, but they also attend to their craft in writing them. Some authors compose journals to record a particular time period or a series of related events, such as a cancer diagnosis, treatment, surviving the disease, and how these experiences have changed or affected them. Other experiences someone might include in a journal are recovering from addiction, journeys of spiritual exploration and discovery, time spent in another country, or anything else someone wants to personally document. Journaling can also be therapeutic, as some people use journals to work through feelings of grief over loss or to wrestle with big decisions.

Examples of Diaries in Literature

The Diary of a Young Girl by Dutch Jew Anne Frank (1947) contains her life-affirming, nonfictional diary entries from 1942-1944 while her family hid in an attic from World War II's genocidal Nazis. *Go Ask Alice* (1971) by Beatrice Sparks is a cautionary, fictional novel in the form of diary entries by Alice, an unhappy, rebellious teen who takes LSD, runs away from home and lives with hippies, and eventually returns home. Frank's writing reveals an intelligent, sensitive, insightful girl, raised by intellectual European parents—a girl who believes in the goodness of human nature despite surrounding atrocities. Alice, influenced by early 1970s counterculture, becomes less optimistic. However, similarities can be found between them: Frank dies in a Nazi concentration camp while the fictitious Alice dies from a drug overdose. Both young women are also unable to escape their surroundings. Additionally, adolescent searches for personal identity are evident in both books.

Review Video: Journals, Diaries, Letters, and Blogs
Visit mometrix.com/academy and enter code: 432845

Letters

Letters are messages written to other people. In addition to letters written between individuals, some writers compose letters to the editors of newspapers, magazines, and other publications, while some write "Open Letters" to be published and read by the general public. Open letters, while intended for everyone to read, may also identify a group of people or a single person whom the letter directly addresses. In everyday use, the most-used forms are business letters and personal or friendly letters. Both kinds share common elements: business or personal letterhead stationery; the writer's return address at the top; the addressee's address next; a salutation, such as "Dear [name]" or some similar opening greeting, followed by a colon in business letters or a comma in personal letters; the body of the letter, with paragraphs as indicated; and a closing, like "Sincerely/Cordially/Best regards/etc." or "Love," in intimate personal letters.

Early Letters

The Greek word for "letter" is *epistolē*, which became the English word "epistle." The earliest letters were called epistles, including the New Testament's epistles from the apostles to the Christians. In ancient Egypt, the writing curriculum in scribal schools included the epistolary genre. Epistolary novels frame a story in the form of letters. Examples of noteworthy epistolary novels include:

- *Pamela* (1740), by 18th-century English novelist Samuel Richardson
- *Shamela* (1741), Henry Fielding's satire of *Pamela* that mocked epistolary writing.
- *Lettres persanes* (1721) by French author Montesquieu
- *The Sorrows of Young Werther* (1774) by German author Johann Wolfgang von Goethe
- *The History of Emily Montague* (1769), the first Canadian novel, by Frances Brooke
- *Dracula* (1897) by Bram Stoker
- *Frankenstein* (1818) by Mary Shelley
- *The Color Purple* (1982) by Alice Walker

Blogs

The word "blog" is derived from "weblog" and refers to writing done exclusively on the internet. Readers of reputable newspapers expect quality content and layouts that enable easy reading. These expectations also apply to blogs. For example, readers can easily move visually from line to line when columns are narrow, while overly wide columns cause readers to lose their places. Blogs must also be posted with layouts enabling online readers to follow them easily. However, because the way people read on computer, tablet, and smartphone screens differs from how they read print on paper, formatting and writing blog content is more complex than writing newspaper articles. Two major principles are the bases for blog-writing rules: The first is while readers of print articles skim to estimate their length, online they must scroll down to scan; therefore, blog layouts need more subheadings, graphics, and other indications of what information follows. The second is onscreen reading can be harder on the eyes than reading printed paper, so legibility is crucial in blogs.

Rules and Rationales for Writing Blogs

1. Format all posts for smooth page layout and easy scanning.
2. Column width should not be too wide, as larger lines of text can be difficult to read
3. Headings and subheadings separate text visually, enable scanning or skimming, and encourage continued reading.
4. Bullet-pointed or numbered lists enable quick information location and scanning.

5. Punctuation is critical, so beginners should use shorter sentences until confident in their knowledge of punctuation rules.
6. Blog paragraphs should be far shorter—two to six sentences each—than paragraphs written on paper to enable "chunking" because reading onscreen is more difficult.
7. Sans-serif fonts are usually clearer than serif fonts, and larger font sizes are better.
8. Highlight important material and draw attention with **boldface**, but avoid overuse. Avoid hard-to-read *italics* and ALL CAPITALS.
9. Include enough blank spaces: overly busy blogs tire eyes and brains. Images not only break up text but also emphasize and enhance text and can attract initial reader attention.
10. Use background colors judiciously to avoid distracting the eye or making it difficult to read.
11. Be consistent throughout posts, since people read them in different orders.
12. Tell a story with a beginning, middle, and end.

Specialized Types of Writing

Editorials

Editorials are articles in newspapers, magazines, and other serial publications. Editorials express an opinion or belief belonging to the majority of the publication's leadership. This opinion or belief generally refers to a specific issue, topic, or event. These articles are authored by a member, or a small number of members, of the publication's leadership and are often written to affect their readers, such as persuading them to adopt a stance or take a particular action.

Resumes

Resumes are brief, but formal, documents that outline an individual's experience in a certain area. Resumes are most often used for job applications. Such resumes will list the applicant's work experience, certification, and achievements or qualifications related to the position. Resumes should only include the most pertinent information. They should also use strategic formatting to highlight the applicant's most impressive experiences and achievements, to ensure the document can be read quickly and easily, and to eliminate both visual clutter and excessive negative space.

Reports

Reports summarize the results of research, new methodology, or other developments in an academic or professional context. Reports often include details about methodology and outside influences and factors. However, a report should focus primarily on the results of the research or development. Reports are objective and deliver information efficiently, sacrificing style for clear and effective communication.

Memoranda

A memorandum, also called a memo, is a formal method of communication used in professional settings. Memoranda are printed documents that include a heading listing the sender and their job title, the recipient and their job title, the date, and a specific subject line. Memoranda often include an introductory section explaining the reason and context for the memorandum. Next, a memorandum includes a section with details relevant to the topic. Finally, the memorandum will conclude with a paragraph that politely and clearly defines the sender's expectations of the recipient.

Technology in the Writing Process

Modern technology has yielded several tools that can be used to make the writing process more convenient and organized. Word processors and online tools, such as databases and plagiarism detectors, allow much of the writing process to be completed in one place, using one device.

Technology for Planning and Drafting

For the planning and drafting stages of the writing process, word processors are a helpful tool. These programs also feature formatting tools, allowing users to create their own planning tools or create digital outlines that can be easily converted into sentences, paragraphs, or an entire essay draft. Online databases and references also complement the planning process by providing convenient access to information and sources for research. Word processors also allow users to keep up with their work and update it more easily than if they wrote their work by hand. Online word processors often allow users to collaborate, making group assignments more convenient. These programs also allow users to include illustrations or other supplemental media in their compositions.

Technology for Revising, Editing, and Proofreading

Word processors also benefit the revising, editing, and proofreading stages of the writing process. Most of these programs indicate errors in spelling and grammar, allowing users to catch minor errors and correct them quickly. There are also websites designed to help writers by analyzing text for deeper errors, such as poor sentence structure, inappropriate complexity, lack of sentence variety, and style issues. These websites can help users fix errors they may not know to look for or may have simply missed. As writers finish these steps, they may benefit from checking their work for any plagiarism. There are several websites and programs that compare text to other documents and publications across the internet and detect any similarities within the text. These websites show the source of the similar information, so users know whether or not they referenced the source and unintentionally plagiarized its contents.

Technology for Publishing

Technology also makes managing written work more convenient. Digitally storing documents keeps everything in one place and is easy to reference. Digital storage also makes sharing work easier, as documents can be attached to an email or stored online. This also allows writers to publish their work easily, as they can electronically submit it to other publications or freely post it to a personal blog, profile, or website.

Chapter Quiz

Ready to see how well you retained what you just read? Scan the QR code to go directly to the chapter quiz interface for this study guide. If you're using a computer, simply visit the online resources page at **mometrix.com/resources719/tabe1314** and click the Chapter Quizzes link.

Mathematics

Numbers and Quantity

Number Basics

Classifications of Numbers

Numbers are the basic building blocks of mathematics. Specific features of numbers are identified by the following terms:

Integer – any positive or negative whole number, including zero. Integers do not include fractions $\left(\frac{1}{3}\right)$, decimals (0.56), or mixed numbers $\left(7\frac{3}{4}\right)$.

Prime number – any whole number greater than 1 that has only two factors, itself and 1; that is, a number that can be divided evenly only by 1 and itself.

Composite number – any whole number greater than 1 that has more than two different factors; in other words, any whole number that is not a prime number. For example: The composite number 8 has the factors of 1, 2, 4, and 8.

Even number – any integer that can be divided by 2 without leaving a remainder. For example: 2, 4, 6, 8, and so on.

Odd number – any integer that cannot be divided evenly by 2. For example: 3, 5, 7, 9, and so on.

Decimal number – any number that uses a decimal point to show the part of the number that is less than one. Example: 1.234.

Decimal point – a symbol used to separate the ones place from the tenths place in decimals or dollars from cents in currency.

Decimal place – the position of a number to the right of the decimal point. In the decimal 0.123, the 1 is in the first place to the right of the decimal point, indicating tenths; the 2 is in the second place, indicating hundredths; and the 3 is in the third place, indicating thousandths.

The **decimal**, or base 10, system is a number system that uses ten different digits (0, 1, 2, 3, 4, 5, 6, 7, 8, 9). An example of a number system that uses something other than ten digits is the **binary**, or base 2, number system, used by computers, which uses only the numbers 0 and 1. It is thought that the decimal system originated because people had only their 10 fingers for counting.

Rational numbers include all integers, decimals, and fractions. Any terminating or repeating decimal number is a rational number.

Irrational numbers cannot be written as fractions or decimals because the number of decimal places is infinite and there is no recurring pattern of digits within the number. For example, pi (π) begins with 3.141592 and continues without terminating or repeating, so pi is an irrational number.

Real numbers are the set of all rational and irrational numbers.

> **Review Video: Classification of Numbers**
> Visit mometrix.com/academy and enter code: 461071
>
> **Review Video: Prime and Composite Numbers**
> Visit mometrix.com/academy and enter code: 565581

Numbers in Word Form and Place Value

When writing numbers out in word form or translating word form to numbers, it is essential to understand how a place value system works. In the decimal or base-10 system, each digit of a number represents how many of the corresponding place value—a specific factor of 10—are contained in the number being represented. To make reading numbers easier, every three digits to the left of the decimal place is preceded by a comma. The following table demonstrates some of the place values:

Power of 10	10^3	10^2	10^1	10^0	10^{-1}	10^{-2}	10^{-3}
Value	1,000	100	10	1	0.1	0.01	0.001
Place	thousands	hundreds	tens	ones	tenths	hundredths	thousandths

For example, consider the number 4,546.09, which can be separated into each place value like this:

4: thousands
5: hundreds
4: tens
6: ones
0: tenths
9: hundredths

This number in word form would be *four thousand five hundred forty-six and nine hundredths.*

> **Review Video: Place Value**
> Visit mometrix.com/academy and enter code: 205433

Number Lines

A number line is a graph to see the distance between numbers. Basically, this graph shows the relationship between numbers. So a number line may have a point for zero and may show negative numbers on the left side of the line. Any positive numbers are placed on the right side of the line. For example, consider the points labeled on the following number line:

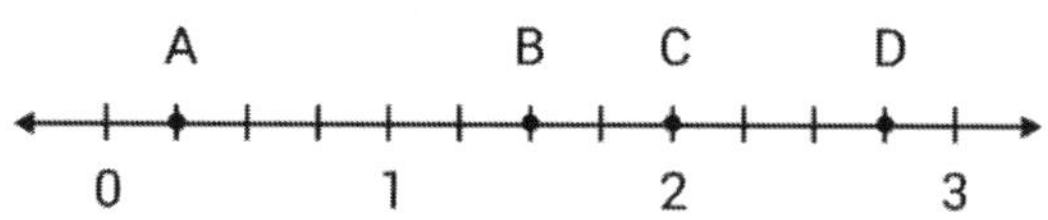

We can use the dashed lines on the number line to identify each point. Each dashed line between two whole numbers is $\frac{1}{4}$. The line halfway between two numbers is $\frac{1}{2}$.

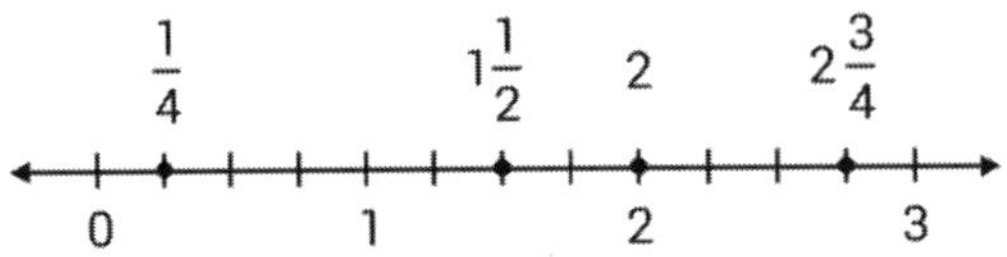

Review Video: The Number Line
Visit mometrix.com/academy and enter code: 816439

Comparing Numbers

Inequality Notation

The symbols < and > mean "is less than" and "is greater than," respectively. For instance, $3 < 5$ means "3 is less than 5," and $7 > 4$ means "7 is greater than 4." Statements like $3 < 5$ and $7 > 4$ are **inequalities**, and the symbols < and > are **inequality symbols**.

Whole Numbers and Decimal Numbers

To compare whole or decimal numbers, we look at the most significant place (the leftmost digit) at which they differ. The number with the larger digit in that place is larger. For instance, $0.3\underline{8}74$ and $0.3\underline{9}$ differ in the hundredths place (underlined). Since 8 is smaller than 9, we see $0.3874 < 0.39$. This is clearer if we make the decimals equal in length by writing extra zeroes: $0.3874 < 0.3900$. Similarly, $2\underline{3}.984 < 2\underline{5}.112$ because 3 is smaller than 5, or 23 is smaller than 25.

Fractions

If fractions have the same denominator, the fraction with the larger numerator is larger. For instance, $\frac{2}{7} < \frac{5}{7}$ since $2 < 5$. We compare fractions with different denominators by finding a common denominator. When comparing the fractions with a common denominator we only compare the numerator, so as a shortcut, we can multiply each numerator by the denominator of the other fraction. The numerator that produces the larger product belongs to the larger fraction. For example, to compare $\frac{7}{8}$ and $\frac{5}{6}$, we note that $7 \cdot 6 = 42$ is larger than $5 \cdot 8 = 40$. Since the numerator 7 produces the larger product, we see $\frac{7}{8} > \frac{5}{6}$. We can also compare fractions by converting them to decimals. For instance, since $\frac{3}{4} = 0.75$ and $\frac{4}{5} = 0.8$ and $0.75 < 0.8$, we conclude $\frac{3}{4} < \frac{4}{5}$.

Mixed Numbers

To compare mixed numbers we compare their whole number parts. If those are equal, then we compare their fractional parts. For instance, $5\frac{3}{8} > 4\frac{7}{8}$ because $5 > 4$, but $3\frac{5}{9} < 3\frac{8}{9}$ because $\frac{5}{9} < \frac{8}{9}$.

Square Roots

To compare square roots, we convert them to decimals, usually with a calculator. To compare two square roots, we compare their radicands. For instance, $\sqrt{11} < \sqrt{14}$ because $11 < 14$.

Negative Numbers

A negative number is always less than a positive number. Two negative numbers compare in the reverse order of their opposites. For instance, $-6 < -2$ (that is, −6 is smaller, more negative, than −2) because $6 > 2$.

Absolute Value

A precursor to working with negative numbers is understanding what **absolute values** are. A number's absolute value is simply the distance away from zero a number is on the number line. The absolute value of a number is always positive and is written $|x|$. For example, the absolute value of 3, written as $|3|$, is 3 because the distance between 0 and 3 on a number line is three units. Likewise, the absolute value of –3, written as $|-3|$, is 3 because the distance between 0 and -3 on a number line is three units. So $|3| = |-3|$.

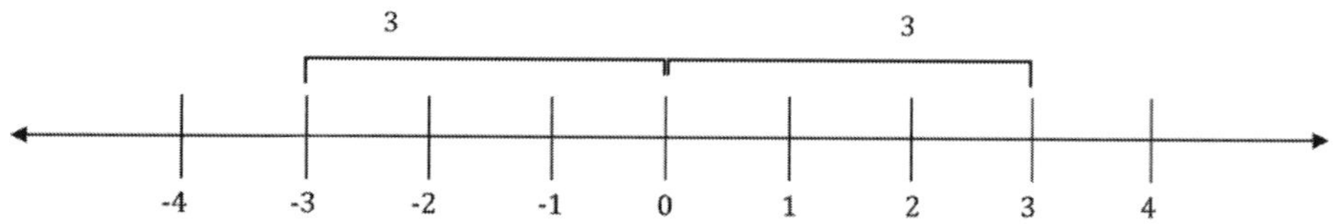

Review Video: Absolute Value
Visit mometrix.com/academy and enter code: 314669

Operations

An **operation** is simply a mathematical process that takes some value(s) as input(s) and produces an output. Elementary operations are often written in the following form: *value operation value*. For instance, in the expression $1 + 2$ the values are 1 and 2 and the operation is addition. Performing the operation gives the output of 3. In this way we can say that $1 + 2$ and 3 are equal, or $1 + 2 = 3$.

Addition

Addition increases the value of one quantity by the value of another quantity (both called **addends**). Example: $2 + 4 = 6$ or $8 + 9 = 17$. The result is called the **sum**. With addition, the order does not matter, $4 + 2 = 2 + 4$.

When adding signed numbers, if the signs are the same simply add the absolute values of the addends and apply the original sign to the sum. For example, $(+4) + (+8) = +12$ and $(-4) + (-8) = -12$. When the original signs are different, take the absolute values of the addends and subtract the smaller value from the larger value, then apply the original sign of the larger value to the difference. Example: $(+4) + (-8) = -4$ and $(-4) + (+8) = +4$.

Subtraction

Subtraction is the opposite operation to addition; it decreases the value of one quantity (the **minuend**) by the value of another quantity (the **subtrahend**). For example, $6 - 4 = 2$ or $17 - 8 = 9$. The result is called the **difference**. Note that with subtraction, the order does matter, $6 - 4 \neq 4 - 6$.

For subtracting signed numbers, change the sign of the subtrahend and then follow the same rules used for addition. Example: $(+4) - (+8) = (+4) + (-8) = -4$

Multiplication

Multiplication can be thought of as repeated addition. One number (the **multiplier**) indicates how many times to add the other number (the **multiplicand**) to itself. Example: $3 \times 2 = 2 + 2 + 2 = 6$. With multiplication, the order does not matter, $2 \times 3 = 3 \times 2$ or $3 + 3 = 2 + 2 + 2$, either way the result (the **product**) is the same.

If the signs are the same, the product is positive when multiplying signed numbers. Example: $(+4) \times (+8) = +32$ and $(-4) \times (-8) = +32$. If the signs are opposite, the product is negative. Example: $(+4) \times (-8) = -32$ and $(-4) \times (+8) = -32$. When more than two factors are multiplied together, the sign of the product is determined by how many negative factors are present. If there are an odd number of negative factors then the product is negative, whereas an even number of negative factors indicates a positive product. Example: $(+4) \times (-8) \times (-2) = +64$ and $(-4) \times (-8) \times (-2) = -64$.

Division

Division is the opposite operation to multiplication; one number (the **divisor**) tells us how many parts to divide the other number (the **dividend**) into. The result of division is called the **quotient**. Example: $20 \div 4 = 5$. If 20 is split into 4 equal parts, each part is 5. With division, the order of the numbers does matter, $20 \div 4 \neq 4 \div 20$.

The rules for dividing signed numbers are similar to multiplying signed numbers. If the dividend and divisor have the same sign, the quotient is positive. If the dividend and divisor have opposite signs, the quotient is negative. Example: $(-4) \div (+8) = -0.5$.

Review Video: Mathematical Operations
Visit mometrix.com/academy and enter code: 208095

Parentheses

Parentheses are used to designate which operations should be done first when there are multiple operations. Example: $4 - (2 + 1) = 1$; the parentheses tell us that we must add 2 and 1, and then subtract the sum from 4, rather than subtracting 2 from 4 and then adding 1 (this would give us an answer of 3).

Review Video: Mathematical Parentheses
Visit mometrix.com/academy and enter code: 978600

Exponents

An **exponent** is a superscript number placed next to another number at the top right. It indicates how many times the base number is to be multiplied by itself. Exponents provide a shorthand way to write what would be a longer mathematical expression. Example: $2^4 = 2 \times 2 \times 2 \times 2$. A number with an exponent of 2 is said to be "squared," while a number with an exponent of 3 is said to be "cubed." The value of a number raised to an exponent is called its power. So 8^4 is read as "8 to the 4th power," or "8 raised to the power of 4."

Review Video: Exponents
Visit mometrix.com/academy and enter code: 600998

Roots

A **root**, such as a square root, is another way of writing a fractional exponent. Instead of using a superscript, roots use the radical symbol ($\sqrt{\ }$) to indicate the operation. A radical will have a number underneath the bar, and may sometimes have a number in the upper left: $\sqrt[n]{a}$, read as "the nth root of a." The relationship between radical notation and exponent notation can be described by this equation:

$$\sqrt[n]{a} = a^{\frac{1}{n}}$$

The two special cases of $n = 2$ and $n = 3$ are called square roots and cube roots. If there is no number to the upper left, the radical is understood to be a square root ($n = 2$). Nearly all of the roots you encounter will be square roots. A square root is the same as a number raised to the one-half power. When we say that a is the square root of b ($a = \sqrt{b}$), we mean that a multiplied by itself equals b: ($a \times a = b$).

A **perfect square** is a number that has an integer for its square root. There are 10 perfect squares from 1 to 100: 1, 4, 9, 16, 25, 36, 49, 64, 81, 100 (the squares of integers 1 through 10).

Review Video: Roots
Visit mometrix.com/academy and enter code: 795655

Review Video: Perfect Squares and Square Roots
Visit mometrix.com/academy and enter code: 648063

Word Problems and Mathematical Symbols

When working on word problems, you must be able to translate verbal expressions or "math words" into math symbols. This chart contains several "math words" and their appropriate symbols:

Phrase	Symbol
equal, is, was, will be, has, costs, gets to, is the same as, becomes	$=$
times, of, multiplied by, product of, twice, doubles, halves, triples	$\times$
divided by, per, ratio of/to, out of	$\div$
plus, added to, sum, combined, and, more than, totals of	$+$
subtracted from, less than, decreased by, minus, difference between	$-$
what, how much, original value, how many, a number, a variable	x, n, etc.

Review Video: Understanding Word Problems
Visit mometrix.com/academy and enter code: 499199

Examples of Translated Mathematical Phrases

- The phrase four more than twice a number can be written algebraically as $2x + 4$.
- The phrase half a number decreased by six can be written algebraically as $\frac{1}{2}x - 6$.
- The phrase the sum of a number and the product of five and that number can be written algebraically as $x + 5x$.
- You may see a test question that says, "Olivia is constructing a bookcase from seven boards. Two of them are for vertical supports and five are for shelves. The height of the bookcase is twice the width of the bookcase. If the seven boards total 36 feet in length, what will be the height of Olivia's bookcase?" You would need to make a sketch and then create the equation to determine the width of the shelves. The height can be represented as double the width. (If x represents the width of the shelves in feet, then the height of the bookcase is $2x$. Since the seven boards total 36 feet, $2x + 2x + x + x + x + x + x = 36$ or $9x = 36$; $x = 4$. The height is twice the width, or 8 feet.)

Subtraction with Regrouping

A great way to make use of some of the features built into the decimal system would be regrouping when attempting longform subtraction operations. When subtracting within a place value, sometimes the minuend is smaller than the subtrahend; **regrouping** enables you to 'borrow' a unit from a place value to the left in order to get a positive difference. For example, consider subtracting 189 from 525 with regrouping.

First, set up the subtraction problem in vertical form:

$$\begin{array}{r} 525 \\ -\ 189 \\ \hline \end{array}$$

Notice that the numbers in the ones and tens columns of 525 are smaller than the numbers in the ones and tens columns of 189. This means you will need to use regrouping to perform subtraction:

$$\begin{array}{rrrr} & 5 & 2 & 5 \\ - & 1 & 8 & 9 \\ \hline \end{array}$$

To subtract 9 from 5 in the ones column you will need to borrow from the 2 in the tens column:

$$\begin{array}{rrrr} & 5 & 1 & 15 \\ - & 1 & 8 & 9 \\ \hline & & & 6 \end{array}$$

Mathematics

Next, to subtract 8 from 1 in the tens column you will need to borrow from the 5 in the hundreds column:

	4	11	15
–	1	8	9
		3	6

Last, subtract the 1 from the 4 in the hundreds column:

	4	11	15
–	1	8	9
	3	3	6

Review Video: Subtracting Large Numbers
Visit mometrix.com/academy and enter code: 603350

Order of Operations

The **order of operations** is a set of rules that dictates the order in which we must perform each operation in an expression so that we will evaluate it accurately. If we have an expression that includes multiple different operations, the order of operations tells us which operations to do first. The most common mnemonic for the order of operations is **PEMDAS**, or "Please Excuse My Dear Aunt Sally." PEMDAS stands for parentheses, exponents, multiplication, division, addition, and subtraction. It is important to understand that multiplication and division have equal precedence, as do addition and subtraction, so those pairs of operations are simply worked from left to right in order.

For example, evaluating the expression $5 + 20 \div 4 \times (2 + 3)^2 - 6$ using the correct order of operations would be done like this:

- **P:** Perform the operations inside the parentheses: $(2 + 3) = 5$
- **E:** Simplify the exponents: $(5)^2 = 5 \times 5 = 25$
    - The expression now looks like this: $5 + 20 \div 4 \times 25 - 6$
- **MD:** Perform multiplication and division from left to right: $20 \div 4 = 5$; then $5 \times 25 = 125$
    - The expression now looks like this: $5 + 125 - 6$
- **AS:** Perform addition and subtraction from left to right: $5 + 125 = 130$; then $130 - 6 = 124$

Review Video: Order of Operations
Visit mometrix.com/academy and enter code: 259675

Properties of Operations

The Commutative Property

The commutative property applies to addition and multiplication and states that these operations can be completed in any order. The **commutative property of addition** states that numbers and terms can be added together in any order to still get the same value. For example, $3 + 4 = 7$ and $4 + 3 = 7$. Also, we can use the commutative property of addition to show that $3x + 4 + 2^2$ is equivalent to $4 + 3x + 2^2$ and $2^2 + 4 + 3x$. When adding terms, you can add in any order and get the same value.

The **commutative property of multiplication** states that numbers and terms can be multiplied in any order to get the same value. For example, 12×3 is equivalent to 3×12. Additionally, we can use the commutative property of multiplication to assume that $(5 + 3) \times (36 - 6)$ is equivalent to $(36 - 6) \times (5 + 3)$. You can multiply terms in any order and still get the same value.

The Associative Property

The **associative property of addition** states that if three or more terms are being added together, the value is the same regardless of the groupings.

For example, given the expression $3 + 4 + 6$, these terms can be grouped and added in any form. $3 + 4 + 6$ is equivalent to $(3 + 4) + 6$ and is also equivalent to $3 + (4 + 6)$. This can be applied to write equivalent expressions in a variety of ways.

For example, suppose we are given the expression $5 + (y + 2) + 4$. We can generate equivalent expressions knowing the associative property. Knowing that when three or more terms are added, the grouping is irrelevant, we can say that this expression is equivalent to $5 + y + (2 + 4)$, and it is equivalent to $(5 + y) + (2 + 4)$. It is even equivalent to $5 + y + 2 + 4$.

The **associative property of multiplication** states that if three or more terms are being multiplied together, the value is the same regardless of the grouping. We can use this property to identify and generate equivalent expressions.

For example, given the expression $2 \times 7 \times 3$, these terms can be grouped in any way and still get the same value. $2 \times 7 \times 3$ is equivalent to $(2 \times 7) \times 3$ or $2 \times (7 \times 3)$.

The Identity Property

The **identity property of multiplication** states that when a number is multiplied by 1, you get the same number. That is, anything multiplied by 1 is itself. For example, $2 \times 1 = 2$, or $1 \times -36 = -36$. Using the identity property of multiplication, we can identify and generate equivalent expressions. Let's say that we are given the expression $15 - (3 \times 4)$. We can generate equivalent expressions using the identity property. One equivalent expression example would be $(15 \times 1) - (3 \times 4)$. Another example would be $15 - (1 \times 3 \times 4)$. We can say these expressions are equivalent because the identity property of multiplication states that we can multiply any portion of an expression by 1 to get the same value.

The **identity property of addition** states that when 0 is added to a number, you get the same number. For example, $2 + 0 = 2$, or $0 + -3 = -3$. We can also use this property to identify and generate equivalent expressions. For example, if we are given the expression $2 \times (1 + 2)$, we could write the equivalent expressions $2 \times (0 + 1 + 2)$ or $(2 + 0) \times (1 + 2)$.

The Inverse Property

The **inverse property of addition** states that the sum of a number and its opposite is always equal to 0. Remember, the opposite of a number is a number that is opposite on the number line from zero, or the same number with the opposite sign. For example, −4 is opposite to 4, and 1,726.9 is opposite to −1,726.9. So, the inverse property of addition states that if you add opposite numbers, their sum is zero. For example, $5 + (-5) = 0$ and $-5 + 5 = 0$.

The **inverse property of multiplication** states that a number multiplied by its reciprocal is always equal to 1. The **reciprocal** of a number is its "flipped" fraction. For example, the reciprocal of 5 is $\frac{1}{5}$, or the reciprocal of $\frac{2}{3}$ is $\frac{3}{2}$. The inverse property of multiplication can be applied for these values, $5 \times \frac{1}{5} = 1$ and $\frac{2}{3} \times \frac{3}{2} = 1$. This is because when you multiply across, you get a fraction that is equal to 1.

$$\frac{2}{3} \times \frac{3}{2} = \frac{6}{6} = 1$$

The Distributive Property

The **distributive property** explains how multiplication and addition interact. It says that when multiplying one number by the sum of two other numbers, the same result can also be obtained by multiplying the one number by each of the numbers individually and then adding the products. For example, to multiply 2 by the sum of 7 and 3, the direct approach says, "the sum of 7 and 3 is 10, and 2 times 10 is 20." This would be expressed as $2 \times (7 + 3) = 2 \times 10 = 20$. On the other hand, the distributive property states that the same answer can be achieved by multiplying each number inside the parentheses and adding the products. That is, "the product of 2 and 7 is 14, the product of 2 and 3 is 6, and the sum of 14 and 6 is 20." This would be expressed as $2 \times (7 + 3) = 2 \times 7 + 2 \times 3 = 14 + 6 = 20$, and it is demonstrated below.

$$2 \times (7 + 3) = 2 \times 7 + 2 \times 3$$

This same concept can be used when multiplying a number by the difference of two numbers. For example, $5 \times (10 - 4) = 5 \times 10 - 5 \times 4$. Since $5 \times 10 = 50$ and $5 \times 4 = 20$, the result is $50 - 20 = 30$. This answer can be checked by subtracting inside the parentheses first and then multiplying: $5 \times (10 - 4) = 5 \times 6 = 30$.

Review Video: Commutative, Associative, and Distributive Properties
Visit mometrix.com/academy and enter code: 483176

Properties of Exponents

The properties of exponents are as follows:

Property	Description
$a^1 = a$	Any number to the power of 1 is equal to itself
$1^n = 1$	The number 1 raised to any power is equal to 1
$a^0 = 1$	Any number raised to the power of 0 is equal to 1
$a^n \times a^m = a^{n+m}$	Add exponents to multiply powers of the same base number
$a^n \div a^m = a^{n-m}$	Subtract exponents to divide powers of the same base number
$(a^n)^m = a^{n \times m}$	When a power is raised to a power, the exponents are multiplied
$(a \times b)^n = a^n \times b^n$ $(a \div b)^n = a^n \div b^n$	Multiplication and division operations inside parentheses can be raised to a power. This is the same as each term being raised to that power.
$a^{-n} = \frac{1}{a^n}$	A negative exponent is the same as the reciprocal of a positive exponent

Note that exponents do not have to be integers. Fractional or decimal exponents follow all the rules above as well. Example: $5^{\frac{1}{4}} \times 5^{\frac{3}{4}} = 5^{\frac{1}{4}+\frac{3}{4}} = 5^1 = 5$.

Review Video: Properties of Exponents
Visit mometrix.com/academy and enter code: 532558

Factors and Multiples

Factors and Greatest Common Factor

A whole number a is a **factor** (or **divisor**) of a whole number b if a divides b evenly. In other words, a is a factor of b if the quotient $b \div a$ is a whole number with a remainder of 0. For instance, 3 is a factor of 12 because $12 \div 3 = 4$ with no remainder. Another way to say this is that a is a factor of b if we can multiply a by another whole number to get b. So, we can also show that 3 is a factor of 12 by noting that $3 \times 4 = 12$.

Every positive whole number has 1 and itself as factors. If a whole number greater than one has *only* 1 and itself as factors, we call it a **prime number**. For instance, 5 is a prime number because its only factors are 1 and 5. The first several prime numbers are 2, 3, 5, 7, 11, and 13.

If a whole number greater than 1 is not prime—that is, if it has factors besides 1 and itself—then it is a **composite number.** For instance, 10 is a composite number because it has factors 2 and 5 in addition to 1 and 10. The first several composite numbers are 4, 6, 8, 9, 10, 12, 14, and 15.

A **prime factor** of a whole number is a factor that is also a prime number. For example, the prime factors of 12 are 2 and 3. The prime factors of 15 are 3 and 5.

A **common factor** of two (or more) whole numbers is a number that is a factor of both (or all) of them. For example, the factors of 12 are 1, 2, 3, 4, 6, and 12, while the factors of 15 are 1, 3, 5, and 15. The common factors (underlined) of 12 and 15 are 1 and 3.

The **greatest common factor** (**GCF**) of two (or more) whole numbers is the largest number that is a factor of both (or all) of them. For example, the factors of 15 are 1, 3, 5, and 15; the factors of 35 are 1, 5, 7, and 35. Therefore, the greatest common factor of 15 and 35 is 5.

Review Video: Factors
Visit mometrix.com/academy and enter code: 920086

Review Video: Prime Numbers and Factorization
Visit mometrix.com/academy and enter code: 760669

Multiples and Least Common Multiple

A whole number b is a **multiple** of a whole number a when a is a factor of b. This means that b is the product of a and another whole number. For example, the multiples of 7 are $0 \times 7 = 0, 1 \times 7 = 7, 2 \times 7 = 14, 3 \times 7 = 21, 4 \times 7 = 28, 5 \times 7 = 35$, ... Dividing 0, 7, 14, 21, 28, and 35 by 7 results in the whole numbers 0, 1, 2, 3, 4, and 5, respectively, showing that 7 is a factor of these numbers.

The least common multiple (**LCM**) of two (or more) whole numbers is the smallest number that is a multiple of both (or all) of them. For example, the multiples of 3 are 3, 6, 9, 12, 15, ...; the multiples of 5 are 5, 10, 15, 20, ... The smallest number that appears in both lists is 15, so the least common multiple of 3 and 5 is 15.

Review Video: Multiples
Visit mometrix.com/academy and enter code: 626738

Review Video: Greatest Common Factor and Least Common Multiple
Visit mometrix.com/academy and enter code: 838699

Fractions

A **fraction** is a number that is expressed as one integer written above another integer, with a dividing line between them $\left(\frac{x}{y}\right)$. It represents the **quotient** of the two numbers "x divided by y." It can also be thought of as x out of y equal parts.

The top number of a fraction is called the **numerator**, and it represents the number of parts under consideration. The 1 in $\frac{1}{4}$ means that 1 part out of the whole is being considered in the calculation. The bottom number of a fraction is called the **denominator**, and it represents the total number of equal parts. The 4 in $\frac{1}{4}$

means that the whole consists of 4 equal parts. A fraction cannot have a denominator of zero; this is referred to as "*undefined.*"

Fractions can be manipulated, without changing the value of the fraction, by multiplying or dividing (but not adding or subtracting) both the numerator and denominator by the same number. If you divide both numbers by a common factor, you are **reducing** or simplifying the fraction. Two fractions that have the same value but are expressed differently are known as **equivalent fractions**. For example, $\frac{2}{10}, \frac{3}{15}, \frac{4}{20}$, and $\frac{5}{25}$ are all equivalent fractions. They can also all be reduced or simplified to $\frac{1}{5}$.

When two fractions are manipulated so that they have the same denominator, this is known as finding a **common denominator**. The number chosen to be that common denominator should be the least common multiple of the two original denominators. Example: $\frac{3}{4}$ and $\frac{5}{6}$; the least common multiple of 4 and 6 is 12. Manipulating to achieve the common denominator: $\frac{3}{4} = \frac{9}{12}; \frac{5}{6} = \frac{10}{12}$.

Review Video: Overview of Fractions
Visit mometrix.com/academy and enter code: 262335

Proper Fractions and Mixed Numbers

A fraction whose denominator is greater than its numerator is known as a **proper fraction**, while a fraction whose numerator is greater than its denominator is known as an **improper fraction**. Proper fractions have values *less than one* and improper fractions have values *greater than one.*

A **mixed number** is a number that contains both an integer and a fraction. Any improper fraction can be rewritten as a mixed number. Example: $\frac{8}{3} = \frac{6}{3} + \frac{2}{3} = 2 + \frac{2}{3} = 2\frac{2}{3}$. Similarly, any mixed number can be rewritten as an improper fraction. Example: $1\frac{3}{5} = 1 + \frac{3}{5} = \frac{5}{5} + \frac{3}{5} = \frac{8}{5}$.

Review Video: Proper and Improper Fractions and Mixed Numbers
Visit mometrix.com/academy and enter code: 211077

Adding and Subtracting Fractions

If two fractions have a common denominator, they can be added or subtracted simply by adding or subtracting the two numerators and retaining the same denominator. If the two fractions do not already have the same denominator, one or both of them must be manipulated to achieve a common denominator before they can be added or subtracted. Example: $\frac{1}{2} + \frac{1}{4} = \frac{2}{4} + \frac{1}{4} = \frac{3}{4}$.

Review Video: Adding and Subtracting Fractions
Visit mometrix.com/academy and enter code: 378080

Multiplying Fractions

Two fractions can be multiplied by multiplying the two numerators to find the new numerator and the two denominators to find the new denominator. Example: $\frac{1}{3} \times \frac{2}{3} = \frac{1 \times 2}{3 \times 3} = \frac{2}{9}$.

Dividing Fractions

Two fractions can be divided by flipping the numerator and denominator of the second fraction and then proceeding as though it were a multiplication problem. Example: $\frac{2}{3} \div \frac{3}{4} = \frac{2}{3} \times \frac{4}{3} = \frac{8}{9}$.

Review Video: Multiplying and Dividing Fractions
Visit mometrix.com/academy and enter code: 473632

Multiplying a Mixed Number by a Whole Number or a Decimal

When multiplying a mixed number by something, it is usually best to convert it to an improper fraction first. Additionally, if the multiplicand is a decimal, it is most often simplest to convert it to a fraction. For instance, to multiply $4\frac{3}{8}$ by 3.5, begin by rewriting each quantity as a whole number plus a proper fraction. Remember, a mixed number is a fraction added to a whole number and a decimal is a representation of the sum of fractions, specifically tenths, hundredths, thousandths, and so on:

$$4\frac{3}{8} \times 3.5 = \left(4 + \frac{3}{8}\right) \times \left(3 + \frac{1}{2}\right)$$

Next, the quantities being added need to be expressed with the same denominator. This is achieved by multiplying and dividing the whole number by the denominator of the fraction. Recall that a whole number is equivalent to that number divided by 1:

$$= \left(\frac{4}{1} \times \frac{8}{8} + \frac{3}{8}\right) \times \left(\frac{3}{1} \times \frac{2}{2} + \frac{1}{2}\right)$$

When multiplying fractions, remember to multiply the numerators and denominators separately:

$$= \left(\frac{4 \times 8}{1 \times 8} + \frac{3}{8}\right) \times \left(\frac{3 \times 2}{1 \times 2} + \frac{1}{2}\right)$$

$$= \left(\frac{32}{8} + \frac{3}{8}\right) \times \left(\frac{6}{2} + \frac{1}{2}\right)$$

Now that the fractions have the same denominators, they can be added:

$$= \frac{35}{8} \times \frac{7}{2}$$

Finally, perform the last multiplication and then simplify:

$$= \frac{35 \times 7}{8 \times 2} = \frac{245}{16} = \frac{240}{16} + \frac{5}{16} = 15\frac{5}{16}$$

Comparing Fractions

It is important to master the ability to compare and order fractions. This skill is relevant to many real-world scenarios. For example, carpenters often compare fractional construction nail lengths when preparing for a project, and bakers often compare fractional measurements to have the correct ratio of ingredients. There are three commonly used strategies when comparing fractions. These strategies are referred to as the common denominator approach, the decimal approach, and the cross-multiplication approach.

Using a Common Denominator to Compare Fractions

The fractions $\frac{2}{3}$ and $\frac{4}{7}$ have different denominators. $\frac{2}{3}$ has a denominator of 3, and $\frac{4}{7}$ has a denominator of 7. In order to precisely compare these two fractions, it is necessary to use a common denominator. A common denominator is a common multiple that is shared by both denominators. In this case, the denominators 3 and 7 share a multiple of 21. In general, it is most efficient to select the least common multiple for the two denominators.

Rewrite each fraction with the common denominator of 21. Then, calculate the new numerators as illustrated below.

$$\frac{2}{3} = \frac{\mathbf{14}}{21} \quad (\times 7) \qquad \frac{4}{7} = \frac{\mathbf{12}}{21} \quad (\times 3)$$

For $\frac{2}{3}$, multiply the numerator and denominator by 7. The result is $\frac{14}{21}$.

For $\frac{4}{7}$, multiply the numerator and denominator by 3. The result is $\frac{12}{21}$.

Now that both fractions have a denominator of 21, the fractions can accurately be compared by comparing the numerators. Since 14 is greater than 12, the fraction $\frac{14}{21}$ is greater than $\frac{12}{21}$. This means that $\frac{2}{3}$ is greater than $\frac{4}{7}$.

Using Decimals to Compare Fractions

Sometimes decimal values are easier to compare than fraction values. For example, $\frac{5}{8}$ is equivalent to 0.625 and $\frac{3}{5}$ is equivalent to 0.6. This means that the comparison of $\frac{5}{8}$ and $\frac{3}{5}$ can be determined by comparing the decimals 0.625 and 0.6. When both decimal values are extended to the thousandths place, they become 0.625 and 0.600, respectively. It becomes clear that 0.625 is greater than 0.600 because 625 thousandths is greater than 600 thousandths. In other words, $\frac{5}{8}$ is greater than $\frac{3}{5}$ because 0.625 is greater than 0.6.

Using Cross-Multiplication to Compare Fractions

Cross-multiplication is an efficient strategy for comparing fractions. This is a shortcut for the common denominator strategy. Start by writing each fraction next to one another. Multiply the numerator of the fraction on the left by the denominator of the fraction on the right. Write down the result next to the fraction on the left. Now multiply the numerator of the fraction on the right by the denominator of the fraction on the left. Write down the result next to the fraction on the right. Compare both products. The fraction with the larger result is the larger fraction.

Consider the fractions $\frac{4}{7}$ and $\frac{5}{9}$.

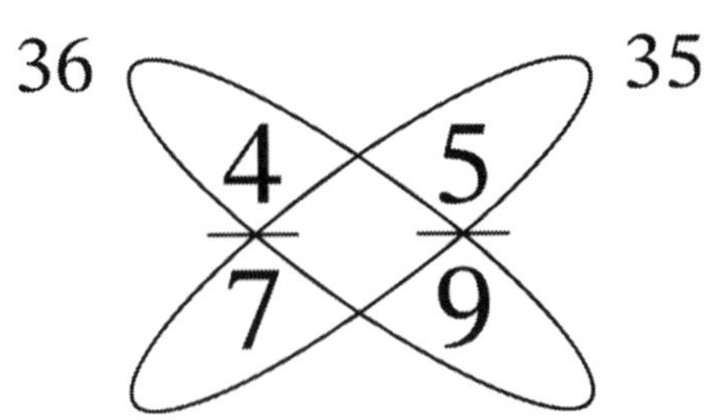

36 is greater than 35. Therefore, $\frac{4}{7}$ is greater than $\frac{5}{9}$.

Decimals

Decimals are one way to represent parts of a whole. Using the place value system, each digit to the right of a decimal point denotes the number of units of a corresponding *negative* power of ten. For example, consider the decimal 0.24. We can use a model to represent the decimal. Since a dime is worth one-tenth of a dollar and a penny is worth one-hundredth of a dollar, one possible model to represent this fraction is to have 2 dimes representing the 2 in the tenths place and 4 pennies representing the 4 in the hundredths place:

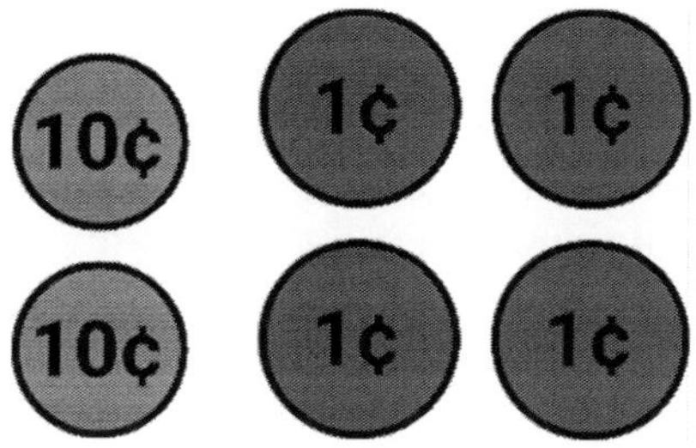

To write the decimal as a fraction, put the decimal in the numerator with 1 in the denominator. Multiply the numerator and denominator by tens until there are no more decimal places. Then simplify the fraction to lowest terms. For example, converting 0.24 to a fraction:

$$0.24 = \frac{0.24}{1} = \frac{0.24 \times 100}{1 \times 100} = \frac{24}{100} = \frac{6}{25}$$

Review Video: Decimals
Visit mometrix.com/academy and enter code: 837268

Operations with Decimals

Adding and Subtracting Decimals

When adding and subtracting decimals, the decimal points must always be aligned. Adding decimals is just like adding regular whole numbers. Example: $4.5 + 2.0 = 6.5$.

If the problem-solver does not properly align the decimal points, an incorrect answer of 4.7 may result. An easy way to add decimals is to align all of the decimal points in a vertical column visually. This will allow you to see exactly where the decimal should be placed in the final answer. Begin adding from right to left. Add each column in turn, making sure to carry the number to the left if a column adds up to more than 9. The same rules apply to the subtraction of decimals.

Review Video: Adding and Subtracting Decimals
Visit mometrix.com/academy and enter code: 381101

Multiplying Decimals

A simple multiplication problem has two components: a **multiplicand** and a **multiplier**. When multiplying decimals, work as though the numbers were whole rather than decimals. Once the final product is calculated, count the number of places to the right of the decimal in both the multiplicand and the multiplier. Then, count that number of places from the right of the product and place the decimal in that position.

For example, 12.3×2.56 has a total of three places to the right of the respective decimals. Multiply 123×256 to get 31,488. Now, beginning on the right, count three places to the left and insert the decimal. The final product will be 31.488.

Review Video: How to Multiply Decimals
Visit mometrix.com/academy and enter code: 731574

Dividing Decimals

Every division problem has a **divisor** and a **dividend**. The dividend is the number that is being divided. In the problem $14 \div 7$, 14 is the dividend and 7 is the divisor. In a division problem with decimals, the divisor must be converted into a whole number. Begin by moving the decimal in the divisor to the right until a whole number is created. Next, move the decimal in the dividend the same number of spaces to the right. For example, 4.9 into 24.5 would become 49 into 245. The decimal was moved one space to the right to create a whole number in the divisor, and then the same was done for the dividend. Once the whole numbers are created, the problem is carried out normally: $245 \div 49 = 5$.

Review Video: Dividing Decimals
Visit mometrix.com/academy and enter code: 560690

Review Video: Dividing Decimals by Whole Numbers
Visit mometrix.com/academy and enter code: 535669

Percentages

Percentages can be thought of as fractions that are based on a whole of 100; that is, one whole is equal to 100%. The word **percent** means "per hundred." Percentage problems are often presented in three main ways:

- Find what percentage of some number another number is.
  - Example: What percentage of 40 is 8?
- Find what number is some percentage of a given number.
  - Example: What number is 20% of 40?
- Find what number another number is a given percentage of.
  - Example: What number is 8 20% of?

There are three components in each of these cases: a **whole** (W), a **part** (P), and a **percentage** (%). These are related by the equation: $P = W \times \%$. This can easily be rearranged into other forms that may suit different questions better: $\% = \frac{P}{W}$ and $W = \frac{P}{\%}$. Percentage problems are often also word problems. As such, a large part of solving them is figuring out which quantities are what. For example, consider the following word problem:

In a school cafeteria, 7 students choose pizza, 9 choose hamburgers, and 4 choose tacos. What percentage of students choose tacos?

To find the whole, you must first add all of the parts: $7 + 9 + 4 = 20$. The percentage can then be found by dividing the part by the whole $\left(\% = \frac{P}{W}\right)$: $\frac{4}{20} = \frac{20}{100} = 20\%$.

Review Video: Computation with Percentages
Visit mometrix.com/academy and enter code: 693099

Calculating Percent Change

Suppose a quantity has a particular value (the *old value*) and then we add something (the *change*) to it to get another value (the *new value*). We can describe this process by the simple equation (old value) + change =

(new value). If we know the old and new values, we can rearrange this equation to find the change, getting change $=$ (new value) $-$ (old value). For instance, if a store's price for a box of computer paper goes from \$20 last week to \$25 this week, this is a change of (new value) $-$ (old value) $= \$25 - \$20 = \$5$. Or, if the size of the freshman class at a college goes from 500 students one year to 440 students the next year, this is a change of (new value) $-$ (old value) $= 440 - 500 = -60$ students. So, we see that change can be positive or negative.

Instead of the word *change*, we sometimes use the words *increase* or *decrease* to specify whether the value goes up or down, respectively. In the examples above, the price of computer paper increases by \$5 and the freshman class decreases by 60 students. Note that the decrease is 60 students and not −60 because the word *decrease* already means that the value goes down. So, *increase* is the same as positive change and *decrease* is the opposite or negative change.

If the changing quantity represents an amount (how much of something there is), we can also calculate the **percent change**. This is the change expressed as a percentage of the old amount. To calculate this, we divide the change by the old amount and express the quotient as a percent. That is, we use the formula percent change $= \frac{\text{change}}{\text{old value}}$, converting the resulting decimal answer to a percent. In the examples above, the price of a box of computer paper has a percent change of $\frac{\text{change in price}}{\text{old price}} = \frac{\$5}{\$20} = 0.25 = 25\%$, and the size of the freshman class at the college has a percent change of $\frac{\text{change in enrollment}}{\text{old enrollment}} = \frac{-60}{500} = -0.12 = -12\%$. We can also use the terms *percent increase* and *percent decrease*, saying that the price of computer paper increases by 25% and the size of the freshman class decreases by 12%. Note that the denominator is always the old amount, never the new amount.

Example: Your landlord raises your rent from \$1,500 to \$1,700 per month. To find the percent change in your rent (rounded to the nearest tenth of a percent), you calculate as follows.

$$\begin{aligned}\text{percent change in rent} &= \frac{\text{change in rent}}{\text{old rent}} = \frac{(\text{new rent}) - (\text{old rent})}{\text{old rent}} \\ &= \frac{\$1{,}700 - \$1{,}500}{\$1{,}500} = \frac{\$200}{\$1{,}500} = 0.1333\ldots \approx 13.3\%\end{aligned}$$

Therefore, the percent change in your rent is approximately 13.3%.

Review Video: Percent Change
Visit mometrix.com/academy and enter code: 907890

Converting Between Percentages, Fractions, and Decimals

Converting decimals to percentages and percentages to decimals is as simple as moving the decimal point. To *convert from a decimal to a percentage*, move the decimal point **two places to the right**. To *convert from a percentage to a decimal*, move it **two places to the left**. It may be helpful to remember that the percentage number will always be larger than the equivalent decimal number. Example:

$$\begin{array}{ccc} 0.23 = 23\% & 5.34 = 534\% & 0.007 = 0.7\% \\ 700\% = 7.00 & 86\% = 0.86 & 0.15\% = 0.0015 \end{array}$$

To convert a fraction to a decimal, simply divide the numerator by the denominator in the fraction. To convert a decimal to a fraction, put the decimal in the numerator with 1 in the denominator. Multiply the numerator

Mathematics

and denominator by tens until there are no more decimal places. Then simplify the fraction to lowest terms. For example, converting 0.24 to a fraction:

$$0.24 = \frac{0.24}{1} = \frac{0.24 \times 100}{1 \times 100} = \frac{24}{100} = \frac{6}{25}$$

Fractions can be converted to a percentage by finding equivalent fractions with a denominator of 100. Example:

$$\frac{7}{10} = \frac{70}{100} = 70\% \quad \frac{1}{4} = \frac{25}{100} = 25\%$$

To convert a percentage to a fraction, divide the percentage number by 100 and reduce the fraction to its simplest possible terms. Example:

$$60\% = \frac{60}{100} = \frac{3}{5} \quad 96\% = \frac{96}{100} = \frac{24}{25}$$

Review Video: Converting Fractions to Percentages and Decimals
Visit mometrix.com/academy and enter code: 306233

Review Video: Converting Percentages to Decimals and Fractions
Visit mometrix.com/academy and enter code: 287297

Review Video: Converting Decimals to Fractions and Percentages
Visit mometrix.com/academy and enter code: 986765

Review Video: Converting Decimals, Improper Fractions, and Mixed Numbers
Visit mometrix.com/academy and enter code: 696924

Rational and Irrational Numbers

The term **rational** means that the number can be expressed as a ratio or fraction. That is, a number, r, is rational if and only if it can be represented by a fraction $\frac{a}{b}$ where a and b are integers and b does not equal 0. The set of rational numbers includes integers and decimals. If there is no finite way to represent a value with a fraction of integers, then the number is **irrational**. Common irrational numbers are π and the square roots of whole numbers that are not perfect squares (e.g., $\sqrt{5}$ or $\sqrt{21}$). The sum or product of an integer and an irrational number is always irrational (e.g., 3π or $7 + \sqrt{6}$).

Review Video: Rational and Irrational Numbers
Visit mometrix.com/academy and enter code: 280645

Review Video: Ordering Rational Numbers
Visit mometrix.com/academy and enter code: 419578

Review Video: Irrational Numbers on a Number Line
Visit mometrix.com/academy and enter code: 433866

Proportions and Ratios

Proportions

There is a **proportion** between two variable quantities if there is a constant relationship between their products or quotients, a relationship that does not change as the quantities themselves change.

Given variable quantities x and y, we say that they are **directly proportional** (or that y **varies directly with** x) if their quotient or *ratio* is constant—that is, if there is a constant k such that $\frac{y}{x} = k$ is always true. Another way of saying this is that y is a constant multiple of x, so that $y = kx$ is always true. We call the number k the **constant of proportionality**. For example, if you drive at a constant 50 miles per hour, then the distance, y, that you travel in miles is 50 times the number of hours, x, that you drive. In symbols, $y = 50x$ miles (or $\frac{y}{x} = 50$ mph). So, the distance you travel, y, is directly proportional to (or varies directly with) the time you travel, x, with constant of proportionality $k = 50$ mph.

The quantities x and y are **inversely proportional** (or y varies inversely with x) if their product is constant—that is, if there is a constant k such that $xy = k$ is always true. Another way of saying this is to say that y is a constant multiple of the reciprocal of x so that $y = \frac{k}{x}$ is always true. For instance, suppose you drive at speed (rate) y mph for x hours, going a total of 120 miles. Since rate × time = distance, we get $xy = 120$ miles (or $y = \frac{120}{x}$ miles per hour). Thus, your driving speed, y, is inversely proportional to (or varies inversely with) your drive time, x, with constant of proportionality $k = 120$ miles.

Review Video: Proportions
Visit mometrix.com/academy and enter code: 505355

Ratios

A **ratio** expresses the sizes of two quantities relative to each other. For instance, suppose we have 3 copies of sheet music to share among 6 singers. We can divide the singers into groups of 2 and give each group 1 copy of the music. Thus, there is 1 copy of the music for every 2 singers, and we say that the **ratio** of sheet music to singers is 1 to 2, which we write either as a fraction $\frac{1}{2}$ or using a colon $1 : 2$. Of course, it is also true there are 3 copies for every 6 singers so that the ratio of sheet music to singers is also 3 to 6, which we write as $\frac{3}{6}$ or $3 : 6$. So, the ratios $\frac{1}{2}$ and $\frac{3}{6}$ express the same relative quantities of music and singers. We say that these ratios are equal or **equivalent**, and we note that ratios are equal precisely when their fractions are equal (so, in this case, $\frac{1}{2} = \frac{3}{6}$ as fractions). We can also express the quantities in the other order and say that the ratio of singers to music is $\frac{2}{1}$ or $2 : 1$ (or $\frac{6}{3}$ or $6 : 3$).

Review Video: Ratios
Visit mometrix.com/academy and enter code: 996914

Constant of Proportionality

If variable quantities x and y are proportional and we know a pair of corresponding values for them, then we can find their constant of proportionality. If they are directly proportional, we use the formula $\frac{y}{x} = k$. If they are inversely proportional, we use the formula $xy = k$.

Example: The cost in dollars, y, of buying fence posts is directly proportional to the number, x, that you buy. If it costs \$51 to buy 17 fence posts, what is the constant of proportionality? Because of direct proportionality, we know that $\frac{y}{x} = k$. Since this works for every pair of corresponding x- and y-values, it also works for $x = 17$ and $y = 51$. This gives us $\frac{51}{17} = k$, which simplifies to $k = 3$. Note also that this is the unit price, namely \$3 per fence post.

Work/Unit Rate

Unit rate expresses a quantity of one thing in terms of one unit of another. For example, if you travel 30 miles every two hours, a unit rate expresses this comparison in terms of one hour: in one hour you travel 15 miles, so your unit rate is 15 miles per hour. Other examples are how much one ounce of food costs (price per ounce) or figuring out how much one egg costs out of the dozen (price per 1 egg, instead of price per 12 eggs). The denominator of a unit rate is always 1. Unit rates are used to compare different situations to solve problems. For example, to make sure you get the best deal when deciding which kind of soda to buy, you can find the unit rate of each. If soda #1 costs $1.50 for a 1-liter bottle, and soda #2 costs $2.75 for a 2-liter bottle, it would be a better deal to buy soda #2, because its unit rate is only $1.375 per liter, which is cheaper than soda #1. Unit rates can also help determine the length of time a given event will take. For example, if you can paint 2 rooms in 4.5 hours, you can determine how long it will take you to paint 5 rooms by solving for the unit rate per room and then multiplying that by 5.

Review Video: Rates and Unit Rates
Visit mometrix.com/academy and enter code: 185363

Cross Multiplication

Finding an Unknown in Equivalent Expressions

It is often necessary to apply information given about a rate or proportion to a new scenario. For example, if you know that Jedha can run a marathon (26.2 miles) in 3 hours, how long would it take her to run 10 miles at the same pace? Start by setting up equivalent expressions:

$$\frac{26.2 \text{ mi}}{3 \text{ hr}} = \frac{10 \text{ mi}}{x \text{ hr}}$$

Now, cross multiply and solve for x:

$$26.2x = 30$$
$$x = \frac{30}{26.2} = \frac{15}{13.1}$$
$$x \approx 1.15 \text{ hrs } or \text{ } 1 \text{ hr } 9 \text{ min}$$

So, at this pace, Jedha could run 10 miles in about 1.15 hours or about 1 hour and 9 minutes.

Review Video: Cross Multiplying Fractions
Visit mometrix.com/academy and enter code: 893904

Slope

Finding Slope Given Graph or Table

On a graph with two points, (x_1, y_1) and (x_2, y_2), the **slope** is found with the formula $m = \frac{y_2 - y_1}{x_2 - x_1}$; where $x_1 \neq x_2$ and m stands for slope. If the value of the slope is **positive**, the line has an *upward direction* from left to right. If the value of the slope is **negative**, the line has a *downward direction* from left to right. Consider the following example:

A new book goes on sale in bookstores and online stores. In the first month, 5,000 copies of the book are sold. Over time, the book continues to grow in popularity. The data for the number of copies sold is in the table below.

# of Months on Sale	1	2	3	4	5
# of Copies Sold (In Thousands)	5	10	15	20	25

So, the number of copies that are sold and the time that the book is on sale is a proportional relationship. In this example, an equation can be used to show the data: $y = 5x$, where x is the number of months that the book is on sale. Also, y is the number of copies sold. So, the slope of the corresponding line is $\frac{\text{rise}}{\text{run}} = \frac{5}{1} = 5$.

FINDING SLOPE GIVEN AN EQUATION

When given an equation of a line, it is necessary to solve for y to determine the slope of the line. Given the equation $6x + 2y = 8$, find the slope. First, subtract $6x$ from both sides of the equation, resulting in $2y = -6x + 8$. Then divide both sides of the equation by 2, resulting in $y = -3x + 4$. This then allows us to conclude that the slope of the line is $m = -3$, the coefficient of x. Once an equation is in the form $y = mx + b$, the slope and y-intercept can easily be determined. For this reason, we refer to the equation $y = mx + b$ as "slope-intercept form" of the equation of a line.

Review Video: Finding the Slope of a Line
Visit mometrix.com/academy and enter code: 766664

Algebraic Concepts

LINEAR EXPRESSIONS

TERMS AND COEFFICIENTS

Mathematical expressions consist of a combination of one or more values arranged in terms that are added together. As such, an expression could be just a single number, including zero. A **variable term** is the product of a real number, also called a **coefficient**, and one or more variables, each of which may be raised to an exponent. Expressions may also include numbers without a variable, called **constants** or **constant terms**. The expression $6s^2$, for example, is a single term where the coefficient is the real number 6 and the variable term is s^2. Note that if a term is written as simply a variable to some exponent, like t^2, then the coefficient is 1, because $t^2 = 1t^2$.

LINEAR EXPRESSIONS

A **single variable linear expression** is the sum of a single variable term, where the variable has no exponent, and a constant, which may be zero. For instance, the expression $2w + 7$ has $2w$ as the variable term and 7 as the constant term. It is important to realize that terms are separated by addition or subtraction. Since an expression is a sum of terms, expressions such as $5x - 3$ can be written as $5x + (-3)$ to emphasize that the constant term is negative. A real-world example of a single variable linear expression is the perimeter of a square, four times the side length, often expressed: $4s$.

In general, a **linear expression** is the sum of any number of variable terms so long as none of the variables have an exponent and none of the terms have two variables multiplied together. For example, $3m + 8n - \frac{1}{4}p + 5.5q - 1$ is a linear expression, but $3y^3$ and $5xy$ are not. In the same way, the expression for the perimeter of a general triangle $(a + b + c)$ is linear, but the expression for the area of a square (s^2) is not.

LINEAR EQUATIONS

Equations like $5x = 100$ and $8x - 120 = 200$ and $6x + 4y = 240$ are **linear equations**. Linear equations are named based off the number of distinct variables they include. For example, the equation $3x + 30 = 8x$ is a **one-variable linear equation** because it involves only the single variable x. It does not matter that x appears more than once. Any equations that can be written as $ax + b = 0$, where $a \neq 0$, falls into this category. Furthermore, the equation $3x - 5y = 14 + 9y$ is a **two-variable linear equation** because it involves the two variables x and y. The equation $7x + 8y - 12z + 14w = 56$ is a linear equation in four variables.

Satisfying the Equation

When given a one-variable linear equation, the goal is typically to solve it. This means that we want to find the number that makes the equation true if we substitute it for the variable. That number is the **solution,** or root, of the equation. For instance, the equation $5x = 10$ has the solution $x = 2$. This is true because when 2 is substituted for x, the result is $5 \cdot 2 = 10$, which is true. On the other hand, $x = 6$ can not be a solution because $5 \cdot 6 \neq 10$, so it is false. Two equations with the same solution are **equivalent equations**. For example, the equations $5x = 10$ and $5x + 3 = 13$ are equivalent because both have the same solution of $x = 2$.

Determining a Solution Set

The **solution set** is the set of all solutions of an equation. In the previous example, the solution set would be 2. Solutions to a linear equation in two variables consist of pairs of numbers. For instance, the equation $6x + 4y = 240$ has the solution $x = 20$ and $y = 30$ since $6 \cdot 20 + 4 \cdot 30 = 240$ is true. We can write this solution as the ordered pair (20,30) and plot it as a point on the coordinate plane. Such equations usually have infinitely many solutions; and if we plot the points for all these solutions we get a line, which is a picture of all the solutions. We call this **graphing the equation**. When an equation has no true solutions, it is referred to as an **empty set**.

Linear Equation Forms

Linear equations can be written many ways. Below is a list of some forms linear equations can take:

- **Standard Form**: $Ax + By = C$; the slope is $\frac{-A}{B}$ and the y-intercept is $\frac{C}{B}$
- **Slope Intercept Form**: $y = mx + b$, where m is the slope and b is the y-intercept
- **Point-Slope Form**: $y - y_1 = m(x - x_1)$, where m is the slope and (x_1, y_1) is a point on the line
- **Two-Point Form**: $\frac{y-y_1}{x-x_1} = \frac{y_2-y_1}{x_2-x_1}$, where (x_1, y_1) and (x_2, y_2) are two points on the given line
- **Intercept Form**: $\frac{x}{x_1} + \frac{y}{y_1} = 1$, where $(x_1, 0)$ is the point at which a line intersects the x-axis, and $(0, y_1)$ is the point at which the same line intersects the y-axis

Review Video: Slope-Intercept and Point-Slope Forms
Visit mometrix.com/academy and enter code: 113216

Review Video: Converting Between Standard and Slope-Intercept Forms
Visit mometrix.com/academy and enter code: 982828

Review Video: Linear Equations Basics
Visit mometrix.com/academy and enter code: 793005

Solving Equations

Manipulating Equations

Like Terms

Like terms are terms in an equation that have the same variable, regardless of whether they also have the same coefficient. This includes terms that *lack* a variable; all constants (i.e., numbers without variables) are considered like terms. If the equation involves terms with a variable raised to different powers, the like terms are those that have the variable raised to the same power.

For example, consider the equation $x^2 + 3x + 2 = 2x^2 + x - 7 + 2x$. In this equation, 2 and -7 are like terms; they are both constants. The terms $3x$, x, and $2x$ are like terms, they all include the variable x raised to the first power. The terms x^2 and $2x^2$ are like terms, they both include the variable x, raised to the second power. The terms $2x$ and $2x^2$ are not like terms; although they both involve the variable x, the variable is not raised to the same power in both terms. The fact that they have the same coefficient, 2, is not relevant.

Review Video: Rules for Manipulating Equations
Visit mometrix.com/academy and enter code: 838871

Carrying Out the Same Operation on Both Sides of an Equation

When solving an equation, the general procedure is to carry out a series of operations on both sides of an equation, choosing operations that simplify the equation when doing so. The reason why the same operation must be carried out on both sides of the equation is because that leaves the meaning of the equation unchanged, and yields a result that is equivalent to the original equation. This would not be the case if we carried out an operation on one side of an equation and not the other. Consider what an equation means: it is a statement that two values or expressions are equal. If we carry out the same operation on both sides of the equation—add 3 to both sides, for example—then the two sides of the equation are changed in the same way, and so remain equal. If we do that to only one side of the equation—add 3 to one side but not the other—then that wouldn't be true; if we change one side of the equation but not the other then the two sides are no longer equal.

Combining Like Terms

Combining like terms refers to adding or subtracting like terms—terms with the same variable—and therefore reducing sets of like terms to a single term. The main advantage of doing this is that it simplifies the equation. Often, combining like terms can be done as the first step in solving an equation, though it can also be done later, such as after distributing terms in a product.

For example, consider the equation $2(x+3)+3(2+x+3)=-4$. The 2 and the 3 in the second set of parentheses are like terms, and we can combine them, yielding $2(x+3)+3(x+5)=-4$. Now we can carry out the multiplications implied by the parentheses, distributing the outer 2 and 3 accordingly: $2x+6+3x+15=-4$. The $2x$ and the $3x$ are like terms, and we can add them together: $5x+6+15=-4$. Now, the constants 6, 15, and –4 are also like terms, and we can combine them as well: subtracting 6 and 15 from both sides of the equation, we get $5x=-4-6-15$, or $5x=-25$, which simplifies further to $x=-5$.

Review Video: Solving Equations by Combining Like Terms
Visit mometrix.com/academy and enter code: 668506

Canceling Terms on Opposite Sides of an Equation

Two terms on opposite sides of an equation can be canceled if and only if they *exactly* match each other. They must have the same variable raised to the same power and the same coefficient. For example, in the equation $3x+2x^2+6=2x^2-6$, $2x^2$ appears on both sides of the equation and can be canceled, leaving $3x+6=-6$. The 6 on each side of the equation *cannot* be canceled, because it is added on one side of the equation and subtracted on the other. While they cannot be canceled, however, the 6 and –6 are like terms and can be combined, yielding $3x=-12$, which simplifies further to $x=-4$.

It's also important to note that the terms to be canceled must be independent terms and cannot be part of a larger term. For example, consider the equation $2(x+6)=3(x+4)+1$. We cannot cancel the x's, because even though they match each other they are part of the larger terms $2(x+6)$ and $3(x+4)$. We must first distribute the 2 and 3, yielding $2x+12=3x+12+1$. Now we see that the terms with the x's do not match, but the 12s do, and can be canceled, leaving $2x=3x+1$, which simplifies to $x=-1$.

Isolating Variables

To isolate a variable means to manipulate the equation so that the variable appears by itself on one side of the equation, and does not appear at all on the other side. Generally, an equation or inequality is considered to be solved once the variable is isolated and the other side of the equation or inequality is simplified as much as possible. In the case of a two-variable equation or inequality, only one variable needs to be isolated; it will not usually be possible to simultaneously isolate both variables.

For a linear equation—an equation in which the variable only appears raised to the first power—isolating a variable can be done by first moving all the terms with the variable to one side of the equation and all other terms to the other side. (*Moving* a term really means adding the inverse of the term to both sides; when a term is *moved* to the other side of the equation its sign is flipped.) Then combine like terms on each side. Finally, divide both sides by the coefficient of the variable, if applicable. The steps need not necessarily be done in this order, but this order will always work.

Review Video: Solving Equations for Specific Variables
Visit mometrix.com/academy and enter code: 130695

Review Video: Solving Equations Involving Algebraic Fractions
Visit mometrix.com/academy and enter code: 237770

Review Video: Solving One-Step Equations
Visit mometrix.com/academy and enter code: 777004

Solving One-Variable Linear Equations

Equations with One Solution (the Usual Case)

To solve a one-variable linear equation, we use the techniques above to isolate the variable.

1. If any coefficients or constants are fractions, it is often helpful first to multiply both sides of the equation by the least common denominator (of all fractions) to clear the fractions.
2. Simplify both sides of the equation by combining any like terms.
3. Put all terms with the variable on one side of the equation and all constant terms on the other side, by adding or subtracting the same terms on both sides of the equation.
4. Divide both sides by the coefficient of the variable (or multiply both sides by its reciprocal).
5. When we have a value for the variable, we can check it by substituting the value into the original equation to make sure it produces a true result.

Consider the following example for solving the equation $\frac{2}{3}x + 8 = 14$:

$3 \cdot \left(\frac{2}{3}x + 8\right) = 3 \cdot 14$	Clear fractions by multiplying both sides by 3.
$2x + 24 = 42$	Simplify, remembering to apply the distributive property.
$2x + 24 - 24 = 42 - 24$	Subtract 24 from both sides to isolate $2x$.
$2x = 18$	Simplify by combining like terms.
$\frac{2x}{2} = \frac{18}{2}$	Divide both sides by 2 to isolate x.
$x = 9$	Simplify

Finally, we check this answer by substituting $x = 9$ into the original equation to make sure we get a true result.

$$\frac{2}{3}x + 8 = \frac{2}{3}(9) + 8 = 6 + 8 = 14$$

This is correct, so the value of x is 9.

Review Video: Solving Equations Using the Distributive Property
Visit mometrix.com/academy and enter code: 765499

Equations with More Than One Solution

Some types of non-linear equations, such as equations involving squares of variables, may have more than one solution. For example, the equation $x^2 = 4$ has two solutions: 2 and –2. Equations with absolute values can also have multiple solutions: $|x| = 1$ has the solutions $x = 1$ and $x = -1$.

It is possible for a linear equation to have more than one solution but only if the equation is true regardless of the value of the variable. We call such an equation an **identity**. In this case, the equation has infinitely many solutions, because every possible value of the variable is a solution. We discover that a linear equation is an identity when our attempts to isolate the variable cause the variable to disappear, leaving a *true* equation involving only constants. For example, consider the equation $2(3x + 5) = x + 5(x + 2)$. Distributing, we get $6x + 10 = x + 5x + 10$; combining like terms gives $6x + 10 = 6x + 10$, and the $6x$-terms cancel to leave $10 = 10$. This is clearly true, so the original equation is an identity. We could also cancel the 10's leaving $0 = 0$, which is also is clearly true—in general if both sides of the equation can be reduced to match one another exactly, the original equation is an identity.

Equations with No Solution

Some types of non-linear equations, such as equations involving squares of variables, may have no solution. For example, the equation $x^2 = -2$ has no solutions in the real numbers because the square of a real number must be positive. Similarly, $|x| = -1$ has no solution because the absolute value of a number is always positive.

It is also possible for a linear equation to have no solution. We call such an equation a **contradiction**. We discover that a linear equation is a contradiction when our attempts to isolate the variable cause the variable to disappear, leaving a *false* equation involving only constants. For example, the equation $2(x + 3) + x = 3x$ has no solution. We can see this by trying to solve it: first we distribute, leaving $2x + 6 + x = 3x$. Combining like terms gives us $3x + 6 = 3x$, and cancelling the term $3x$ on both sides leaves us with $6 = 0$. This is clearly false, so the original equation is a contradiction, having no solutions.

Features of Equations That Require Special Treatment

A linear equation is an equation in which variables only appear by themselves: not multiplied together, not with exponents other than one, and not inside absolute value signs or any other functions. For example, the equation $x + 1 - 3x = 5 - x$ is a linear equation; while x appears multiple times, it never appears with an exponent other than one, or inside any function. The two-variable equation $2x - 3y = 5 + 2x$ is also a linear equation. In contrast, the equation $x^2 - 5 = 3x$ is *not* a linear equation, because it involves the term x^2. The equation $\sqrt{x} = 5$ is not linear, because it involves a square root. The equation $(x - 1)^2 = 4$ is not linear because even though there's no exponent on the x directly, it appears as part of an expression that is squared. The two-variable equation $x + xy - y = 5$ is not linear because it includes the term xy, where two variables are multiplied together.

As we see above, linear equations can always be solved (or shown to have no solution) by combining like terms and performing simple operations on both sides of the equation. Some non-linear equations can be solved by similar methods, but others may require more advanced methods of solution, if they can be solved analytically at all.

Solving Equations Involving Roots

In an equation involving roots, the first step is to isolate the term with the root, if possible, and then raise both sides of the equation to the appropriate power to eliminate it. Consider an example equation, $2\sqrt{x+1}-1=3$. In this case, begin by adding 1 to both sides, yielding $2\sqrt{x+1}=4$, and then dividing both sides by 2, yielding $\sqrt{x+1}=2$. Now square both sides, yielding $x+1=4$. Finally, subtracting 1 from both sides yields $x=3$.

Squaring both sides of an equation (or raising both sides to any *even* power) may, however, yield a spurious solution—a solution to the squared equation that is *not* a solution of the original equation. It's therefore necessary to plug the solution back into the original equation to make sure it works. In this case, it does: $2\sqrt{3+1}-1=2\sqrt{4}-1=2(2)-1=4-1=3$.

The same procedure applies for other roots as well. For example, given the equation $3+\sqrt[3]{2x}=5$, we can first subtract 3 from both sides, yielding $\sqrt[3]{2x}=2$ and isolating the root. Raising both sides to the third power yields $2x=2^3$; i.e., $2x=8$. We can now divide both sides by 2 to get $x=4$.

Review Video: Solving Equations Involving Roots
Visit mometrix.com/academy and enter code: 297670

Solving Equations with Exponents

In solving an equation with powers of a variable, sometimes it is possible to eliminate all but one term involving the variable. In that case, we can isolate the power of the variable and then take the appropriate root of both sides to eliminate the exponent. For instance, for the equation $2x^3+17=5x^3-7$, we can subtract $5x^3$ from both sides to get $-3x^3+17=-7$, and then subtract 17 from both sides to get $-3x^3=-24$. Finally, we can divide both sides by –3 to get $x^3=8$. Since this isolates the cube of the variable, we can take the cube root of both sides to get $x=\sqrt[3]{8}=2$.

One important but often overlooked point is that equations with an exponent greater than 1 may have more than one answer. The solution to $x^2=9$ isn't simply $x=3$; it's $x=\pm 3$ (that is, $x=3$ or $x=-3$). For a slightly more complicated example, consider the equation $(x-1)^2-1=3$. Adding 1 to both sides yields $(x-1)^2=4$; taking the square root of both sides yields $x-1=2$. We can then add 1 to both sides to get $x=3$. However, there's a second solution. We also have the possibility that $x-1=-2$, in which case $x=-1$. Both $x=3$ and $x=-1$ are valid solutions, as can be verified by substituting them both into the original equation.

Review Video: Solving Equations with Exponents
Visit mometrix.com/academy and enter code: 514557

Review Video: Adding and Subtracting with Exponents
Visit mometrix.com/academy and enter code: 875756

Solving Equations with Absolute Values

When solving an equation with an absolute value, the first step is to isolate the absolute value term. We then consider two possibilities: when the expression inside the absolute value is positive or when it is negative. In the former case, the expression in the absolute value equals the expression on the other side of the equation; in the latter, it equals the additive inverse of that expression—the expression times negative one. We consider each case separately and finally check for spurious solutions.

For instance, consider solving $|2x-1|+x=5$ for x. We can first isolate the absolute value by moving the x to the other side: $|2x-1|=-x+5$. Now, we have two possibilities. First, that $2x-1$ is positive, and hence $2x-1=-x+5$. Rearranging and combining like terms yields $3x=6$, and hence $x=2$. The other possibility is that $2x-1$ is negative, and hence $2x-1=-(-x+5)=x-5$. In this case, rearranging and combining like terms yields $x=-4$. Substituting $x=2$ and $x=-4$ back into the original equation, we see that they are both valid solutions.

Note that the absolute value of a sum or difference applies to the sum or difference as a whole, not to the individual terms; in general, $|2x - 1|$ is not equal to $|2x + 1|$ or to $|2x| - 1$.

Review Video: Solving Absolute Value Equations
Visit mometrix.com/academy and enter code: 501208

EXTRANEOUS SOLUTIONS

An **extraneous solution** may arise when we square both sides of an equation (or raise both sides to an even power) as a step in solving it or under certain other operations on the equation. It is a solution to the squared or otherwise modified equation that is *not* a solution of the original equation. To identify an extraneous solution, it's useful when you solve an equation involving roots or absolute values to plug the solution back into the original equation to make sure it's valid.

TWO-VARIABLE EQUATIONS

Similar to methods for a one-variable equation, solving a two-variable equation involves isolating a variable: manipulating the equation so that a variable appears by itself on one side of the equation, and not at all on the other side. However, in a two-variable equation, you will usually only be able to isolate one of the variables; the other variable may appear on the other side along with constant terms, or with exponents or other functions. If an equation has multiple variables, the problem should tell you which variable to isolate.

Review Video: Solving Equations with Variables on Both Sides
Visit mometrix.com/academy and enter code: 402497

GRAPHING EQUATIONS

GRAPHICAL SOLUTIONS TO EQUATIONS

When equations are shown graphically, they are usually shown on a **Cartesian coordinate plane**. The Cartesian coordinate plane consists of two number lines placed perpendicular to each other and intersecting at the zero point, also known as the origin. The horizontal number line is known as the x-axis, with positive values to the right of the origin, and negative values to the left of the origin. The vertical number line is known as the y-axis, with positive values above the origin, and negative values below the origin. Any point on the plane can be identified by an ordered pair in the form (x, y), called coordinates. The x-value of the coordinate is called the abscissa, and the y-value of the coordinate is called the ordinate. The two number lines divide the plane into **four quadrants**: I, II, III, and IV.

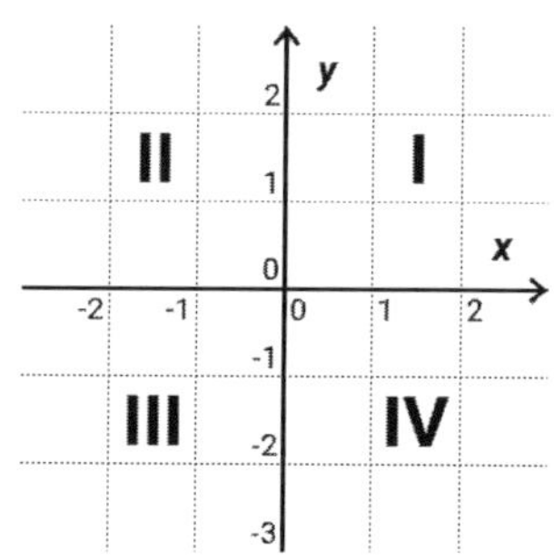

Note that in quadrant I $x > 0$ and $y > 0$, in quadrant II $x < 0$ and $y > 0$, in quadrant III $x < 0$ and $y < 0$, and in quadrant IV $x > 0$ and $y < 0$.

Recall that if the value of the slope of a line is positive, the line slopes upward from left to right. If the value of the slope is negative, the line slopes downward from left to right. If the y-coordinates are the same for two points on a line, the slope is 0 and the line is a **horizontal line**. If the x-coordinates are the same for two points on a line, there is no slope and the line is a **vertical line**. Two or more lines that have equivalent slopes are **parallel lines**. **Perpendicular lines** have slopes that are negative reciprocals of each other, such as $\frac{a}{b}$ and $\frac{-b}{a}$.

Review Video: Cartesian Coordinate Plane and Graphing
Visit mometrix.com/academy and enter code: 115173

GRAPHING EQUATIONS IN TWO VARIABLES

One way of graphing an equation in two variables is to plot enough points to get an idea for its shape and then draw the appropriate curve through those points. A point can be plotted by substituting in a value for one variable and solving for the other. If the equation is linear, we only need two points and can then draw a straight line between them.

For example, consider the equation $y = 2x - 1$. This is a linear equation—both variables only appear raised to the first power—so we only need two points. When $x = 0, y = 2(0) - 1 = -1$. When $x = 2, y = 2(2) - 1 = 3$. We can therefore choose the points $(0, -1)$ and $(2, 3)$, and draw a line between them:

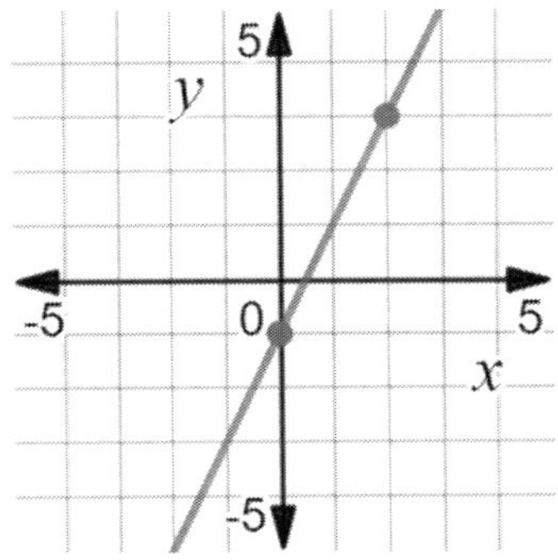

INEQUALITIES

Commonly in algebra and other upper-level fields of math you find yourself working with mathematical expressions that do not equal each other. The statement comparing such expressions with symbols such as $<$ (less than) or $>$ (greater than) is called an *inequality*. An example of an inequality is $7x > 5$. To solve for x, simply divide both sides by 7 and the solution is shown to be $x > \frac{5}{7}$. Graphs of the solution set of inequalities are represented on a number line. Open circles are used to show that an expression approaches a number but is never quite equal to that number.

Review Video: Solving One-Step Inequalities
Visit mometrix.com/academy and enter code: 229684

Review Video: Solving Multi-Step Inequalities
Visit mometrix.com/academy and enter code: 347842

Review Video: Solving Inequalities Using All 4 Basic Operations
Visit mometrix.com/academy and enter code: 401111

TYPES OF INEQUALITIES

Conditional inequalities are those with certain values for the variable that will make the condition true and other values for the variable where the condition will be false. **Absolute inequalities** can have any real number as the value for the variable to make the condition true, while there is no real number value for the variable that will make the condition false. Solving inequalities is done by following the same rules for solving equations with the exception that when multiplying or dividing by a negative number the direction of the inequality sign must be flipped or reversed. **Double inequalities** are situations where two inequality statements apply to the same variable expression. Example: $-c < ax + b < c$.

> **Review Video: Conditional and Absolute Inequalities**
> Visit mometrix.com/academy and enter code: 980164

SOLVING INEQUALITIES

DETERMINING SOLUTIONS TO INEQUALITIES

To determine whether a coordinate is a solution of an inequality, you can substitute the values of the coordinate into the inequality, simplify, and check whether the resulting statement holds true. For instance, to determine whether $(-2,4)$ is a solution of the inequality $y \geq -2x + 3$, substitute the values into the inequality, $4 \geq -2(-2) + 3$. Simplify the right side of the inequality and the result is $4 \geq 7$, which is a false statement. Therefore, the coordinate is not a solution of the inequality. You can also use this method to determine which part of the graph of an inequality is shaded. The graph of $y \geq -2x + 3$ includes the solid line $y = -2x + 3$ and, since it excludes the point $(-2,4)$ to the left of the line, it is shaded to the right of the line.

> **Review Video: Graphing Linear Inequalities**
> Visit mometrix.com/academy and enter code: 439421
>
> **Review Video: Graphing Solutions to Inequalities**
> Visit mometrix.com/academy and enter code: 391281

FLIPPING INEQUALITY SIGNS

When given an inequality, we can always turn the entire inequality around, swapping the two sides of the inequality and changing the inequality sign. For instance, $x + 2 > 2x - 3$ is equivalent to $2x - 3 < x + 2$. Aside from that, normally the inequality does not change if we carry out the same operation on both sides of the inequality. There is, however, one principal exception: if we *multiply* or *divide* both sides of the inequality by a *negative number*, the inequality is flipped. For example, if we take the inequality $-2x < 6$ and divide both sides by -2, the inequality flips and we are left with $x > -3$. This *only* applies to multiplication and division, and only with negative numbers. Multiplying or dividing both sides by a positive number, or adding or subtracting any number regardless of sign, does not flip the inequality. Another special case that flips the inequality sign is when reciprocals are used. For instance, $3 > 2$ but the relation of the reciprocals is $\frac{1}{3} < \frac{1}{2}$.

COMPOUND INEQUALITIES

A **compound inequality** is an equality that consists of two inequalities combined with *and* or *or*. The two components of a proper compound inequality must be of opposite type: that is, one must be greater than (or greater than or equal to), the other less than (or less than or equal to). For instance, "$x + 1 < 2$ or $x + 1 > 3$" is a compound inequality, as is "$2x \geq 4$ and $2x \leq 6$." An *and* inequality can be written more compactly by having one inequality on each side of the common part: "$2x \geq 1$ and $2x \leq 6$," can also be written as $1 \leq 2x \leq 6$.

In order for the compound inequality to be meaningful, the two parts of an *and* inequality must overlap; otherwise, no numbers satisfy the inequality. On the other hand, if the two parts of an *or* inequality overlap, then *all* numbers satisfy the inequality and as such the inequality is usually not meaningful.

Solving a compound inequality requires solving each part separately. For example, given the compound inequality "$x + 1 < 2$ or $x + 1 > 3$," the first inequality, $x + 1 < 2$, reduces to $x < 1$, and the second part, $x + 1 > 3$, reduces to $x > 2$, so the whole compound inequality can be written as "$x < 1$ or $x > 2$." Similarly, $1 \leq 2x \leq 6$ can be solved by dividing each term by 2, yielding $\frac{1}{2} \leq x \leq 3$.

> **Review Video: Compound Inequalities**
> Visit mometrix.com/academy and enter code: 786318

Solving Inequalities Involving Absolute Values

To solve an inequality involving an absolute value, first isolate the term with the absolute value. Then proceed to treat the two cases separately as with an absolute value equation, but flipping the inequality in the case where the expression in the absolute value is negative (since that essentially involves multiplying both sides by −1.) The two cases are then combined into a compound inequality; if the absolute value is on the greater side of the inequality, then it is an *or* compound inequality, if on the lesser side, then it's an *and*.

Consider the inequality $2 + |x - 1| \geq 3$. We can isolate the absolute value term by subtracting 2 from both sides: $|x - 1| \geq 1$. Now, we're left with the two cases $x - 1 \geq 1$ or $x - 1 \leq -1$: note that in the latter, negative case, the inequality is flipped. $x - 1 \geq 1$ reduces to $x \geq 2$, and $x - 1 \leq -1$ reduces to $x \leq 0$. Since in the inequality $|x - 1| \geq 1$ the absolute value is on the greater side, the two cases combine into an *or* compound inequality, so the final, solved inequality is "$x \leq 0$ or $x \geq 2$."

Review Video: Solving Absolute Value Inequalities
Visit mometrix.com/academy and enter code: 997008

Solving Inequalities Involving Square Roots

Solving an inequality with a square root involves two parts. First, we solve the inequality as if it were an equation, isolating the square root and then squaring both sides of the equation. Second, we restrict the solution to the set of values of x for which the value inside the square root sign is non-negative.

For example, in the inequality, $\sqrt{x - 2} + 1 < 5$, we can isolate the square root by subtracting 1 from both sides, yielding $\sqrt{x - 2} < 4$. Squaring both sides of the inequality yields $x - 2 < 16$, so $x < 18$. Since we can't take the square root of a negative number, we also require the part inside the square root to be non-negative. In this case, that means $x - 2 \geq 0$. Adding 2 to both sides of the inequality yields $x \geq 2$. Our final answer is a compound inequality combining the two simple inequalities: $x \geq 2$ and $x < 18$, or $2 \leq x < 18$.

Note that we only get a compound inequality if the two simple inequalities are in opposite directions; otherwise, we take the one that is more restrictive.

The same technique can be used for other even roots, such as fourth roots. It is *not*, however, used for cube roots or other odd roots—negative numbers *do* have cube roots, so the condition that the quantity inside the root sign cannot be negative does not apply.

Review Video: Solving Inequalities Involving Square Roots
Visit mometrix.com/academy and enter code: 800288

Special Circumstances

Sometimes an inequality involving an absolute value or an even exponent is true for all values of x, and we don't need to do any further work to solve it. This is true if the inequality, once the absolute value or exponent term is isolated, says that term is greater than a negative number (or greater than or equal to zero). Since an absolute value or a number raised to an even exponent is *always* non-negative, this inequality is always true.

Graphing Inequalities

Graphing Simple Inequalities

To graph a simple inequality, we first mark on the number line the value that signifies the end point of the inequality. If the inequality is strict (involves a less than or greater than), we use a hollow circle; if it is not strict (less than or equal to or greater than or equal to), we use a solid circle. We then fill in the part of the number line that satisfies the inequality: to the left of the marked point for less than (or less than or equal to), to the right for greater than (or greater than or equal to).

For example, we would graph the inequality $x < 5$ by putting a hollow circle at 5 and filling in the part of the line to the left:

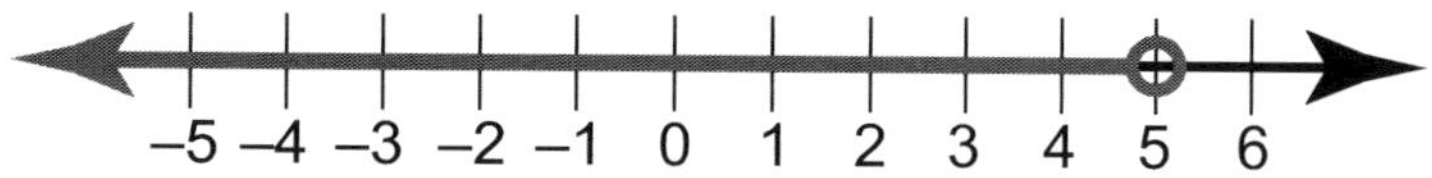

Graphing Compound Inequalities

To graph a compound inequality, we fill in both parts of the inequality for an *or* inequality, or the overlap between them for an *and* inequality. More specifically, we start by plotting the endpoints of each inequality on the number line. For an *or* inequality, we then fill in the appropriate side of the line for each inequality. Typically, the two component inequalities do not overlap, which means the shaded part is *outside* the two points. For an *and* inequality, we instead fill in the part of the line that meets both inequalities.

For the inequality "$x \leq -3$ or $x > 4$," we first put a solid circle at –3 and a hollow circle at 4. We then fill the parts of the line *outside* these circles:

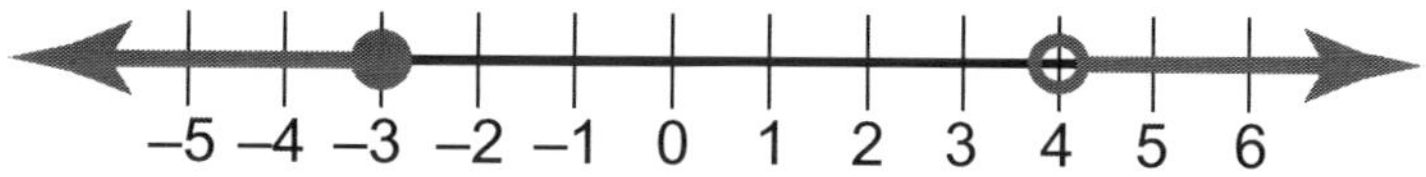

Graphing Inequalities Including Absolute Values

An inequality with an absolute value can be converted to a compound inequality. To graph the inequality, first convert it to a compound inequality, and then graph that normally. If the absolute value is on the greater side of the inequality, we end up with an *or* inequality; we plot the endpoints of the inequality on the number line and fill in the part of the line *outside* those points. If the absolute value is on the smaller side of the inequality, we end up with an *and* inequality; we plot the endpoints of the inequality on the number line and fill in the part of the line *between* those points.

For example, the inequality $|x + 1| \geq 4$ can be rewritten as $x \geq 3$ or $x \leq -5$. We place solid circles at the points 3 and –5 and fill in the part of the line *outside* them:

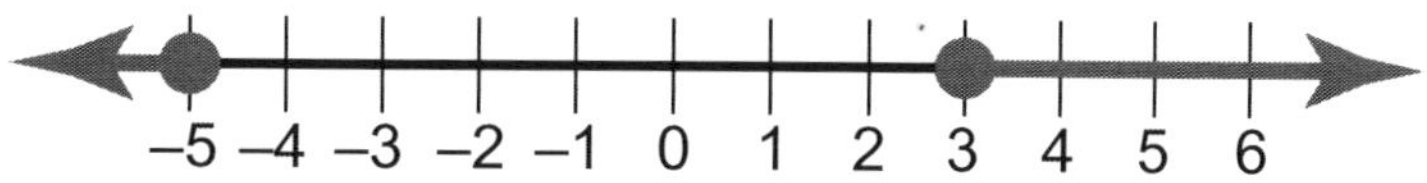

Graphing Inequalities in Two Variables

To graph an inequality in two variables, we first graph the border of the inequality. This means graphing the equation that we get if we replace the inequality sign with an equals sign. If the inequality is strict ($>$ or $<$), we graph the border with a dashed or dotted line; if it is not strict ($\geq$ or $\leq$), we use a solid line. We can then test any point not on the border to see if it satisfies the inequality. If it does, we shade in that side of the border; if not, we shade in the other side. As an example, consider $y > 2x + 2$. To graph this inequality, we first graph the border, $y = 2x + 2$. Since it is a strict inequality, we use a dashed line. Then, we choose a test point. This can be any point not on the border; in this case, we will choose the origin, (0,0). (This makes the calculation easy and is generally a good choice unless the border passes through the origin.) Putting this into the original inequality,

Mathematics

we get $0 > 2(0) + 2$, i.e., $0 > 2$. This is *not* true, so we shade in the side of the border that does *not* include the point (0,0):

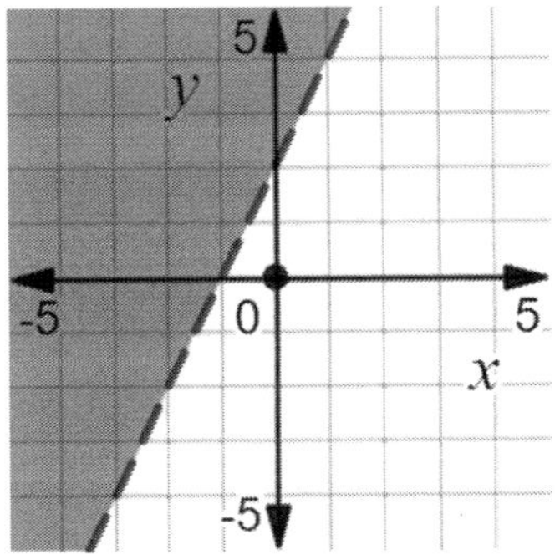

GRAPHING COMPOUND INEQUALITIES IN TWO VARIABLES

One way to graph a compound inequality in two variables is to first graph each of the component inequalities. For an *and* inequality, we then shade in only the parts where the two graphs overlap; for an *or* inequality, we shade in any region that pertains to either of the individual inequalities.

Consider the graph of "$y \geq x - 1$ and $y \leq -x$":

We first shade in the individual inequalities:

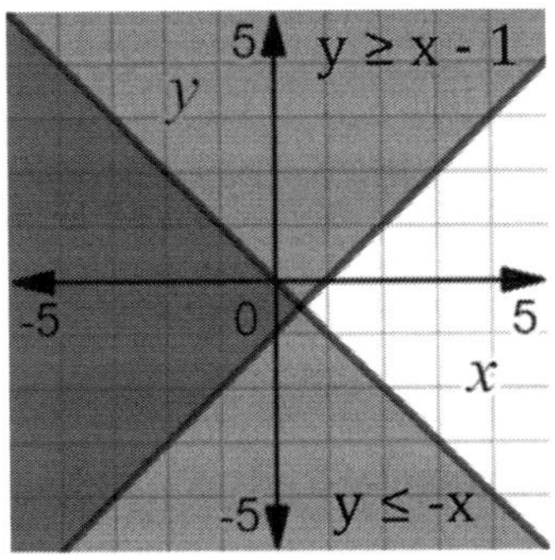

Now, since the compound inequality has an *and*, we only leave shaded the overlap—the part that pertains to *both* inequalities:

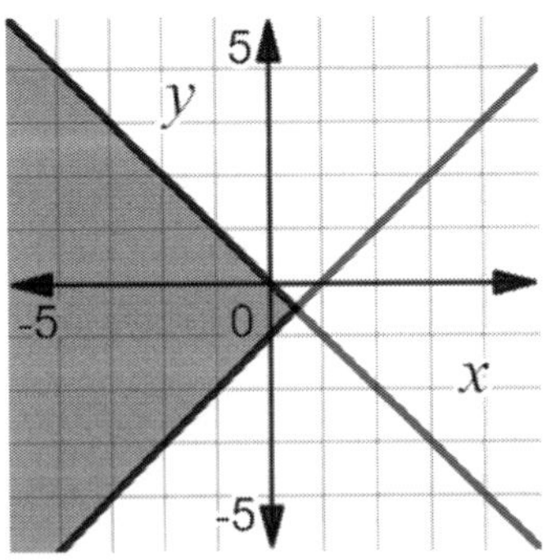

If instead the inequality had been "$y \geq x - 1$ or $y \leq -x$," our final graph would involve the *total* shaded area:

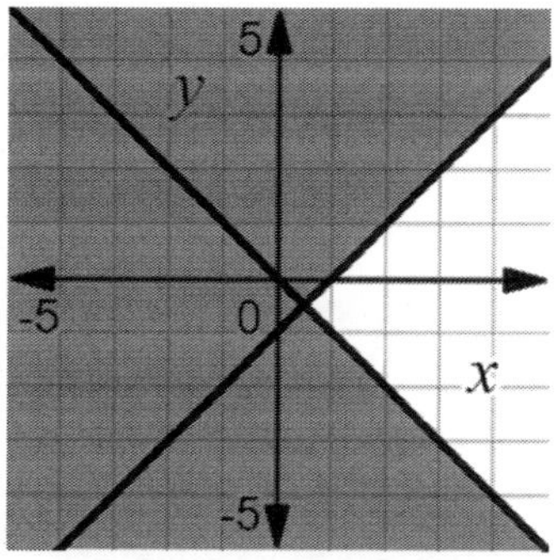

Review Video: Graphing Solutions to Inequalities
Visit mometrix.com/academy and enter code: 391281

SYSTEMS OF EQUATIONS

SOLVING SYSTEMS OF EQUATIONS

A **system of equations** is a set of simultaneous equations that all use the same variables. A solution to a system of equations must be true for each equation in the system. **Consistent systems** are those with at least one solution. **Inconsistent systems** are systems of equations that have no solution.

Review Video: Solving Systems of Linear Equations
Visit mometrix.com/academy and enter code: 746745

SUBSTITUTION

To solve a system of linear equations by **substitution**, start with the easier equation and solve for one of the variables. Express this variable in terms of the other variable. Substitute this expression in the other equation and solve for the other variable. The solution should be expressed in the form (x, y). Substitute the values into both of the original equations to check your answer. Consider the following system of equations:

$$\begin{aligned} x + 6y &= 15 \\ 3x - 12y &= 18 \end{aligned}$$

Solving the first equation for x: $x = 15 - 6y$

Substitute this value in place of x in the second equation, and solve for y:

$$\begin{aligned} 3(15 - 6y) - 12y &= 18 \\ 45 - 18y - 12y &= 18 \\ 30y &= 27 \\ y &= \frac{27}{30} = \frac{9}{10} = 0.9 \end{aligned}$$

Mathematics

Plug this value for y back into the first equation to solve for x:

$$x = 15 - 6(0.9) = 15 - 5.4 = 9.6$$

Check both equations if you have time:

$$\begin{aligned} 9.6 + 6(0.9) &= 15 \\ 9.6 + 5.4 &= 15 \\ 15 &= 15 \end{aligned} \qquad \begin{aligned} 3(9.6) - 12(0.9) &= 18 \\ 28.8 - 10.8 &= 18 \\ 18 &= 18 \end{aligned}$$

Therefore, the solution is $(9.6,0.9)$.

Review Video: The Substitution Method
Visit mometrix.com/academy and enter code: 565151

Review Video: Substitution and Elimination
Visit mometrix.com/academy and enter code: 958611

Elimination

To solve a system of equations using **elimination**, begin by rewriting both equations in standard form $Ax + By = C$. Check to see if the coefficients of one pair of like variables add to zero. If not, multiply one or both of the equations by a non-zero number to make one set of like variables add to zero. Add the two equations to solve for one of the variables. Substitute this value into one of the original equations to solve for the other variable. Check your work by substituting into the other equation. Now, let's look at solving the following system using the elimination method:

$$\begin{aligned} 5x + 6y &= 4 \\ x + 2y &= 4 \end{aligned}$$

If we multiply the second equation by -3, we can eliminate the y-terms:

$$\begin{aligned} 5x + 6y &= 4 \\ -3x - 6y &= -12 \end{aligned}$$

Add the equations together and solve for x:

$$\begin{aligned} 2x &= -8 \\ x &= \frac{-8}{2} = -4 \end{aligned}$$

Plug the value for x back in to either of the original equations and solve for y:

$$\begin{aligned} -4 + 2y &= 4 \\ y &= \frac{4 + 4}{2} = 4 \end{aligned}$$

Check both equations if you have time:

$$\begin{aligned} 5(-4) + 6(4) &= 4 \\ -20 + 24 &= 4 \\ 4 &= 4 \end{aligned} \qquad \begin{aligned} -4 + 2(4) &= 4 \\ -4 + 8 &= 4 \\ 4 &= 4 \end{aligned}$$

Therefore, the solution is $(-4,4)$.

Review Video: The Elimination Method
Visit mometrix.com/academy and enter code: 449121

GRAPHICALLY

To solve a system of linear equations **graphically**, plot both equations on the same graph. The solution of the equations is the point where both lines cross. If the lines do not cross (are parallel), then there is **no solution**.

For example, consider the following system of equations:

$$y = 2x + 7$$
$$y = -x + 1$$

Since these equations are given in slope-intercept form, they are easy to graph; the y-intercepts of the lines are (0,7) and (0,1). The respective slopes are 2 and –1, thus the graphs look like this:

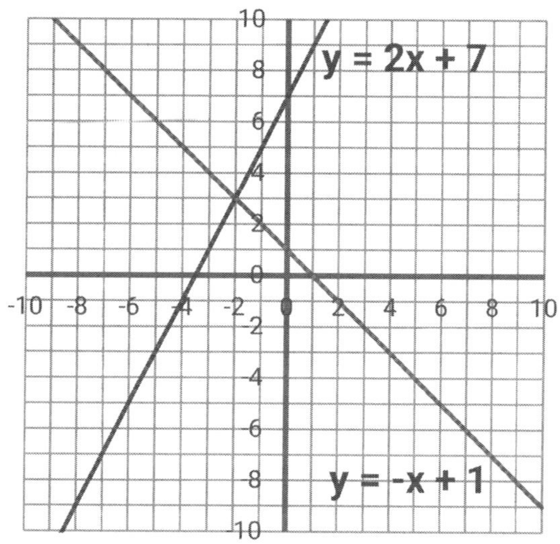

The two lines intersect at the point $(-2,3)$, thus this is the solution to the system of equations.

Solving a system graphically is generally only practical if both coordinates of the solution are integers; otherwise the intersection will lie between gridlines on the graph and the coordinates will be difficult or impossible to determine exactly. It also helps if, as in this example, the equations are in slope-intercept form or some other form that makes them easy to graph. Otherwise, another method of solution (by substitution or elimination) is likely to be more useful.

Review Video: Solving Systems by Graphing
Visit mometrix.com/academy and enter code: 634812

SOLVING SYSTEMS OF EQUATIONS USING THE TRACE FEATURE

Using the trace feature on a calculator requires that you rewrite each equation, isolating the y-variable on one side of the equal sign. Enter both equations in the graphing calculator and plot the graphs simultaneously. Use the trace cursor to find where the two lines cross. Use the zoom feature if necessary to obtain more accurate results. Always check your answer by substituting into the original equations. The trace method is likely to be less accurate than other methods due to the resolution of graphing calculators but is a useful tool to provide an approximate answer.

Advanced Systems of Equations

Solving a System of Equations with a Linear Equation and a Quadratic Equation

Algebraically

Generally, the simplest way to solve a system of equations consisting of a linear equation and a quadratic equation algebraically is through the method of substitution. One possible strategy is to solve the linear equation for y and then substitute that expression into the quadratic equation. After expansion and combining like terms, this will result in a new quadratic equation for x, which, like all quadratic equations, may have zero, one, or two solutions. Plugging each solution for x back into one of the original equations will then produce the corresponding value of y.

For example, consider the following system of equations:

$$x + y = 1$$
$$y = (x + 3)^2 - 2$$

We can solve the linear equation for y to yield $y = -x + 1$. Substituting this expression into the quadratic equation produces $-x + 1 = (x + 3)^2 - 2$. We can simplify this equation:

$$\begin{aligned} -x + 1 &= (x + 3)^2 - 2 \\ -x + 1 &= x^2 + 6x + 9 - 2 \\ -x + 1 &= x^2 + 6x + 7 \\ 0 &= x^2 + 7x + 6 \end{aligned}$$

This quadratic equation can be factored as $(x + 1)(x + 6) = 0$. It therefore has two solutions: $x_1 = -1$ and $x_2 = -6$. Plugging each of these back into the original linear equation yields $y_1 = -x_1 + 1 = -(-1) + 1 = 2$ and $y_2 = -x_2 + 1 = -(-6) + 1 = 7$. Thus, this system of equations has two solutions, $(-1,2)$ and $(-6,7)$.

It may help to check your work by putting each x- and y-value back into the original equations and verifying that they do provide a solution.

Graphically

To solve a system of equations consisting of a linear equation and a quadratic equation graphically, plot both equations on the same graph. The linear equation will, of course, produce a straight line, while the quadratic equation will produce a parabola. These two graphs will intersect at zero, one, or two points; each point of intersection is a solution of the system.

For example, consider the following system of equations:

$$y = -2x + 2$$
$$y = -2x^2 + 4x + 2$$

The linear equation describes a line with a y-intercept of $(0,2)$ and a slope of -2.

To graph the quadratic equation, we can first find the vertex of the parabola: the x-coordinate of the vertex is $h = -\frac{b}{2a} = -\frac{4}{2(-2)} = 1$, and the y-coordinate is $k = -2(1)^2 + 4(1) + 2 = 4$. Thus, the vertex lies at $(1,4)$. To get a feel for the rest of the parabola, we can plug in a few more values of x to find more points; by putting in

$x = 2$ and $x = 3$ in the quadratic equation, we find that the points (2,2) and $(3, -4)$ lie on the parabola; by symmetry, so must $(0, 2)$ and $(-1, -4)$. We can now plot both equations:

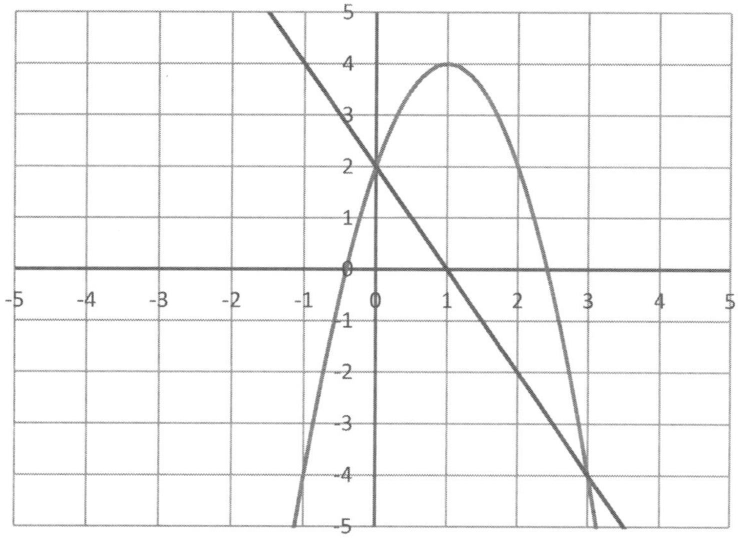

These two curves intersect at the points (0,2) and $(3, -4)$, thus these are the solutions of the equation.

Review Video: Parabolas
Visit mometrix.com/academy and enter code: 129187

Review Video: Vertex of a Parabola
Visit mometrix.com/academy and enter code: 272300

Review Video: Solving a System of Linear and Quadratic Equations
Visit mometrix.com/academy and enter code: 194870

Midpoint and Distance Formulas

If you know the coordinates of the endpoints of a line segment, you can calculate the midpoint and length of the line segment. Conveniently, the length of the line segment is also the distance between the two endpoints.

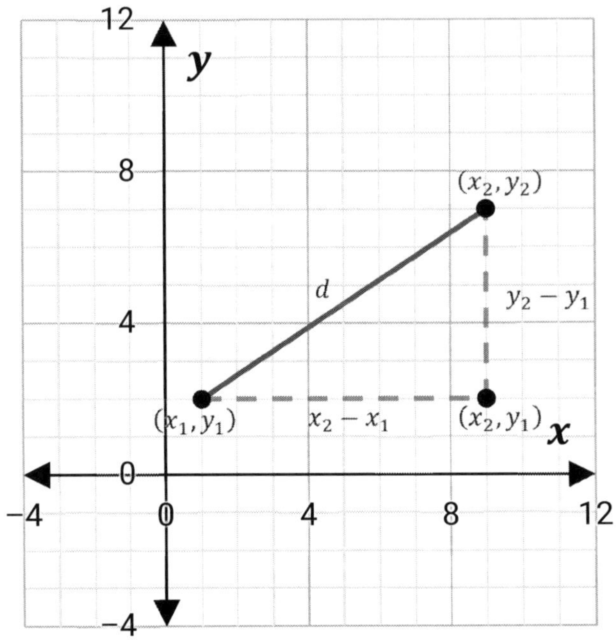

To find the **midpoint** of the line segment with endpoints (x_1, y_1) and (x_2, y_2), average the x-coordinates to get the x-coordinate of the midpoint, and average the y-coordinates to get the y-coordinate of the midpoint. Thus, the **midpoint formula** is:

$$\left(\frac{x_1 + x_2}{2}, \frac{y_1 + y_2}{2}\right)$$

The **distance** between points (x_1, y_1) and (x_2, y_2) is the same as the length of the hypotenuse of a right triangle with the two given points as endpoints, and the two sides of the right triangle parallel to the x-axis and y-axis, respectively. The length of the segment parallel to the x-axis is the difference between the x-coordinates of the two points. The length of the segment parallel to the y-axis is the difference between the y-coordinates of the two points. Use the Pythagorean theorem $a^2 + b^2 = c^2$ or $c = \sqrt{a^2 + b^2}$ to find the distance. Thus, the **distance formula** is:

$$d = \sqrt{(x_2 - x_1)^2 + (y_2 - y_1)^2}$$

Review Video: Calculations Using Points on a Graph
Visit mometrix.com/academy and enter code: 883228

Polynomials

Monomials and Polynomials

A **monomial** is a single constant, variable, or product of constants and variables, such as 7, x, $2x$, or x^3y. There will never be addition or subtraction symbols in a monomial. Like monomials have like variables, but they may have different coefficients. A **polynomial** is a monomial or the result of combining two or more monomials by sums or differences. In a polynomial we call each monomial a **term**. Two terms make a **binomial** (e.g., $2x + 3y$), three terms make a **trinomial** (e.g., $5x^2 - 4x + 9$). The **degree of a monomial** is the sum of the exponents of the variables. The **degree of a polynomial** is the highest degree of any individual term.

Review Video: Polynomials
Visit mometrix.com/academy and enter code: 305005

Simplifying Polynomials

Simplifying polynomials requires combining like terms. The like terms in a polynomial expression are those that have the same variables raised to the same powers. It is often helpful to connect the like terms with arrows or lines in order to separate them from the other monomials. Once you have determined the like terms, you can rearrange the polynomial by placing them together. Remember to include the sign that is in front of each term. Once the like terms are placed together, you can apply each operation and simplify. When adding and subtracting polynomials, only add and subtract the **coefficients**, or the number part; the variable and exponent stay the same.

Adding Polynomials

To add polynomials, you need to add like terms. These terms have the same variable part. For example, the terms $4x^2$ and $3x^2$ both include x^2 terms. To find the sum of like terms, find the sum of the coefficients. Then, keep the same variable part. You can use the distributive property to distribute the plus sign to each term of the polynomial. For example:

$(4x^2 - 5x + 7) + (3x^2 + 2x + 1) =$
$(4x^2 - 5x + 7) + 3x^2 + 2x + 1 =$
$(4x^2 + 3x^2) + (-5x + 2x) + (7 + 1) =$
$7x^2 - 3x + 8$

Subtracting Polynomials

To subtract polynomials, you need to subtract like terms. To find the difference of like terms, find the difference of the coefficients. Then, keep the same variable part. You can use the distributive property to distribute the minus sign to each term of the polynomial. For example:

$(-2x^2 - x + 5) - (3x^2 - 4x + 1) =$
$(-2x^2 - x + 5) - 3x^2 + 4x - 1 =$
$(-2x^2 - 3x^2) + (-x + 4x) + (5 - 1) =$
$-5x^2 + 3x + 4$

Review Video: Adding and Subtracting Polynomials
Visit mometrix.com/academy and enter code: 124088

Multiplying Polynomials

In general, multiplying polynomials is done by multiplying each term in one polynomial by each term in the other and adding the results. In the specific case for multiplying binomials, there is a useful acronym, FOIL, that can help you make sure to cover each combination of terms. The **FOIL method** for $(Ax + By)(Cx + Dy)$ would be:

F	Multiply the *first* terms of each binomial	$(\overbrace{Ax}^{first} + By)(\overbrace{Cx}^{first} + Dy)$	ACx^2
O	Multiply the *outer* terms	$(\overbrace{Ax}^{outer} + By)(Cx + \overbrace{Dy}^{outer})$	$ADxy$
I	Multiply the *inner* terms	$(Ax + \overbrace{By}^{inner})(\overbrace{Cx}^{inner} + Dy)$	$BCxy$
L	Multiply the *last* terms of each binomial	$(Ax + \overbrace{By}^{last})(Cx + \overbrace{Dy}^{last})$	BDy^2

Then, add up the result of each and combine like terms: $ACx^2 + (AD + BC)xy + BDy^2$.

For example, using the FOIL method on binomials $(x + 2)$ and $(x - 3)$:

$$\begin{aligned}
&\text{First:} && (\boxed{x} + 2)(\boxed{x} + (-3)) && \rightarrow && (x)(x) &&= x^2 \\
&\text{Outer:} && (\boxed{x} + 2)(x + \boxed{(-3)}) && \rightarrow && (x)(-3) &&= -3x \\
&\text{Inner:} && (x + \boxed{2})(\boxed{x} + (-3)) && \rightarrow && (2)(x) &&= 2x \\
&\text{Last:} && (x + \boxed{2})(x + \boxed{(-3)}) && \rightarrow && (2)(-3) &&= -6
\end{aligned}$$

This results in: $(x^2) + (-3x) + (2x) + (-6)$

Combine like terms: $x^2 + (-3 + 2)x + (-6) = x^2 - x - 6$

Review Video: Multiplying Polynomials
Visit mometrix.com/academy and enter code: 598293

Review Video: Multiplying Terms Using the FOIL Method
Visit mometrix.com/academy and enter code: 854792

DIVIDING POLYNOMIALS

Use long division to divide a polynomial by either a monomial or another polynomial of equal or lesser degree.

When **dividing by a monomial**, divide each term of the polynomial by the monomial.

Review Video: Dividing Monomials
Visit mometrix.com/academy and enter code: 584409

When **dividing by a polynomial**, begin by arranging the terms of each polynomial in order of one variable. You may arrange in ascending or descending order, but be consistent with both polynomials. To get the first term of the quotient, divide the first term of the dividend by the first term of the divisor. Multiply the first term of the quotient by the entire divisor and subtract that product from the dividend. Repeat for the second and successive terms until you either get a remainder of zero or a remainder whose degree is less than the degree of the divisor. If the quotient has a remainder, write the answer as a mixed expression in the form:

$$\text{quotient} + \frac{\text{remainder}}{\text{divisor}}$$

For example, we can evaluate the following expression in the same way as long division:

$$\frac{x^3 - 3x^2 - 2x + 5}{x - 5}$$

$$\begin{array}{r}
x^2 \quad + 2x \quad + 8 \\
x - 5 \,\overline{)\; x^3 \; - 3x^2 \; - 2x \; + 5} \\
-\underline{(x^3 - 5x^2)} \qquad\qquad \\
2x^2 \; - 2x \qquad \\
\underline{-(2x^2 - 10x)} \qquad \\
8x \; + 5 \\
\underline{-(8x - 40)} \\
45
\end{array}$$

$$\frac{x^3 - 3x^2 - 2x + 5}{x - 5} = x^2 + 2x + 8 + \frac{45}{x - 5}$$

Review Video: Dividing Polynomials by Monomials
Visit mometrix.com/academy and enter code: 253551

Review Video: Dividing Trinomials by Binomials
Visit mometrix.com/academy and enter code: 651465

When **factoring** a polynomial, first see whether you can factor out a nontrivial greatest common factor (GCF). For example, the trinomial $3x^5 - 18x^4 + 15x^3$ has a GCF of $3x^3$ since the GCF of 3, 18, and 15 is 3 and the GCF of x^5, x^4, and x^3 is x^3. Factoring out the GCF simplifies the expression to $3x^3(x^2 - 6x + 5)$.

To factor a quadratic trinomial (this comes up frequently), first check whether it is a perfect square trinomial (see bulleted list below). If not, see if you can factor it by trial and error by making clever choices of values for a and b (or a, b, c, and d) in the formulas below (this amounts to trying to use the FOIL mnemonic backwards):

$$x^2 + (a + b)x + ab = (x + a)(x + b)$$
$$(ac)x^2 + (ad + bc)x + bd = (ax + b)(cx + d)$$

For instance, you would try to factor the trinomial $x^2 - 6x + 5$ using the equation $x^2 + (a + b)x + ab = (x + a)(x + b)$. This means that you need to find integers a and b such that $a + b = -6$ and $ab = 5$. Starting with $ab = 5$, you can see that the only ways to write 5 as a product of integers are $(1)(5) = 5$ and $(-1)(-5) = 5$. So, it is easy to see that you want $a = -1$ and $b = -5$ since $a + b = -1 + (-5) = -6$ and $ab = (-1)(-5) = 5$. This tells you that $x^2 - 6x + 5 = (x - 1)(x - 5)$.

For polynomials with four terms (usually a cubic polynomial), sometimes factoring by grouping works: You group the two higher-power terms and the two lower-power terms, factor the GCF out of each group, and then factor out the resulting common binomial factor, if there is one. For example, $x^3 + 5x^2 + 3x + 15 = (x^3 + 5x^2) + (3x + 15) = x^2(x + 5) + 3(x + 5) = (x^2 + 3)(x + 5)$.

Once you have found the factors, write the original polynomial as the product of all the factors. Make sure all of the factors are either monomials, or else linear or irreducible quadratic polynomials (*irreducible* means they have no real zeros, which is easy to check with the quadratic formula). Check your work by multiplying the factors to make sure you get the original polynomial.

Review Video: Factoring Out Common Monomial Factors
Visit mometrix.com/academy and enter code: 398578

Review Video: Factoring Trinomials of the Form x^2+bx+c
Visit mometrix.com/academy and enter code: 270556

Below are patterns of some special products to remember to help make factoring easier:

- Perfect square trinomials: $x^2 + 2xy + y^2 = (x + y)^2$ or $x^2 - 2xy + y^2 = (x - y)^2$. For example, $x^2 + 10x + 25 = (x + 5)^2$.
- Difference between two squares: $x^2 - y^2 = (x + y)(x - y)$. For example, $x^2 - 9 = (x + 3)(x - 3)$.
- Sum of two cubes: $x^3 + y^3 = (x + y)(x^2 - xy + y^2)$. For example, $x^3 + 27 = (x + 3)(x^2 - 3x + 9)$.
    - Note: the second factor is *not* the same as a perfect square trinomial, so do not try to factor it further.
- Difference between two cubes: $x^3 - y^3 = (x - y)(x^2 + xy + y^2)$. For example, $x^3 - 1000 = (x - 10)(x^2 + 10x + 100)$.
    - Again, the second factor is *not* the same as a perfect square trinomial.
- Perfect cubes: $x^3 + 3x^2y + 3xy^2 + y^3 = (x + y)^3$ and $x^3 - 3x^2y + 3xy^2 - y^3 = (x - y)^3$

Review Video: Factoring the Difference of Two Squares
Visit mometrix.com/academy and enter code: 128954

Rational and Irrational Expressions

Rational Expressions

Rational expressions are fractions with polynomials in both the numerator and the denominator; the value of the polynomial in the denominator cannot be equal to zero. Be sure to keep track of values that make the denominator of the original expression zero as the final result inherits the same restrictions. For example, a denominator of $x - 3$ indicates that the expression is not defined when $x = 3$ and, as such, regardless of any operations done to the expression, it remains undefined there.

To **add or subtract** rational expressions, first find the common denominator, then rewrite each fraction as an equivalent fraction with the common denominator. Finally, add or subtract the numerators to get the numerator of the answer, and keep the common denominator as the denominator of the answer.

When **multiplying** rational expressions, factor each polynomial and cancel like factors (a factor which appears in both the numerator and the denominator). Then, multiply all remaining factors in the numerator to get the numerator of the product, and multiply the remaining factors in the denominator to get the denominator of the product. Remember: cancel entire factors, not individual terms.

To **divide** rational expressions, take the reciprocal of the divisor (the rational expression you are dividing by) and multiply by the dividend.

Review Video: Rational Expressions
Visit mometrix.com/academy and enter code: 415183

Simplifying Rational Expressions

To simplify a rational expression, factor the numerator and denominator completely. Factors that are the same and appear in the numerator and denominator have a ratio of 1. For example, look at the following expression:

$$\frac{x-1}{1-x^2}$$

The denominator, $(1-x^2)$, is a difference of squares. It can be factored as $(1-x)(1+x)$. The factor $1-x$ and the numerator $x-1$ are opposites and have a ratio of –1. Rewrite the numerator as $-1(1-x)$. So, the rational expression can be simplified as follows:

$$\frac{x-1}{1-x^2} = \frac{-1(1-x)}{(1-x)(1+x)} = \frac{-1}{1+x}$$

Note that since the original expression is only defined for $x \neq \{-1, 1\}$, the simplified expression has the same restrictions.

> **Review Video: Reducing Rational Expressions**
> Visit mometrix.com/academy and enter code: 788868
>
> **Review Video: Simplifying Algebraic Expressions with Parentheses**
> Visit mometrix.com/academy and enter code: 850843

Irrational Expressions

Irrational expressions are mathematical expressions that contain an irrational number and cannot be simplified into a rational form. Usually, this includes expressions that contain radicals or constants such as π. Most commonly, you will encounter these in the forms of expressions containing roots of non-perfect squares.

Basic Operations on Radical Expressions

To add or subtract radical numbers, the numbers within the radicals must match, similar to finding a common denominator in fractions:

$$a\sqrt{x} + b\sqrt{x} = (a+b)\sqrt{x}$$

$$a\sqrt{x} - b\sqrt{x} = (a-b)\sqrt{x}$$

To multiply radicals, the numbers outside the radical are multiplied together and the numbers inside the radical are multiplied together:

$$a\sqrt{x} \times b\sqrt{y} = ab\sqrt{xy}$$

To divide radicals, the radical must be eliminated from the denominator by multiplying both numerator and denominator by a value that will make the denominator a rational number:

$$\frac{a\sqrt{x}}{b\sqrt{y}} = \frac{a\sqrt{x}\sqrt{y}}{b\sqrt{y}\sqrt{y}} = \frac{a\sqrt{xy}}{by}$$

> **Review Video: Adding and Subtracting Radical Expressions**
> Visit mometrix.com/academy and enter code: 752176

EXAMPLE

To solve $\frac{(3\sqrt{6})(2\sqrt{3})}{4\sqrt{5}}$, we first multiply the numerator, inside the radical and out: $3 \times 2\sqrt{6 \times 3} = 6\sqrt{18} = 18\sqrt{2}$. To divide, we multiply both numerator and denominator by a value that will eliminate the radical:

$$\frac{18\sqrt{2} \times \sqrt{5}}{4\sqrt{5} \times \sqrt{5}} = \frac{18\sqrt{10}}{4 \times 5} = \frac{18\sqrt{10}}{20} = \frac{9\sqrt{10}}{10}$$

ALGEBRAIC THEOREMS

According to the **fundamental theorem of algebra**, every non-constant, single-variable polynomial has exactly as many roots as the polynomial's highest exponent. For example, if x^4 is the largest exponent of a term, the polynomial will have exactly 4 roots. However, some of these roots may have multiplicity or be complex numbers. For instance, in the polynomial function $f(x) = x^4 - 4x + 3$, the only real root is 1, though it has multiplicity of 2 – that is, it occurs twice. The other two roots, $(-1 - i\sqrt{2})$ and $(-1 + i\sqrt{2})$, are complex, consisting of both real and non-real components.

The **remainder theorem** is useful for determining the remainder when a polynomial is divided by a binomial. The remainder theorem states that if a polynomial function $f(x)$ is divided by a binomial $x - a$, where a is a real number, the remainder of the division will be the value of $f(a)$. If $f(a) = 0$, then a is a root of the polynomial.

The **factor theorem** is related to the remainder theorem and states that if $f(a) = 0$ then $(x - a)$ is a factor of the function.

According to the **rational root theorem,** any rational root of a polynomial function $f(x) = a_n x^n + a_{n-1}x^{n-1} + \cdots + a_1 x + a_0$ with integer coefficients will, when reduced to its lowest terms, be a positive or negative fraction such that the numerator is a factor of a_0 and the denominator is a factor of a_n. For instance, if the polynomial function $f(x) = x^3 + 3x^2 - 4$ has any rational roots, the numerators of those roots can only be factors of 4 (1, 2, 4), and the denominators can only be factors of 1 (1). The function in this example has roots of 1 (or $\frac{1}{1}$) and –2 (or $\frac{-2}{1}$).

QUADRATICS

SOLVING QUADRATIC EQUATIONS

A quadratic equation is an equation that can be written (possibly after simplification) in the form $ax^2 + bx + c = 0$. Thus, the **solutions** of this equation are precisely the **zeros** of the quadratic polynomial $P(x) = ax^2 + bx + c$. On the graph of this polynomial the zeros, if any, appear as x-intercepts. There are several ways to find these solutions including the quadratic formula, factoring, completing the square, and graphing the function.

> **Review Video: Quadratic Equations Overview**
> Visit mometrix.com/academy and enter code: 476276
>
> **Review Video: Solutions of a Quadratic Equation on a Graph**
> Visit mometrix.com/academy and enter code: 328231

QUADRATIC FORMULA

The **quadratic formula** gives the zeros of a quadratic polynomial. It always works, but it is sometimes a little harder to use than other methods. To use it to solve a quadratic equation, rewrite the equation in the form $ax^2 + bx + c = 0$, where a, b, and c are coefficients. Now, as explained above, the solutions of the equation are the zeros of the quadratic polynomial $P(x) = ax^2 + bx + c$. To find them, substitute the values of a, b, and c into the Quadratic Formula:

$$x = \frac{-b \pm \sqrt{b^2 - 4ac}}{2a}$$

After simplification this formula produces two, one, or zero real solutions, depending on whether the **discriminant** (the number $b^2 - 4ac$ under the radical) is positive, zero, or negative. It is a good practice to check each solution by substituting it into the original equation. Incidentally, if the discriminant is negative, then the equation does have two complex solutions, but you often ignore these as meaningless in real-world settings.

Review Video: Using the Quadratic Formula
Visit mometrix.com/academy and enter code: 163102

FACTORING

To solve a quadratic equation by factoring, begin by rewriting the equation in the standard form, $ax^2 + bx + c = 0$. In the important special case that $a = 1$, the goal of factoring is to find numbers f and g such that $x^2 + bx + c = (x + f)(x + g) = x^2 + (f + g)x + fg$. In other words, you want to choose f and g to make $fg = c$ and $f + g = b$. To do this, find pairs of numbers (factors) whose product is c and look for a pair whose sum is b.

For example, suppose you want to find the solutions of the equation $x^2 + 6x - 16 = 0$ by factoring. Here $b = 6$ and $c = -16$. First, you find the pairs of numbers whose product is -16. These are -4 and 4, -8 and 2, -2 and 8, -1 and 16, and 1 and -16. The pair -2 and 8 has a sum of 6. This means $f = -2$ and $g = 8$. So, the factorization is $x^2 + 6x - 16 = (x + f)(x + g) = (x - 2)(x + 8)$, allowing you to rewrite the original equation as $(x - 2)(x + 8) = 0$. The only way for a product to equal zero is for one of the factors to equal zero; so, either $x - 2 = 0$ (in which case $x = 2$) or $x + 8 = 0$ (in which case $x = -8$). Thus, the equation has the solution $x = 2$ or $x = -8$.

In the case that $a \neq 1$, you can attempt to factor the quadratic polynomial $ax^2 + bx + c$ in the form $(mx + f)(nx + g)$ by a similar trial-and-error procedure, but the work tends to be much harder.

Review Video: Factoring Quadratic Equations
Visit mometrix.com/academy and enter code: 336566

COMPLETING THE SQUARE

The technique of completing the square comes from a simple observation: Suppose you have the expression $x^2 + bx$. If you take half the linear coefficient, b, square it, and add the result to the expression, the result is always a perfect square trinomial:

$$x^2 + bx + \left(\frac{b}{2}\right)^2 = \left(x + \frac{b}{2}\right)^2$$

For example, if you begin with $x^2 + 6x$ and add the square of half of 6 (half of 6 is 3, and $3^2 = 9$), then you get a perfect square trinomial:

$$x^2 + 6x + 9 = (x + 3)^2$$

This also works if b is negative. For instance, if you begin with the expression $x^2 - 10x$ and complete the square by adding 25 (half of -10 is -5, and $(-5)^2 = 25$), then you get another perfect square trinomial:

$$x^2 - 10x + 25 = (x - 5)^2$$

Now, suppose you want to solve the equation $x^2 + bx + c = 0$. Subtract c from both sides, to get the equation $x^2 + bx = -c$. Complete the square on the left side by adding $(b/2)^2$, but also add this same term to the right side so that the new equation is equivalent to the old one:

$$x^2 + bx + \left(\frac{b}{2}\right)^2 = -c + \left(\frac{b}{2}\right)^2$$
$$\left(x + \frac{b}{2}\right)^2 = -c + \left(\frac{b}{2}\right)^2$$

Take square roots of both sides:

$$x + \frac{b}{2} = \pm\sqrt{-c + \left(\frac{b}{2}\right)^2}$$

Remember to include $\pm$ since every positive number has both a positive and a negative square root. Subtract $b/2$ from both sides to isolate the variable x to finish the problem:

$$x = -\frac{b}{2} \pm \sqrt{-c + \left(\frac{b}{2}\right)^2}$$

This may sound complicated, but in practice it is not hard. For example, suppose you want to solve the equation $x^2 + 6x - 16 = 0$ by completing the square. First, add 16 to both sides:

$$x^2 + 6x = 16$$

Half of 6 is 3 and $3^2 = 9$, so complete the square by adding 9 to both sides of the equation:

$$x^2 + 6x + 9 = 16 + 9$$
$$(x + 3)^2 = 25$$

Now take square root of both sides, remembering to include the $\pm$:

$$\sqrt{(x + 3)^2} = \pm\sqrt{25}$$
$$x + 3 = \pm 5$$
$$x = -3 \pm 5$$

So we see that the two solutions to the equation are $x = 2$ and $x = -8$.

Review Video: Completing the Square
Visit mometrix.com/academy and enter code: 982479

Using Given Solutions to Find a Quadratic Equation

To find a quadratic equation with given numbers as solutions, simply find a quadratic polynomial that has those numbers as zeros and set that polynomial equal to zero. This is easy because a polynomial has the number p as a zero precisely when it has the binomial $x - p$ as a factor. Thus, for instance, to find a quadratic polynomial with zeros at $x = 3$ and $x = -5$, construct the polynomial $P(x) = (x - 3)(x - (-5)) = (x - 3)(x + 5) = x^2 + 2x - 15$. Setting this equal to zero produces an equation, $x^2 + 2x - 15 = 0$, whose solutions are $x = 3$ and $x = -5$.

Of course, any constant multiple $P(x) = a(x - 3)(x + 5)$ will also have the same zeros. For instance, if you choose $a = 4$, then you get the polynomial $P(x) = 4(x - 3)(x + 5) = 4x^2 + 8x - 60$, which also has zeros at

$x = 3$ and $x = -5$. From this you can get another equation, $4x^2 + 8x - 60 = 0$, with solutions $x = 3$ and $x = -5$.

Basics of Functions

Definition of a Function

A function is a rule that assigns to every number in a given set (called the **domain**) exactly one corresponding value. For example, if our domain is the set $\{-2,1,2,3\}$, we can define a function by assigning to each number its square. This function assigns to -2 the value 4, to 1 the value 1, to 2 the value 4, and to 3 the value 9 (since $(-2)^2 = 4$, $1^2 = 1$, $2^2 = 4$, and $3^2 = 9$). The set of all the values assigned by a function is the **range** of the function. The range of the function in our example is the set $\{1, 4, 9\}$. We may think of a function as a kind of machine: we give it a number as an input, and it uses its rule to produce a number as an output. In the squaring function above, the input 3 produces the output 9.

Review Video: What is a Function?
Visit mometrix.com/academy and enter code: 784611

Function Notation

We usually name a function by a letter, often the letter f (for *function*—if we need to talk about more than one function, we name the second one g, the third one h, etc.). To specify the value (the output) corresponding to a particular number in the domain (the input), we write the function letter followed by the input number in parentheses. For instance, in the example above the notation $f(3)$ means the value that the function assigns to the number 3, namely 9—that is, $f(3) = 9$. We read the symbols $f(3)$ as, "f of 3," and we call 3 the **argument** of the function and 9 the **value** of the function (so *argument* means *input* and *value* means *output*).

Using function notation we can define the squaring function above by listing the values the function assigns to each argument in the domain: $f(-2) = 4$. $f(1) = 1$, $f(2) = 4$, and $f(3) = 9$. More efficiently, we can define the function by the single equation $f(x) = x^2$, which says that if x is a number from the domain, then we calculate the value assigned to it by substituting the number x in the formula x^2. For instance, we calculate $f(5) = 5^2 = 25$. Similarly, if we define a function g by the equation $g(x) = x^2 - 4x + 7$, then we calculate the value $g(3)$ by substituting 3 for each x in the formula: $g(3) = 3^2 - 4 \cdot 3 + 7 = 9 - 12 + 7 = 4$.

Other Ways to Define Functions

Instead of denoting the value of the function by $f(x)$, sometimes we simply use another letter, usually y. For instance, instead of defining the squaring function by the equation $f(x) = x^2$, we might use the equation $y = x^2$. In this case, we refer to x (the input) as the **independent variable** and y (the output) as the **dependent variable** because the value, y, depends on the number we choose for x.

A formula (with y or $f(x)$) is the most common way to define a function; but sometimes, if the domain is small enough, we prefer to list explicitly the possible inputs and their corresponding outputs. Some ways of doing this appear above, but a more common approach is to put the input-output pairs in a table. For instance, we can define the squaring function above by the table

x	-2	1	2	3
y	4	1	4	9

We see that the domain of this function is the set of all numbers in the x-row and the range is the set of all numbers in the y-row. We note that numbers cannot repeat in the x-row (because a function assigns exactly one value to each argument in the domain) but they can repeat in the y-row (because the function can assign the same value to multiple arguments—for instance, the number 4 appears twice in the y-row).

We can also define a function by writing the inputs and corresponding outputs as ordered pairs of x- and y-values. For instance, we can write the squaring function above as the set of ordered pairs

$\{(-2,4), (1,1), (2,4), (3,9)\}$. Further, by treating these ordered pairs as coordinates and plotting the corresponding points on the coordinate plane, we get the **graph** of the function:

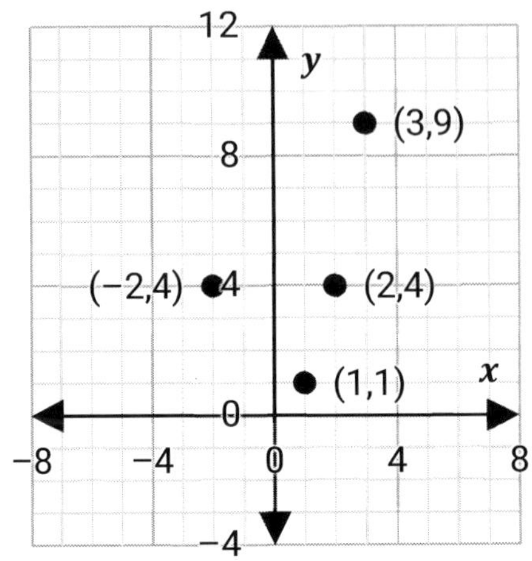

Turning this around, we can potentially use a graph to define a function, namely the function consisting of the coordinate pairs of all the points in the graph. This always works unless the graph has two points with the same x-coordinate (because then the function would assign two different y-values to the same x). It is easy to detect such points: because they have the same x-coordinate, a vertical line passes through both of them. Thus, a graph always defines a function unless it is possible to draw a vertical line that intersects the graph in two or more points. We call this condition the **vertical line test**. For example, if our graph is a circle, then by the Vertical Line Test the graph does not define a function because there are vertical lines that will intersect the circle in two different points.

More on Domains and Ranges

When we define a function by a formula and do not specify the domain, then by default the domain consists of all real numbers for which the formula produces an answer. For instance, suppose we define a function f by the formula $f(x) = 1/x$. If $x = 0$, then $1/x = 1/0$, which is undefined. But if x is any other real number, then we can calculate the value of $1/x$. So, the default domain of this function is all real numbers except zero. Because of this domain convention, the graph of a function defined by a formula usually consists of infinitely many points that “connect to” each other in a way that produces a line or curve (see examples below) rather than the isolated points we see in the squaring function above.

If we have the graph of a function, its domain consists of all numbers on the x-axis with corresponding points on the graph and its range consists of all numbers on the y-axis with corresponding points on the graph. For example, consider the function $f(x) = x^2 + 3$:

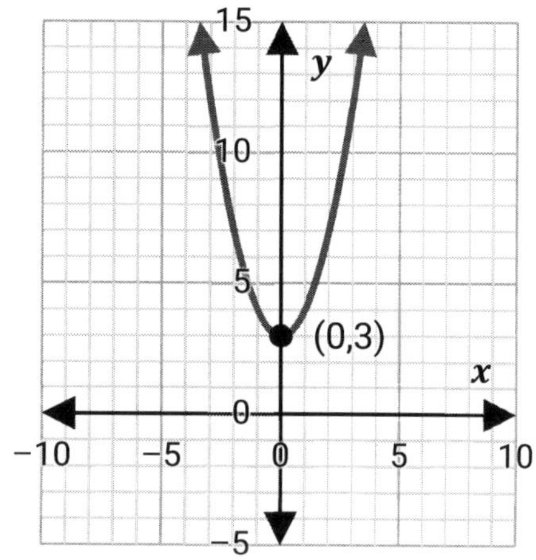

Since the graph continues infinitely to the left and right beyond what we can see, every point on the x-axis has a corresponding point on the graph; so, the domain of this function is all real numbers. On the other hand, the lowest point on this graph has a y-value of 3, and the graph passes through all higher y-values. So, the range of this function is all real numbers greater than or equal to 3, which we can denote algebraically by $y \geq 3$ or, using interval notation, by $[3, \infty)$.

Review Video: How to Find Domain and Range
Visit mometrix.com/academy and enter code: 778133

Review Video: Domain and Range of Quadratic Functions
Visit mometrix.com/academy and enter code: 331768

Monotonic and Even/Odd Functions

A function, f, is **increasing** if it always assigns larger values to larger arguments. It is **decreasing** if it always assigns smaller values to larger arguments. That is, f is increasing if $a < b$ always guarantees $f(a) < f(b)$, and it is decreasing if $a < b$ always guarantees $f(a) > f(b)$. The graph of an increasing function consistently rises from left to right, and the graph of a decreasing function consistently falls from left to right. For example, the function $f(x) = 2x$ is an increasing function because doubling a larger number always gives us a larger result

Mathematics

than doubling a smaller number. The graph of $f(x) = 2x$ is a line with slope $m = 2$, which, as we expect, rises from left to right. We call a function **monotonic** if it is either increasing or decreasing.

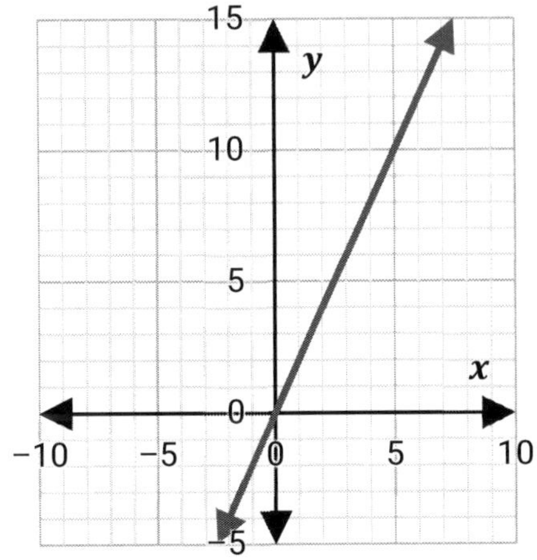

A function, f, is **even** if changing the sign of its argument produces the same value. It is **odd** if changing the sign of its argument produces the same value except with the opposite sign. That is, f is even if $f(-x) = f(x)$ and odd if $f(-x) = -f(x)$ for every argument x. The function $f(x) = x^2 + 3$ is even because substituting opposite arguments always produces the same value. For instance, $f(5) = 28$ and $f(-5) = 28$ because $5^2 + 3 = 25 + 3 = 28$ and $(-5)^2 + 3 = 25 + 3 = 28$. The function $f(x) = 2x$ is odd because substituting opposite arguments always produces opposite values. For instance, $f(10) = 20$ and $f(-10) = -20$ because $2(10) = 20$ and $2(-10) = -20$. The graph of an even function is always symmetric with respect to the y-axis, making the left and right halves of the graph mirror images of each other, as in the graph of the even function $f(x) = x^2 + 3$ above. The graph of an odd function is always symmetric with respect to the origin. This means that if we rotate the graph 180° around the origin (think of sticking a pin through the origin on a sheet of graph paper and rotating the paper halfway around) the graph looks the same, as in the graph of the odd function $f(x) = 2x$ above.

It is worth noting that most functions are neither increasing nor decreasing (that is, they are not monotonic) and most functions are neither even nor odd. For example, the function $f(x) = x^2 - x$ is neither increasing nor decreasing and neither even nor odd: its graph neither rises nor falls consistently, and it is symmetric with respect to neither the y-axis nor the origin.

Review Video: Even and Odd Functions
Visit mometrix.com/academy and enter code: 278985

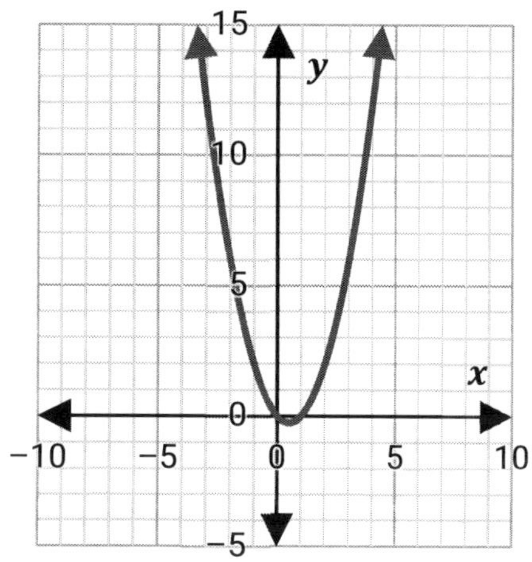

INVERTIBLE (ONE-TO-ONE) FUNCTIONS

A function, f, is one-to-one if it never assigns the same value to different arguments—that is, if $f(a)$ and $f(b)$ are different whenever a and b are different. The graph of a one-to-one function never has two points that lie on the same horizontal line because such points would have different x-values but the same y-value. Thus, a function is one-to-one if it is impossible to draw a horizontal line that intersects its graph in more than one point. We call this condition the **horizonal line test**. For example, the graph of the function $f(x) = 2x$ above is a line that rises from left to right. Every horizontal line intersects this line in exactly one point, so the function $f(x) = 2x$ is one-to-one. This is also clear without the graph because it is impossible to double two different numbers and get the same answer.

When a function, f, is one-to-one, it is possible to define its inverse function, f^{-1}, that "undoes" what f does, assigning to each output from f the input that produced it. That is, for each x in the domain of f, if $y = f(x)$, then $f^{-1}(y) = x$. For example, the inverse of the function $f(x) = 2x$ above is $f^{-1}(y) = y/2$. So, for instance, $f(5) = 2 \cdot 5 = 10$, and $f^{-1}(10) = 10/2 = 5$ (and similarly for every other value of x). Thus, the domain of f^{-1} is the range of f and vice versa. If a function, f, has an inverse, we say that f is **invertible**. Since a function has an inverse precisely when it is one-to-one, the terms *invertible* and *one-to-one* are synonyms.

If f is an invertible function defined by a formula, then to find its inverse we simply write the equation $y = f(x)$ and solve it for x (that is, we isolate the x). The result will be the equation $f^{-1}(y) = x$. For instance, starting with the function $f(x) = 2x$, we write $y = 2x$ and isolate the x by dividing both sides of the equation by 2. This gives us $y/2 = x$, so we know that $f^{-1}(y) = y/2$. Although this procedure is theoretically simple, in practice the algebra can be difficult.

COMMON FUNCTIONS

Certain functions and certain kinds of functions are particularly useful, coming up frequently in mathematics and its applications. Once we know some basic function terminology and concepts, it is useful to begin developing a mental library of the most common and useful functions.

Review Video: Common Functions
Visit mometrix.com/academy and enter code: 629798

Mathematics

CONSTANT FUNCTIONS

A function of the form $f(x) = a$, where a is a real number, is a **constant function**. This function assigns the same value, a, to every real argument x. For instance, given the constant function $f(x) = 5$, we have $f(2) = 5$, $f(100) = 5$, and $f(-7.1) = 5$.

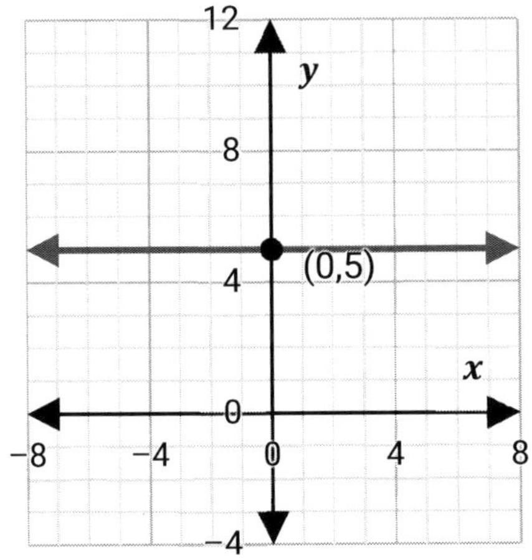

The domain of a constant function is the set of all real numbers, and the range is the set containing the single number a. Its graph is a horizontal line passing through the number $y = a$ on the y-axis (we call the number at which a function's graph intersects the y-axis the ***y*-intercept** of the function).

THE IDENTITY FUNCTION

The function $f(x) = x$ is the **identity function**. Its value always equals its argument. Thus, for instance, $f(2) = 2$, $f(100) = 100$, and $f(-7.1) = -7.1$.

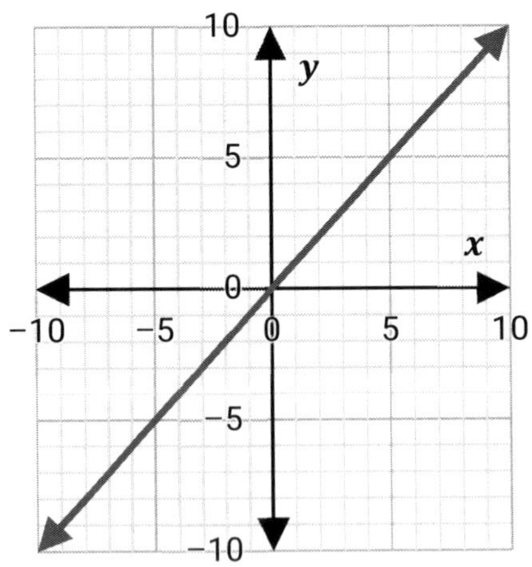

Its domain and range are the set of all real numbers. It is both an increasing function and an odd function. Its graph is a line that passes through the origin and rises from left to right at a 45° angle to the horizontal. Since it passes through the origin, its y intercept is $y = 0$ and it also has an ***x*-intercept** (a number at which the function's graph intersects the x-axis) of $x = 0$.

LINEAR FUNCTIONS

A function of the form $f(x) = ax + b$, where a and b are real numbers (with $a \neq 0$), is a **linear function** (the identity function is a linear function with $a = 1$ and $b = 0$). Its domain and range are the set of all real numbers. Its graph is a line (the word *linear* contains the root word *line*) with one x-intercept (at $x = -b/a$), with a y-intercept at $y = b$, and with a direction and steepness that depend on the coefficient a, which we call the **slope**. Specifically, the slope a is the amount the y-value increases for each increase of 1 in the x-value. Thus, for $a > 0$, the line rises from left to right (making f an increasing function), and larger values of a produce steeper ascents. Similarly, for $a < 0$, the line falls from left to right (making f a decreasing function), and smaller (more negative) values of a produce steeper descents. For instance, the graph of the linear function $f(x) = (1/2)x + 3$ is a line that passes through the point $y = 3$ on the y-axis and that rises by $1/2$ unit for every unit that x increases.

Review Video: Linear Functions
Visit mometrix.com/academy and enter code: 200735

Review Video: Graphing Linear Functions
Visit mometrix.com/academy and enter code: 699478

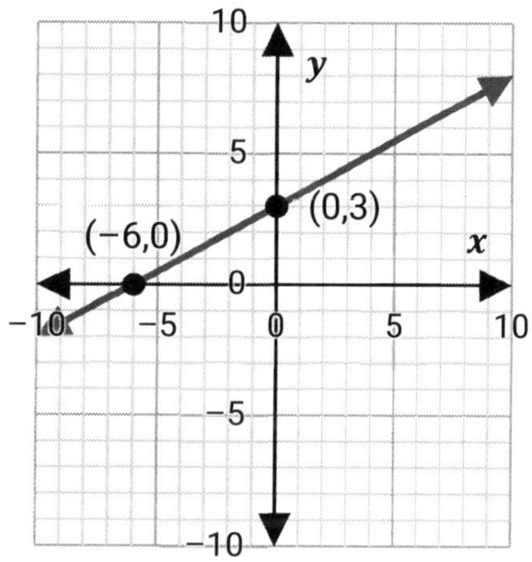

In many contexts it is standard to use the letter m for slope and thus to write the general form of a linear function as $f(x) = mx + b$, known as **slope-intercept form**.

THE SQUARING FUNCTION

The function $f(x) = x^2$ is the **squaring function**.

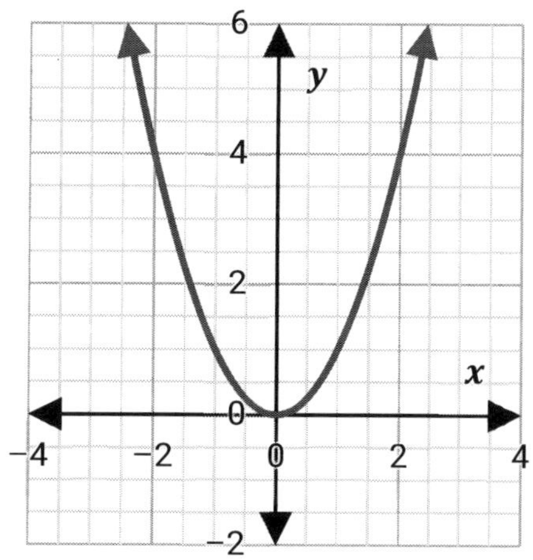

Its graph is U-shaped, opening upward as shown, a shape known as a **parabola**. It has a lowest point, its **vertex**, at the origin, which is also the location of its single x-intercept and single y-intercept. Thus, its **minimum** is $y = 0$, its domain is the set of all real numbers, and its range is the set of nonnegative real numbers (that is, $y \geq 0$). It is an even function and thus symmetric with respect to the y-axis (which we call the **axis of symmetry**), meaning that the left half of the graph is the mirror image of the right half, with the mirror standing on the y-axis.

Quadratic Functions

A function of the form $f(x) = ax^2 + bx + c$, where a, b, and c are real numbers (with $a \neq 0$), is a **quadratic function** (the squaring function is a quadratic function with $a = 1, b = 0$, and $c = 0$). Its domain is the set of all real numbers, and its graph is a parabola. It is symmetric with respect to its axis of symmetry, the vertical line $x = -b/(2a)$. If $a > 0$, the parabola opens upward, so that its vertex is at its lowest point (its minimum) and its range consists of all real numbers greater than or equal to this minimum y-value. If $a < 0$, the parabola opens downward, so that its vertex is at its highest point (its maximum) and its range consists of all real numbers less than or equal to this maximum y-value. Its y-intercept is $y = c$ since $f(0) = c$, and it may have zero, one, or two x-intercepts. For example, the function $f(x) = x^2 - 6x + 5$ has $a = 1, b = -6$, and $c = 5$.

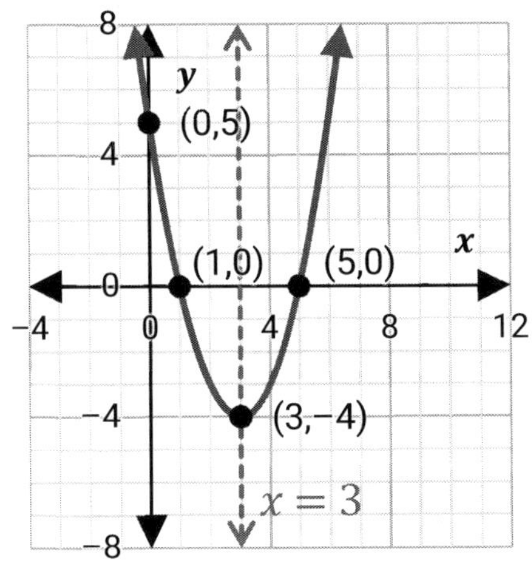

Its graph opens upward (because $a > 0$) and its axis of symmetry is the vertical line $x = 3$ (since $-b/(2a) = -(-6)/(2 \cdot 1) = 3$). Its y-intercept is at $y = 5$. It turns out to have its vertex at the point $(3, -4)$, making its minimum value $y = -4$. So, its domain is the set of all real numbers, and its range is $y \geq -4$. It also turns out to have two x-intercepts, at $x = 1$ and at $x = 5$ (since $f(1) = 0$ and $f(5) = 0$).

Polynomial Functions

A function of the form $f(x) = a^n x^n + a^{n-1} x^{n-1} + \cdots + a_2 x^2 + a_1 x + a_0$, where n is a whole number and $a_0, a_1, a_2, \ldots a_{n-1}, a_n$ are real numbers, is a **polynomial function of degree n**. Its domain is the set of all real numbers (it is complicated to describe its range in general), and its y-intercept is $y = a_0$ (since $f(0) = a_0$). Constant functions, linear functions, and quadratic functions are polynomial functions of degrees 0, 1, and 2, respectively. In general, a polynomial function of degree n has up to n zeros (x-intercepts) and up to $n - 1$ "bends." For example, the fourth degree polynomial function $f(x) = x^4 - 11x^3 + 41x^2 - 61x + 30$, whose graph appears here, has four x-intercepts (at $x = 1, x = 2, x = 3$, and $x = 5$) and three "bends," and its y-intercept (not visible on the graph) is at $y = 30$.

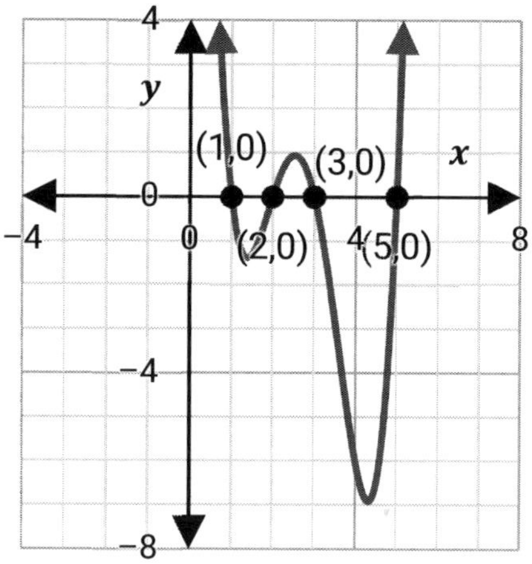

RATIONAL FUNCTIONS

A function of the form $f(x) = P(x)/Q(x)$, where P and Q are polynomials, is a rational function (we note that the word *rational* includes the root word *ratio*, indicating that a rational function is a ratio of polynomial functions). The domain of a rational function is all real numbers except the zeros of $Q(x)$ since division by zero is undefined (the range can be difficult to describe in general). Its y-intercept is $f(0)$, if this is defined; and its x-intercepts are the zeros of $P(x)$ that are in the domain of f, if there are any. A rational function may also have vertical asymptotes (vertical lines that the graph approaches without crossing) and a horizontal asymptote (a horizontal line that the curve approaches as x becomes very small or very large (toward the left and right edges of the graph). For example, the rational function $f(x) = (2x^2 + x - 1)/(x^2 + x - 2)$ has as its domain the set of all real numbers except $x = -2$ and $x = 1$ (since those numbers make the denominator zero).

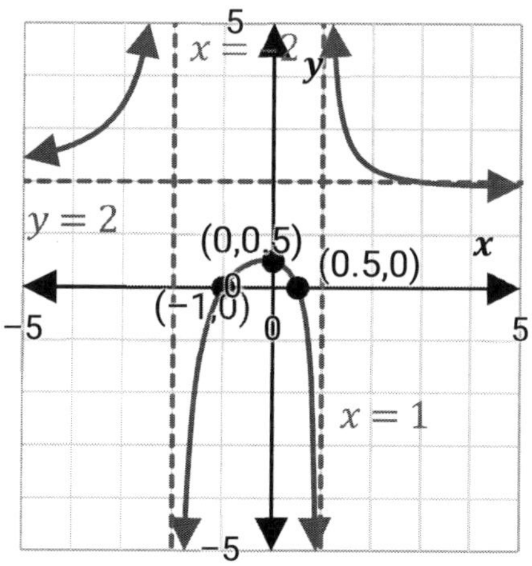

It has a y-intercept of $y = 1/2$ since $f(0) = (-1)/(-2) = 1/2$, and it has x-intercepts at $x = -1$ and at $x = 1/2$ since those numbers make the numerator zero. It has vertical asymptotes at $x = -2$ and $x = 1$ (not coincidentally, these are the numbers omitted from the domain) and a horizontal asymptote at $y = 2$. It is important to note that vertical asymptotes cannot be crossed in rational functions, but horizontal asymptotes

Mathematics

can be crossed if the function tends near the asymptote at infinity and does not go past all possible turning points.

Review Video: Simplifying Rational Polynomial Functions
Visit mometrix.com/academy and enter code: 351038

Review Video: Horizontal Asymptotes
Visit mometrix.com/academy and enter code: 747796

THE SQUARE ROOT FUNCTION

The function $f(x) = \sqrt{x}$ is the square root function.

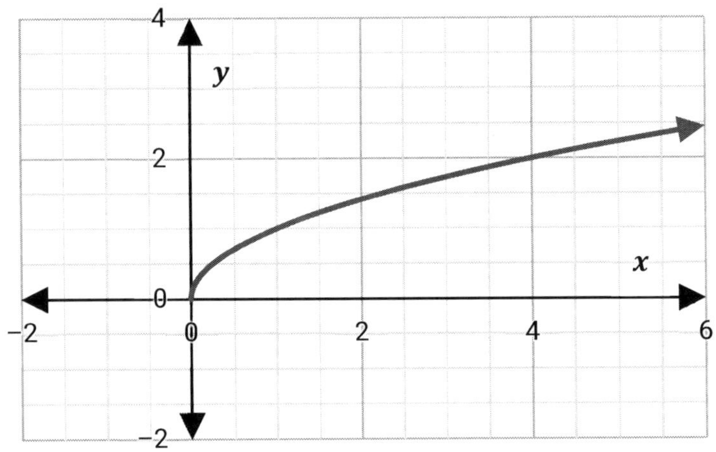

It is an increasing function, and its domain and range are both the set of all nonnegative real numbers. It has one x-intercept and one y-intercept, both appearing at the origin. Its graph is the upper half of a parabola opening to the right. The square root function is the inverse of the squaring function with domain restricted to the nonnegative real numbers (that is, $f(x) = x^2$ for $x \geq 0$).

PIECEWISE-DEFINED FUNCTIONS

As the name suggests, a **piecewise-defined function** (or, simply, a **piecewise function**) is a function defined by different rules on different pieces of the domain. We define such a function using the following form:

Function Name	Rule to Apply	Piece of the Domain on Which the Rule Applies
$f(x) =$	Rule 1,	First Piece of the Domain
	Rule 2,	Second Piece of the Domain
	Rule 3,	Third Piece of the Domain
	etc.,	etc.

The pieces of the domain should not overlap, and together they should cover the whole domain. For example, we might craft a piecewise-defined function by

$$f(x) = \begin{cases} x^2, & \text{if } x < 2 \\ 3x - 5, & \text{if } x \geq 2 \end{cases}$$

The two pieces of the domain—namely, $x < 2$ and $x \geq 2$—do not overlap, and together they include all real numbers. To evaluate the function for a particular argument x, we determine which piece of the domain includes x and then apply the corresponding rule. For instance, to find $f(4)$, we note that $4 \geq 2$; so, we apply the rule $3x - 5$ to get the value $f(4) = 3 \cdot 4 - 5 = 7$. Similarly, to find $f(-6)$, we note that $-6 < 2$; so, we apply the rule x^2 to get the value $f(-6) = (-6)^2 = 36$.

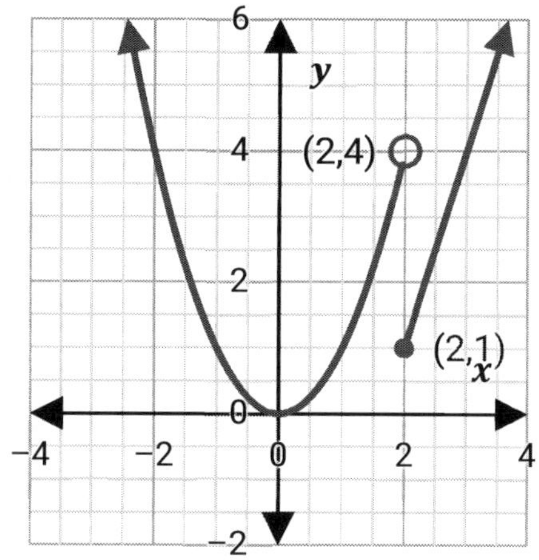

To graph this function, we sketch the graph of the parabola $y = x^2$ on the part of the plane where $x < 2$ and we sketch the line $y = 3x - 5$ on the part of the plane where $x \geq 2$. This produces a graph with a jump at $x = 2$ (a discontinuity—piecewise-defined functions are useful for producing graphs with discontinuities). We plot an open circle at the point (2,4), the end of the left part of the graph, to show that this point is not part of the graph. And we plot a solid dot at the point (2,1), the start of the right part of the graph, to show that this point *is* part of the graph.

Review Video: Piecewise Functions
Visit mometrix.com/academy and enter code: 707921

The Absolute Value Function

A particularly useful piecewise-defined function is the absolute value function. It is so important that instead of naming it $f(x)$ or $g(x)$, we denote it using the special notation $|x|$. Its definition is

$$|x| = \begin{cases} -x, & \text{if } x < 0 \\ x, & \text{if } x \geq 0 \end{cases}$$

For instance, $|8| = 8$ (since $8 \geq 0$) and $|-5| = -(-5) = 5$, since $-5 < 0$. So, the absolute value function acts like the identity function for nonnegative numbers (it leaves them unchanged), and it gives the opposite of negative numbers (it effectively strips off the minus sign). Thus, we can think of the absolute value of a real number as its distance from zero on the number line, without taking into consideration whether the number is larger than or smaller than zero. For instance, $|-3| = 3$ and $|3| = 3$, showing that both -3 and 3 are three units away from zero. The absolute value function is an even function with a V-shaped graph that looks like the line $y = x$ (the identity function) on the right "half" of the plane (for $x \geq 0$) and the line $y = -x$ on the left "half" of the plane (for $x < 0$).

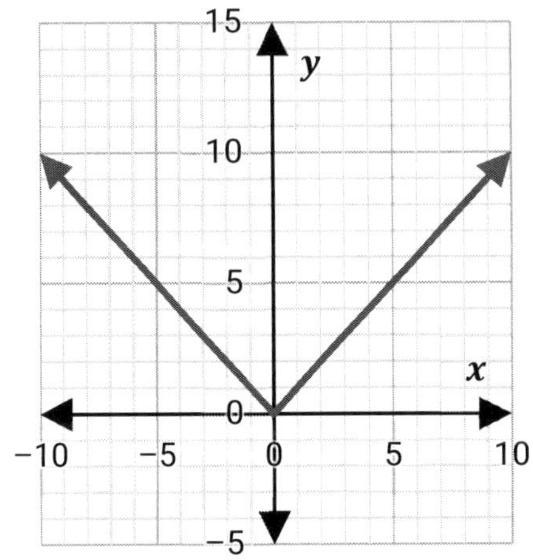

WORKING WITH FUNCTIONS

MANIPULATION OF FUNCTIONS

Translation occurs when values are added to or subtracted from the x- or y-values. If a constant is added to the y-portion of each point, the graph shifts up. If a constant is subtracted from the y-portion of each point, the graph shifts down. This is represented by the expression $f(x) \pm k$, where k is a constant. If a constant is added to the x-portion of each point, the graph shifts left. If a constant is subtracted from the x-portion of each point, the graph shifts right. This is represented by the expression $f(x \pm k)$, where k is a constant.

Stretching, compression, and reflection occur when different parts of a function are multiplied by different groups of constants. If the function as a whole is multiplied by a real number constant greater than 1, $(k \times f(x))$, the graph is stretched vertically. If k in the previous equation is greater than zero but less than 1, the graph is compressed vertically. If k is less than zero, the graph is reflected about the x-axis, in addition to being either stretched or compressed vertically if k is less than or greater than –1, respectively. If instead, just the x-term is multiplied by a constant greater than 1 $(f(k \times x))$, the graph is compressed horizontally. If k in the previous equation is greater than zero but less than 1, the graph is stretched horizontally. If k is less than zero, the graph is reflected about the y-axis, in addition to being either stretched or compressed horizontally if k is greater than or less than –1, respectively.

> **Review Video: Manipulation of Functions**
> Visit mometrix.com/academy and enter code: 669117

APPLYING THE BASIC OPERATIONS TO FUNCTIONS

For each of the basic operations, we will use these functions as examples: $f(x) = x^2$ and $g(x) = x$.

To find the sum of two functions f and g, assuming the domains are compatible, simply add the two functions together: $(f + g)(x) = f(x) + g(x) = x^2 + x$.

To find the difference of two functions f and g, assuming the domains are compatible, simply subtract the second function from the first: $(f - g)(x) = f(x) - g(x) = x^2 - x$.

To find the product of two functions f and g, assuming the domains are compatible, multiply the two functions together: $(f \times g)(x) = f(x) \times g(x) = x^2 \times x = x^3$.

To find the quotient of two functions f and g, assuming the domains are compatible, divide the first function by the second: $\left(\frac{f}{g}\right)(x) = \frac{f(x)}{g(x)} = \frac{x^2}{x} = x\,; x \neq 0$.

The example given in each case is fairly simple, but on a given problem, if you are looking only for the value of the sum, difference, product, or quotient of two functions at a particular x-value, it may be simpler to solve the functions individually and then perform the given operation using those values.

The composite of two functions f and g, written as $(f \circ g)(x)$ simply means that the output of the second function is used as the input of the first. This can also be written as $f(g(x))$. In general, this can be solved by substituting $g(x)$ for all instances of x in $f(x)$ and simplifying. Using the example functions $f(x) = x^2 - x + 2$ and $g(x) = x + 1$, we can find that $(f \circ g)(x)$ or $f(g(x))$ is equal to $f(x + 1) = (x + 1)^2 - (x + 1) + 2$, which simplifies to $x^2 + x + 2$.

It is important to note that $(f \circ g)(x)$ is not necessarily the same as $(g \circ f)(x)$. The process is not always commutative like addition or multiplication expressions. It *can* be commutative, but most often this is not the case.

Evaluating Linear Functions

A **function** can be expressed as an equation that relates an input to an output where each input corresponds to exactly one output. The input of a function is defined by the x-variable, and the output is defined by the y-variable. For example, consider the function $y = 2x + 6$. The value of y, the output, is determined by the value of the x, the input. If the value of x is 3, the value of y is $y = 2(3) + 6 = 6 + 6 = 12$. This means that when $x = 3, y = 12$. This can be expressed as the ordered pair (3,12).

It is common for function equations to use the form $f(x) =$ instead of $y =$. However, $f(x)$ and y represent the same thing. We read $f(x)$ as "f of x." The expression "f of x" implies that the value of f depends on the value of x. The function used in the example above could be expressed as $y = 2x + 6$ or $f(x) = 2x + 6$. Both functions represent the same line when graphed.

Functions that are expressed in the form $f(x) =$ are evaluated in the same way the equations are evaluated in the form $y =$. For example, when evaluating the function $f(x) = 3x - 2$ for $f(6)$, substitute 6 in for x, and simplify. In this case, $f(x) = 3x - 2$ becomes $f(6) = 3(6) - 2 = 18 - 2 = 16$. When x is 6, $f(x)$ is 16.

Example: To find the value of $f(8)$, calculate as follows:

$$f(x) = 3x - 2$$
$$f(8) = 3(8) - 2$$
$$f(8) = 22$$

Review Video: Evaluating Functions
Visit mometrix.com/academy and enter code: 588515

Advanced Functions

Step Functions

The double brackets indicate a step function. For a step function, the value inside the double brackets is rounded down to the nearest integer. The graph of the function $f_0(x) = [\![x]\!]$ appears on the left graph. In comparison $f(x) = 2\left[\!\left[\frac{1}{3}(x - 1)\right]\!\right]$ is on the right graph. The coefficient of 2 shows that it's stretched vertically by a factor of 2 (so there's a vertical distance of 2 units between successive "steps"). The coefficient of $\frac{1}{3}$ in front

Mathematics

of the x shows that it's stretched horizontally by a factor of 3 (so each "step" is three units long), and the $x - 1$ shows that it's displaced one unit to the right.

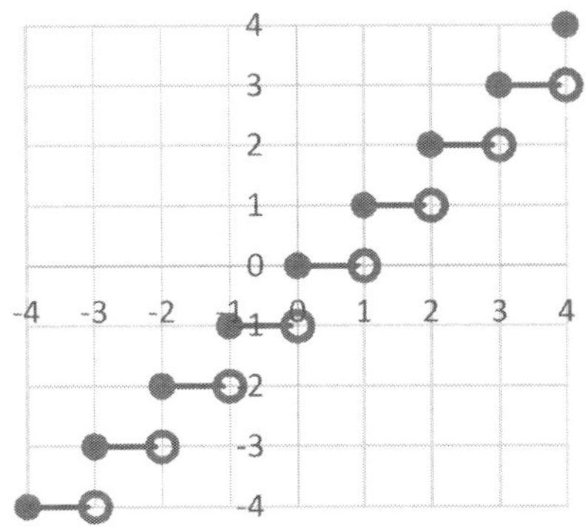

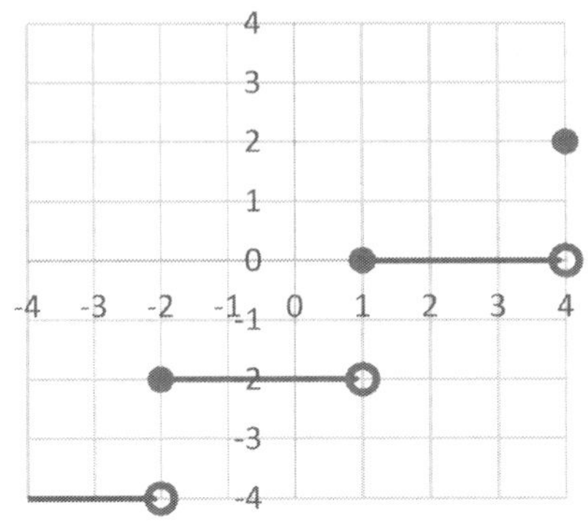

Transcendental Functions

Roughly speaking, algebraic functions are functions defined by formulas involving numbers and variables combined by addition, subtraction, multiplication, division, powers (but not variable powers), and roots. **Transcendental functions** are functions that are not algebraic. A function that includes logarithms, trigonometric functions, or variables as exponents, is transcendental, not algebraic, even if the function also includes polynomials or roots.

Exponential Functions

Exponential functions are functions that have the form $y = b^x$, where base $b > 0$ and $b \neq 1$. The exponential function can also be written $f(x) = b^x$. The following properties apply to exponential expressions:

Property	Description
$a^x a^y = a^{x+y}$	The product of exponentials with the same base equals the base raised to the sum of the powers
$a^x/a^y = a^{x-y}$	The quotient of exponentials with the same base equals the base raised to the difference of the powers
$(a^x)^y = a^{xy}$	An exponential raised to a power equals the base raised to the product of the powers
$(ab)^x = a^x b^x$	Exponentiation distributes over multiplication
$(a/b)^x = a^x/b^x$	Exponentiation distributes over division

The graph of an example exponential function, $f(x) = 2^x$, is below:

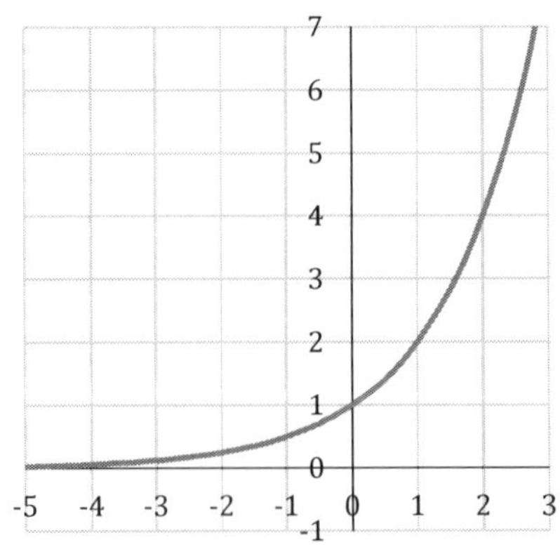

Note in the graph that the y-value approaches zero to the left and infinity to the right. One of the key features of an exponential function is that there will be one end that goes off to infinity and another that asymptotically approaches a lower bound. Common forms of exponential functions include the following:

Geometric sequences: The terms of a geometric sequence have the form $a_n = a_1 \times r^{n-1}$, where a_n is the value of the nth term, a_1 is the initial term, and r is the common ratio between succesive terms. Note that $a_1 \times r^{1-1} = a_1 \times r^0 = a_1 \times 1 = a_1$

Review Video: Geometric Sequences
Visit mometrix.com/academy and enter code: 140779

General exponential growth or decay: The general exponential growth or decay function is $f(t) = a(1+r)^t$, where the value of $f(t)$ is the amount (of whatever quantity we are measuring) at time t, the constant a is the initial amount (the amount at time $t = 0$), and the constant r is the fixed rate of increase (if $r > 0$) or decrease (if $r < 0$) per unit time. For example, if we invest \$1000 at an interest rate of 6% interest compounded annually and we measure time in years, then our investment will grow according to an exponential model with $a = \$1000$ and $r = 6\% = 0.06$. Thus, after t years the value of our investment will be $f(t) = \$1000(1+0.06)^t$. After 5 years, for instance, the investment will grow to $f(5) = \$1000(1+0.06)^5 \approx \$1338.23$.

Compound interest: We can modify the general exponential growth function above slightly to get a formula for interest compounded n times per year. Replacing the constant a with P (for principal, the initial amount we invest), the total value of our investment after t years is $f(t) = P\left(1+\frac{r}{n}\right)^{nt}$, where r is the nominal annual interest rate. Thus, if we change our \$1000 investment above by having the interest rate be 6% compounded *semiannually* (two times per year—so $n = 2$), the value of our investment after t years is $f(t) = \$1000\left(1+\frac{0.06}{2}\right)^{2t} = \$1000(1+0.03)^{2t}$. After 5 years, for instance, the investment will grow to $f(5) = \$1000(1+0.03)^{10} \approx \$1343.92$. This is slightly higher than the previous investment because the interest compounds twice as often.

Review Video: Compound Interest Formula
Visit mometrix.com/academy and enter code: 100366

Review Video: Interest Functions
Visit mometrix.com/academy and enter code: 559176

Population growth and continuously compounded interest: When a quantity grows (or decays) continuously at a rate that stays constant relative to the size the quantity has already attained, then we can model its size at time t with the function $f(t) = ae^{rt}$, where a is the initial amount, r is the relative growth rate (which we often call simply the **growth rate**), and e is the irrational constant known as Euler's number (approximately 2.718; scientific calculators have a button for finding e^x, which is known as the **natural exponential function**). For instance, under some circumstances, if an initial population (of people, plants, or animals, for example) of size a grows at constant relative rate r, then the size of the population at time t is $f(t) = ae^{rt}$. Similarly, if we invest principal P (instead of a) for t years at nominal annual interest rate r compounded *continuously*, then after t years the value of the investment is $f(t) = Pe^{rt}$.

For example, suppose the initial population of a town is $a = 1{,}200$ people and the relative annual growth rate is $r = 5\% = 0.05$. Then the population of the town after t years is $f(t) = ae^{rt} = 1200e^{0.05t}$. After 10 years, for instance, the town population is $f(10) = 1200e^{0.05 \cdot 10} = 1200e^{0.5} \approx 1978$ people.

Review Video: Population Growth
Visit mometrix.com/academy and enter code: 109278

Mathematics

LOGARITHMIC FUNCTIONS

The **logarithmic function base b** is the function $y = \log_b x$ or $f(x) = \log_b x$, where the base b may be any positive number except one. The most common bases for logarithms are base 10 (the **common logarithm**) and base e (the **natural logarithm**). We usually write the common logarithm as $y = \log x$ (that is, $\log x$, with no base listed, means $\log_{10} x$) and the natural logarithm as $y = \ln x$ (that is, $\ln x$ means $\log_e x$).

Exponential functions and logarithmic functions with the same base are inverse functions. That is, if $f(x) = b^x$, then $f^{-1}(x) = \log_b x$. This means that the two equations $y = b^x$ (exponential form) and $x = \log_b y$ (logarithmic form) express the same relationship between the quantities x and y. We often solve problems involving logarithms by rewriting them in exponential form, and vice versa. Also, because of this inverse relationship, logarithms and exponentials cancel each other. That is, $\log_b b^x = x$ and $b^{\log_b x} = x$.

The following properties apply to logarithmic expressions:

Property	Description
$\log_b 1 = 0$	The log of 1 is equal to 0 for any base
$\log_b b = 1$	The log of the base is equal to 1
$\log_b b^p = p$	The log of the base raised to a power is equal to that power
$\log_b MN = \log_b M + \log_b N$	The log of a product is the sum of the log of each factor
$\log_b \frac{M}{N} = \log_b M - \log_b N$	The log of a quotient is equal to the log of the dividend minus the log of the divisor
$\log_b M^p = p \log_b M$	The log of a value raised to a power is equal to the power times the log of the value

Logarithms are helpful in solving equations in which the variable appears in an exponent. For instance, consider the example above in which we model the population of a town by the function $f(t) = 1200e^{0.05t}$. Suppose we want to know how long it will take the population of the town to double to 2400 people from its original value of 1200. We find this by solving the equation $1200e^{0.05t} = 2400$. First, we divide both sides of the equation by 1200 to get $e^{0.05t} = 2$. Then we take natural logarithms of both sides to get $\ln e^{0.05t} = \ln 2$, which simplifies (because natural logarithms and natural exponentials are inverse functions) to $0.05t = \ln 2$. Finally, we divide both sides by 0.05 to get $t = (\ln 2)/0.05$, which we evaluate with a calculator to get $t \approx$ 13.9 years.

The graph of an example logarithmic function, $f(x) = \log_2(x + 2)$, is below:

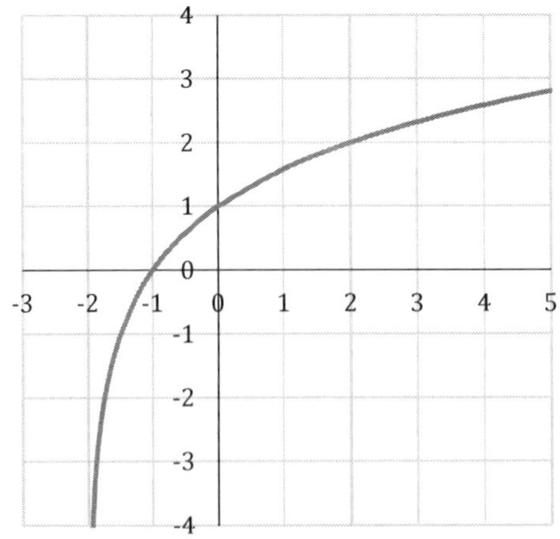

Review Video: Logarithmic Function
Visit mometrix.com/academy and enter code: 658985

Geometry

Points, Lines, and Planes

Points and Lines

A **point** is a fixed location in space, has no size or dimensions, and is commonly represented by a dot. A **line** is a set of points that extends infinitely in two opposite directions. It has length, but no width or depth. A line can be defined by any two distinct points that it contains. A **line segment** is a portion of a line that has definite endpoints. A **ray** is a portion of a line that extends from a single point on that line in one direction along the line. It has a definite beginning, but no ending.

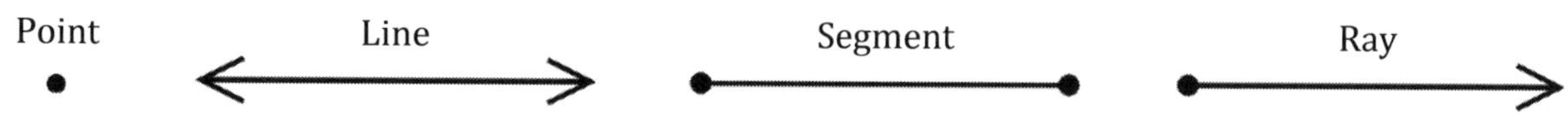

Points are **collinear** if there is a single line that passes through all of them. Otherwise, they are noncollinear. Two points are always collinear since two points define a line. Three points may be noncollinear. For example, the three vertices of a triangle are noncollinear since there is no line that goes through all three of them.

Interactions Between Lines

Intersecting lines are lines that have exactly one point in common. **Concurrent lines** are multiple lines that intersect at a single point. **Perpendicular lines** are lines that intersect at right angles. They are represented by the symbol ⊥. The shortest distance from a line to a point not on the line is a perpendicular segment from the point to the line. **Parallel lines** are lines in the same plane that have no points in common and never meet. Two distinct lines in a given plane are always either intersecting or parallel. **Skew lines** are two distinct lines in a three dimensional space that do not intersect and may also not be parallel because there is no single plane that contains them both.

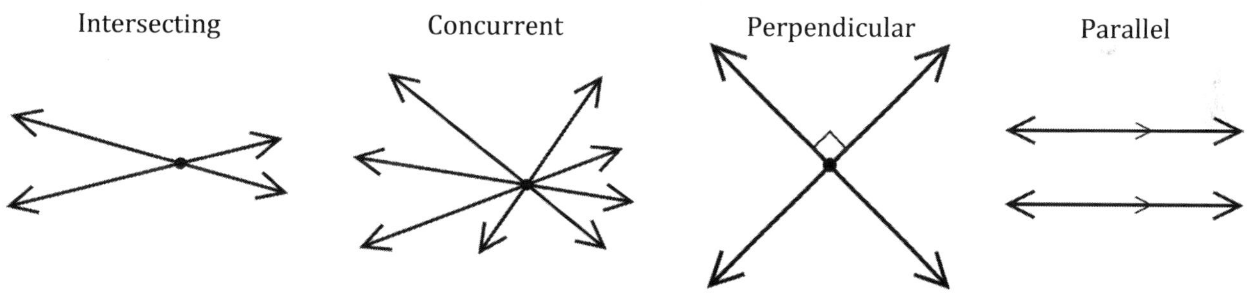

Review Video: Parallel and Perpendicular Lines
Visit mometrix.com/academy and enter code: 815923

A **transversal** is a line that intersects at least two other lines, which may or may not be parallel to one another. A transversal that intersects parallel lines is a common occurrence in geometry. A **bisector** is a line or line segment that divides another line segment into two equal lengths. A **perpendicular bisector** of a line segment is composed of points that are equidistant from the endpoints of the segment it is dividing.

Transversal

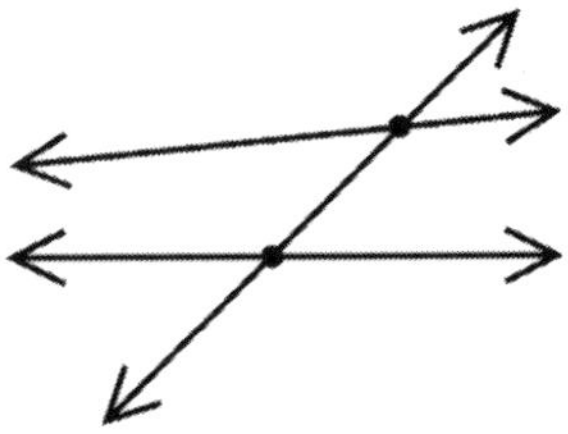

Bisector

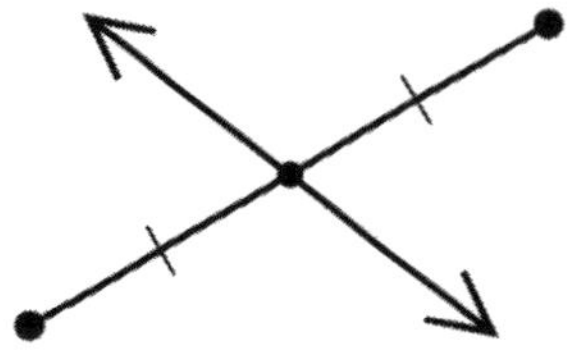

Perpendicular bisector

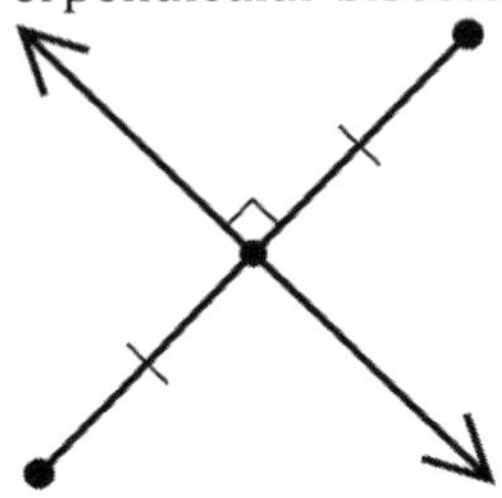

The **projection of a point on a line** is the point at which a perpendicular line drawn from the given point to the given line intersects the line. This is also the shortest distance from the given point to the line. The **projection of a segment on a line** is a segment whose endpoints are the points formed when perpendicular lines are drawn from the endpoints of the given segment to the given line. This is similar to the length a diagonal line appears to be when viewed from above.

Projection of a point on a line

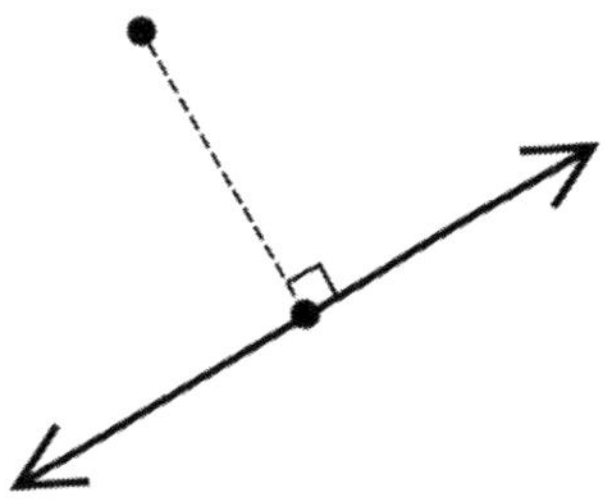

Projection of a segment on a line

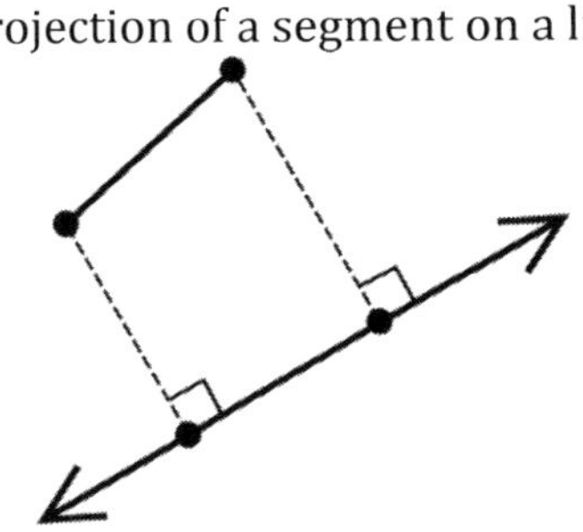

Planes

A **plane** is a two-dimensional flat surface defined by three non-collinear points. A plane extends an infinite distance in all directions in those two dimensions. It contains an infinite number of points, parallel lines and segments, intersecting lines and segments, as well as parallel or intersecting rays. A plane will never contain a three-dimensional figure or skew lines. Two given planes are either parallel or they intersect at a line. A plane may intersect a circular conic surface to form **conic sections**, such as a parabola, hyperbola, circle or ellipse.

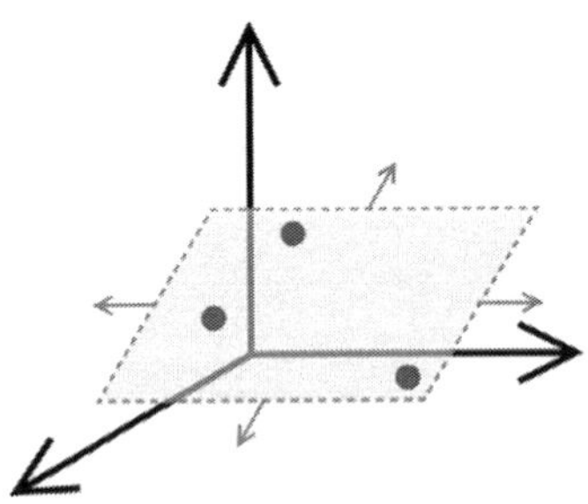

Review Video: Lines and Planes Visit mometrix.com/academy and enter code: 554267

Angles

Angles and Vertices

An **angle** is formed when two lines or line segments meet at a common point. It may be a common starting point for a pair of segments or rays, or it may be the intersection of lines. Angles are represented by the symbol ∠.

The **vertex** is the point at which two segments or rays meet to form an angle. If the angle is formed by intersecting rays, lines, and/or line segments, the vertex is the point at which four angles are formed. The pairs of angles opposite one another are called vertical angles, and their measures are equal.

- An **acute** angle is an angle with a degree measure less than 90°.
- A **right** angle is an angle with a degree measure of exactly 90°.
- An **obtuse** angle is an angle with a degree measure greater than 90° but less than 180°.
- A **straight angle** is an angle with a degree measure of exactly 180°.
- A **reflex angle** is an angle with a degree measure greater than 180° but less than 360°.
- A **full angle** is an angle with a degree measure of exactly 360°.

Review Video: Angles
Visit mometrix.com/academy and enter code: 264624

Relationships Between Angles

Two angles whose sum is exactly 90° are said to be **complementary**. The two angles may or may not be adjacent. In a right triangle, the two acute angles are complementary.

Two angles whose sum is exactly 180° are said to be **supplementary**. The two angles may or may not be adjacent. Two intersecting lines always form two pairs of supplementary angles. Adjacent supplementary angles will always form a straight line.

Two angles that have the same vertex and share a side are said to be **adjacent**. Vertical angles are not adjacent because they share a vertex but no common side.

Review Video: Adjacent Angles
Visit mometrix.com/academy and enter code: 100375

Adjacent
Share vertex and side

Not adjacent
Share part of a side, but not vertex

When two lines are cut by a transversal, the angles that are between the two lines are **interior angles**. In the diagram below, angles 3, 4, 5, and 6 are interior angles.

When two lines are cut by a transversal, the angles that are outside the lines are **exterior angles**. In the diagram below, angles 1, 2, 7, and 8 are exterior angles.

When two lines are cut by a transversal, the angles that are in the same position relative to the transversal and the cut lines are **corresponding angles**. The diagram below has four pairs of corresponding angles: angles 1 and 5, angles 2 and 6, angles 3 and 7, and angles 4 and 8. Corresponding angles formed by parallel lines are congruent.

When two lines are cut by a transversal, the two interior angles that are on opposite sides of the transversal are called **alternate interior angles**. In the diagram below, there are two pairs of alternate interior angles:

angles 3 and 6, and angles 4 and 5. Alternate interior angles formed by parallel lines are congruent. Similarly, the two interior angles on the same side of the transversal (angles 3 and 5, and angles 4 and 6) are supplementary when the transversed lines are parallel. Some books call these angles **same side interior angles**.

When two lines are cut by a transversal, the two exterior angles that are on opposite sides of the transversal are called **alternate exterior angles.** In the diagram below, there are two pairs of alternate exterior angles: angles 1 and 8, and angles 2 and 7. Alternate exterior angles formed by parallel lines are congruent. Similarly, the two exterior angles on the same side of the transversal (angles 1 and 7, and angles 2 and 8) are supplementary when the transversed lines are parallel. Some books call these angles **same side exterior angles**.

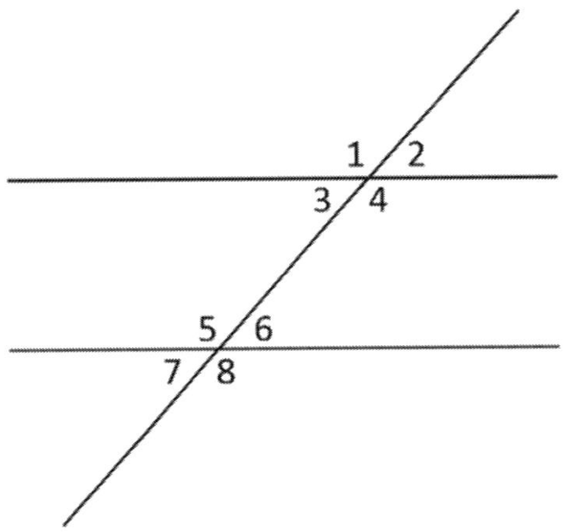

When two lines intersect, four angles are formed. The non-adjacent angles at this vertex are called vertical angles. Vertical angles are congruent. In the diagram, $\angle ABD \cong \angle CBE$ and $\angle ABC \cong \angle DBE$. The other pairs of angles, $(\angle ABC, \angle CBE)$ and $(\angle ABD, \angle DBE)$, are supplementary, meaning the pairs sum to 180°.

Review Video: Congruent Angles
Visit mometrix.com/academy and enter code: 642874

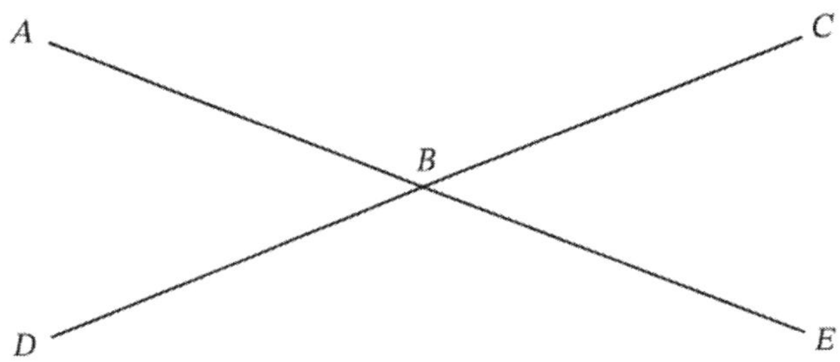

Polygons

A **polygon** is a closed, two-dimensional figure with three or more straight line segments called **sides.** The point at which two sides of a polygon intersect is called the **vertex**. In a polygon, the number of sides is always equal to the number of vertices. A polygon with all sides congruent and all angles equal is called a **regular polygon**. Common polygons are:

Triangle = 3 sides
Quadrilateral = 4 sides
Pentagon = 5 sides
Hexagon = 6 sides
Heptagon = 7 sides
Octagon = 8 sides
Nonagon = 9 sides
Decagon = 10 sides
Dodecagon = 12 sides

More generally, an n-gon is a polygon that has n angles and n sides.

Review Video: Intro to Polygons
Visit mometrix.com/academy and enter code: 271869

The sum of the interior angles of an n-sided polygon is $(n - 2) \times 180°$. For example, in a triangle $n = 3$. So the sum of the interior angles is $(3 - 2) \times 180° = 180°$. In a quadrilateral, $n = 4$, and the sum of the angles is $(4 - 2) \times 180° = 360°$.

Review Video: Sum of Interior Angles
Visit mometrix.com/academy and enter code: 984991

Convex and Concave Polygons

A **convex polygon** is a polygon whose diagonals all lie within the interior of the polygon. A **concave polygon** is a polygon with at least one diagonal that is outside the polygon. In the diagram below, quadrilateral $ABCD$ is concave because diagonal $\overline{AC}$ lies outside the polygon and quadrilateral $EFGH$ is convex because both diagonals lie inside the polygon.

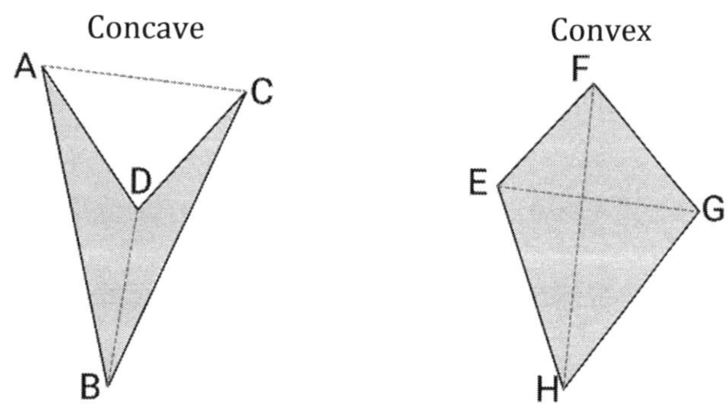

Apothem and Radius

A line segment from the center of a regular polygon that is perpendicular to a side of the polygon is called the **apothem**. A line segment from the center of a regular polygon to a vertex of the polygon is called a **radius.** In a regular polygon, the apothem can be used to find the area of the polygon using the formula $A = \frac{1}{2}ap$, where a is the apothem, and p is the perimeter.

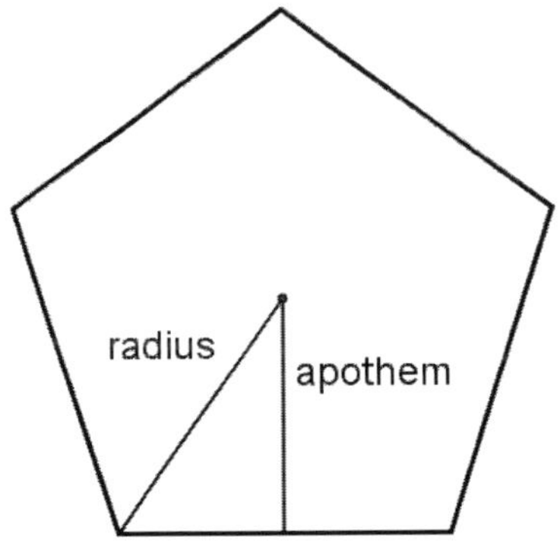

A **diagonal** is a line segment that joins two non-adjacent vertices of a polygon. The number of diagonals a polygon has can be found by using the formula:

$$\text{number of diagonals} = \frac{n(n-3)}{2}$$

Note that n is the number of sides in the polygon. This formula works for all polygons, not just regular polygons.

Congruence and Similarity

Congruent figures are geometric figures that have the same size and shape. For congruent polygons all corresponding angle measures are equal, and all corresponding side lengths are equal. Congruence is indicated by the symbol $\cong$. For instance, the expression $ABC \cong DEF$ indicates that the triangles below are congruent. The order of the letters is important, indicating which parts of the polygons correspond to each other. For example, since the letters A and D both come first, $\angle A$ and $\angle D$ have the same measure.

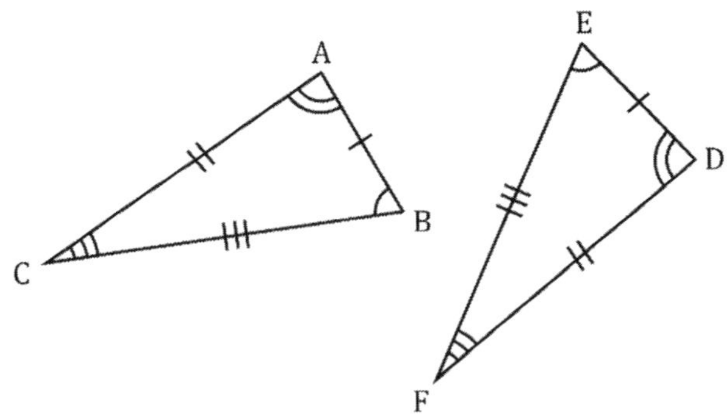

Similar figures are geometric figures that have the same shape, but do not necessarily have the same size. For similar polygons all corresponding angle measures are equal, and all corresponding side lengths are proportional, but they do not have to be equal. It is indicated by the symbol $\sim$. For instance, the expression

$ABC{\sim}DEF$ indicates that the triangles below are similar. Again, the order of the letters indicates which parts of the polygons correspond to each other.

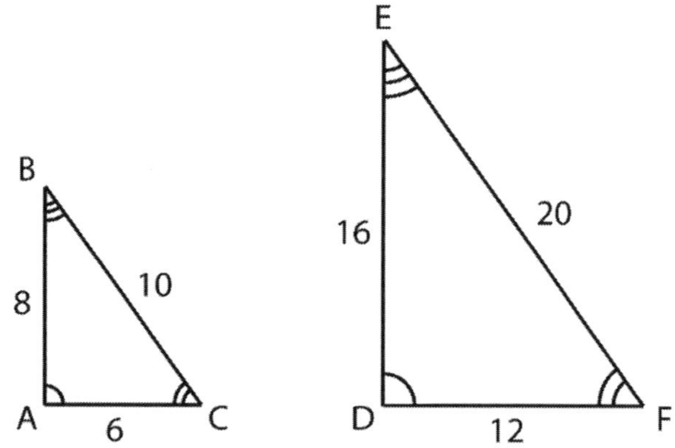

Note that all congruent figures are also similar, but not all similar figures are congruent.

Review Video: Congruent Shapes
Visit mometrix.com/academy and enter code: 492281

LINE OF SYMMETRY

A line that divides a figure or object into congruent parts that are mirror images of each other across the line is called a **line of symmetry**. An object may have no lines of symmetry, one line of symmetry, or multiple (i.e., more than one) lines of symmetry.

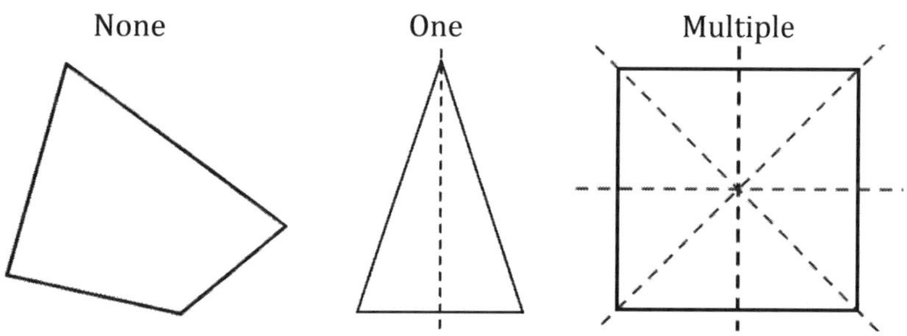

Review Video: Symmetry
Visit mometrix.com/academy and enter code: 528106

Mathematics

TRIANGLES

A triangle is a three-sided figure with the sum of its interior angles being 180°. The **perimeter of any triangle** is found by summing the three side lengths; $P = a + b + c$. For an equilateral triangle, this is the same as $P = 3a$, where a is any side length, since all three sides are the same length.

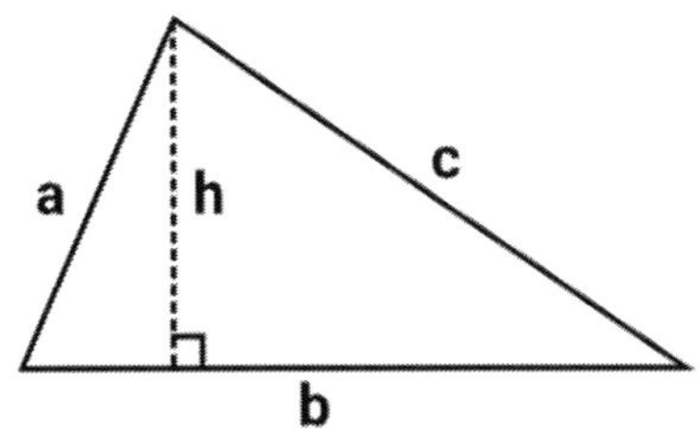

Review Video: Proof that a Triangle is 180 Degrees
Visit mometrix.com/academy and enter code: 687591

Review Video: Area and Perimeter of a Triangle
Visit mometrix.com/academy and enter code: 853779

The **area of any triangle** can be found by taking half the product of one side length referred to as the base, often given the variable b and the perpendicular distance from that side to the opposite vertex called the altitude or height and given the variable h. In equation form that is $A = \frac{1}{2}bh$. Another formula that works for any triangle is $A = \sqrt{s(s-a)(s-b)(s-c)}$, where s is the semiperimeter: $\frac{a+b+c}{2}$, and a, b, and c are the lengths of the three sides. Special cases include isosceles triangles, $A = \frac{1}{2}b\sqrt{a^2 - \frac{b^2}{4}}$, where b is the unique side and a is the length of one of the two congruent sides, and equilateral triangles, $A = \frac{\sqrt{3}}{4}a^2$, where a is the length of a side.

Review Video: Area of Any Triangle
Visit mometrix.com/academy and enter code: 138510

PARTS OF A TRIANGLE

An **altitude** of a triangle is a line segment drawn from one vertex perpendicular to the opposite side. In the diagram that follows, $\overline{BE}$, $\overline{AD}$, and $\overline{CF}$ are altitudes. The length of an altitude is also called the height of the triangle. The three altitudes in a triangle are always concurrent. The point of concurrency of the altitudes of a triangle, O, is called the **orthocenter**. Note that in an obtuse triangle, the orthocenter will be outside the triangle, and in a right triangle, the orthocenter is the vertex of the right angle.

A **median** of a triangle is a line segment drawn from one vertex to the midpoint of the opposite side. In the diagram that follows, $\overline{BH}$, $\overline{AG}$, and $\overline{CI}$ are medians. This is not the same as the altitude, except the altitude to the base of an isosceles triangle and all three altitudes of an equilateral triangle. The point of concurrency of the medians of a triangle, T, is called the **centroid**. This is the same point as the orthocenter only in an equilateral triangle. Unlike the orthocenter, the centroid is always inside the triangle. The centroid can also be considered the exact center of the triangle. Any shape triangle can be perfectly balanced on a tip placed at the centroid. The centroid is also the point that is two-thirds the distance from the vertex to the opposite side.

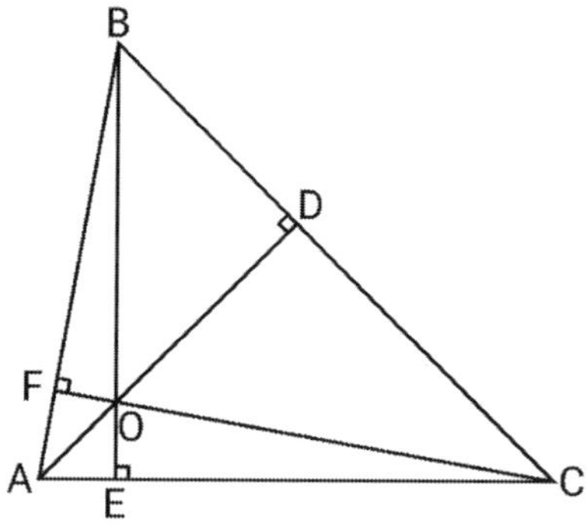

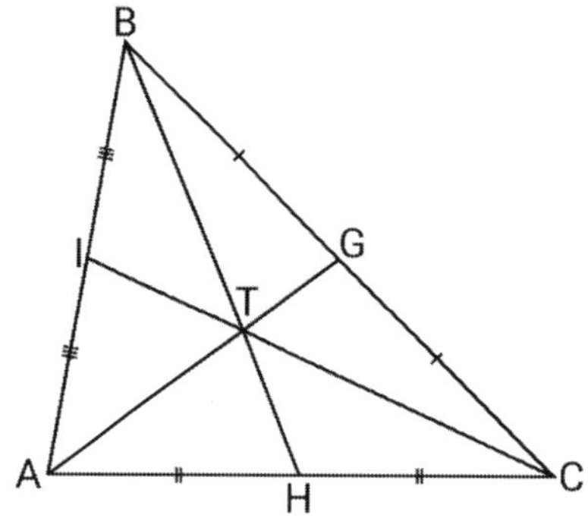

Review Video: Centroid, Incenter, Circumcenter, and Orthocenter
Visit mometrix.com/academy and enter code: 598260

TRIANGLE PROPERTIES

CLASSIFICATIONS OF TRIANGLES

A **scalene triangle** is a triangle with no congruent sides. A scalene triangle will also have three angles of different measures. The angle with the largest measure is opposite the longest side, and the angle with the smallest measure is opposite the shortest side. An **acute triangle** is a triangle whose three angles are all less than 90°. If two of the angles are equal, the acute triangle is also an **isosceles triangle**. An isosceles triangle will also have two congruent angles opposite the two congruent sides. If the three angles are all equal, the acute triangle is also an **equilateral triangle**. An equilateral triangle will also have three congruent angles, each 60°. All equilateral triangles are also acute triangles. An **obtuse triangle** is a triangle with exactly one angle greater than 90°. The other two angles may or may not be equal. If the two remaining angles are equal, the obtuse triangle is also an isosceles triangle. A **right triangle** is a triangle with exactly one angle equal to 90°. All right triangles follow the Pythagorean theorem. A right triangle can never be acute or obtuse.

The table below illustrates how each descriptor places a different restriction on the triangle:

Angles / Sides	Acute: All angles < 90°	Obtuse: One angle > 90°	Right: One angle = 90°
Scalene: No equal side lengths	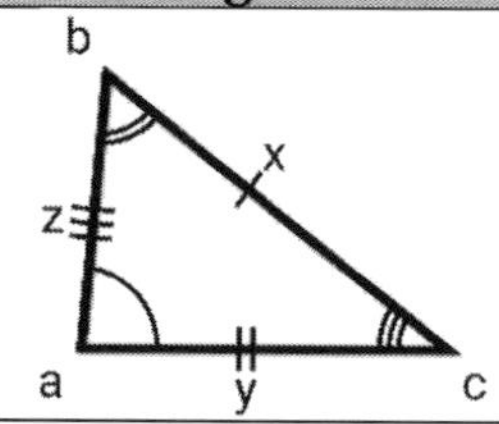	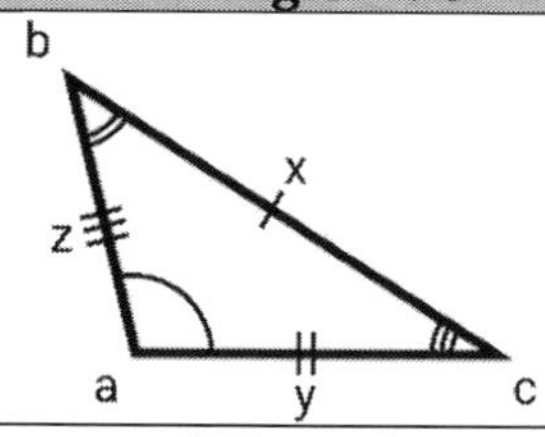	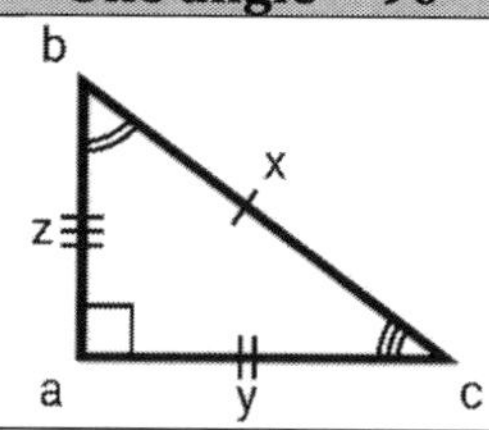
	$90° > \angle a > \angle b > \angle c$ $x > y > z$	$\angle a > 90° > \angle b > \angle c$ $x > y > z$	$90° = \angle a > \angle b > \angle c$ $x > y > z$
Isosceles: Two equal side lengths	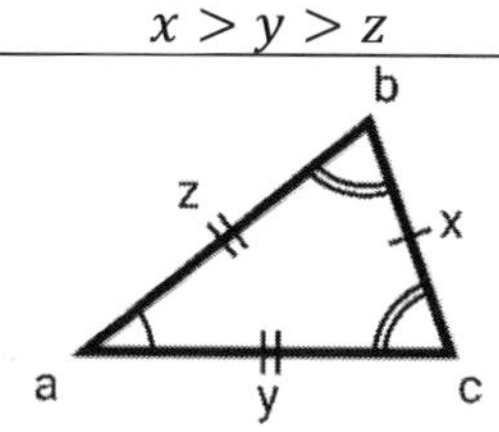	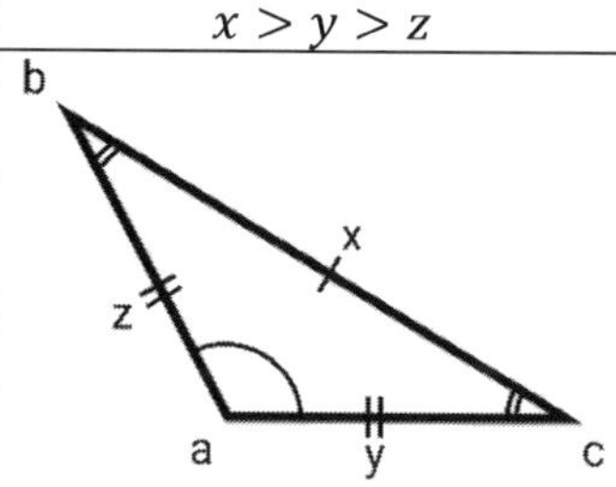	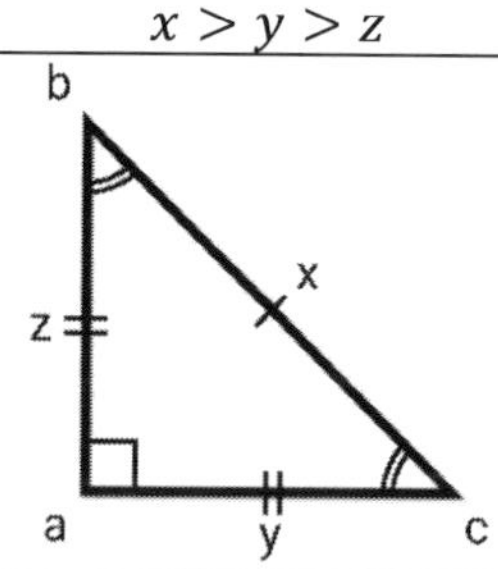

Mathematics

Angles / Sides	**Acute:** **All angles < 90°**	**Obtuse:** **One angle > 90°**	**Right:** **One angle = 90°**
	$90° > \angle a, \angle b, or \angle c$ $\angle b = \angle c, \quad y = z$	$\angle a > 90° > \angle b = \angle c$ $x > y = z$	$\angle a = 90°$ $\angle b = \angle c = 45°$ $x > y = z$
Equilateral: Three equal side lengths	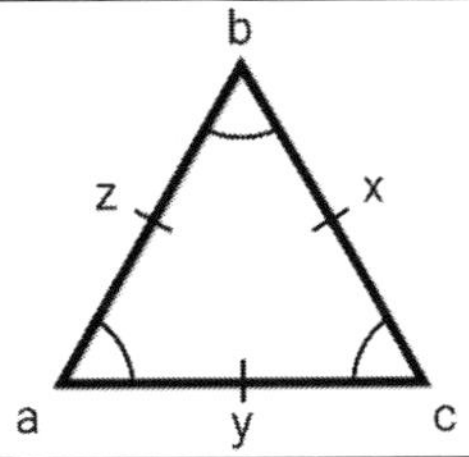 		
	$60° = \angle a = \angle b = \angle c$ $x = y = z$		

Review Video: Introduction to Types of Triangles
Visit mometrix.com/academy and enter code: 511711

General Rules for Triangles

The **triangle inequality theorem** states that the sum of the measures of any two sides of a triangle is always greater than the measure of the third side. If the sum of the measures of two sides were equal to the third side, a triangle would be impossible because the two sides would lie flat across the third side and there would be no vertex. If the sum of the measures of two of the sides was less than the third side, a closed figure would be impossible because the two shortest sides would never meet. In other words, for a triangle with sides lengths A, B, and C: $A + B > C$, $B + C > A$, and $A + C > B$.

The sum of the measures of the interior angles of a triangle is always 180°. Therefore, a triangle can never have more than one angle greater than or equal to 90°.

In any triangle, the angles opposite congruent sides are congruent, and the sides opposite congruent angles are congruent. The largest angle is always opposite the longest side, and the smallest angle is always opposite the shortest side.

The line segment that joins the midpoints of any two sides of a triangle is always parallel to the third side and exactly half the length of the third side.

Review Video: General Rules (Triangle Inequality Theorem)
Visit mometrix.com/academy and enter code: 166488

Similarity and Congruence Rules

Similar triangles are triangles whose corresponding angles are equal and whose corresponding sides are proportional. Represented by AAA. Similar triangles whose corresponding sides are congruent are also congruent triangles.

Triangles can be shown to be **congruent** in 5 ways:

- **SSS**: Three sides of one triangle are congruent to the three corresponding sides of the second triangle.
- **SAS**: Two sides and the included angle (the angle formed by those two sides) of one triangle are congruent to the corresponding two sides and included angle of the second triangle.
- **ASA**: Two angles and the included side (the side that joins the two angles) of one triangle are congruent to the corresponding two angles and included side of the second triangle.

- **AAS**: Two angles and a non-included side of one triangle are congruent to the corresponding two angles and non-included side of the second triangle.
- **HL**: The hypotenuse and leg of one right triangle are congruent to the corresponding hypotenuse and leg of the second right triangle.

Review Video: Similar Triangles
Visit mometrix.com/academy and enter code: 398538

QUADRILATERALS

A **quadrilateral** is a closed two-dimensional geometric figure that has four straight sides. The sum of the interior angles of any quadrilateral is 360°.

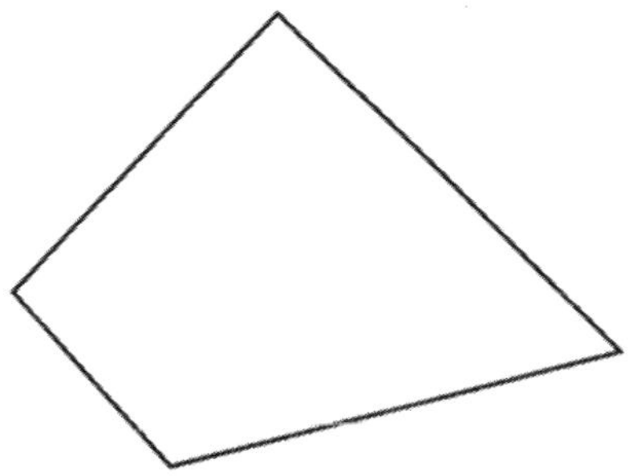

Review Video: Diagonals of Parallelograms, Rectangles, and Rhombi
Visit mometrix.com/academy and enter code: 320040

KITE

A **kite** is a quadrilateral with two pairs of adjacent sides that are congruent. A result of this is perpendicular diagonals. A kite can be concave or convex and has one line of symmetry.

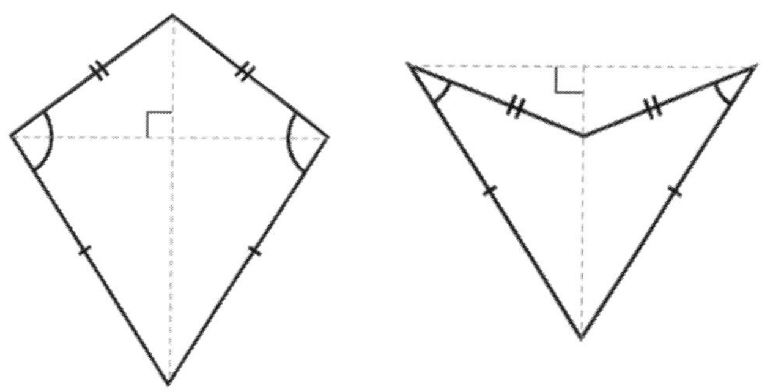

TRAPEZOID

Trapezoid: A trapezoid is defined as a quadrilateral that has at least one pair of parallel sides. There are no rules for the second pair of sides. So, there are no rules for the diagonals and no lines of symmetry for a trapezoid.

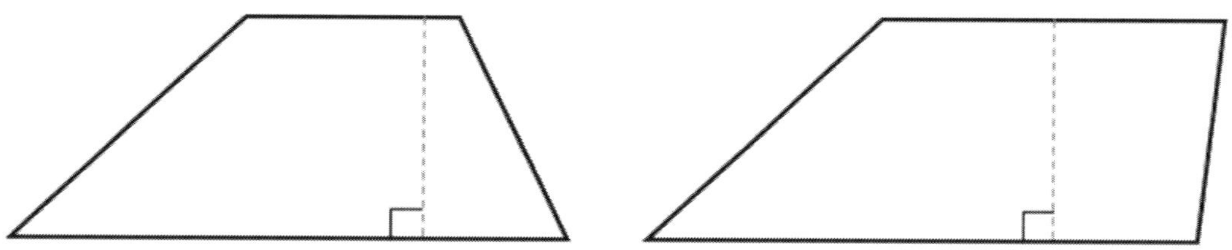

The **area of a trapezoid** is found by the formula $A = \frac{1}{2}h(b_1 + b_2)$, where h is the height (segment joining and perpendicular to the parallel bases), and b_1 and b_2 are the two parallel sides (bases). Do not use one of the other two sides as the height unless that side is also perpendicular to the parallel bases.

The **perimeter of a trapezoid** is found by the formula $P = a + b_1 + c + b_2$, where a, b_1, c, and b_2 are the four sides of the trapezoid.

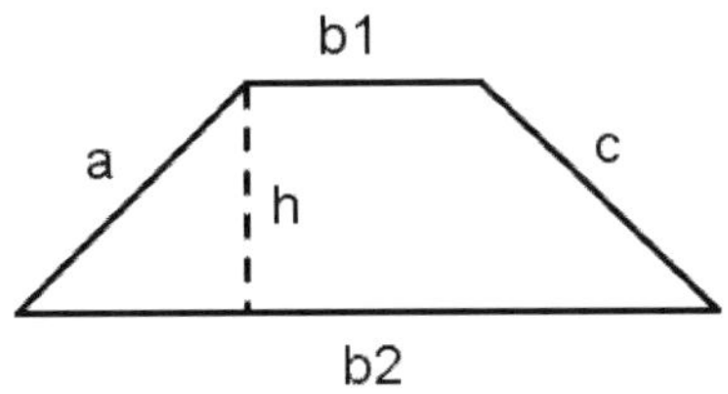

Review Video: Area and Perimeter of a Trapezoid
Visit mometrix.com/academy and enter code: 587523

Isosceles trapezoid: A trapezoid with equal base angles. This gives rise to other properties including: the two nonparallel sides have the same length, the two non-base angles are also equal, and there is one line of symmetry through the midpoints of the parallel sides.

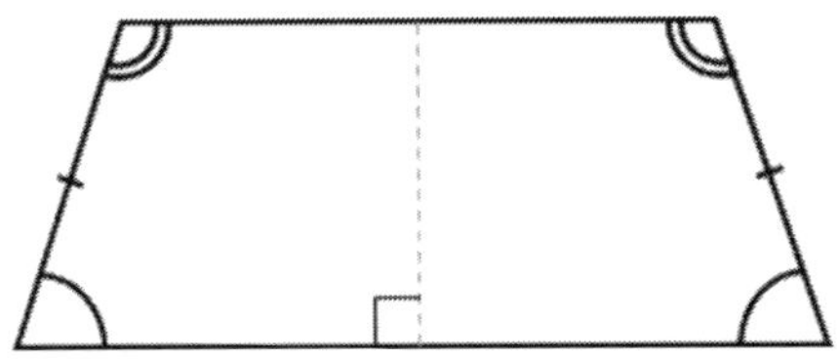

PARALLELOGRAM

A **parallelogram** is a quadrilateral that has two pairs of opposite parallel sides. As such it is a special type of trapezoid. The sides that are parallel are also congruent. The opposite interior angles are always congruent, and the consecutive interior angles are supplementary. The diagonals of a parallelogram divide each other. Each diagonal divides the parallelogram into two congruent triangles. A parallelogram has no line of symmetry, but does have 180-degree rotational symmetry about the midpoint.

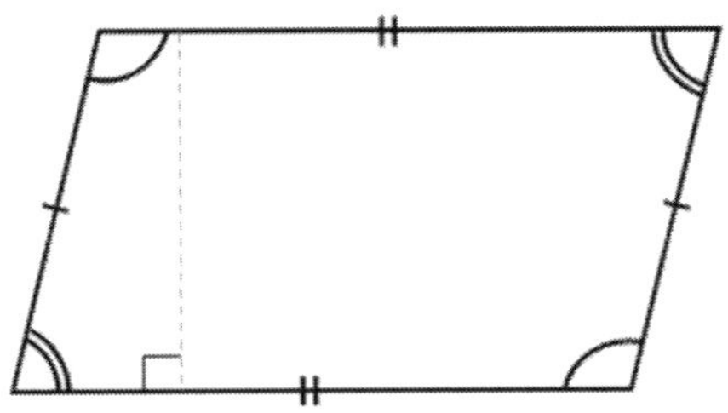

The **area of a parallelogram** is found by the formula $A = bh$, where b is the length of the base, and h is the height. Note that the base and height correspond to the length and width in a rectangle, so this formula would apply to rectangles as well. Do not confuse the height of a parallelogram with the length of the second side. The two are only the same measure in the case of a rectangle.

The **perimeter of a parallelogram** is found by the formula $P = 2a + 2b$ or $P = 2(a + b)$, where a and b are the lengths of the two sides.

Review Video: Area and Perimeter of a Parallelogram
Visit mometrix.com/academy and enter code: 718313

RECTANGLE

A **rectangle** is a quadrilateral with four right angles. All rectangles are parallelograms and trapezoids, but not all parallelograms or trapezoids are rectangles. The diagonals of a rectangle are congruent. Rectangles have two lines of symmetry (through each pair of opposing midpoints) and 180-degree rotational symmetry about the midpoint.

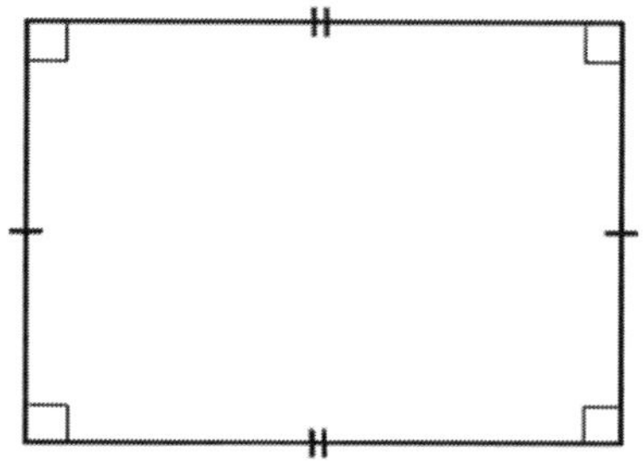

The **area of a rectangle** is found by the formula $A = lw$, where A is the area of the rectangle, l is the length (usually considered to be the longer side) and w is the width (usually considered to be the shorter side). The numbers for l and w are interchangeable.

The **perimeter of a rectangle** is found by the formula $P = 2l + 2w$ or $P = 2(l + w)$, where l is the length, and w is the width. It may be easier to add the length and width first and then double the result, as in the second formula.

RHOMBUS

A **rhombus** is a quadrilateral with four congruent sides. All rhombuses are parallelograms and kites; thus, they inherit all the properties of both types of quadrilaterals. The diagonals of a rhombus are perpendicular to each other. Rhombi have two lines of symmetry (along each of the diagonals) and 180° rotational symmetry. The **area of a rhombus** is half the product of the diagonals: $A = \frac{d_1 d_2}{2}$ and the perimeter of a rhombus is: $P = 2\sqrt{(d_1)^2 + (d_2)^2}$.

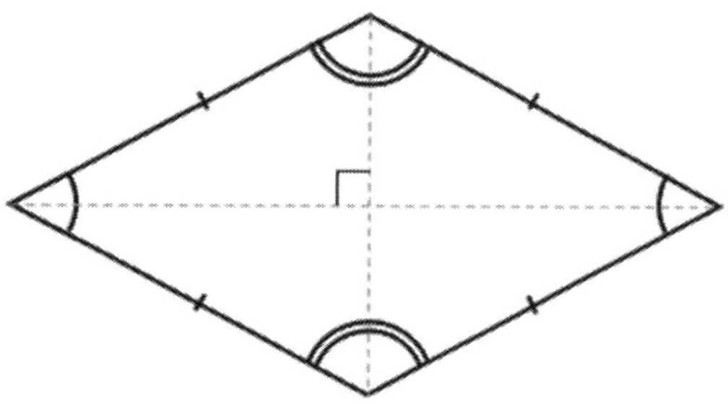

SQUARE

A **square** is a quadrilateral with four right angles and four congruent sides. Squares satisfy the criteria of all other types of quadrilaterals. The diagonals of a square are congruent and perpendicular to each other.

Mathematics

Squares have four lines of symmetry (through each pair of opposing midpoints and along each of the diagonals) as well as 90° rotational symmetry about the midpoint.

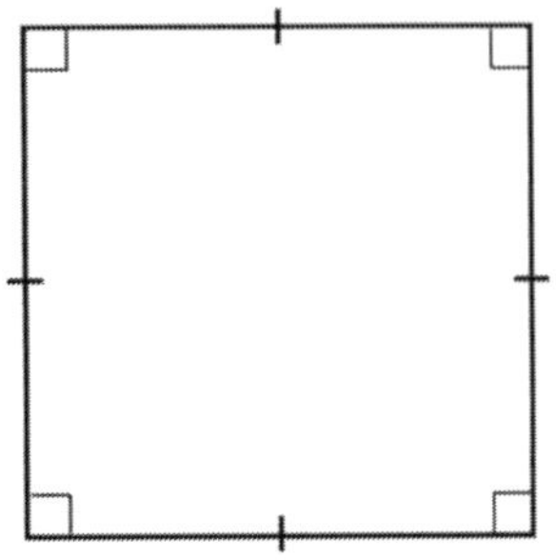

The **area of a square** is found by using the formula $A = s^2$, where s is the length of one side. The **perimeter of a square** is found by using the formula $P = 4s$, where s is the length of one side. Because all four sides are equal in a square, it is faster to multiply the length of one side by 4 than to add the same number four times. You could use the formulas for rectangles and get the same answer.

Review Video: Area and Perimeter of Rectangles and Squares
Visit mometrix.com/academy and enter code: 428109

HIERARCHY OF QUADRILATERALS

The hierarchy of quadrilaterals is as follows:

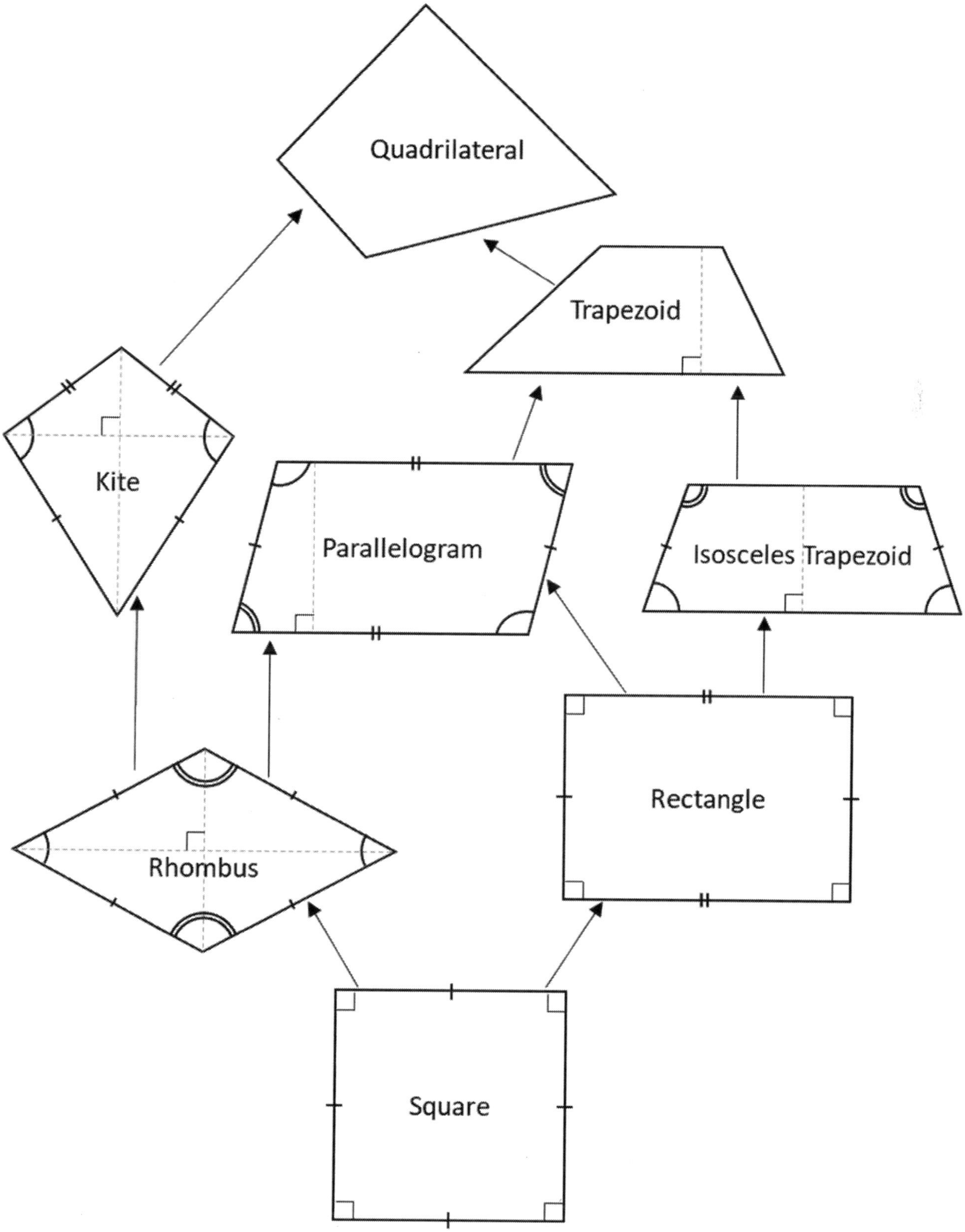

CIRCLES

The **center** of a circle is the single point from which every point on the circle is **equidistant**. The **radius** is a line segment that joins the center of the circle and any one point on the circle. All radii of a circle are equal. Circles that have the same center but not the same length of radii are **concentric**. The **diameter** is a line segment that passes through the center of the circle and has both endpoints on the circle. The length of the diameter is exactly twice the length of the radius. Point O in the diagram below is the center of the circle, segments $\overline{OX}$, $\overline{OY}$, and $\overline{OZ}$ are radii; and segment $\overline{XZ}$ is a diameter.

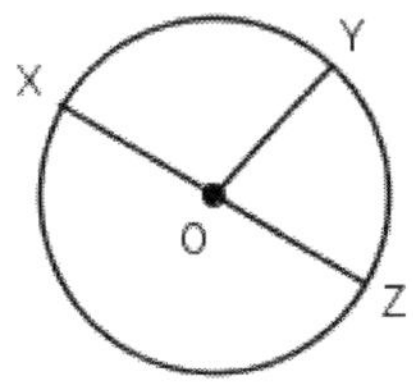

Review Video: Points of a Circle
Visit mometrix.com/academy and enter code: 420746

Review Video: Diameter, Radius, and Circumference
Visit mometrix.com/academy and enter code: 448988

The **area of a circle** is found by the formula $A = \pi r^2$, where r is the length of the radius. If the diameter of the circle is given, remember to divide it in half to get the length of the radius before proceeding.

The **circumference** of a circle is found by the formula $C = 2\pi r$, where r is the radius. Again, remember to convert the diameter if you are given that measure rather than the radius.

Review Video: Area and Circumference of a Circle
Visit mometrix.com/academy and enter code: 243015

INSCRIBED AND CIRCUMSCRIBED FIGURES

These terms can both be used to describe a given arrangement of figures, depending on perspective. If each of the vertices of figure A lie on figure B, then it can be said that figure A is **inscribed** in figure B, but it can also be said that figure B is **circumscribed** about figure A. The following table and examples help to illustrate the concept. Note that the figures cannot both be circles, as they would be completely overlapping and neither would be inscribed or circumscribed.

Given	Description	Equivalent Description	Figures
Each of the sides of a pentagon is tangent to a circle	The circle is inscribed in the pentagon	The pentagon is circumscribed about the circle	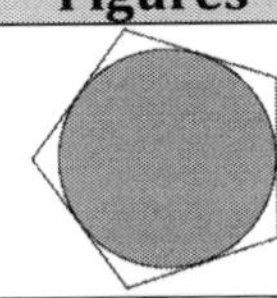
Each of the vertices of a pentagon lie on a circle	The pentagon is inscribed in the circle	The circle is circumscribed about the pentagon	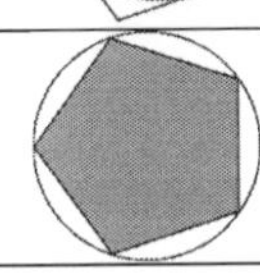

TRANSFORMATIONS

ROTATION

A **rotation** is a transformation that turns a figure around a point called the **center of rotation**, which can lie anywhere in the plane. If a line is drawn from a point on a figure to the center of rotation, and another line is drawn from the center to the rotated image of that point, the angle between the two lines is the **angle of rotation**. The vertex of the angle of rotation is the center of rotation.

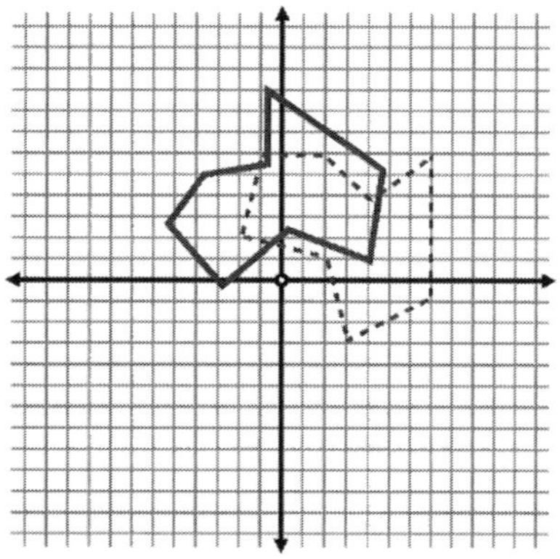

Review Video: Rotation
Visit mometrix.com/academy and enter code: 602600

Translation and Dilation

A **translation** is a transformation which slides a figure from one position in the plane to another position in the plane. The original figure and the translated figure have the same size, shape, and orientation. A **dilation** is a transformation which proportionally stretches or shrinks a figure by a **scale factor**. The dilated image is the same shape and orientation as the original image but a different size. A polygon and its dilated image are similar.

Translation

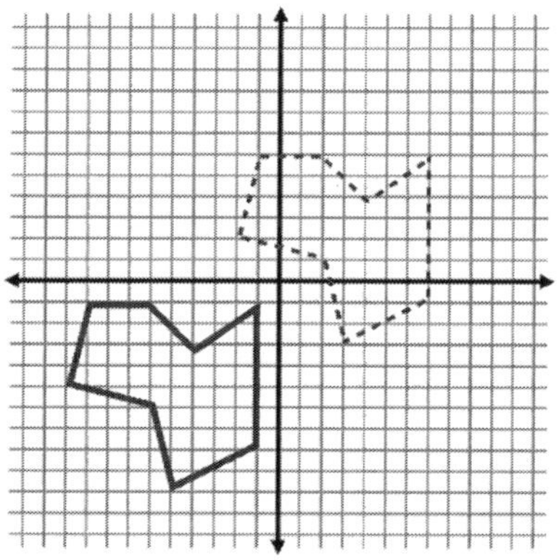

Dilation

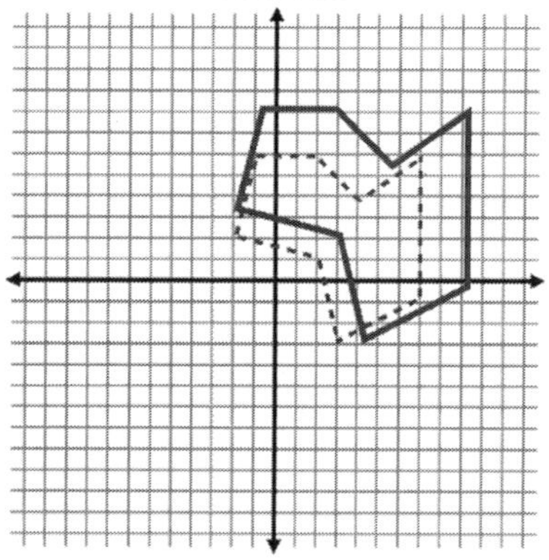

Review Video: Translation
Visit mometrix.com/academy and enter code: 718628

Review Video: Dilation
Visit mometrix.com/academy and enter code: 471630

A **reflection of a figure over a line** (a "flip") creates a congruent image that is the same distance from the line as the original figure but on the opposite side. The **line of reflection** is the perpendicular bisector of any line segment drawn from a point on the original figure to its reflected image (unless the point and its reflected image happen to be the same point, which happens when a figure is reflected over one of its own sides). A **reflection of a figure over a point** (an inversion) in two dimensions is the same as the rotation of the figure 180° about that point. The image of the figure is congruent to the original figure. The **point of reflection** is the midpoint of a line segment which connects a point in the figure to its image (unless the point and its reflected image happen to be the same point, which happens when a figure is reflected in one of its own points).

Reflection of a figure over a line

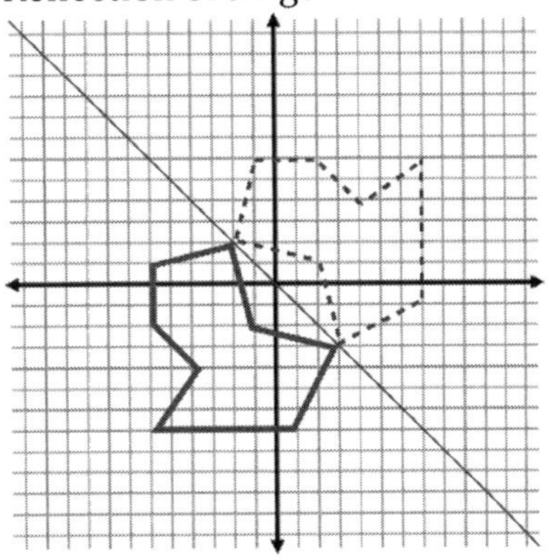

Reflection of a figure over a point

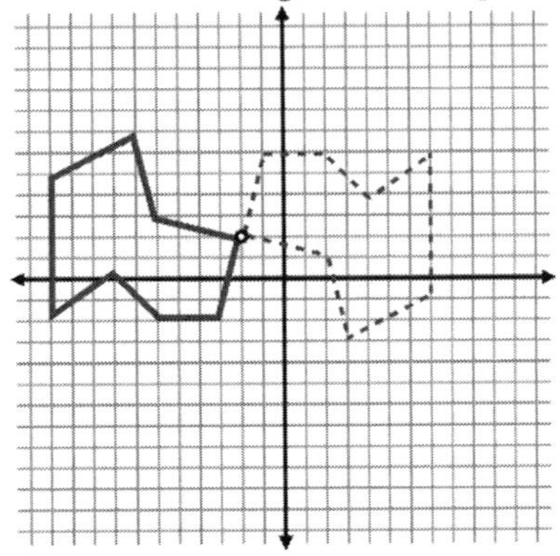

Review Video: Reflection
Visit mometrix.com/academy and enter code: 955068

3D Shapes

Solids

The **surface area of a solid object** is the area of all sides or exterior surfaces. For objects such as prisms and pyramids, a further distinction is made between base surface area (B) and lateral surface area (LA). For a prism, the total surface area (SA) is $SA = LA + 2B$. For a pyramid or cone, the total surface area is $SA = LA + B$.

The **surface area of a sphere** can be found by the formula $A = 4\pi r^2$, where r is the radius. The volume is given by the formula $V = \frac{4}{3}\pi r^3$, where r is the radius. Both quantities are generally given in terms of π.

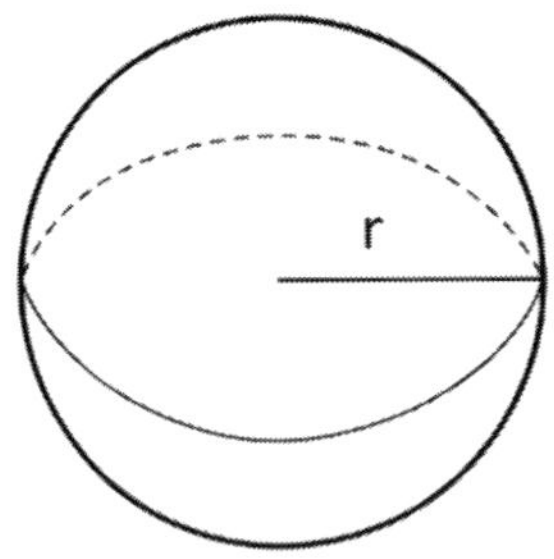

Review Video: Volume and Surface Area of a Sphere
Visit mometrix.com/academy and enter code: 786928

Review Video: How to Calculate the Volume of 3D Objects
Visit mometrix.com/academy and enter code: 163343

The **volume of any prism** is found by the formula $V = Bh$, where B is the area of the base, and h is the height (perpendicular distance between the bases). The surface area of any prism is the sum of the areas of both bases and all sides. It can be calculated as $SA = 2B + Ph$, where P is the perimeter of the base.

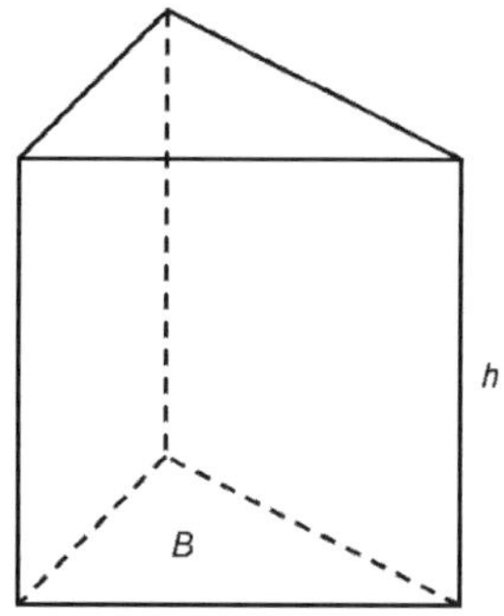

Review Video: Volume and Surface Area of a Prism
Visit mometrix.com/academy and enter code: 420158

For a **rectangular prism**, the volume can be found by the formula $V = lwh$, where V is the volume, l is the length, w is the width, and h is the height. The surface area can be calculated as $SA = 2lw + 2hl + 2wh$ or $SA = 2(lw + hl + wh)$.

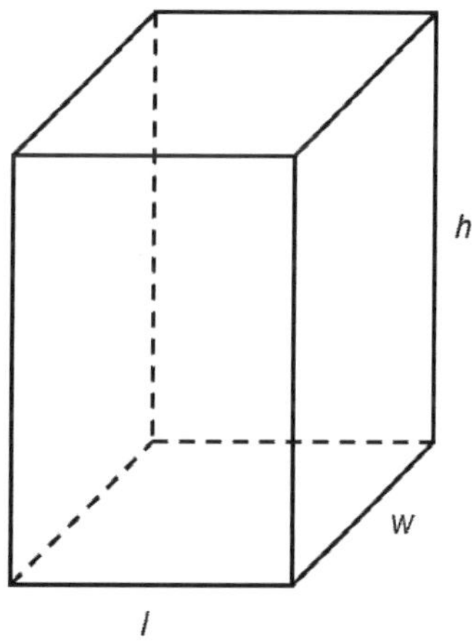

Review Video: Volume and Surface Area of a Rectangular Prism
Visit mometrix.com/academy and enter code: 282814

The **volume of a cube** can be found by the formula $V = s^3$, where s is the length of a side. The surface area of a cube is calculated as $SA = 6s^2$, where SA is the total surface area and s is the length of a side. These formulas are the same as the ones used for the volume and surface area of a rectangular prism, but simplified since all three quantities (length, width, and height) are the same.

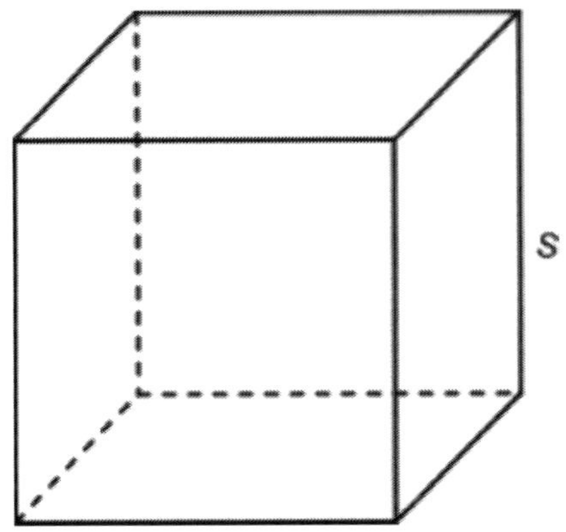

Review Video: Volume and Surface Area of a Cube
Visit mometrix.com/academy and enter code: 664455

The **volume of a cylinder** can be calculated by the formula $V = \pi r^2 h$, where r is the radius, and h is the height. The surface area of a cylinder can be found by the formula $SA = 2\pi r^2 + 2\pi rh$. The first term is the base area multiplied by two, and the second term is the perimeter of the base multiplied by the height.

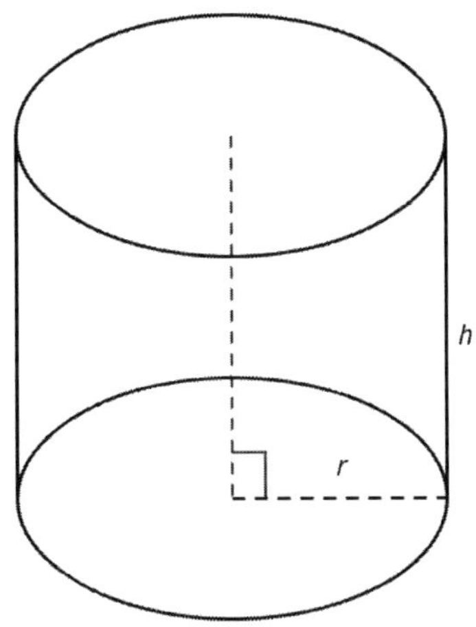

Review Video: Volume and Surface Area of a Right Circular Cylinder
Visit mometrix.com/academy and enter code: 226463

The **volume of a pyramid** is found by the formula $V = \frac{1}{3}Bh$, where B is the area of the base, and h is the height (perpendicular distance from the vertex to the base). Notice this formula is the same as $\frac{1}{3}$ times the volume of a prism. Like a prism, the base of a pyramid can be any shape.

Finding the **surface area of a pyramid** is not as simple as the other shapes we've looked at thus far. If the pyramid is a right pyramid, meaning the base is a regular polygon and the vertex is directly over the center of that polygon, the surface area can be calculated as $SA = B + \frac{1}{2}Ph_s$, where P is the perimeter of the base, and h_s

is the slant height (distance from the vertex to the midpoint of one side of the base). If the pyramid is irregular, the area of each triangle side must be calculated individually and then summed, along with the base.

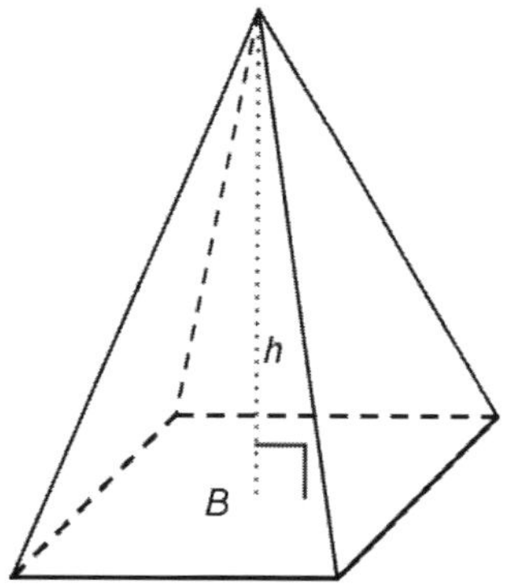

Review Video: Volume and Surface Area of a Pyramid
Visit mometrix.com/academy and enter code: 621932

The **volume of a cone** is found by the formula $V = \frac{1}{3}\pi r^2 h$, where r is the radius, and h is the height. Notice this is the same as $\frac{1}{3}$ times the volume of a cylinder. The surface area can be calculated as $SA = \pi r^2 + \pi rs$, where s is the slant height. The slant height can be calculated using the Pythagorean theorem to be $\sqrt{r^2 + h^2}$, so the surface area formula can also be written as $SA = \pi r^2 + \pi r\sqrt{r^2 + h^2}$.

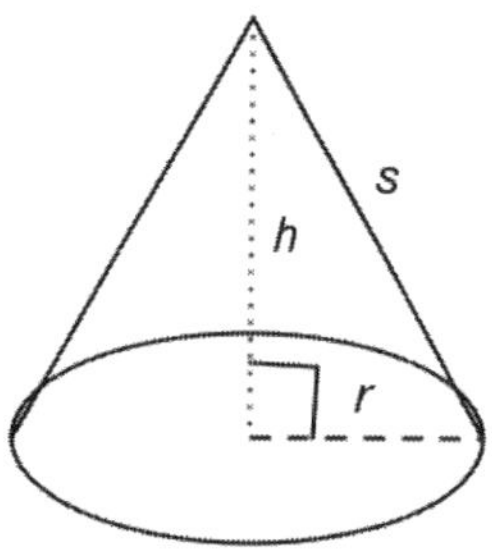

Review Video: Volume and Surface Area of a Right Circular Cone
Visit mometrix.com/academy and enter code: 573574

Pythagorean Theorem

The side of a triangle opposite the right angle is called the **hypotenuse**. The other two sides are called the legs. The Pythagorean theorem states a relationship among the legs and hypotenuse of a right triangle: $(a^2 + b^2 = c^2)$, where a and b are the lengths of the legs of a right triangle, and c is the length of the hypotenuse. Note that this formula will only work with right triangles.

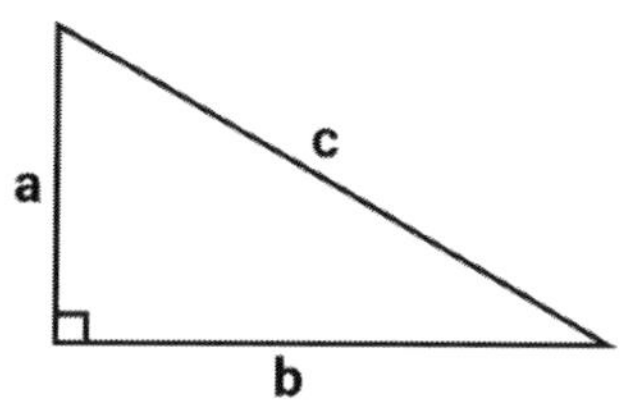

Review Video: Pythagorean Theorem
Visit mometrix.com/academy and enter code: 906576

Trigonometric Formulas

In the diagram below, angle C is the right angle, and side c is the hypotenuse. Side a is the side opposite to angle A and side b is the side opposite to angle B. Using ratios of side lengths as a means to calculate the sine, cosine, and tangent of an acute angle only works for right triangles.

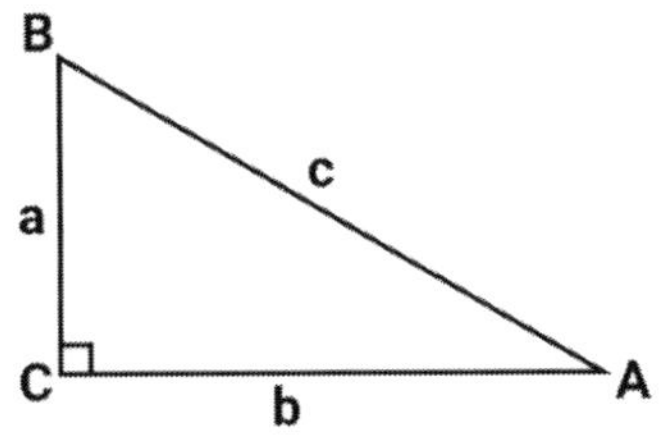

$$\sin A = \frac{\text{opposite side}}{\text{hypotenuse}} = \frac{a}{c} \qquad \csc A = \frac{1}{\sin A} = \frac{\text{hypotenuse}}{\text{opposite side}} = \frac{c}{a}$$

$$\cos A = \frac{\text{adjacent side}}{\text{hypotenuse}} = \frac{b}{c} \qquad \sec A = \frac{1}{\cos A} = \frac{\text{hypotenuse}}{\text{adjacent side}} = \frac{c}{b}$$

$$\tan A = \frac{\text{opposite side}}{\text{adjacent side}} = \frac{a}{b} \qquad \cot A = \frac{1}{\tan A} = \frac{\text{adjacent side}}{\text{opposite side}} = \frac{b}{a}$$

Laws of Sines and Cosines

The **law of sines** states that $\frac{\sin A}{a} = \frac{\sin B}{b} = \frac{\sin C}{c}$, where A, B, and C are the angles of a triangle, and a, b, and c are the sides opposite their respective angles. This formula will work with all triangles, not just right triangles.

The **law of cosines** is given by the formula $c^2 = a^2 + b^2 - 2ab(\cos C)$, where a, b, and c are the sides of a triangle, and C is the angle opposite side c. This is a generalized form of the Pythagorean theorem that can be used on any triangle.

Review Video: Law of Sines
Visit mometrix.com/academy and enter code: 206844

Review Video: Law of Cosines
Visit mometrix.com/academy and enter code: 158911

Measurement, Data, and Probability

Rounding and Estimation

Rounding is reducing the digits in a number while still trying to keep the value similar. The result will be less accurate but in a simpler form and easier to use. Whole numbers can be rounded to the nearest ten, hundred, or thousand, for instance.

To round a number, we make it a little smaller (rounding down) or a little larger (rounding up) to get a number that ends in zeros. We specify the number of zeros by naming the last place that we will not "zero out." For example, to round 8,327 to the nearest hundred, we round down to 8,300, zeroing out every digit to the right of the hundreds place. To round 4,728 to the nearest thousand, we round up to 5,000, increasing the thousands digit by one (to make the number larger) and zeroing out every digit to the right of the thousands place.

We decide whether to round down or up by looking at the first digit we are going to zero out. If it is less than 5 (namely, 0, 1, 2, 3, or 4) we round down. If it is greater than or equal to 5 (namely, 5, 6, 7, 8, or 9) we round up by adding 1 to the place we are rounding to. So, rounding 8,327 to the nearest hundred, we round down to 8,300 because the tens digit, 2, is less than 5. And rounding 4,728 to the nearest thousand, we round up to 5,000, increasing the thousands digit by 1, because the hundreds digit, 7, is greater than or equal to 5.

This even works with decimals. For example, rounding 39.7426 to the nearest tenth, we round down to 39.7000 (or simply 39.7) because the hundredths digit, 4, is less than 5. And rounding 0.019823 to the nearest thousandth, we round up to 0.020000 (or simply 0.02) by increasing the thousandths digit by 1, because the ten-thousandths digit, 8, is greater than or equal to 5.

When you are asked to estimate the solution to a problem, you will need to provide only an approximate figure or **estimation** for your answer. In this situation, you will need to round each number in the calculation to the level indicated (nearest hundred, nearest thousand, etc.) or to a level that makes sense for the numbers involved. When estimating a sum **all numbers must be rounded to the same level**. You cannot round one number to the nearest thousand while rounding another to the nearest hundred.

For instance, suppose you are considering buying four pieces of equipment for your home office. Their prices are $485, $1,217, $750, and $643. To estimate their total cost, you might round each price to the nearest hundred and add the rounded figures, getting an estimate of $500 + $1,200 + $800 + $600 = $3,100. By estimating instead of making an exact calculation, you give up a little accuracy to get a simpler calculation.

Review Video: Rounding and Estimation
Visit mometrix.com/academy and enter code: 126243

Scientific Notation

Scientific notation is a way of writing large numbers in a shorter form. The form $a \times 10^n$ is used in scientific notation, where a is greater than or equal to 1 but less than 10, and n is the number of places the decimal must move to get from the original number to a. Example: The number 230,400,000 is cumbersome to write. To write the value in scientific notation, place a decimal point between the first and second numbers, and include all digits through the last non-zero digit ($a = 2.304$). To find the appropriate power of 10, count the number of places the decimal point had to move ($n = 8$). The number is positive if the decimal moved to the left, and negative if it moved to the right. We can then write 230,400,000 as 2.304×10^8. If we look instead at the number 0.00002304, we have the same value for a, but this time the decimal moved 5 places to the right ($n = -5$). Thus, 0.00002304 can be written as 2.304×10^{-5}. Using this notation makes it simple to compare very large or very small numbers. By comparing exponents, it is easy to see that 3.28×10^4 is smaller than 1.51×10^5, because 4 is less than 5.

Review Video: Scientific Notation
Visit mometrix.com/academy and enter code: 976454

Metric and Customary Measurements

Metric Measurement Prefixes

Giga-	One billion	1 *giga*watt is one billion watts
Mega-	One million	1 *mega*hertz is one million hertz
Kilo-	One thousand	1 *kilo*gram is one thousand grams
Deci-	One-tenth	1 *deci*meter is one-tenth of a meter
Centi-	One-hundredth	1 *centi*meter is one-hundredth of a meter
Milli-	One-thousandth	1 *milli*liter is one-thousandth of a liter
Micro-	One-millionth	1 *micro*gram is one-millionth of a gram

Review Video: How the Metric System Works
Visit mometrix.com/academy and enter code: 163709

Measurement Conversion

When converting between units, the goal is to maintain the same meaning but change the way it is displayed. In order to go from a larger unit to a smaller unit, multiply the number of the known amount by the equivalent amount. When going from a smaller unit to a larger unit, divide the number of the known amount by the equivalent amount.

For complicated conversions, it may be helpful to set up conversion fractions. In these fractions, one fraction is the **conversion factor**. The other fraction has the unknown amount in the numerator. So, the known value is placed in the denominator. Sometimes, the second fraction has the known value from the problem in the numerator and the unknown in the denominator. Multiply the two fractions to get the converted measurement. Note that since the numerator and the denominator of the factor are equivalent, the value of the fraction is 1. That is why we can say that the result in the new units is equal to the result in the old units even though they have different numbers.

It can often be necessary to chain known conversion factors together. As an example, consider converting 512 square inches to square meters. We know that there are 2.54 centimeters in an inch and 100 centimeters in a meter, and we know we will need to square each of these factors to achieve the conversion we are looking for.

$$\frac{512\text{ in}^2}{1} \times \left(\frac{2.54\text{ cm}}{1\text{ in}}\right)^2 \times \left(\frac{1\text{ m}}{100\text{ cm}}\right)^2 = \frac{512\,\cancel{\text{in}^2}}{1} \times \left(\frac{6.4516\,\cancel{\text{cm}^2}}{1\,\cancel{\text{in}^2}}\right) \times \left(\frac{1\text{ m}^2}{10{,}000\,\cancel{\text{cm}^2}}\right) = 0.330\text{ m}^2$$

Review Video: Measurement Conversions
Visit mometrix.com/academy and enter code: 316703

Review Video: Converting Kilograms to Pounds
Visit mometrix.com/academy and enter code: 241463

Common Units and Equivalents

Metric Equivalents

1000 μg (microgram)	1 mg
1000 mg (milligram)	1 g
1000 g (gram)	1 kg
1000 kg (kilogram)	1 metric ton
1000 mL (milliliter)	1 L
1000 μm (micrometer)	1 mm
1000 mm (millimeter)	1 m
100 cm (centimeter)	1 m
1000 m (meter)	1 km

Distance and Area Measurement

Unit	Abbreviation	US equivalent	Metric equivalent
Inch	in	1 inch	2.54 centimeters
Foot	ft	12 inches	0.305 meters
Yard	yd	3 feet	0.914 meters
Mile	mi	5280 feet	1.609 kilometers
Acre	ac	4840 square yards	0.405 hectares
Square Mile	sq. mi. or mi.^{2}	640 acres	2.590 square kilometers

Capacity Measurements

Unit	Abbreviation	US equivalent	Metric equivalent
Fluid Ounce	fl oz	8 fluid drams	29.573 milliliters
Cup	c	8 fluid ounces	0.237 liter
Pint	pt.	16 fluid ounces	0.473 liter
Quart	qt.	2 pints	0.946 liter
Gallon	gal.	4 quarts	3.785 liters
Teaspoon	t or tsp.	1 fluid dram	5 milliliters
Tablespoon	T or tbsp.	4 fluid drams	15 or 16 milliliters
Cubic Centimeter	cc or cm^3	0.271 drams	1 milliliter

Weight Measurements

Unit	Abbreviation	US equivalent	Metric equivalent
Ounce	oz	16 drams	28.35 grams
Pound	lb	16 ounces	453.6 grams
Ton	tn.	2,000 pounds	907.2 kilograms

Volume and Weight Measurement Clarifications

Always be careful when using ounces and fluid ounces. They are not equivalent.

1 pint = 16 fluid ounces	1 fluid ounce ≠ 1 ounce
1 pound = 16 ounces	1 pint ≠ 1 pound

Having one pint of something does not mean you have one pound of it. In the same way, just because something weighs one pound does not mean that its volume is one pint.

In the United States, the word "ton" by itself refers to a short ton or a net ton. Do not confuse this with a long ton (also called a gross ton) or a metric ton (also spelled *tonne*), which have different measurement equivalents.

1 US ton = 2000 pounds ≠ 1 metric ton = 1000 kilograms

Precision, Accuracy, and Error

Measurements of physical quantities (e.g., length, area, volume, weight, mass, and time) in the real world are never perfect. Measurements miss the true value, and repeated measurements produce different values. For this reason, fields that depend on good measurement have technical terms, precision and accuracy, that describe how particular ways of measuring a quantity produce good or bad results. Note that these terms apply not to single measurements but to repeated measurements of the same quantity using the same procedure.

Precision describes the consistency of measurements. Measurements that cluster closely together, with little variation from one measurement to the next, have high precision. Measurements that vary a great deal from one measurement to the next have low precision.

Accuracy describes the closeness of measurements to the true value of the quantity being measured or, more technically, the tendency of measurements to cluster around the true value (though we do not usually know the true value; otherwise, we would not bother to measure it).

An analogy from archery may help. An outstanding archer aiming at the center of the target (the true value) produces a tight cluster of arrows around the center (high accuracy, high precision). Under the same circumstances a modestly good archer produces a loose cluster around the center (high accuracy, low precision). If, however, there is a strong crosswind and the archers do nothing to compensate for it, the outstanding archer's shots will cluster tightly around a point away from the center (low accuracy, high precision); and the modestly good archer's shots will cluster loosely around a point away from the center (low accuracy, low precision).

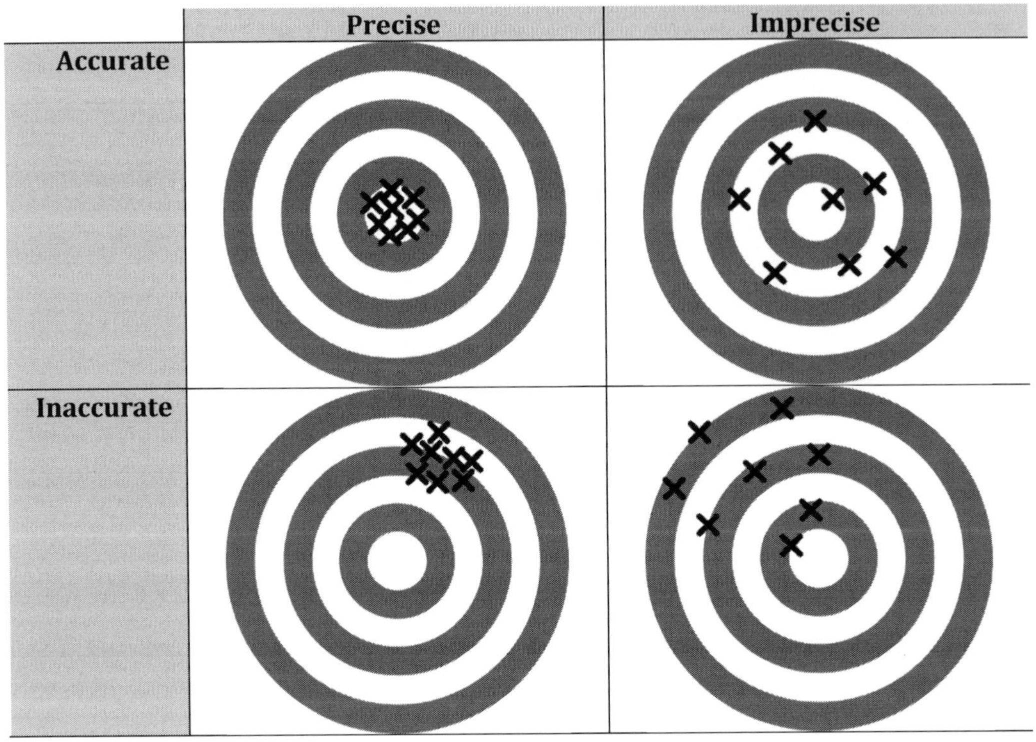

Error in measurement is not a mistake but simply the difference between the true value and the measured value. Since we seldom know the true value, we seldom know the exact error; but sometimes we know a limit on how big the error can be (an error bound), in which case we can use the plus-or-minus sign, $\pm$, to indicate how far the true value might lie from the measured value. For instance, if we measure the length of a metal bar as 25.6 cm and we know the error in our measurement is no more than 0.03 cm (some sources call this **approximate error**), then we might report the length of the bar as 25.6 ± 0.03 cm, which means it lies between 25.57 cm and 25.63 cm.

A particularly important application of this comes from the necessity of rounding whenever we make a measurement. For instance, if we measure the length of a pencil using a ruler marked off in whole inches (no fractions), then we must round our measurement to the nearest inch. Thus, if we report the length as 8 inches, it means that the actual value lies somewhere between 7.5 inches and 8.5 inches, which is to say 8 ± 0.5 inches. This built-in error bound due to rounding is called the **maximum possible error**, and it is always half the magnitude of the smallest unit used in the measurement. Determining the smallest unit can be somewhat subtle, involving the rules for significant figures commonly used in physics, chemistry, and other fields.

Review Video: Precision, Accuracy, and Error
Visit mometrix.com/academy and enter code: 520377

PROBABILITY

Probability is the likelihood of a certain outcome occurring for a given event. An **event** is any situation that produces a result. It could be something as simple as flipping a coin or as complex as launching a rocket. Determining the probability of an outcome for an event can be equally simple or complex. As such, there are specific terms used in the study of probability that need to be understood:

- **Compound event**—an event that involves two or more independent events (rolling a pair of dice and taking the sum)
- **Desired outcome** (or success)—an outcome that meets a particular set of criteria (a roll of 1 or 2 if we are looking for numbers less than 3)
- **Independent events**—two or more events whose outcomes do not affect one another (two coins tossed at the same time)
- **Dependent events**—two or more events whose outcomes affect one another (two cards drawn consecutively from the same deck)
- **Certain outcome**—probability of outcome is 100% or 1
- **Impossible outcome**—probability of outcome is 0% or 0
- **Mutually exclusive outcomes**—two or more outcomes whose criteria cannot all be satisfied in a single event (a coin coming up heads and tails on the same toss)
- **Random variable**—refers to all possible outcomes of a single event which may be discrete or continuous.

Review Video: Intro to Probability
Visit mometrix.com/academy and enter code: 212374

SAMPLE SPACE

The total set of all possible results of a test or experiment is called a **sample space**, or sometimes a universal sample space. The sample space, represented by one of the variables S, Ω, or U (for universal sample space) has individual elements called outcomes. Other terms for outcome that may be used interchangeably include elementary outcome, simple event, or sample point. The number of outcomes in a given sample space could be infinite or finite, and some tests may yield multiple unique sample sets. For example, tests conducted by drawing playing cards from a standard deck would have one sample space of the card values, another sample space of the card suits, and a third sample space of suit-denomination combinations. For most tests, the sample spaces considered will be finite.

An **event**, represented by the variable E, is a portion of a sample space. It may be one outcome or a group of outcomes from the same sample space. If an event occurs, then the test or experiment will generate an outcome that satisfies the requirement of that event. For example, given a standard deck of 52 playing cards as the sample space, and defining the event as the collection of face cards, then the event will occur if the card drawn is a J, Q, or K. If any other card is drawn, the event is said to have not occurred.

For every sample space, each possible outcome has a specific likelihood, or probability, that it will occur. The probability measure, also called the **distribution**, is a function that assigns a real number probability, from zero to one, to each outcome. For a probability measure to be accurate, every outcome must have a real number probability measure that is greater than or equal to zero and less than or equal to one. Also, the probability measure of the sample space must equal one, and the probability measure of the union of multiple outcomes must equal the sum of the individual probability measures.

Probabilities of events are expressed as real numbers from zero to one. They give a numerical value to the chance that a particular event will occur. The probability of an event occurring is the sum of the probabilities of the individual elements of that event. For example, in a standard deck of 52 playing cards as the sample space and the collection of face cards as the event, the probability of drawing a specific face card is $\frac{1}{52} = 0.019$, but the probability of drawing any one of the twelve face cards is $12(0.019) = 0.228$. Note that rounding of numbers can generate different results. If you multiplied 12 by the fraction $\frac{1}{52}$ before converting to a decimal, you would get the answer $\frac{12}{52} = 0.231$.

Theoretical and Experimental Probability

Theoretical probability can usually be determined without actually performing the event. The likelihood of an outcome occurring, or the probability of an outcome occurring, is given by the formula:

$$P(A) = \frac{\text{Number of acceptable outcomes}}{\text{Number of possible outcomes}}$$

Note that $P(A)$ is the probability of an outcome A occurring, and each outcome is just as likely to occur as any other outcome. If each outcome has the same probability of occurring as every other possible outcome, the outcomes are said to be equally likely to occur. The total number of acceptable outcomes must be less than or equal to the total number of possible outcomes. If the two are equal, then the outcome is certain to occur and the probability is 1. If the number of acceptable outcomes is zero, then the outcome is impossible and the probability is 0. For example, if there are 20 marbles in a bag and 5 are red, then the theoretical probability of randomly selecting a red marble is 5 out of 20, $\left(\frac{5}{20} = \frac{1}{4}, 0.25, \text{or } 25\%\right)$.

If the theoretical probability is unknown or too complicated to calculate, it can be estimated by an experimental probability. **Experimental probability**, also called empirical probability, is an estimate of the likelihood of a certain outcome based on repeated experiments or collected data. In other words, while theoretical probability is based on what *should* happen, experimental probability is based on what *has* happened. Experimental probability is calculated in the same way as theoretical probability, except that actual outcomes are used instead of possible outcomes. The more experiments performed or datapoints gathered, the better the estimate should be.

Theoretical and experimental probability do not always line up with one another. Theoretical probability says that out of 20 coin-tosses, 10 should be heads. However, if we were actually to toss 20 coins, we might record just 5 heads. This doesn't mean that our theoretical probability is incorrect; it just means that this particular experiment had results that were different from what was predicted. A practical application of empirical probability is the insurance industry. There are no set functions that define lifespan, health, or safety. Insurance companies look at factors from hundreds of thousands of individuals to find patterns that they then use to set the formulas for insurance premiums.

Review Video: Empirical Probability
Visit mometrix.com/academy and enter code: 513468

Objective and Subjective Probability

Objective probability is based on mathematical formulas and documented evidence. Examples of objective probability include raffles or lottery drawings where there is a pre-determined number of possible outcomes and a predetermined number of outcomes that correspond to an event. Other cases of objective probability include probabilities of rolling dice, flipping coins, or drawing cards. Most gambling games are based on objective probability.

In contrast, **subjective probability** is based on personal or professional feelings and judgments. Often, there is a lot of guesswork following extensive research. Areas where subjective probability is applicable include sales trends and business expenses. Attractions set admission prices based on subjective probabilities of attendance based on varying admission rates in an effort to maximize their profit.

COMPLEMENT OF AN EVENT

Sometimes it may be easier to calculate the possibility of something not happening, or the **complement of an event**. Represented by the symbol $\bar{A}$, the complement of A is the probability that event A does not happen. When you know the probability of event A occurring, you can use the formula $P(\bar{A}) = 1 - P(A)$, where $P(\bar{A})$ is the probability of event A not occurring, and $P(A)$ is the probability of event A occurring.

ADDITION RULE

The **addition rule** for probability is used for finding the probability of a compound event. Use the formula $P(A \cup B) = P(A) + P(B) - P(A \cap B)$, where $P(A \cap B)$ is the probability of both events occurring to find the probability of a compound event. The probability of both events occurring at the same time must be subtracted to eliminate any overlap in the first two probabilities.

CONDITIONAL PROBABILITY

Given two events A and B, the **conditional probability** $P(A|B)$ is the probability that event A will occur, given that event B has occurred. The conditional probability cannot be calculated simply from $P(A)$ and $P(B)$; these probabilities alone do not give sufficient information to determine the conditional probability. It can, however, be determined if you are also given the probability of the intersection of events A and B, $P(A \cap B)$, the probability that events A and B both occur. Specifically, $P(A|B) = \frac{P(A \cap B)}{P(B)}$. For instance, suppose you have a jar containing two red marbles and two blue marbles, and you draw two marbles at random. Consider event A being the event that the first marble drawn is red, and event B being the event that the second marble drawn is blue. If we want to find the probability that B occurs given that A occurred, $P(B|A)$, then we can compute it using the fact that $P(A)$ is $\frac{1}{2}$, and $P(A \cap B)$ is $\frac{1}{3}$. (The latter may not be obvious, but may be determined by finding the product of $\frac{1}{2}$ and $\frac{2}{3}$). Therefore $P(B|A) = \frac{P(A \cap B)}{P(A)} = \frac{1/3}{1/2} = \frac{2}{3}$.

CONDITIONAL PROBABILITY IN EVERYDAY SITUATIONS

Conditional probability often arises in everyday situations in, for example, estimating the risk or benefit of certain activities. The conditional probability of having a heart attack given that you exercise daily may be smaller than the overall probability of having a heart attack. The conditional probability of having lung cancer given that you are a smoker is larger than the overall probability of having lung cancer. Note that changing the order of the conditional probability changes the meaning: the conditional probability of having lung cancer given that you are a smoker is a very different thing from the probability of being a smoker given that you have lung cancer. In an extreme case, suppose that a certain rare disease is caused only by eating a certain food, but even then, it is unlikely. Then the conditional probability of having that disease given that you eat the dangerous food is nonzero but low, but the conditional probability of having eaten that food given that you have the disease is 100%!

Review Video: Conditional Probability
Visit mometrix.com/academy and enter code: 397924

INDEPENDENCE

The conditional probability $P(A|B)$ is the probability that event A will occur given that event B occurs. If the two events are independent, we do not expect that whether or not event B occurs should have any effect on whether or not event A occurs. In other words, we expect $P(A|B) = P(A)$.

This can be proven using the usual equations for conditional probability and the joint probability of independent events. The conditional probability $P(A|B) = \frac{P(A \cap B)}{P(B)}$. If A and B are independent, then $P(A \cap B) = P(A)P(B)$. So $P(A|B) = \frac{P(A)P(B)}{P(B)} = P(A)$. By similar reasoning, if A and B are independent then $P(B|A) = P(B)$.

Multiplication Rule

The **multiplication rule** can be used to find the probability of two independent events occurring using the formula $P(A \cap B) = P(A) \times P(B)$, where $P(A \cap B)$ is the probability of two independent events occurring, $P(A)$ is the probability of the first event occurring, and $P(B)$ is the probability of the second event occurring.

The multiplication rule can also be used to find the probability of two dependent events occurring using the formula $P(A \cap B) = P(A) \times P(B|A)$, where $P(A \cap B)$ is the probability of two dependent events occurring and $P(B|A)$ is the probability of the second event occurring after the first event has already occurred.

Use a **combination of the multiplication** rule and the rule of complements to find the probability that at least one outcome of the element will occur. This is given by the general formula $P(\text{at least one event occurring}) = 1 - P(\text{no outcomes occurring})$. For example, to find the probability that at least one even number will show when a pair of dice is rolled, find the probability that two odd numbers will be rolled (no even numbers) and subtract from one. You can always use a tree diagram or make a chart to list the possible outcomes when the sample space is small, such as in the dice-rolling example, but in most cases it will be much faster to use the multiplication and complement formulas.

Review Video: Multiplication Rule
Visit mometrix.com/academy and enter code: 782598

Union and Intersection of Two Sets of Outcomes

If A and B are each a set of elements or outcomes from an experiment, then the **union** (symbol ∪) of the two sets is the set of elements found in set A or set B. For example, if $A = \{2, 3, 4\}$ and $B = \{3, 4, 5\}$, $A \cup B = \{2, 3, 4, 5\}$. Note that the outcomes 3 and 4 appear only once in the union. For statistical events, the union is equivalent to "or"; $P(A \cup B)$ is the same thing as $P(A \text{ or } B)$. The **intersection** (symbol ∩) of two sets is the set of outcomes common to both sets. For the above sets A and B, $A \cap B = \{3, 4\}$. For statistical events, the intersection is equivalent to "and"; $P(A \cap B)$ is the same thing as $P(A \text{ and } B)$. It is important to note that union and intersection operations commute. That is:

$$A \cup B = B \cup A \text{ and } A \cap B = B \cap A$$

Permutations and Combinations in Probability

When trying to calculate the probability of an event using the $\frac{\text{desired outcomes}}{\text{total outcomes}}$ formula, you may frequently find that there are too many outcomes to individually count them. **Permutation** and **combination formulas** offer a shortcut to counting outcomes. A permutation is an arrangement of a specific number of a set of objects in a specific order. The number of **permutations** of r items given a set of n items can be calculated as ${}_nP_r = \frac{n!}{(n-r)!}$. Combinations are similar to permutations, except there are no restrictions regarding the order of the elements. While ABC is considered a different permutation than BCA, ABC and BCA are considered the same combination. The number of **combinations** of r items given a set of n items can be calculated as ${}_nC_r = \frac{n!}{r!(n-r)!}$ or ${}_nC_r = \frac{{}_nP_r}{r!}$.

Suppose you want to calculate how many different 5-card hands can be drawn from a deck of 52 cards. This is a combination since the order of the cards in a hand does not matter. There are 52 cards available, and 5 to be selected. Thus, the number of different hands is ${}_{52}C_5 = \frac{52!}{5! \times 47!} = 2{,}598{,}960$.

Review Video: Probability - Permutation and Combination
Visit mometrix.com/academy and enter code: 907664

TREE DIAGRAMS

For a simple sample space, possible outcomes may be determined by using a **tree diagram** or an organized chart. In either case, you can easily draw or list out the possible outcomes. For example, to determine all the possible ways three objects can be ordered, you can draw a tree diagram:

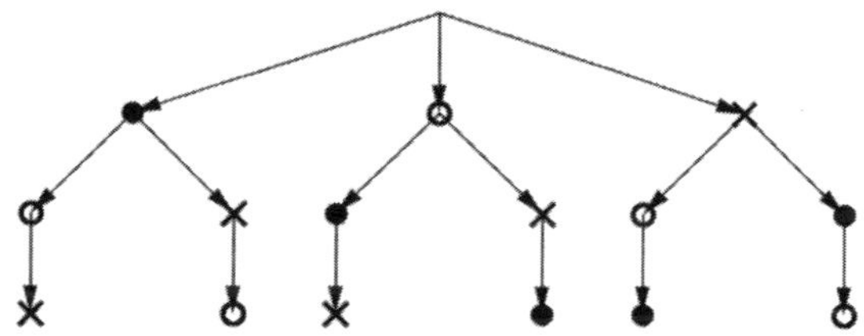

Review Video: Tree Diagrams
Visit mometrix.com/academy and enter code: 829158

You can also make a chart to list all the possibilities:

First object	Second object	Third object
●	x	o
●	o	x
o	●	x
o	x	●
x	●	o
x	o	●

Either way, you can easily see there are six possible ways the three objects can be ordered.

If two events have no outcomes in common, they are said to be **mutually exclusive**. For example, in a standard deck of 52 playing cards, the event of all card suits is mutually exclusive to the event of all card values. If two events have no bearing on each other so that one event occurring has no influence on the probability of another event occurring, the two events are said to be independent. For example, rolling a standard six-sided die multiple times does not change that probability that a particular number will be rolled from one roll to the next. If the outcome of one event does affect the probability of the second event, the two events are said to be dependent. For example, if cards are drawn from a deck, the probability of drawing an ace after an ace has been drawn is different than the probability of drawing an ace if no ace (or no other card, for that matter) has been drawn.

In probability, the **odds in favor of an event** are the number of times the event will occur compared to the number of times the event will not occur. To calculate the odds in favor of an event, use the formula $\frac{P(A)}{1-P(A)}$, where $P(A)$ is the probability that the event will occur. Many times, odds in favor is given as a ratio in the form $\frac{a}{b}$ or $a{:}\,b$, where a is the probability of the event occurring and b is the complement of the event, the probability of the event not occurring. If the odds in favor are given as 2:5, that means that you can expect the event to occur two times for every 5 times that it does not occur. In other words, the probability that the event will occur is $\frac{2}{2+5} = \frac{2}{7}$.

In probability, the **odds against an event** are the number of times the event will not occur compared to the number of times the event will occur. To calculate the odds against an event, use the formula $\frac{1-P(A)}{P(A)}$, where $P(A)$ is the probability that the event will occur. Many times, odds against is given as a ratio in the form $\frac{b}{a}$ or $b: a$, where b is the probability the event will not occur (the complement of the event) and a is the probability the event will occur. If the odds against an event are given as 3:1, that means that you can expect the event to not occur 3 times for every one time it does occur. In other words, 3 out of every 4 trials will fail.

Two-Way Frequency Tables

If we have a two-way frequency table, it is generally a straightforward matter to read off the probabilities of any two events A and B, as well as the joint probability of both events occurring, $P(A \cap B)$. We can then find the conditional probability $P(A|B)$ by calculating $P(A|B) = \frac{P(A \cap B)}{P(B)}$. We could also check whether or not events are independent by verifying whether $P(A)P(B) = P(A \cap B)$.

For example, a certain store's recent T-shirt sales:

	Small	Medium	Large	Total
Blue	25	40	35	100
White	27	25	22	74
Black	8	23	15	46
Total	60	88	72	220

Suppose we want to find the conditional probability that a customer buys a black shirt (event A), given that the shirt he buys is size small (event B). From the table, the probability $P(B)$ that a customer buys a small shirt is $\frac{60}{220} = \frac{3}{11}$. The probability $P(A \cap B)$ that he buys a small, black shirt is $\frac{8}{220} = \frac{2}{55}$. The conditional probability $P(A|B)$ that he buys a black shirt, given that he buys a small shirt, is therefore $P(A|B) = \frac{2/55}{3/11} = \frac{2}{15}$.

Similarly, if we want to check whether the event a customer buys a blue shirt, A, is independent of the event that a customer buys a medium shirt, B. From the table, $P(A) = \frac{100}{220} = \frac{5}{11}$ and $P(B) = \frac{88}{220} = \frac{4}{10}$. Also, $P(A \cap B) = \frac{40}{220} = \frac{2}{11}$. Since $\left(\frac{5}{11}\right)\left(\frac{4}{10}\right) = \frac{20}{110} = \frac{2}{11}$, $P(A)P(B) = P(A \cap B)$ and these two events are indeed independent.

Expected Value

Expected value is a method of determining the expected outcome in a random situation. It is a sum of the weighted probabilities of the possible outcomes. Multiply the probability of an event occurring by the weight assigned to that probability (such as the amount of money won or lost). A practical application of the expected value is to determine whether a game of chance is really fair. If the sum of the weighted probabilities is equal to zero, the game is generally considered fair because the player has a fair chance to at least break even. If the expected value is less than zero, then players are expected to lose more than they win. For example, a lottery drawing might allow the player to choose any three-digit number, 000–999. The probability of choosing the winning number is 1:1000. If it costs \$1 to play, and a winning number receives \$500, the expected value is $\left(-\$1 \times \frac{999}{1,000}\right) + \left(\$499 \times \frac{1}{1,000}\right) = -\$0.50$. You can expect to lose on average 50 cents for every dollar you spend.

Review Video: Expected Value
Visit mometrix.com/academy and enter code: 643554

Expected Value and Simulators

A die roll simulator will show the results of n rolls of a die. The result of each die roll may be recorded. For example, suppose a die is rolled 100 times. All results may be recorded. The numbers of 1s, 2s, 3s, 4s, 5s, and 6s, may be counted. The experimental probability of rolling each number will equal the ratio of the frequency of the rolled number to the total number of rolls. As the number of rolls increases, or approaches infinity, the experimental probability will approach the theoretical probability of $\frac{1}{6}$. Thus, the expected value for the roll of a die is shown to be $\left(1 \times \frac{1}{6}\right) + \left(2 \times \frac{1}{6}\right) + \left(3 \times \frac{1}{6}\right) + \left(4 \times \frac{1}{6}\right) + \left(5 \times \frac{1}{6}\right) + \left(6 \times \frac{1}{6}\right)$, or 3.5.

Introduction to Statistics

Statistics is the branch of mathematics that deals with collecting, recording, interpreting, illustrating, and analyzing large amounts of **data**. The following terms are often used in the discussion of data and **statistics**:

- **Data** – the collective name for pieces of information (singular is datum)
- **Quantitative data** – measurements (such as length, mass, and speed) that provide information about quantities in numbers
- **Qualitative data** – information (such as colors, scents, tastes, and shapes) that cannot be measured using numbers
- **Discrete data** – information that can be expressed only by a specific value, such as whole or half numbers. (e.g., since people can be counted only in whole numbers, a population count would be discrete data.)
- **Continuous data** – information (such as time and temperature) that can be expressed by any value within a given range
- **Primary data** – information that has been collected directly from a survey, investigation, or experiment, such as a questionnaire or the recording of daily temperatures. (Primary data that has not yet been organized or analyzed is called **raw data**.)
- **Secondary data** – information that has been collected, sorted, and processed by the researcher
- **Ordinal data** – information that can be placed in numerical order, such as age or weight
- **Nominal data** – information that *cannot* be placed in numerical order, such as names or places

Data Collection

Population

In statistics, the **population** is the entire collection of people, plants, etc., that data can be collected from. For example, a study to determine how well students in local schools perform on a standardized test would have a population of all the students enrolled in those schools, although a study may include just a small sample of students from each school. A **parameter** is a numerical value that gives information about the population, such as the mean, median, mode, or standard deviation. Remember that the symbol for the mean of a population is μ and the symbol for the standard deviation of a population is σ.

SAMPLE

A **sample** is a portion of the entire population. Whereas a parameter helped describe the population, a **statistic** is a numerical value that gives information about the sample, such as mean, median, mode, or standard deviation. Keep in mind that the symbols for mean and standard deviation are different when they are referring to a sample rather than the entire population. For a sample, the symbol for mean is $\bar{x}$ and the symbol for standard deviation is s. The mean and standard deviation of a sample may or may not be identical to that of the entire population due to a sample only being a subset of the population. However, if the sample is random and large enough, statistically significant values can be attained. Samples are generally used when the population is too large to justify including every element or when acquiring data for the entire population is impossible.

INFERENTIAL STATISTICS

Inferential statistics is the branch of statistics that uses samples to make predictions about an entire population. This type of statistic is often seen in political polls, where a sample of the population is questioned about a particular topic or politician to gain an understanding of the attitudes of the entire population of the country. Often, exit polls are conducted on election days using this method. Inferential statistics can have a large margin of error if you do not have a valid sample.

SAMPLING DISTRIBUTION

Statistical values calculated from various samples of the same size make up the **sampling distribution**. For example, if several samples of identical size are randomly selected from a large population and then the mean of each sample is calculated, the distribution of values of the means would be a sampling distribution.

The **sampling distribution of the mean** is the distribution of the sample mean, $\bar{x}$, derived from random samples of a given size. It has three important characteristics. First, the mean of the sampling distribution of the mean is equal to the mean of the population that was sampled. Second, assuming the standard deviation is non-zero, the standard deviation of the sampling distribution of the mean equals the standard deviation of the sampled population divided by the square root of the sample size. This is sometimes called the standard error. Finally, as the sample size gets larger, the sampling distribution of the mean gets closer to a normal distribution via the central limit theorem.

SURVEY STUDY

A **survey study** is a method of gathering information from a small group in an attempt to gain enough information to make accurate general assumptions about the population. Once a survey study is completed, the results are then put into a summary report.

Survey studies are generally in the format of surveys, interviews, or questionnaires as part of an effort to find opinions of a particular group or to find facts about a group.

It is important to note that the findings from a survey study are only as accurate as the sample chosen from the population.

CORRELATIONAL STUDIES

Correlational studies seek to determine how much one variable is affected by changes in a second variable. For example, correlational studies may look for a relationship between the amount of time a student spends studying for a test and the grade that student earned on the test or between student scores on college admissions tests and student grades in college.

It is important to note that correlational studies cannot show a cause and effect, but rather can show only that two variables are or are not potentially correlated.

Experimental Studies

Experimental studies take correlational studies one step farther, in that they attempt to prove or disprove a cause-and-effect relationship. These studies are performed by conducting a series of experiments to test the hypothesis. For a study to be scientifically accurate, it must have both an experimental group that receives the specified treatment and a control group that does not get the treatment. This is the type of study pharmaceutical companies do as part of drug trials for new medications. Experimental studies are only valid when the proper scientific method has been followed. In other words, the experiment must be well-planned and executed without bias in the testing process, all subjects must be selected at random, and the process of determining which subject is in which of the two groups must also be completely random.

Observational Studies

Observational studies are the opposite of experimental studies. In observational studies, the tester cannot change or in any way control all of the variables in the test. For example, a study to determine which gender does better in math classes in school is strictly observational. You cannot change a person's gender, and you cannot change the subject being studied. The big downfall of observational studies is that you have no way of proving a cause-and-effect relationship because you cannot control outside influences. Events outside of school can influence a student's performance in school, and observational studies cannot take that into consideration.

Random Samples

For most studies, a **random sample** is necessary to produce valid results. Random samples should not have any particular influence to cause sampled subjects to behave one way or another. The goal is for the random sample to be a **representative sample**, or a sample whose characteristics give an accurate picture of the characteristics of the entire population. To accomplish this, you must make sure you have a proper **sample size**, or an appropriate number of elements in the sample.

Biases

In statistical studies, biases must be avoided. **Bias** is an error that causes the study to favor one set of results over another. For example, if a survey to determine how the country views the president's job performance only speaks to registered voters in the president's party, the results will be skewed because a disproportionately large number of responders would tend to show approval, while a disproportionately large number of people in the opposite party would tend to express disapproval. **Extraneous variables** are, as the name implies, outside influences that can affect the outcome of a study. They are not always avoidable but could trigger bias in the result.

Data Analysis

Dispersion

A **measure of dispersion** is a single value that helps to "interpret" the measure of central tendency by providing more information about how the data values in the set are distributed about the measure of central tendency. The measure of dispersion helps to eliminate or reduce the disadvantages of using the mean, median, or mode as a single measure of central tendency, and give a more accurate picture of the dataset as a whole. To have a measure of dispersion, you must know or calculate the range, standard deviation, or variance of the data set.

Range

The **range** of a set of data is the difference between the greatest and lowest values of the data in the set. To calculate the range, you must first make sure the units for all data values are the same, and then identify the greatest and lowest values. If there are multiple data values that are equal for the highest or lowest, just use one of the values in the formula. Write the answer with the same units as the data values you used to do the calculations.

Review Video: Statistical Range
Visit mometrix.com/academy and enter code: 778541

SAMPLE STANDARD DEVIATION

Standard deviation is a measure of dispersion that compares all the data values in the set to the mean of the set to give a more accurate picture. To find the **standard deviation of a sample**, use the formula

$$s = \sqrt{\frac{\sum_{i=1}^{n}(x_i - \bar{x})^2}{n - 1}}$$

Note that s is the standard deviation of a sample, x_i represents the individual values in the data set, $\bar{x}$ is the mean of the data values in the set, and n is the number of data values in the set. The higher the value of the standard deviation is, the greater the variance of the data values from the mean. The units associated with the standard deviation are the same as the units of the data values.

> **Review Video: Standard Deviation**
> Visit mometrix.com/academy and enter code: 419469

SAMPLE VARIANCE

The **variance of a sample** is the square of the sample standard deviation (denoted s^2). While the mean of a set of data gives the average of the set and gives information about where a specific data value lies in relation to the average, the variance of the sample gives information about the degree to which the data values are spread out and tells you how close an individual value is to the average compared to the other values. The units associated with variance are the same as the units of the data values squared.

PERCENTILE

Percentiles and quartiles are other methods of describing data within a set. **Percentiles** tell what percentage of the data in the set fall below a specific point. For example, achievement test scores are often given in percentiles. A score at the 80th percentile is one which is equal to or higher than 80 percent of the scores in the set. In other words, 80 percent of the scores were lower than that score.

Quartiles are percentile groups that make up quarter sections of the data set. The first quartile is the 25th percentile. The second quartile is the 50th percentile; this is also the median of the dataset. The third quartile is the 75th percentile.

SKEWNESS

Skewness is a way to describe the symmetry or asymmetry of the distribution of values in a dataset. If the distribution of values is symmetrical, there is no skew. In general the closer the mean of a data set is to the median of the data set, the less skew there is. Generally, if the mean is to the right of the median, the data set is *positively skewed*, or right-skewed, and if the mean is to the left of the median, the data set is *negatively skewed*, or left-skewed. However, this rule of thumb is not infallible. When the data values are graphed on a curve, a set with no skew will be a perfect bell curve.

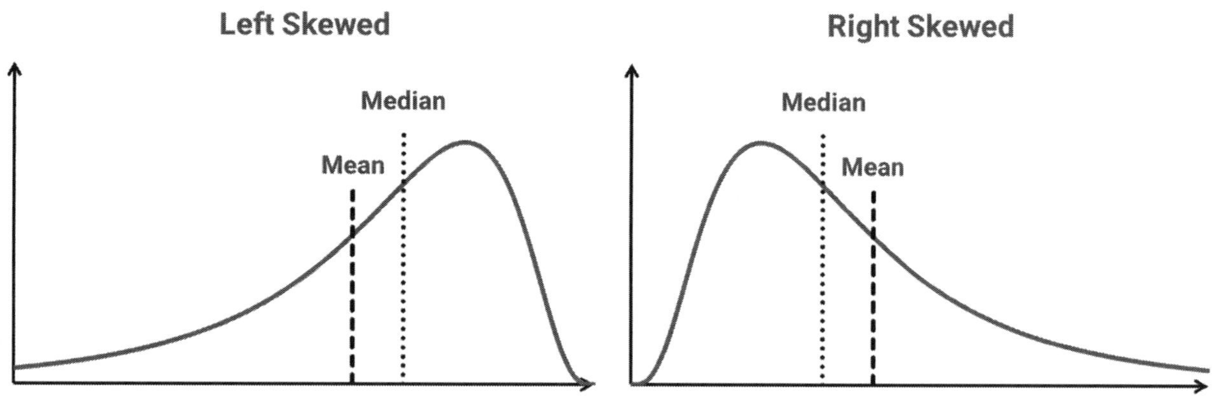

To estimate skew, use the formula:

$$\text{skew} = \frac{\sqrt{n(n-1)}}{n-2}\left(\frac{\frac{1}{n}\sum_{i=1}^{n}(x_i-\bar{x})^3}{\left(\frac{1}{n}\sum_{i=1}^{n}(x_i-\bar{x})^2\right)^{\frac{3}{2}}}\right)$$

Note that n is the datapoints in the set, x_i is the ith value in the set, and $\bar{x}$ is the mean of the set.

Review Video: Skew
Visit mometrix.com/academy and enter code: 661486

Unimodal vs. Bimodal

If a distribution has a single peak, it would be considered **unimodal**. If it has two discernible peaks it would be considered **bimodal**. Bimodal distributions may be an indication that the set of data being considered is actually the combination of two sets of data with significant differences. A **uniform distribution** is a distribution in which there is *no distinct peak or variation* in the data. No values or ranges are particularly more common than any other values or ranges.

Outlier

An outlier is an extremely high or extremely low value in the data set. It may be the result of measurement error, in which case, the outlier is not a valid member of the data set. However, it may also be a valid member of the distribution. Unless a measurement error is identified, the experimenter cannot know for certain if an outlier is or is not a member of the distribution. There are arbitrary methods that can be employed to designate an extreme value as an outlier. One method designates an outlier (or possible outlier) to be any value less than $Q_1 - 1.5(IQR)$ or any value greater than $Q_3 + 1.5(IQR)$.

Data Analysis

Simple Regression

In statistics, **simple regression** is using an equation to represent a relation between independent and dependent variables. The independent variable is also referred to as the explanatory variable or the predictor and is generally represented by the variable x in the equation. The dependent variable, usually represented by the variable y, is also referred to as the response variable. The equation may be any type of function – linear, quadratic, exponential, etc. The best way to handle this task is to use the regression feature of your graphing calculator. This will easily give you the curve of best fit and provide you with the coefficients and other information you need to derive an equation.

Line of Best Fit

In a scatter plot, the **line of best fit** is the line that best shows the trends of the data. The line of best fit is given by the equation $\hat{y} = ax + b$, where a and b are the regression coefficients. The regression coefficient a is also the slope of the line of best fit, and b is also the y-coordinate of the point at which the line of best fit crosses the y-axis. Not every point on the scatter plot will be on the line of best fit. The differences between the y-values of the points in the scatter plot and the corresponding y-values according to the equation of the line of best fit are the residuals. The line of best fit is also called the least-squares regression line because it is also the line that has the lowest sum of the squares of the residuals.

Correlation Coefficient

The **correlation coefficient** is the numerical value that indicates how strong the relationship is between the two variables of a linear regression equation. A correlation coefficient of −1 is a perfect negative correlation. A correlation coefficient of +1 is a perfect positive correlation. Correlation coefficients close to −1 or +1 are very strong correlations. A correlation coefficient equal to zero indicates there is no correlation between the two variables. This test is a good indicator of whether or not the equation for the line of best fit is accurate. The formula for the correlation coefficient is

$$r = \frac{\sum_{i=1}^{n}(x_i - \bar{x})(y_i - \bar{y})}{\sqrt{\sum_{i=1}^{n}(x_i - \bar{x})^2}\sqrt{\sum_{i=1}^{n}(y_i - \bar{y})^2}}$$

where r is the correlation coefficient, n is the number of data values in the set, (x_i, y_i) is a point in the set, and $\bar{x}$ and $\bar{y}$ are the means.

Z-Score

A **z-score** is an indication of how many standard deviations a given value falls from the sample mean. To calculate a z-score, use the formula:

$$\frac{x - \bar{x}}{\sigma}$$

In this formula x is the data value, $\bar{x}$ is the mean of the sample data, and σ is the standard deviation of the population. If the z-score is positive, the data value lies above the mean. If the z-score is negative, the data value falls below the mean. These scores are useful in interpreting data such as standardized test scores, where every piece of data in the set has been counted, rather than just a small random sample. In cases where standard deviations are calculated from a random sample of the set, the z-scores will not be as accurate.

Central Limit Theorem

According to the **central limit theorem**, regardless of what the original distribution of a sample is, the distribution of the means tends to get closer and closer to a normal distribution as the sample size gets larger and larger (this is necessary because the sample is becoming more all-encompassing of the elements of the population). As the sample size gets larger, the distribution of the sample mean will approach a normal distribution with a mean of the population mean and a variance of the population variance divided by the sample size.

Measures of Central Tendency

A **measure of central tendency** is a statistical value that gives a reasonable estimate for the center of a group of data. There are several different ways of describing the measure of central tendency. Each one has a unique way it is calculated, and each one gives a slightly different perspective on the data set. Whenever you give a measure of central tendency, always make sure the units are the same. If the data has different units, such as hours, minutes, and seconds, convert all the data to the same unit, and use the same unit in the measure of central tendency. If no units are given in the data, do not give units for the measure of central tendency.

MEAN

The **statistical mean** of a group of data is the same as the arithmetic average of that group. To find the mean of a set of data, first convert each value to the same units, if necessary. Then find the sum of all the values, and count the total number of data values, making sure you take into consideration each individual value. If a value appears more than once, count it more than once. Divide the sum of the values by the total number of values and apply the units, if any. Note that the mean does not have to be one of the data values in the set, and may not divide evenly.

$$\text{mean} = \frac{\text{sum of the data values}}{\text{quantity of data values}}$$

For instance, the mean of the data set {88, 72, 61, 90, 97, 68, 88, 79, 86, 93, 97, 71, 80, 84, 89} would be the sum of the fifteen numbers divided by 15:

$$\frac{88 + 72 + 61 + 90 + 97 + 68 + 88 + 79 + 86 + 93 + 97 + 71 + 80 + 84 + 89}{15} = \frac{1242}{15} = 82.8$$

While the mean is relatively easy to calculate and averages are understood by most people, the mean can be very misleading if it is used as the sole measure of central tendency. If the data set has outliers (data values that are unusually high or unusually low compared to the rest of the data values), the mean can be very distorted, especially if the data set has a small number of values. If unusually high values are countered with unusually low values, the mean is not affected as much. For example, if five of twenty students in a class get a 100 on a test, but the other 15 students have an average of 60 on the same test, the class average would appear as 70. Whenever the mean is skewed by outliers, it is always a good idea to include the median as an alternate measure of central tendency.

A **weighted mean**, or weighted average, is a mean that uses "weighted" values. The formula is weighted mean $= \frac{w_1x_1+w_2x_2+w_3x_3...+w_nx_n}{w_1+w_2+w_3+\cdots+w_n}$. Weighted values, such as $w_1, w_2, w_3, ... w_n$ are assigned to each member of the set $x_1, x_2, x_3, ... x_n$. When calculating the weighted mean, make sure a weight value for each member of the set is used.

Review Video: All About Averages
Visit mometrix.com/academy and enter code: 176521

MEDIAN

The **statistical median** is the value in the middle of the set of data. To find the median, list all data values in order from smallest to largest or from largest to smallest. Any value that is repeated in the set must be listed the number of times it appears. If there are an odd number of data values, the median is the value in the middle of the list. If there is an even number of data values, the median is the arithmetic mean of the two middle values.

For example, the median of the data set {88, 72, 61, 90, 97, 68, 88, 79, 86, 93, 97, 71, 80, 84, 88} is 86 since the ordered set is {61, 68, 71, 72, 79, 80, 84, **86**, 88, 88, 88, 90, 93, 97, 97}.

The big disadvantage of using the median as a measure of central tendency is that is relies solely on a value's relative size as compared to the other values in the set. When the individual values in a set of data are evenly dispersed, the median can be an accurate tool. However, if there is a group of rather large values or a group of rather small values that are not offset by a different group of values, the information that can be inferred from the median may not be accurate because the distribution of values is skewed.

MODE

The **statistical mode** is the data value that occurs the greatest number of times in the data set. It is possible to have exactly one mode, more than one mode, or no mode. To find the mode of a set of data, arrange the data like you do to find the median (all values in order, listing all multiples of data values). Count the number of times each value appears in the data set. If all values appear an equal number of times, there is no mode. If one value appears more than any other value, that value is the mode. If two or more values appear the same number of times, but there are other values that appear fewer times and no values that appear more times, all of those values are the modes.

For example, the mode of the data set {**88**, 72, 61, 90, 97, 68, **88**, 79, 86, 93, 97, 71, 80, 84, **88**} is 88.

The main disadvantage of the mode is that the values of the other data in the set have no bearing on the mode. The mode may be the largest value, the smallest value, or a value anywhere in between in the set. The mode only tells which value or values, if any, occurred the greatest number of times. It does not give any suggestions about the remaining values in the set.

Review Video: Mean, Median, and Mode
Visit mometrix.com/academy and enter code: 286207

DISPLAYING INFORMATION

FREQUENCY TABLES

Frequency tables show how frequently each unique value appears in a set. A **relative frequency table** is one that shows the proportions of each unique value compared to the entire set. Relative frequencies are given as percentages; however, the total percent for a relative frequency table will not necessarily equal 100 percent due to rounding. An example of a frequency table with relative frequencies is below.

Favorite Color	Frequency	Relative Frequency
Blue	4	13%
Red	7	22%
Green	3	9%
Purple	6	19%
Cyan	12	38%

Review Video: Data Interpretation of Graphs
Visit mometrix.com/academy and enter code: 200439

CIRCLE GRAPHS

Circle graphs, also known as *pie charts*, provide a visual depiction of the relationship of each type of data compared to the whole set of data. The circle graph is divided into sections by drawing radii to create central angles whose percentage of the circle is equal to the individual data's percentage of the whole set. Each 1% of data is equal to 3.6° in the circle graph. Therefore, data represented by a 90° section of the circle graph makes up 25% of the whole. When complete, a circle graph often looks like a pie cut into uneven wedges. The pie chart below shows the data from the frequency table referenced earlier where people were asked their favorite color.

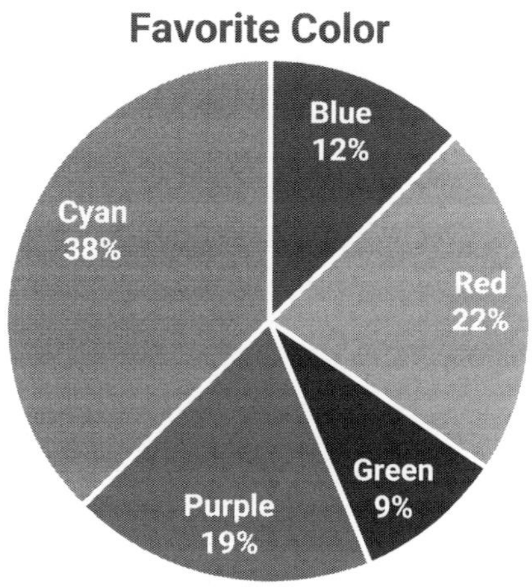

PICTOGRAPHS

A **pictograph** is a graph, generally in the horizontal orientation, that uses pictures or symbols to represent the data. Each pictograph must have a key that defines the picture or symbol and gives the quantity each picture or symbol represents. Pictures or symbols on a pictograph are not always shown as whole elements. In this case, the fraction of the picture or symbol shown represents the same fraction of the quantity a whole picture or symbol stands for. For example, a row with $3\frac{1}{2}$ ears of corn, where each ear of corn represents 100 stalks of corn in a field, would equal $3\frac{1}{2} \times 100 = 350$ stalks of corn in the field.

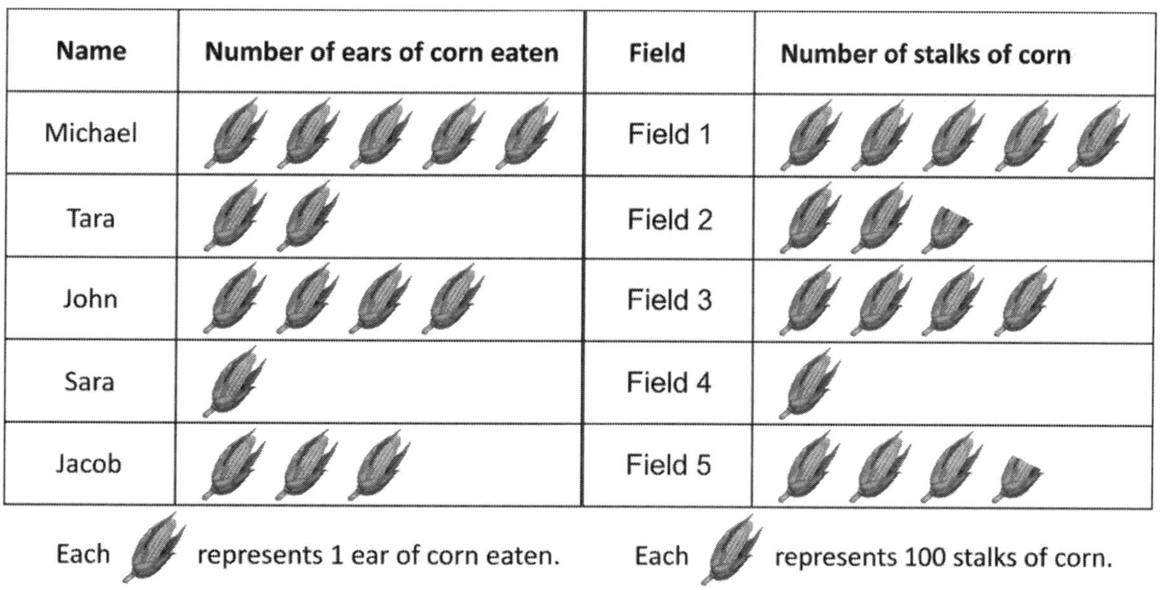

Review Video: Pictographs
Visit mometrix.com/academy and enter code: 147860

LINE GRAPHS

Line graphs have one or more lines of varying styles (solid or broken) to show the different values for a set of data. The individual data are represented as ordered pairs, much like on a Cartesian plane. In this case, the x- and y-axes are defined in terms of their units, such as dollars or time. The individual plotted points are joined by line segments to show whether the value of the data is increasing (line sloping upward), decreasing (line sloping downward), or staying the same (horizontal line). Multiple sets of data can be graphed on the same line graph to give an easy visual comparison. An example of this would be graphing achievement test scores for different groups of students over the same time period to see which group had the greatest increase or decrease in performance from year to year (as shown below).

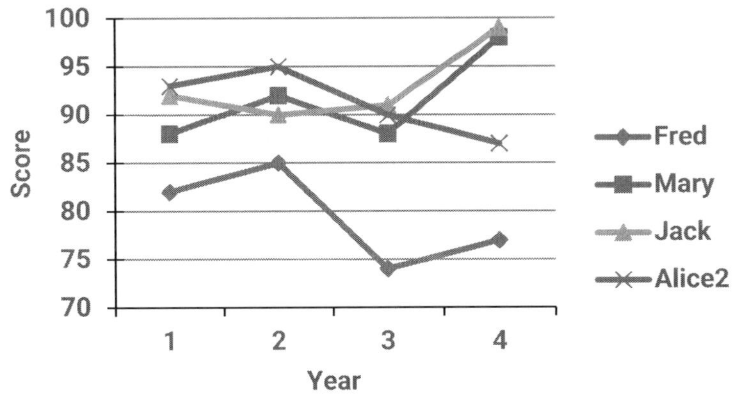

Review Video: How to Create a Line Graph
Visit mometrix.com/academy and enter code: 480147

Line Plots

A **line plot**, also known as a *dot plot*, has plotted points that are not connected by line segments. In this graph, the horizontal axis lists the different possible values for the data, and the vertical axis lists the number of times the individual value occurs. A single dot is graphed for each value to show the number of times it occurs. This graph is more closely related to a bar graph than a line graph. Do not connect the dots in a line plot or it will misrepresent the data.

Review Video: Line Plot
Visit mometrix.com/academy and enter code: 754610

Stem and Leaf Plots

A **stem and leaf plot** is useful for depicting groups of data that fall into a range of values. Each piece of data is separated into two parts: the first, or left, part is called the stem; the second, or right, part is called the leaf. Each stem is listed in a column from smallest to largest. Each leaf that has the common stem is listed in that stem's row from smallest to largest. For example, in a set of two-digit numbers, the digit in the tens place is the stem, and the digit in the ones place is the leaf. With a stem and leaf plot, you can easily see which subset of numbers (10s, 20s, 30s, etc.) is the largest. This information is also readily available by looking at a histogram, but a stem and leaf plot also allows you to look closer and see exactly which values fall in that range. Using a sample set of test scores (82, 88, 92, 93, 85, 90, 92, 95, 74, 88, 90, 91, 78, 87, 98, 99), we can assemble a stem and leaf plot like the one below.

Test Scores

7	4	8							
8	2	5	7	8	8				
9	0	0	1	2	2	3	5	8	9

Review Video: Stem and Leaf Plots
Visit mometrix.com/academy and enter code: 302339

BAR GRAPHS

A **bar graph** is one of the few graphs that can be drawn correctly in two different configurations – both horizontally and vertically. A bar graph is similar to a line plot in the way the data is organized on the graph. Both axes must have their categories defined for the graph to be useful. Rather than placing a single dot to mark the point of the data's value, a bar, or thick line, is drawn from zero to the exact value of the data, whether it is a number, percentage, or other numerical value. Longer bar lengths correspond to greater data values. To read a bar graph, read the labels for the axes to find the units being reported. Then, look where the bars end in relation to the scale given on the corresponding axis and determine the associated value.

The bar chart below represents the responses from our favorite-color survey.

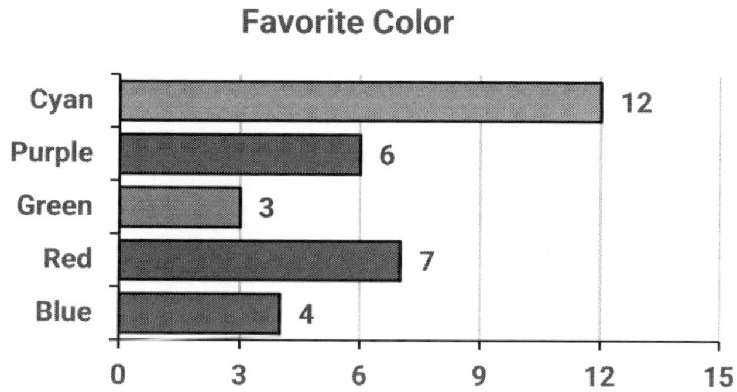

HISTOGRAMS

At first glance, a **histogram** looks like a vertical bar graph. The difference is that a bar graph has a separate bar for each piece of data and a histogram has one continuous bar for each *range* of data. For example, a histogram may have one bar for the range 0–9, one bar for 10–19, etc. While a bar graph has numerical values on one axis, a histogram has numerical values on both axes. Each range is of equal size, and they are ordered left to right from lowest to highest. The height of each column on a histogram represents the number of data values within that range. Like a stem and leaf plot, a histogram makes it easy to glance at the graph and quickly determine which range has the greatest quantity of values. A simple example of a histogram is below.

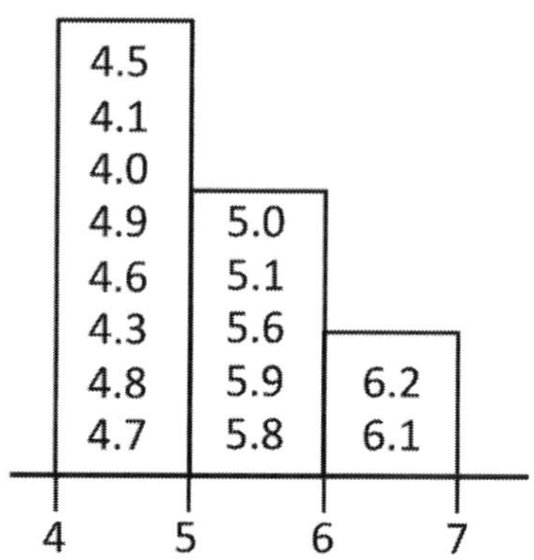

5-NUMBER SUMMARY

The **5-number summary** of a set of data gives a very informative picture of the set. The five numbers in the summary include the minimum value, maximum value, and the three quartiles. This information gives the reader the range and median of the set, as well as an indication of how the data is spread about the median.

Box and Whisker Plots

A **box-and-whiskers plot** is a graphical representation of the 5-number summary. To draw a box-and-whiskers plot, plot the points of the 5-number summary on a number line. Draw a box whose ends are through the points for the first and third quartiles. Draw a vertical line in the box through the median to divide the box in half. Draw a line segment from the first quartile point to the minimum value, and from the third quartile point to the maximum value.

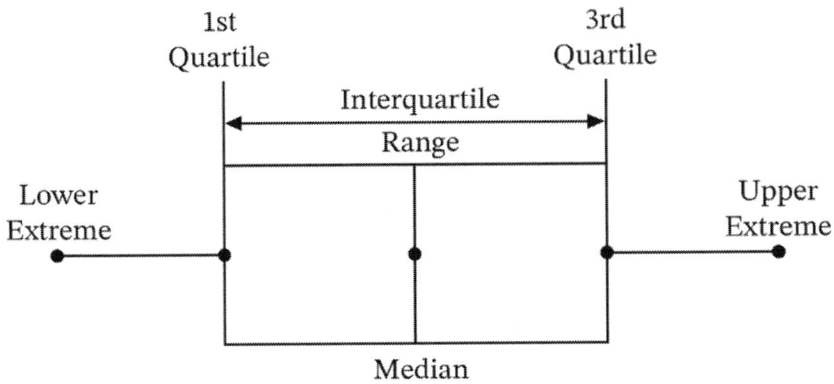

Review Video: Box and Whisker Plots
Visit mometrix.com/academy and enter code: 810817

Example

Given the following data (32, 28, 29, 26, 35, 27, 30, 31, 27, 32), we first sort it into numerical order: 26, 27, 27, 28, 29, 30, 31, 32, 32, 35. We can then find the median. Since there are ten values, we take the average of the 5th and 6th values to get 29.5. We find the lower quartile by taking the median of the data smaller than the median. Since there are five values, we take the 3rd value, which is 27. We find the upper quartile by taking the median of the data larger than the overall median, which is 32. Finally, we note our minimum and maximum, which are simply the smallest and largest values in the set: 26 and 35, respectively. Now we can create our box plot:

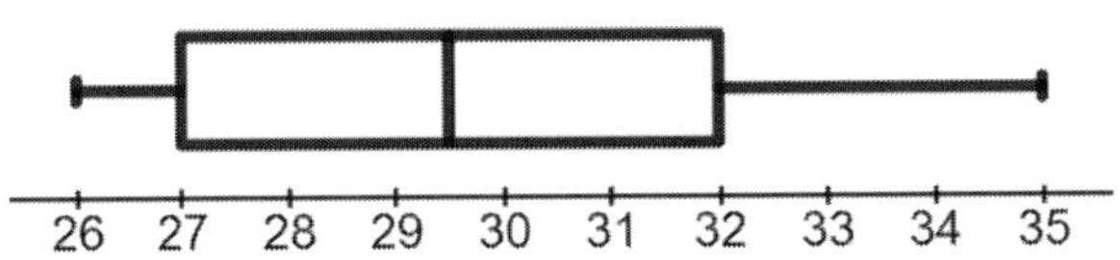

This plot is fairly "long" on the right whisker, showing one or more unusually high values (but not quite outliers). The other quartiles are similar in length, showing a fairly even distribution of data.

Interquartile Range

The **interquartile range, or IQR**, is the difference between the upper and lower quartiles. It measures how the data is dispersed: a high IQR means that the data is more spread out, while a low IQR means that the data is clustered more tightly around the median. To find the IQR, subtract the lower quartile value (Q_1) from the upper quartile value (Q_3).

Example

To find the upper and lower quartiles, we first find the median and then take the median of all values above it and all values below it. In the following data set (16, 18, 13, 24, 16, 51, 32, 21, 27, 39), we first rearrange the values in numerical order: 13, 16, 16, 18, 21, 24, 27, 32, 39, 51. There are 10 values, so the median is the average of the 5th and 6th: $\frac{21+24}{2} = \frac{45}{2} = 22.5$. We do not actually need this value to find the upper and lower quartiles. We look at the set of numbers below the median: 13, 16, 16, 18, 21. There are five values, so the 3rd is the median (16), or the value of the lower quartile (Q_1). Then we look at the numbers above the median: 24, 27, 32, 39, 51. Again there are five values, so the 3rd is the median (32), or the value of the upper quartile (Q_3). We find the IQR by subtracting Q_1 from Q_3: $32 - 16 = 16$.

68-95-99.7 Rule

The **68–95–99.7 rule** describes how a normal distribution of data should appear when compared to the mean. This is also a description of a normal bell curve. According to this rule, 68 percent of the data values in a normally distributed set should fall within one standard deviation of the mean (34 percent above and 34 percent below the mean), 95 percent of the data values should fall within two standard deviations of the mean (47.5 percent above and 47.5 percent below the mean), and 99.7 percent of the data values should fall within three standard deviations of the mean, again, equally distributed on either side of the mean. This means that only 0.3 percent of all data values should fall more than three standard deviations from the mean. On the graph below, the normal curve is centered on the y-axis. The x-axis labels are how many standard deviations away from the center you are. Therefore, it is easy to see how the 68-95-99.7 rule can apply.

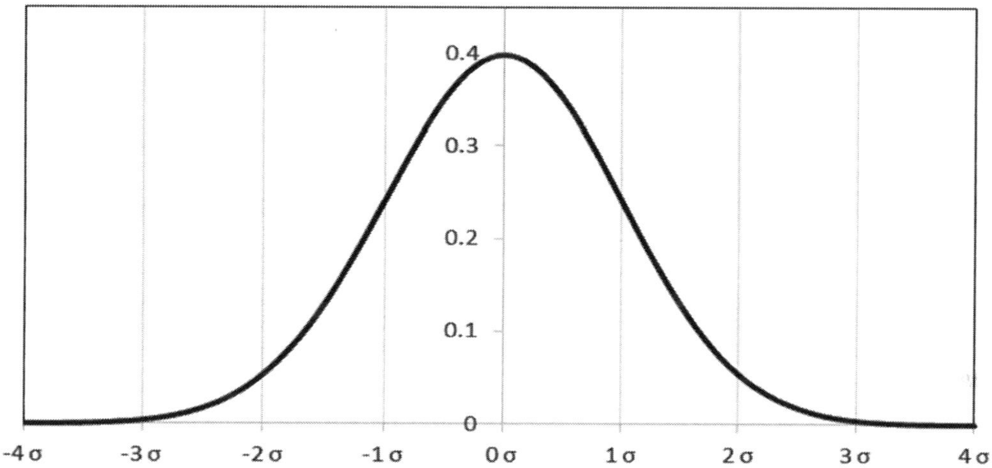

Scatter Plots

Bivariate Data

Bivariate data is simply data from two different variables. (The prefix *bi-* means *two.*) In a *scatter plot,* each value in the set of data is plotted on a grid similar to a Cartesian plane, where each axis represents one of the two variables. By looking at the pattern formed by the points on the grid, you can often determine whether or not there is a relationship between the two variables, and what that relationship is, if it exists. The variables may be directly proportionate, inversely proportionate, or show no proportion at all. It may also be possible to determine if the data is linear, and if so, to find an equation to relate the two variables. The following scatter plot shows the relationship between preference for brand "A" and the age of the consumers surveyed.

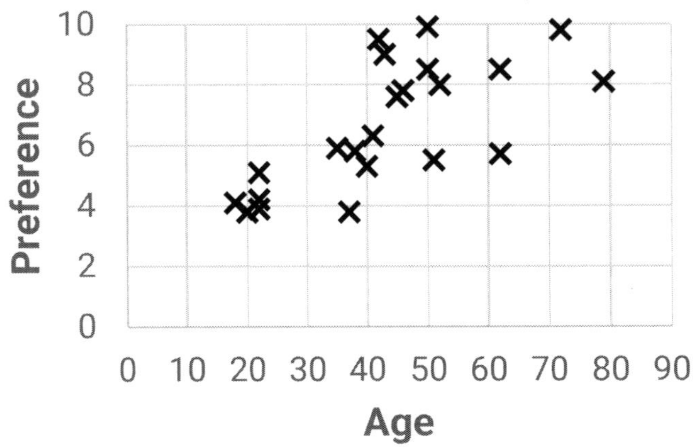

SCATTER PLOTS

Scatter plots are also useful in determining the type of function represented by the data and finding the simple regression. Linear scatter plots may be positive or negative. Nonlinear scatter plots are generally exponential or quadratic. Below are some common types of scatter plots:

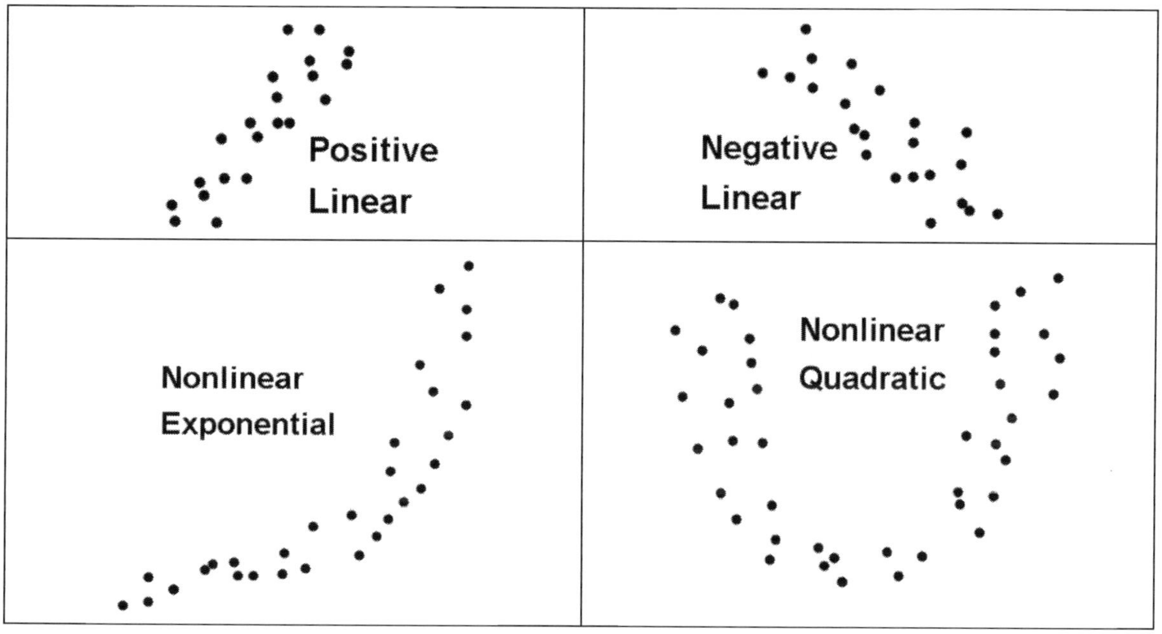

Review Video: Scatter Plot
Visit mometrix.com/academy and enter code: 596526

Chapter Quiz

Ready to see how well you retained what you just read? Scan the QR code to go directly to the chapter quiz interface for this study guide. If you're using a computer, simply visit the online resources page at **mometrix.com/resources719/tabe1314** and click the Chapter Quizzes link.

Mathematics

TABE Practice Test #1

Want to take this practice test in an online interactive format?
Check out the online resources page, which includes interactive practice questions and much more: **mometrix.com/resources719/tabe1314**

Reading

Refer to the following for questions 1–4:

Annelids

The phylum Annelida, named for the Latin word *anellus*, meaning "ring," includes earthworms, leeches, and other similar organisms. In their typical form, these animals exhibit bilateral symmetry, a cylindrical cross section, and an elongate body divided externally into segments (*metameres*) by a series of rings (*annuli*). They are segmented internally as well, with most of the internal organs repeated in series in each segment. This organization is termed *metamerism*. Metameric segmentation is the distinguishing feature of this phylum, and provides it with a degree of evolutionary plasticity in that certain segments can be modified and specialized to perform specific functions. For example, in some species certain of the locomotor *parapodia*, or feet, may be modified for grasping, and some portions of the gut may evolve digestive specializations.

The gut is a straight, muscular tube that functions independently of the muscular activity in the body wall. The Annelida resemble the nematodes, another worm phylum, in possessing a fluid-filled internal cavity separating the gut from the body wall. In both phyla, this cavity is involved in locomotion. However, in the annelids, this space is formed at a much later time during the development of the embryo, and presumably evolved much later as well. This fluid-filled internal space is called a true *coelom*.

The annelid excretory and circulatory systems are well developed, and some members of the phylum have evolved respiratory organs. The nervous system offers a particular example of metameric specialization. It is concentrated anteriorly into enlarged cerebral ganglia connected to a ventral nerve cord that extends posteriorly and is organized into repeating segmental ganglia.

This phylum includes members bearing adaptations required for aquatic (marine or freshwater) or terrestrial habitats. They may be free-living entities or exist as parasites. Among the best known are the earthworm *Lumbricus*, the water leech *Hirudo*, and the marine worm *Nereis*.

1. What is the purpose of this passage?

a. To describe the annelid nervous system
b. To describe the annelid digestive system
c. To introduce distinctive features of annelid anatomy
d. To define metamerism

2. What is meant by the term *parapodia*?

a. Specialization
b. Grasping appendages
c. Locomotion
d. Feet

3. Which of the following is one evolutionary advantage of segmentation?

a. Segmented animals have many feet.
b. Segmented animals have a fluid-filled coelom.
c. Parts of some segments can become specialized to perform certain functions.
d. Segments can evolve.

4. A group of worms other than the Annelida are called:

a. Lumbricus
b. Nematodes
c. Leeches
d. Parapodia

Refer to the following for questions 5–10:

Selection of "The Gettysburg Address" *by Abraham Lincoln*

Four score and seven years ago our fathers brought forth, upon this continent, a new nation, conceived in Liberty, and dedicated to the proposition that all men are created equal.

Now we are engaged in a great civil war, testing whether that nation, or any nation so conceived, and so dedicated, can long endure. We are met here on a great battlefield of that war. We have come to dedicate a portion of it as a final resting place for those who here gave their lives that that nation might live. It is altogether fitting and proper that we should do this.

But in a larger sense we cannot dedicate—we cannot consecrate—we cannot hallow this ground. The brave men, living and dead, who struggled here, have consecrated it far above our poor power to add or detract. The world will little note, nor long remember, what we say here, but can never forget what they did here.

It is for us, the living, rather to be dedicated here to the unfinished work which they have, thus far, so nobly carried on. It is rather for us to be here dedicated to the great task remaining before us—that from these honored dead we take increased devotion to that cause for which they here gave the last full measure of devotion—that we here highly resolve that these dead shall not have died in vain; that this nation shall have a new birth of freedom; and that this government of the people, by the people, for the people, shall not perish from the earth.

5. What is the main message of this speech?

a. Those who died in this battle honor this land we are dedicating today better than anyone else.
b. As we honor those who died in this battle, we should move forward with renewed dedication to ensuring the nation our founding fathers created continues to function the way they intended.
c. We need to put the regrets of the past aside, without remembering the sacrifices of those who gave their lives for our country.
d. The war we are fighting is far from over, as evidenced by the number of lives lost in this battle.

6. The phrase "the world will little note" means what?

a. The world will not soon forget.
b. The world will record what we say here.
c. The world will not pay much attention.
d. The world will recall what we do with perfect accuracy.

7. There were nearly 100 years between the American Revolution and the Civil War. The speech connects ideas about these two conflicts by saying that the ideas of the Civil War:

a. Threaten those of the Revolution.
b. Are similar to those of the Revolution.
c. Are newer than those of the Revolution.
d. Are better than those of the Revolution.

8. Why does Lincoln most likely talk about the past before he talks about the present?

a. To incite listeners of his message to protest
b. To remember what has been lost in the past
c. To establish context for his main message
d. To try to get listeners to side with his position

9. What is the following sentence addressing?

Now we are engaged in a great civil war, testing whether that nation, or any nation so conceived, and so dedicated, can long endure.

a. Whether or not a nation based on ideas of freedom and equality can survive for any significant length of time
b. Whether or not the Union will be able to preserve the existing structure of the United States by preventing the Confederacy from seceding
c. Whether or not the Confederacy will be successful in seceding from the United States and surviving on its own
d. Whether or not Lincoln should continue dedicating troops to the war

10. In paragraph 4, the word *vain* most nearly means:

a. Decisive
b. Frivolous
c. Momentous
d. Practical

Refer to the following for questions 11–15:

Food Storage Containers

Plastic is one of the most common materials used for food storage. Plastic containers, bags and boxes, are inexpensive, lightweight, and convenient. But is plastic safe? The answer to this question may not be a simple one, as there are many different varieties of plastic, manufactured by different processes. Some of these processes employ phthalates, a type of chemical used to soften the plastic so that it may be molded. And, there is mounting evidence that phthalates may be toxic.

The most common phthalate is bis-phenol A, commonly known as BPA. BPA has been declared safe for food storage by the Food and Drug Administration, but the FDA relied on information supplied by the chemical industry to reach that conclusion. Recent evidence has called its decision into doubt, and the agency has announced that it will review its earlier determination.

The concern about BPA's toxicity is widespread, especially when food is stored for young children. Its use in baby bottles has been banned in Canada and in several states in the U.S., and Connecticut has prohibited it in all reusable food containers.

Traces of BPA can be found in foods that have been stored in containers made of polycarbonate and other plastic materials. But these are not limited to baby bottles or to reusable plastic food-storage containers. Canned foods are also found to be contaminated, since plastic linings are often used in food cans to protect the product from taking on the flavor of the metal. The use of plastics in the food industry is widespread, and calls for its elimination have led to predictable protests.

A particular concern is the use of plastic storage containers to microwave food that is to be warmed before serving. BPA has been found to leach from polycarbonates and form other plastics during this process. Caroline Baier-Anderson, a health scientist and an assistant professor in the Department of Epidemiology and Preventive Medicine at the University of Maryland, Baltimore, told the Washington Post: "It is best not to microwave plastics, particularly since alternatives are widely available."

So how can you avoid the potential problems with plastic food storage? You have three major options when it comes to selecting our food storage containers.

1. Use glass containers. Many of these are available with either glass or plastic lids. Some of the plastic lids are BPA-free, but since the lid comes into only limited contact with the product, the presence of BPA is a lesser concern here.

2. Use stainless steel containers. While glass and steel are expensive, they can be used over many times, so that the cost is eventually amortized. They are heavier than plastic, however.

3. Use safer plastic containers. Some manufacturers have responded to consumer concerns by marketing plastics that are BPA-free. There have been some misleading claims however, so that consumers are advised to seek third-party reviews of particular products. One source of information is ftc.gov/news-events/topics/truth-advertising/green-guides, a website by the Federal Trade Commission. It has reviews of specific brands of plastic storage products that have been tested for the presence of BPA.

11. What is the main purpose of this article?

a. To describe the use of plastic in storing food.
b. To warn readers about a potential danger in using plastic containers for food storage.
c. To list a variety of different containers that can be used to store food.
d. To tell readers not to microwave food in plastic containers.

12. Which of the following statements is true, according to the text?

a. Canada has banned the use of plastics in baby bottles.
b. Canada has banned the use of plastics in reusable food containers.
c. Canada has banned the use of BPA in plastics.
d. Canada has banned the use of BPA in reusable baby bottles.

13. Which of the following statements best reflects the author's point of view in writing this article?

a. The author feels that all BPA-containing plastics should be banned.
b. The author feels that BPA-containing plastics should be banned from use in food containers.
c. The author wants to offer consumers alternatives to using BPA-containing food storage containers.
d. The author feels that stainless steel food storage containers are the best for all uses.

14. According to the passage, why are phthalates are used in manufacturing plastics?

a. To facilitate molding
b. To make them toxic
c. To allow them to be microwaved
d. To make them safer

15. What action does the author suggest as a way to avoid potential problems with food storage containers?

a. Avoiding all plastics
b. Carefully selecting materials
c. Never using plastics in microwave ovens
d. Avoiding plastic baby bottles

Refer to the following for questions 16–20:

Leatherback Turtle Populations Recover

The Pacific leatherback turtle arrives in California during the late summer to feed on offshore jellyfish populations. In recent years, egg poaching and accidental capture of adults by fishing nets have led to severe reductions of leatherback populations throughout the Pacific. Conservation of remaining populations of this endangered species became a priority for the U.S. Fish and Wildlife Service.

Since leatherbacks nest on tropical beaches, it was long thought that the California visitors originated from nearby colonies in Mexico and Central America. But research during the past decade has shown that these populations actually come from nesting colonies in the western Pacific.

The western populations were also shown to be comprised of several groups with distinct feeding and migratory patterns. Although they are genetically identical, some groups feed on California beaches, while others visit beaches in the eastern and southern Pacific. These results have caused the Fish and Wildlife Service to alter its approach to conserving the species.

"To help protect the leatherbacks, we have expanded our central California work to include a variety of conservation and research initiatives in western Pacific island nations," said Jeff Seminoff, head of the Southwest Fisheries Center Marine Turtle Ecology and Assessment Team. "We recently conducted aerial surveys in Papua New Guinea, Papua (Indonesia) and the Solomon Islands, confirming that large numbers of nesting leatherbacks remain only on a few beaches in Papua. This underscores the need to protect these last remaining rookeries before it is too late."

A program of sustained beach conservation efforts is now in progress in Papua and throughout the western Pacific. This project coordinates contributions from local organizations, government and university biologists, World Wildlife Fund researchers and fishery management organizations. Local residents are being trained to monitor the nesting beaches and to evaluate hatching success. Early results have inspired a cautious optimism: leatherback turtle populations seem to be recovering.

An important part of local folklore, the leatherback is known by many names throughout the western Pacific: trousel, tabob, penyubelimbing, leddebak. Once an important food source, it figures in the legends of many island peoples. With the new awareness that the turtles travel broadly across the ocean, the new partnership is now working within the international community to ensure survival of the leatherback for future generations.

Continued success of these conservation efforts will require a more complete understanding of the entire ecosystem in which the turtles live. These highly mobile marine reptiles move freely across one third of the globe, roaming the entire Pacific Ocean. An effective program necessitates a broad approach that includes the restoration of feeding grounds, nesting beaches, and the migratory routes that connect them.

As leatherback turtles journey from one edge of the Pacific to the other, these gentle marine ambassadors are bringing governments, communities and people together to share a common cause of preserving vibrant marine ecosystems for future generations.

16. Which of the following is the passage is primarily concerned with?

a. Beach conservation efforts in the western Pacific
b. The occurrence of leatherback turtles in the legends of island peoples
c. The geographic origins of California leatherback populations
d. International efforts to protect leatherback habitats

17. The author's tone in this passage is best described as which of the following?

a. Hectoring
b. Factual
c. Mobilizing
d. Dismissive

18. Why were California's leatherbacks thought to come from beaches in Mexico?

a. These beaches are relatively close
b. They prefer warm water
c. They are poor swimmers
d. They are genetic variants

19. What does this article tell us about the current state of leatherback turtle populations?

a. They are recovering rapidly due to conservation efforts.
b. They are an important source of food for many native populations.
c. They are highly mobile.
d. They are recovering on a small scale.

20. The article implies that effective measures to protect the leatherback turtle will require an understanding of which of the following?

a. Native myths
b. The diet of Third World people
c. A combination of interacting factors
d. Foreign governments

Refer to the following for questions 21–25:

Have you ever bought your child a toy to calm a tantrum? Most parents experience moments like this, moments where money comes into play. But money doesn't always buy happiness, especially when it comes to kids.

Kids start learning about money from a very early age. In fact, today's children have more money than ever: extra income spent on snacks, toys, and clothing. It is estimated that more than 10 million youths between the ages of 10 and 18 receive regular allowances from their parents, averaging over $50 per week.

While today's young people may have more money to spend than ever before, their understanding of savings and values hasn't improved. For example, most young people don't know how to calculate the interest earned on a savings account. For the most part, they don't understand how to manage debt or invest for future expenses like college tuition.

Educators say that parents should teach their children about financial responsibility. Early lessons will go a long way toward fostering positive attitudes and habits later in life. Young children learn about money through everyday activities like grocery shopping, and watching their parents pay bills and withdraw cash from the ATM. Family discussions can also help. Take the time to explain the basics to your child: that there is a certain amount of money that comes into the household and a certain amount of money that goes out, and that essential expenses-food, utilities, and clothing- must be paid from that money.

Most children have no idea where money comes from. Ask them, and they will say, "From the ATM machine." Take the time to explain to your children that you must work to earn your money, that you must put it into the bank before you can withdraw it from the ATM machine. Giving a child an allowance tied to the performance of certain family chores is an excellent way to teach this concept.

Here are some ideas for interacting with your children on the subject of money:

Talk money. Routinely discuss how money is earned and spent. Explain your purchasing decisions: "We are buying apples because they are on sale" or "We need electricity so I have to pay the bill."

Model behavior. Children develop their attitudes from what they see you do, not what they hear you say. A lesson on the value of money might also involve family activities: "Let's rent a movie instead of all going to the theater. We can save for our family vacation."

Set limits. Even if you can buy everything your child asks for, consider the wisdom of setting some boundaries. Learn to say no to your child and be firm.

Provide freedom. As your children grow up and learn more, let them make their own decisions about money and personal finances. Support their decision-making with advice, but gradually cede the final decision.

Teach saving. For young children, a personal piggy bank is a good way to introduce concepts of money and savings. Early opportunities to save help develop a lifelong respect for the value of money. Money can be set aside for a favorite toy, as well as for future goals like college or a car.

21. This passage is best described as which of the following?

a. Humorous
b. Factual
c. Advising
d. Dramatic

22. What is the purpose of the first paragraph?

a. To capture attention by relating the topic to something in the reader's personal experience
b. To introduce the topic of tantrums
c. To suggest that rich children are not happy
d. To show how money can be used to induce children to behave well

23. The article argues which of the following?

a. Young children should not be trusted with money.
b. Parents should discuss money with children from an early age.
c. Children should be given ATM cards.
d. Parents should buy children whatever they can afford.

24. Which of the following is suggested in the article regarding allowances?

a. They should be generous
b. They should not be given
c. They should be tied to some responsibilities
d. They should be given on a monthly basis

25. Which of the following best describes the opinion of the author?

a. Children should be given no say in money matters.
b. Children should be allowed to spend their own money however they wish.
c. Children should not be given money at all.
d. Children should be given increasing freedom to make their own decisions about how to spend money.

Refer to the following for questions 26–29:

The Nigerian Letter Fraud

Nigerian letter frauds are variations of advance fee schemes in which a letter, mailed from Nigeria, offers the recipient the "opportunity" to share in millions of dollars that the author, a self-proclaimed government official, is trying to transfer illegally out of Nigeria. The victim receives a letter or email asking him to send personal information: blank letterhead stationery, bank name and account numbers and other identifying information. Eventually, the scheme attempts to get the willing victim, who has demonstrated a propensity for larceny by responding to the invitation, to send money to the author of the letter in Nigeria in several installments of increasing amounts for a variety of reasons. Payment of taxes, bribes to government officials, and legal fees are often described in great detail with the promise that all expenses will be reimbursed as soon as the funds are spirited out of Nigeria. In reality, the millions of dollars do not exist and the victim gets nothing. In fact, once the victim stops sending money, the perpetrators have been known to use the personal information that they received to impersonate the victim, draining bank accounts and credit card balances. While such an invitation strikes most of us as a laughable hoax, millions of dollars in losses are caused by these schemes annually.

26. This paragraph is best described as which of the following?

a. Factual reporting
b. Humor
c. Fiction
d. Poetry

27. What is a "propensity for larceny?"

a. A desire for compensation
b. A proclivity for theft
c. A talent for robbery
d. A disinclination for pilferage

28. The hoax described in the paragraph attempts to get the victim to send money to the perpetrator for what reason?

a. To show good faith
b. To pay Nigerian taxes
c. To buy stationery
d. To help the perpetrator escape persecution

29. What does the author conclude about the Nigerian letter gambit?

a. It is a laughable attempt to defraud people that has little chance of success.
b. It is a good reason not to open email attachments.
c. It is sometimes legitimate.
d. It is surprisingly successful.

Refer to the following for questions 30–31:

Application Instructions: American Institute for the Written Arts, Grants and Awards Program (excerpt)

WORK SAMPLES

Manuscripts must be submitted by applicants in Screenwriting, Playwriting, and Literature (poetry, fiction, and creative nonfiction).

Manuscripts should include a title page with your name, address, and year the work was completed. All pages must be numbered. All writing samples, including previously published work, must be submitted in 12-point.

Photocopied excerpts from books or periodicals in published form are not accepted. Instead, publication, performance, or production information must be restricted to the résumé.

Fiction and creative nonfiction writers must submit 10-20 pages from several short works, or a portion from no more than two larger works, and they must be labeled fiction or nonfiction. If your work is an excerpt, include a one-page statement in the manuscript about where it fits into the whole to orient the reviewers. Poets must submit 10-15 pages of poetry. Shorter poems should be printed one to a page.

Fellowship and Writer-in-Residence applicants must submit one copy of work with applicant name throughout and one copy without applicant name. There should be no identifying marks on the anonymous copy.

Writer-in-Residence applicants must also include one standard size audiotape or CD with up to ten minutes of the applicant reading aloud from his or her own work. The case must be labeled with applicant's name, title of work, and date written. Do not use your name on the audio portion of your reading. (Work samples will not be returned.)

Screenwriters and playwrights must submit 10 to 20 pages from one or two works. Applicants are encouraged to include a one-page synopsis. If screenwriters and playwrights are submitting produced works, they must submit a videotape work sample.

30. Which of the following must be true regarding information describing publication or other production of the work samples?

a. It must be included with the sample.
b. It must be prominently displayed.
c. It must be kept separate from the sample.
d. It must be submitted as an audio tape.

31. Excerpts must be accompanied by which of the following?

a. An anonymous copy
b. A videotape work sample
c. A label indicating whether the work is fiction or nonfiction
d. A statement indicating where the text fits into the larger work

Refer to the following for questions 32–36:

Forest Manager

Salvage logging is removing dead or dying forest stands that are left behind by a fire or disease. This practice has been used for several decades. These dead or dying trees become fuel that feeds future fires. The best way to lower the risk of forest fires is to remove the dead timber from the forest floor. Salvage logging followed by replanting ensures the reestablishment of desirable tree species.

For example, planting conifers accelerates the return of fire-resistant forests. Harvesting timber helps forests by reducing fuel load, thinning the forest stands, and relieving competition between trees. Burned landscapes leave black surfaces and ash layers that have very high soil temperatures. These high soil temperatures can kill many plant species. Logging mixes the soil. So, this lowers surface temperatures to more normal levels. The shade from material that is left behind by logging also helps to lower surface temperatures. After an area has been salvage logged, seedlings in the area start to grow almost immediately. However, this regrowth can take several years in areas that are not managed well.

Ecology Professor

Salvage logging moves material like small, broken branches to the forest floor. These pieces can become fuel for more fires. The removal of larger, less flammable trees leaves behind small limbs and increases the risk of forest fires. In unmanaged areas, these pieces are found more commonly on the tops of trees where they are unavailable to fires. Logging destroys old forests that are more resistant to wildfires. So, this creates younger forests that are more open to fires. In old forests, branches of bigger trees are higher above the floor where fires may not reach.

Replanting after wildfires creates monoculture plantations where only a single crop is planted. This monoculture allows less biological diversity. Also, it allows plants to be less resistant to disease. So, this increases the chance of fire. Salvage logging also upsets natural forest regrowth by killing most of the seedlings that grow after a wildfire. It breaks up the soil and increases erosion. Also, it removes most of the shade that is needed for young seedlings to grow.

32. According to the professor, why are the broken branches in unmanaged forests preferable to those in logged areas for wildfire resistance?

a. They are left on the forest floor and bring nutrients to the soil.
b. They are left on the forest floor and serve as fuel for fires.
c. They are left on the tops of trees where fires cannot reach.
d. They are spread more evenly across the forest floor.

33. A study compared two plots of land that were managed differently after a fire. Plot A was salvage logged. Plot B was left unmanaged. After a second fire, they compared two plant groups between Plots A and B. They found that both plant groups burned worse in Plot A than in Plot B. Whose viewpoint do these results support?

a. Only the manager
b. Only the professor
c. Both the manager and professor
d. Neither the manager nor the professor

34. What is the main idea of the forest manager's argument?

a. Salvage logging is helpful because it removes dead or dying timber from the forest floor. So, this lowers the risk of future fires.
b. Salvage logging is helpful because it has been practiced for many decades.
c. Salvage logging is harmful because it raises soil temperatures above normal levels. So, this threatens the health of plant species.
d. Salvage logging is helpful because it gives shade for seedlings to grow after a wildfire.

35. Which of the following statements does NOT agree with the professor?

a. In younger forests, small branches are closer to the forest floor and more available for fires.
b. Old growth forests have taller trees, so branches are high up and fires cannot reach them.
c. Monoculture forests have less biological diversity and fewer disease-resistant trees.
d. Larger trees are common in old growth forests and serve as the main fuel source for fires.

36. Which of the following is NOT a supporting detail for the forest manager's argument?

a. "This practice has been used for decades."
b. "Logging mixes the soil. So, this lowers surface temperatures to more normal levels."
c. "After an area has been salvage logged, seedlings in the area start to grow almost immediately."
d. "Salvage logging is removing dead or dying forest stands that are left behind by a fire or disease."

Refer to the following for questions 37–40:

One of the key features of the music scene in the past decade has been the increasing popularity of outsiders, especially those with a career. In previous decades, amateur status was seen as a lower calling or, at best, a step on the way to professional status, but many musical insiders now believe that amateurs actually constitute an elite group within the music scene, with greater chances of eventual success. Professionals, once able to fully devote themselves to the advancement of their musical careers, now find themselves hamstrung by a variety of factors that were not issues even a decade ago, giving the edge to people who do not depend on music for a livelihood. A number of technological, demographic, and economic factors are to blame for this change.

Full-time musicians always had difficulties making ends meet, but these difficulties have been vastly increased by a changing music scene. The increased popularity of electronic music, mega-bands, and other acts that rely heavily on marketing, theatrics, and expensive effects has made it harder than ever for local acts to draw crowds. The decreasing crowds at coffee houses, bars, and other small venues leave the owners without the ability to pay for live music. Amateurs can still play the same coffee houses as ever, and the lack of a hundred-dollar paycheck at the end of the night is hardly noticed. Professionals, however, have to fight more desperately than ever for those few lucrative gigs.

An even bigger factor has been the rise of digital media in general and digital file sharing in particular. People have been trading copies of music for decades, but in the days of analog tapes there was always a loss. The tape one fan burned for another would be of lesser quality than the original, prompting the recipient to go out and buy the album. Now that music fans can make full-quality copies for little or nothing and distribute them all over the world, it can be very hard for bands to make any money on music sales. Again, this does not make much difference to amateurs, but it robs the professionals of what has traditionally been one of their biggest sources of revenue.

All of this results in a situation so dire for professional musicians that their extra experience often doesn't balance out their lack of economic resources. The amateurs are the only ones who can afford to buy new gear and fix broken equipment, keep their cars in working order to get to shows, and pay to promote their shows. The professionals tend to have to fall back on "day jobs," typically at lower rates and with less opportunity for advancement. Even those professional musicians who are able to supplement their incomes with music lessons, wedding shows, and other traditional jobs are often living at such a low level that they cannot afford to buy the professional equipment they need to keep the higher-paying gigs. A fairly skilled amateur, by contrast, may not have the same level of virtuosity but will be able to fake his way through most of what a professional does at a more competitive rate, which will allow him to play professional shows.

37. The author of this essay is mainly:

a. Arguing for a return to a climate more favorable to professional musicians
b. Examining the causes of the increasing success of amateur musicians over professionals
c. Revealing the psychological toll the current economy takes on professional musicians
d. Disputing the claim that unsuccessful professional musicians simply don't work hard enough

38. Which of the following statements about musicians does the essay most directly support?

a. Bars and coffee houses should be willing to pay a fair wage to professional musicians.
b. The most popular professional bands have not been affected by the changes that plague most professional musicians.
c. It is much easier for amateur musicians to book shows than it was a decade ago.
d. Professional musicians have recently lost some of their most important sources of income.

39. In his discussion of professional musicians in the last paragraph, the author:

a. Indicates that amateurs deserve their new, higher status
b. Shows that in the current climate, professionals may not have the ability to purchase and maintain the tools that they need
c. Points out the decrease in the market for wedding gigs and lessons
d. Predicts a decline in the number of professional musicians

40. According to the essay, amateur musicians are becoming more successful at both amateur and professional gigs because professionals:

a. Exclusively performs high-paying gigs and are unwilling to play in clubs
b. Are not able to relate to ordinary people as well as amateurs can
c. Have financial needs that they are not able to meet in the current musical climate
d. Are in an industry that is particularly susceptible to economic changes

Language

1. Which of the following sentences is written correctly?

a. Michael had been studying for this exam for two weeks; but still could not pass.
b. Michael had been studying for this exam for two weeks: but still could not pass.
c. Michael had been studying for this exam for two weeks, but still could not pass.
d. Michael had been studying for this exam for two weeks but still could not pass.

2. Which choice completes the text with the most logical and precise word or phrase?

The concept of community-based participatory research has gained prominence as a means of fostering collaborative efforts between indigenous communities and academic institutions. An illuminating example of such a partnership can be found in the collaboration between the Navajo Nation and the University of Arizona, which serves as a beacon of success in this field. Navajo citizens actively participated in the formulation of research methodologies, and they continue to play an integral role in data collection. This model of cooperation effectively __________ the principles of community-based participatory research.

a. circumvents
b. eclipses
c. fabricates
d. exemplifies

3. Choose the best word to complete the following sentence.

Barney did really ________ and finished in the top three in the competition.

a. excellent
b. well
c. good
d. fine

4. Which choice completes the text with the most logical and precise word or phrase?

Given the intricate relationships in the coral reef ecosystem, it's not surprising that the impact of climate change has lacked __________ explanation. Marine biologists have conducted extensive research, and Dr. Olivia Chang's recent findings offer hope for the preservation of these fragile ecosystems.

a. an intricate
b. an elusive
c. a conclusive
d. a clear

5. Which choice completes the text with the most logical transition?

Famous authors like William Shakespeare, Jane Austen, and Mark Twain have gained international acclaim for their literary contributions, leaving an indelible mark on the world of literature. _______, lesser-recognized but equally talented writers like Zora Neale Hurston, Kazuo Ishiguro, and Octavia Butler have produced exceptional works that are sometimes hidden in the shadows of their more celebrated counterparts. While the literary canon often highlights a select few, there is an abundance of hidden gems waiting to be discovered by avid readers.

a. Similarly
b. For instance
c. In particular
d. On the other hand

6. Which choice completes the text with the most logical and precise word or phrase?

The remarkable ability of chameleons to change the color of their skin has long puzzled scientists. Recent findings by Dr. Michel Milinkovitch and his team suggest that chameleons achieve their color-changing magic by controlling the arrangement of nanocrystals in their skin cells. This enables them to achieve perfect ______ with their surroundings.

a. prediction
b. moderation
c. synchronization
d. hibernation

7. Which of the following sentences is written correctly?

a. Do you know the poem "Wait Until Later?"
b. "Of all the stories in this book," she said, "this is my favorite."
c. Jack mentioned the poem Ode to a Nightingale in his letter.
d. Mike's father asked him "what was wrong."

8. Which TWO of the following sentences are written correctly?

a. In the local currency, yen, everything seemed to be more expensive.
b. My new car a Honda.
c. I don't understand why she keeps calling me?
d. Is there anyone here with change of a dollar?

9. Which of the following sentences is written correctly?

a. Got a couple of friends to help me.
b. "Canada" is a country in North America.
c. She was feeling weak and almost fainted.
d. When boating I always wear a life vest.

10. Select the answer that best combines the following two sentences into one.

The center fielder broke the season record for home runs.
He was handsomely rewarded.

a. The handsome center fielder was rewarded for breaking the season record for home runs.
b. The center fielder was handsomely rewarded, breaking the season record for home runs.
c. The center fielder was handsomely rewarded for breaking the season record for home runs.
d. The handsomely rewarded center fielder broke the season record for home runs.

11. Select the TWO best answers that combine the following two sentences into one.

The mechanic performed a number of diagnostic tests on the car.
The mechanic used a computer to perform the diagnostic tests.

a. While performing a number of diagnostic tests on the car, the mechanic used a computer to perform the tests.
b. With his computer, the mechanic performed a number of diagnostic tests on the car.
c. Because he used a computer, the mechanic performed a number of diagnostic tests on the car.
d. The mechanic used a computer to perform a number of diagnostic tests on the car.

12. Choose the best sentence to fill in the blank in the following paragraph.

Most banks offer checking accounts for their customers. Usually, they require an initial deposit before establishing a new account, along with identification and proof of address. You may opt for a no-frills checking account, which doesn't charge fees, or choose one that pays interest but requires maintaining a high minimum balance. ______________________________

a. A bank is an institution that provides financial services to its customers.
b. Banks are licensed by the government.
c. There may also be surcharges for ATM usage and other services.
d. Banking is a rewarding profession.

13. Choose the best sentence to fill in the blank in the following paragraph.

The Florida Everglades cover thousands of square miles between the east and west coasts of Florida. Everglades National Park is the centerpiece of the region, but there are other great places to explore. ______________________________ The weather is mild, birds are abundant, and there are fewer mosquitoes than at other times of year.

a. The best time to visit is during the winter, from November through early April.
b. The park is run by the National Parks Service.
c. Many visitors come to see the alligators.
d. One way to see the Everglades is by boat.

14. Choose the TWO best sentences to fill in the blank in the following paragraph.

Organic food standards are defined by a 2002 federal law. ______________________________ Use of pesticides and other synthetic chemicals is forbidden. As a result of this law, wherever you go in the fifty states you can be certain that produce carrying an organic label was grown in accordance with the same standards. That fact has helped increase organic food sales.

a. To protect consumers, regulations were established for food labeled organic.
b. Many other laws were passed in 2002.
c. Organic foods are sometimes more expensive.
d. It outlines how products must be grown in order to be certified organic.

15. Choose the best sentence to follow and develop this topic sentence.

More than 200 people were rescued after an Egyptian ferry sank in the Red Sea.

a. The Red Sea is a popular tourist destination in the Middle East.
b. Egypt is the most populous country in North Africa.
c. Authorities blamed rough seas and overloading of the ferry.
d. January is the coldest month in these waters.

16. Select the sentence that does not belong in the following paragraph.

(1) Vegetable oil can be used as fuel in diesel-powered automobiles. (2) There are almost 250 million automobiles in the U.S. (3) It can even be used as is, without being converted to biodiesel. (4) The difficulty is that straight vegetable oil is much more viscous than conventional diesel fuel or biodiesel: studies have found that it can damage engines. (5) But it can be used if you get a professional engine conversion.

a. Sentence 1
b. Sentence 2
c. Sentence 3
d. Sentence 4

17. Consider the following sentence:

Did either Tracy or Vanessa realize that her degree would be so valuable to future employers?

Select the best version of the underlined portion.

a. NO CHANGE
b. Tracy or Vanessa realize that each of their degree was
c. Tracy or Vanessa realize that her or her degree would be
d. Tracy or Vanessa realize that their degree would be

18. Consider the following sentence:

If he stops to consider the ramifications of this decision, it is probable that he will rethink his original decision a while longer.

Select the best version of the underlined portion.

a. NO CHANGE
b. he will rethink his original decision over again.
c. he probably will rethink his original decision.
d. he will most likely rethink his original decision for a bit.

19. Consider the following sentence:

Mr. King, an individual of considerable influence, created a personal fortune and gave back to the community.

Select the best version of the underlined portion.

a. NO CHANGE
b. an individual of considerable influence, he created a personal fortune and gave back
c. an individual of considerable influence created a personal fortune and gave back
d. an individual of considerable influence, created a personal fortune and gave it back

20. Consider the following sentence:

Although most persons prefer traditional pets, like cats and dogs, others gravitate towards exotic animals, like snakes and lizards.

Select the best version of the underlined portion.

a. NO CHANGE
b. Because most people
c. While most people
d. Maybe some persons

Refer to the following for questions 21–24:

Norway's economy relies heavy upon oil and gas. Exports of these commodities account for roughly half of all export earnings. Other exports include metals ships and fish. Norway is one of the world's top 10 fishing nations. Agriculture is diversified and is a great deal of livestock, though more than half of the country's food needs are imported.

21. Select the best replacement for the underlined sentence.

Norway's economy relies heavy upon oil and gas.

a. Norway's economy relies upon heavy oil and gas.
b. Norway's economy relies heavily upon oil and gas.
c. Norways economy relies heavy upon oil and gas.
d. Norways economy relies heavily upon oil and gas.

22. Select the best replacement for the underlined sentence.

Other exports include metals ships and fish.

a. Other exports include metal ships and fish.
b. Other exports includes metals ships and fish.
c. Other exports include metals ships and fishes.
d. Other exports include metals, ships, and fish.

23. Select the best replacement for the underlined phrase.

Agriculture is diversified and is a great deal of livestock, though more than half of the country's food needs are imported.

a. Agriculture is diversified and there is a great deal of livestock
b. Agriculture is diversified and with a great deal of livestock
c. Agriculture is diversified and includes a great deal of livestock
d. Agriculture is diversified and has a great deal of livestock

24. Select the TWO best replacements for the underlined phrase.

Agriculture is diversified and is a great deal of livestock, though more than half of the country's food needs are imported.

a. more than half of the country's food is imported
b. more than half of the countries food needs are imported
c. the country imports more than half of its food
d. the country imports more than half of its food needs

25. Which TWO of the following sentences are most correct in terms of style, clarity, and punctuation?

a. The possible side effects of the medication that Lucinda's doctor had prescribed for her concerned her, but she continued to take the medication.
b. The medication that the doctor prescribed had side effects concerning Lucinda who continued to take it.
c. Lucinda was concerned about side effects from the medication that her doctor had prescribed, so she continued to take it.
d. Although Lucinda was concerned about the possible side effects, she continued to take the medication that her doctor had prescribed for her.

26. Which of the following sentences shows the correct way to separate the items in the series?

a. These are actual cities in the United States: Unalaska, Alaska; Yreka, California; Two Egg, Florida; and Boring, Maryland.
b. These are actual cities in the United States: Unalaska; Alaska, Yreka; California, Two Egg; Florida, and Boring; Maryland.
c. These are actual cities in the United States: Unalaska, Alaska, Yreka, California, Two Egg, Florida, and Boring, Maryland.
d. These are actual cities in the United States: Unalaska Alaska, Yreka California, Two Egg Florida, and Boring Maryland.

27. Which choice completes the text with the most logical and precise word or phrase?

Jane Austen's novels are celebrated for their keen social judgment, and her witty observations provide readers with an insightful _________ on the society and manners of her time.

a. endorsement
b. perspective
c. commentary
d. refusal

28. Which choice completes the text with the most logical transition?

Carlsbad Caverns, a world-renowned natural wonder located in New Mexico, is celebrated for its immense underground chambers and spectacular limestone formations. Explorers are greeted by a breathtaking descent into a subterranean realm filled with awe-inspiring stalactites and stalagmites. __________, the cave system is home to a unique ecosystem with diverse species adapted to the darkness, including thousands of Mexican free-tailed bats, making it a destination of both geological and biological significance.

a. Additionally
b. Therefore
c. For instance
d. Specifically

29. Which choice completes the text with the most logical and precise word or phrase?

William Shakespeare is a timeless figure whose writings have left a lasting impact. His amazing skill in creating characters with complex personalities and deep emotions has made storytelling an art form. Every character in his plays is carefully crafted, and their dialogue in his stories reflects what it's like to be human. Shakespeare's work doesn't just entertain; it also beautifully __________ the depth of human life.

a. avoids
b. captures
c. mirrors
d. diminishes

30. Which of the answer choices is the closest in meaning to the underlined word in the following sentence?

Finlay flatly refused to take part in the piano recital, so his parents had to cajole him with the promise of a trip to his favorite toy store.

a. Prevent
b. Threaten
c. Insist
d. Coax

31. Which choice completes the text with the most logical and precise word or phrase?

Critics have debated the ____ nature of the protagonist in this novel, with some viewing the character as a symbol of hope and others as a representation of despair.

a. complex
b. one-dimensional
c. unambiguous
d. predictable

32. Which of the following best approximates the meaning of the underlined word?

The discussion over the new park had begun well, but it soon descended into an acrimonious debate over misuse of tax revenues.

a. Shocking
b. Childish
c. Rancorous
d. Revealing

33. Considering both style and clarity, which of the answer choices best combines the following sentences?

Fenella wanted to attend the concert. She also wanted to attend the reception at the art gallery. She tried to find a way to do both in one evening. She failed.

a. Although Fenella wanted to attend the concert, she also wanted to attend the reception at the art gallery, so she tried to find a way to do both in one evening. She failed.
b. Fenella wanted to attend both the concert and the reception at the art gallery, but she failed to find a way to do both in one evening.
c. Fenella failed to find a way to attend both the concert and the reception at the art gallery.
d. Because Fenella wanted to attend both the concert and the reception at the art gallery, she tried to find a way to do both in one evening. Unfortunately, she failed.

Mathematics

1. Sunil uses his cell phone an average of 1,200 minutes per month. Which of the following cell phone monthly payment plans will be the least expensive for him? Select the THREE that apply.

a. 10¢ per minute with no base fee
b. $48 base fee for 600 minutes; 12¢ for each additional minute
c. $75 base fee for 900 minutes; 16¢ for each additional minute
d. $100 for 1,000 minutes; 10¢ for each additional minute

Refer to the following for question 2:

In the figure below, lines L1 and L2 are parallel to each other.

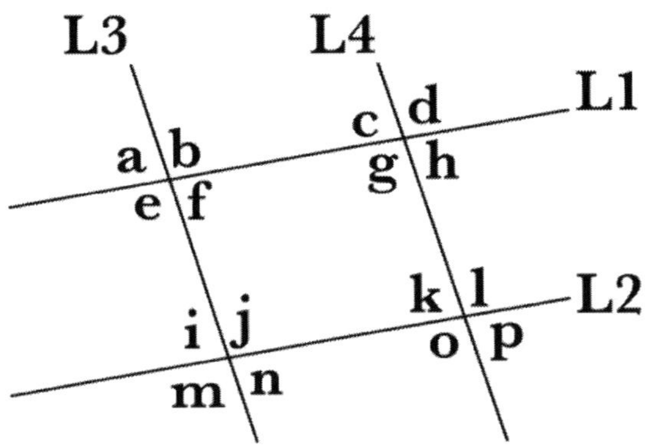

2. If ∠n is congruent to ∠p, which of the following statements must be TRUE? Select the TWO that apply.

a. Line L3 is perpendicular to line L4
b. Line L3 is parallel to line L4
c. Line L3 must eventually intersect line L4
d. ∠m is congruent to ∠o

3. A culture of yeast cells doubles in number every half hour. After 3 hours, there are 6,400 yeast cells in the culture. How many were there when the culture was started?

a. 100
b. 200
c. 400
d. 800

4. During a 60-minute television show, the entertainment portion lasted 15 minutes less than 4 times the advertising portion. How long was the entertainment portion?

a. 30 minutes
b. 40 minutes
c. 45 minutes
d. 50 minutes

5. Which set of figures is congruent?

a. 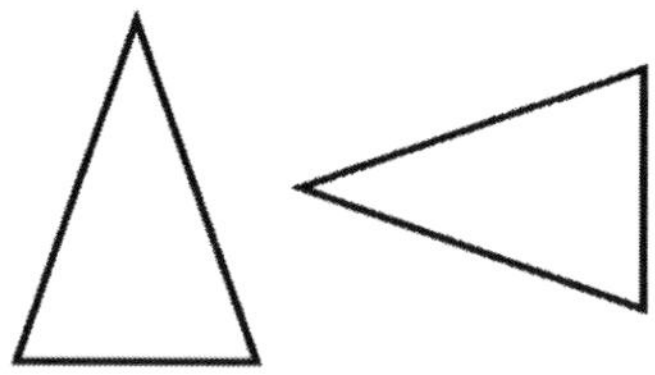

b. 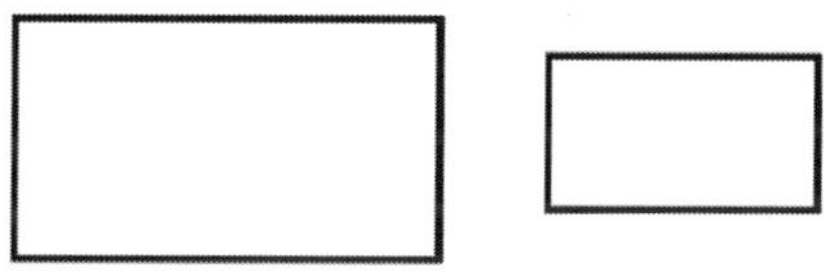

c. 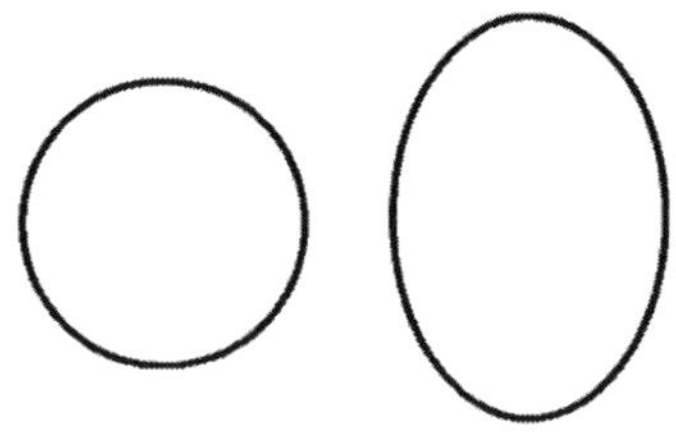

d. 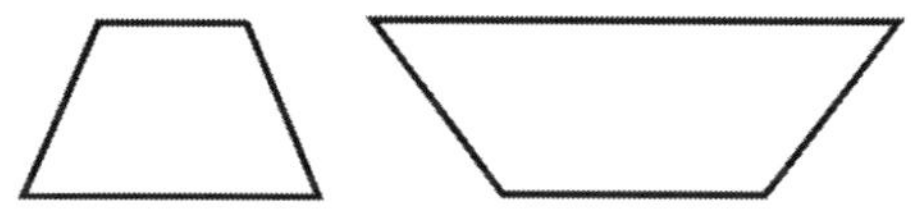

Refer to the following for question 6:

In the figure below, lines L1 and L2 are parallel to each other.

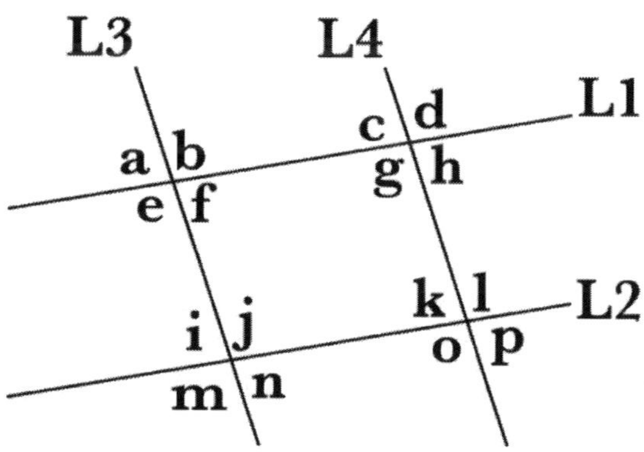

6. If ∠a has a measure of 70°, what is the measure of ∠i?

a. 30°
b. 60°
c. 70°
d. 110°

7. Kasie is filling glasses with water. Each glass is cylindrical with a radius of 1.25 inches and a height of 6 inches. If she fills them to a height of 5 inches, how many glasses can she fill with 3 quarts of water (1 gallon = 231 cubic inches)? Use 3.14 for π.

a. 3
b. 5
c. 7
d. 9

8. Thirty-five boys went out for the soccer team. Of these, $\frac{5}{7}$ made the team. Of the boys who made the team, $\frac{4}{5}$ showed up for practice on Wednesday. How many boys were at the Wednesday practice?

a. 18
b. 20
c. 22
d. 25

9. The price-earnings (PE) ratio of a stock is the ratio of the share price divided by the annual earnings per share. Company A has issued 3 million shares of stock, which are selling at $6.00 per share. If the PE ratio is 12, how much did Company A earn in the past year?

a. $1.5 million
b. $3.0 million
c. $4.5 million
d. $6.0 million

10. Bob buys the newspaper every day for $1.50. If he subscribes, he pays only $3.50 per week for seven issues. How much will his weekly savings be if he subscribes?

a. $2.00
b. $4.50
c. $5.00
d. $7.00

11. A bag of coffee costs $9.85 and contains 16 ounces of coffee. Which of the following best represents the cost per ounce?

a. $0.67
b. $0.64
c. $0.65
d. $0.62

Refer to the following for question 12:

Look at the table below, which compares the orbits of the planets in our solar system.

Property	Mercury	Venus	Earth	Mars	Jupiter	Saturn	Uranus	Neptune
Diameter (km)	4,878	12,104	12,756	6,787	142,800	120,000	51,118	49,528
Mass (Relative to Earth)	0.055	0.815	1	0.107	318	95	15	17
Average distance from Sun (Relative to Earth)	0.39	0.72	1	1.52	5.20	9.54	19.18	30.06
Orbital period (Earth years)	0.24	0.62	1	1.88	11.86	29.46	84.01	164.8
Average orbital speed (km/sec)	47.89	35.03	29.79	24.13	13.06	9.64	6.81	5.43
Gravity (Relative to Earth)	0.38	0.9	1	0.38	2.64	0.93	0.89	1.12

12. Which of the following statements is true? Select the two that apply.

a. The shorter a planet's orbital period, the faster its orbital speed.
b. The closer a planet is to the Sun, the faster its orbital speed.
c. The smaller a planet's diameter, the faster its orbital speed.
d. The smaller a planet's mass, the faster its orbital speed.

13. Which of the following is listed in order from GREATEST to LEAST?

a. $2\frac{1}{4}, \frac{32}{5}, \frac{4}{5}, -5, -2$
b. $\frac{32}{5}, 2\frac{1}{4}, \frac{4}{5}, -2, -5$
c. $-5, -2, \frac{32}{5}, \frac{4}{5}, 2\frac{1}{4}$
d. $\frac{32}{5}, 2\frac{1}{4}, \frac{4}{5}, -5, -2$

14. Alfredo works 40 hours per week at an hourly wage of $20. For any overtime, he makes $30 per hour. This week Alfredo made $950. How many hours did he work?

a. 40
b. 42
c. 45
d. 48

15. Tamara has 3 pairs of socks in her drawer. Each pair is a different color. If she pulls out two socks at random, one at a time, what is the probability that they will be of matching colors? Select the TWO that apply.

a. 0.25
b. $33\frac{1}{3}\%$
c. $\frac{1}{5}$
d. 20%

16. The first three members of a four-man swimming team swim their laps in 22.4 seconds, 23.8 seconds, and 21.9 seconds, respectively. To keep the average pace at exactly 22 seconds, which of the following times would the fourth man have to achieve?

a. 21.0 seconds
b. 19.9 seconds
c. 19.5 seconds
d. 20.2 seconds

Refer to the following for question 17:

Look at the table below, which compares the orbits of the planets in our solar system.

Property	Mercury	Venus	Earth	Mars	Jupiter	Saturn	Uranus	Neptune
Diameter (km)	4,878	12,104	12,756	6,787	142,800	120,000	51,118	49,528
Mass (Relative to Earth)	0.055	0.815	1	0.107	318	95	15	17
Average distance from Sun (Relative to Earth)	0.39	0.72	1	1.52	5.20	9.54	19.18	30.06
Orbital period (Earth years)	0.24	0.62	1	1.88	11.86	29.46	84.01	164.8
Average orbital speed (km/sec)	47.89	35.03	29.79	24.13	13.06	9.64	6.81	5.43
Gravity (Relative to Earth)	0.38	0.9	1	0.38	2.64	0.93	0.89	1.12

17. The mass of the Earth is approximately 6.0×10^{24} kg. What is the mass of Venus?

a. 4.9×10^{24} kg
b. 4.9×10^{23} kg
c. 8.1×10^{23} kg
d. 8.1×10^{24} kg

Refer to the following for question 18:

Look at the following table, which shows the prices of five company stocks at the close of trading on the stock market one day in April.

Company	Price
IBM	127
Intel	23
Cisco	23
Apple	127
Microsoft	30

18. What is the mode share price of the stocks shown in the table? Select the TWO that apply.

a. 23
b. 30
c. 82
d. 127

Refer to the following for question 19:

Look at the table below, which compares the orbits of the planets in our solar system.

Property	Mercury	Venus	Earth	Mars	Jupiter	Saturn	Uranus	Neptune
Diameter (km)	4,878	12,104	12,756	6,787	142,800	120,000	51,118	49,528
Mass (Relative to Earth)	0.055	0.815	1	0.107	318	95	15	17
Average distance from Sun (Relative to Earth)	0.39	0.72	1	1.52	5.20	9.54	19.18	30.06
Orbital period (Earth years)	0.24	0.62	1	1.88	11.86	29.46	84.01	164.8
Average orbital speed (km/sec)	47.89	35.03	29.79	24.13	13.06	9.64	6.81	5.43
Gravity (Relative to Earth)	0.38	0.9	1	0.38	2.64	0.93	0.89	1.12

19. Which of the following statements is true? Select the TWO that apply.

a. The greater a planet's mass, the longer its orbital period.
b. The larger a planet's diameter, the greater its gravity.
c. The further a planet is from the Sun, the longer its orbital period.
d. The greater a planet's orbital period, the lower its average orbital speed.

20. A jar contains 200 marbles. Thirty of them are blue, 80 are red, and the remainder are yellow. If Natasha reaches blindly into the jar and withdraws a marble at random, what is the probability that it will be blue? Select the TWO that apply.

a. 30%
b. $\frac{3}{20}$
c. 15%
d. 0.18

21. Rachel spent $24.15 on produce. She bought 2 pounds of onions, 3 pounds of carrots, and $1\frac{1}{2}$ pounds of mushrooms. If the onions cost $3.69 per pound and the carrots cost $4.29 per pound, what is the price per pound of mushrooms?

a. $2.25
b. $2.60
c. $2.80
d. $3.10

TABE Practice Test #1

Refer to the following for question 22:

Look at the table below, which compares the orbits of the planets in our solar system.

Property	Mercury	Venus	Earth	Mars	Jupiter	Saturn	Uranus	Neptune
Diameter (km)	4,878	12,104	12,756	6,787	142,800	120,000	51,118	49,528
Mass (Relative to Earth)	0.055	0.815	1	0.107	318	95	15	17
Average distance from Sun (Relative to Earth)	0.39	0.72	1	1.52	5.20	9.54	19.18	30.06
Orbital period (Earth years)	0.24	0.62	1	1.88	11.86	29.46	84.01	164.8
Average orbital speed (km/sec)	47.89	35.03	29.79	24.13	13.06	9.64	6.81	5.43
Gravity (Relative to Earth)	0.38	0.9	1	0.38	2.64	0.93	0.89	1.12

22. The average distance from the Earth to the Sun is 149, 600, 000 km. What is the average distance from Mercury to the Sun?

a. 5.8×10^6 km
b. 5.8×10^7 km
c. 3.9×10^6 km
d. 3.9×10^5 km

23. Jamal hosts a dinner in a restaurant for a number of his customers and the bill comes to $1,128.08. The restaurant always adds an 18% tip for large groups, and this is included in the total. How much was the total before the tip was added?

a. $1,010.08
b. $925.02
c. $956.00
d. $988.05

Refer to the following for question 24:

In the figure below, lines L1 and L2 are parallel to each other.

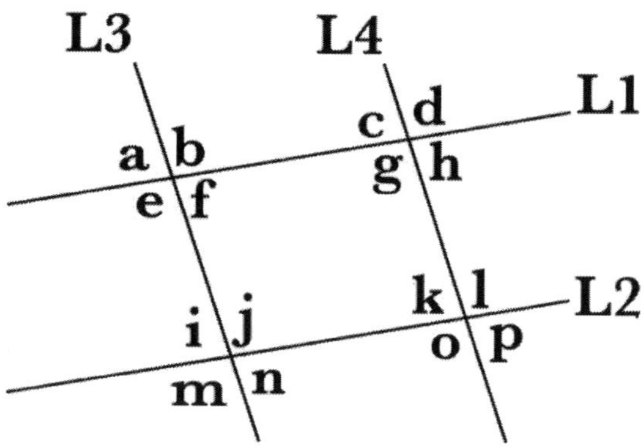

24. If line L3 is parallel to line L4, which of the following statements must be TRUE?

a. ∠f is congruent to ∠k, and ∠a is congruent to ∠p
b. ∠e is congruent to ∠l, and ∠g is congruent to ∠p
c. ∠e is congruent to ∠o, and ∠g is congruent to ∠h
d. ∠f is congruent to ∠l, and ∠g is congruent to ∠n

25. Morgan plans to replace the floor in his bedroom with square tiles that have a side of 12 inches. The bedroom is 15 feet wide and 18 feet long, and Morgan can lay 9 tiles per hour. How long will the job take?

a. 30 hours
b. 18 hours
c. 10.5 hours
d. 12 hours

26. Mischa drives from Town A to Town B at 90 kilometers per hour. Brenda drives the same route at 60 kilometers per hour and it takes her 3 hours longer. How far apart are Town A and Town B?

a. 540 km
b. 600 km
c. 480 km
d. 510 km

27. Kevin pays $12.95 for a text messaging service plus $0.07 for each text message he sends. Which of the following equations could be used to represent the total cost, *y*, when *x* represents the number of text messages sent? Select the TWO that apply.

a. $y - \$12.95 = \$0.07x$
b. $y(\$0.07) = \$12.95x$
c. $y = \frac{\$12.95}{\$0.07}x$
d. $y = \$0.07x + \$12.95$

28. Evaluate $x^2 - (2y - 3)$ if $x = 4$ and $y = 3$.

a. 12
b. 13
c. 10
d. 8

29. Two hikers start at a ranger station and leave at the same time. One hiker heads due west at 3 mph. The other hiker heads due north at 4 mph. How far apart are the hikers after 2 hours of hiking?

a. 5 miles
b. 7 miles
c. 10 miles
d. 14 miles

30. What is the next term in the number series 3, 6, 12, 24, ____?

a. 30
b. 36
c. 42
d. 48

31. Rouenna has to drive 500 miles to Portland. Her car gets 25 miles per gallon and gasoline costs \$3 per gallon. What will the trip cost?

a. \$20
b. \$60
c. \$75
d. \$150

32. Evaluate the following expression if $u = 3$ and $v = 4$: $\frac{1}{3}u^2 + \frac{3v}{4} =$

a. 21
b. 18
c. 12
d. 6

Refer to the following for question 33:

Look at the following table, which shows the results of a qualification exam given to applicants for public service jobs in Montgomery County.

Score	Under 65	65–74	75–85	85–94	95–100	Totals
Men	3	16	24	12	0	55
Women	3	18	20	20	2	63
Totals	6	34	44	32	2	118

33. Approximately what percentage of men passed the exam if 75 is considered to be the cutoff passing grade?

a. 55%
b. 65%
c. 75%
d. 85%

34. If an average American spends a total of $40,000 per year, how much would he or she spend on clothing, according to the chart?

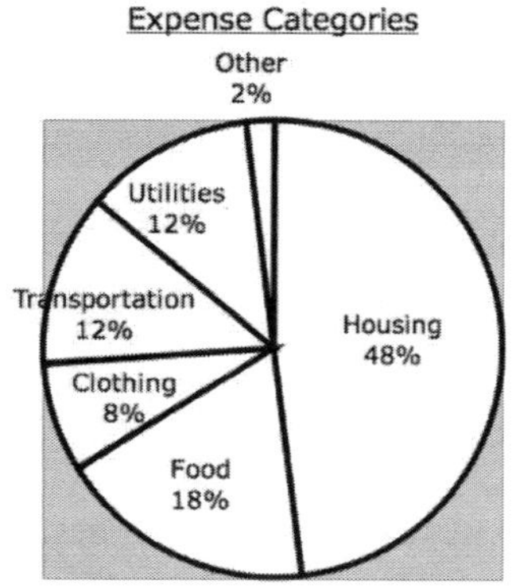

a. $32,000
b. $3,200
c. $320
d. $2,400

Refer to the following for question 35:

Look at the following table, which shows the results of a qualification exam given to applicants for public service jobs in Montgomery County.

Score	Under 65	65–74	75–85	85–94	95–100	Totals
Men	3	16	24	12	0	55
Women	3	18	20	20	2	63
Totals	6	34	44	32	2	118

35. Based on the table, how many women received a grade that was higher than that of the highest-scoring man?

a. 0
b. At least 2
c. At least 4
d. 22

36. Solve the following proportion for x: $-\frac{3}{x} = \frac{2}{8}$.

a. $x = 3$
b. $x = 12$
c. $x = -2$
d. $x = -12$

Refer to the following for question 37:

In the figure below, lines L1 and L2 are parallel to each other.

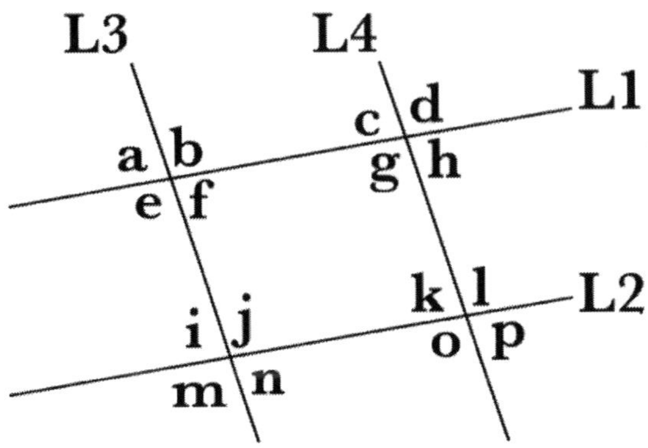

37. If ∠a has a measure of 70°, what is the measure of ∠b?

a. 30°
b. 90°
c. 100°
d. 110°

Refer to the following for question 38:

Look at the following table, which shows the prices of five company stocks at the close of trading on the stock market one day in April.

Company	Price
IBM	127
Intel	23
Cisco	23
Apple	127
Microsoft	30

38. What is the mean share price of the stocks shown in the table?

a. 23
b. 330
c. 66
d. 30

Refer to the following for question 39:

Joshua has to earn more than 92 points on the state test in order to qualify for an academic scholarship. Each question is worth 4 points, and the test has a total of 30 questions. Let x represent the number of test questions Joshua answers correctly.

39. Which of the following inequalities can be solved to determine the number of questions Joshua must answer correctly?

a. $4x < 30$
b. $4x < 92$
c. $4x > 30$
d. $4x > 92$

40. Which pair of figures below is similar?

a.
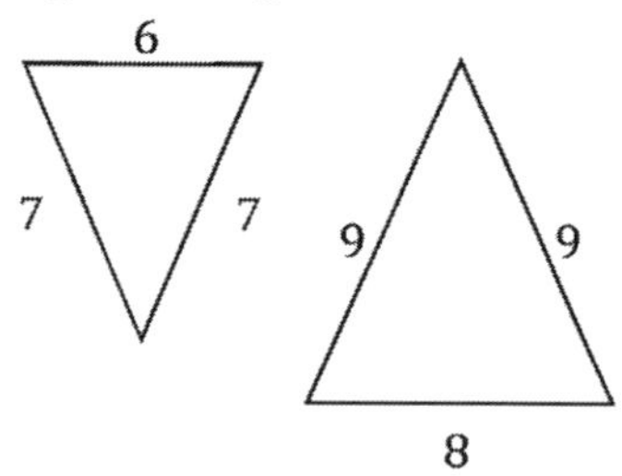

b.
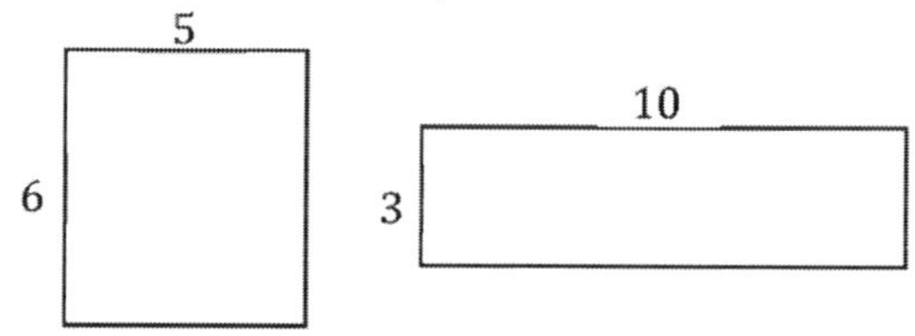

c.
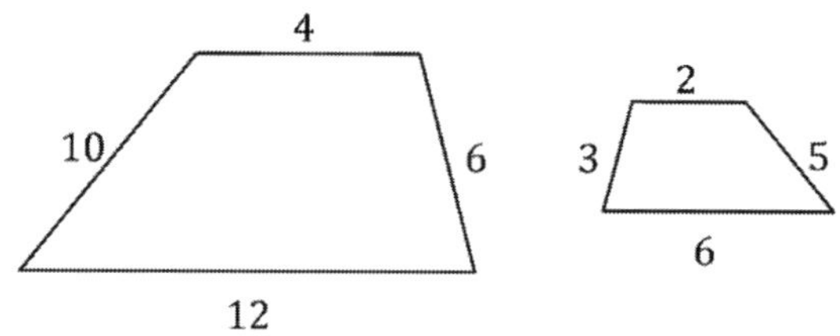

d.
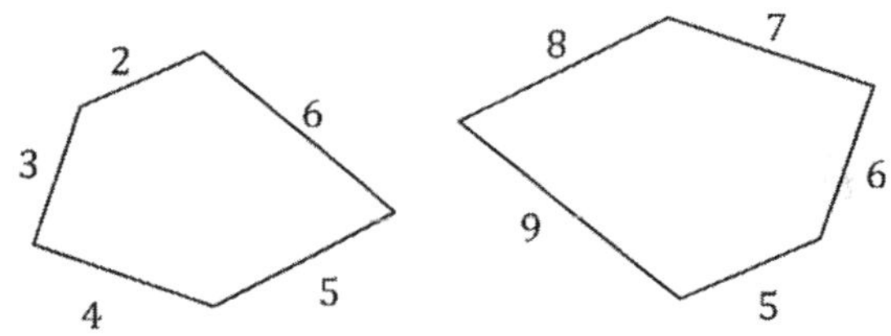

Answer Key and Explanations for Test #1

Reading

1. C: The passage describes several distinctive features of annelid anatomy and tells how some of them differ from other worms.

2. D: The term is defined in the text between commas.

3. C: The text gives the example of feet specializing into grasping organs to illustrate this evolutionary advantage of segmental plasticity.

4. B: *Nematodes* differ from the annelids in the structure of the coelum. *Lumbricus* and leeches are both members of the Annelida.

5. B: Lincoln begins this speech by discussing the founding of the US and what the original purpose of the US was. Then, he goes on to talk about how the US is currently engaged in a war intended to fracture the nation, and he states that the battle being discussed was one large tragedy that came out of the war. Next, Lincoln says that his speech and even the memorial itself can't truly honor those who died, and that it's up to those who survived to continue the fight to ensure the nation does not break apart. Choice B best communicates this message.

6. C: The sentence in which this phrase is found is: "The world will little note, nor long remember, what we say here, but can never forget what they did here." In this context, the phrase "the world will little note" means that no one outside of those in attendance or possibly those outside the country will pay attention to the speech or the ceremony. This eliminates all of the choices except choice C.

7. A: The ideals of the revolution are addressed in the first paragraph: "Four score and seven years ago our fathers brought forth, upon this continent, a new nation, conceived in Liberty, and dedicated to the proposition that all men are created equal." This introduces the point that Lincoln is trying to make about the battle at hand and the war as a whole: the Civil War is threatening the ideas upon which the nation was created.

8. C: There is a comparison between the ideas of the Revolution and the Civil War in this speech. To facilitate understanding of this comparison, Lincoln has to set the stage by telling his audience about the past event he is referencing. This establishes the context of his message.

9. A: This line directly references the idea in the previous paragraph, which is that the US is a nation that was created to ensure liberty and equality. This sentence talks about how the Civil War is testing whether or not a nation that was created to ensure liberty and equality can really survive.

10. B: When President Lincoln argues that the people who died at Gettysburg did not die in vain, he asserts that their passing was not frivolous or unimportant or meaningless.

11. B: The article informs the reader that most plastic food containers contain BPA, that BPA has been detected in stored foods, and that it is a material that may be toxic. Several alternative container types are listed to enable the reader to avoid containers with BPA.

12. D: The second paragraph tells us that, due to concern about its toxicity, Canada has banned the use of BPA in baby bottles. It has not banned the use of BPA in plastic products other than baby bottles, as suggested by choice C.

13. C: While the author states that certain countries and states have banned BPA for these applications, he does not take a stand on this issue in the article. Nor is it suggested that stainless steel is the best material: it is merely listed as one of several alternatives. The author simply provides the reader with several different types of container that can be used.

14. A: According to the text, phthalates, including BPA, are used to soften plastics so that they may be molded. They do not make the plastics safer, nor do they permit the use of plastic containers in microwave ovens.

15. B: At the end of the text, the author provides a list of three ways to avoid potential problems with food storage containers. These involve selecting containers made of glass, stainless steel, or BPA-free plastics.

16. D: The text describes how the migratory patterns of these turtles move them around the entire Pacific. As a result, researchers from the Fish and Wildlife Service were obliged to expand their conservation efforts beyond the beaches of California to encompass sites in the western Pacific as well.

17. B: The author refrains from trying to enlist the reader's efforts in work to protect the leatherbacks, and does not appear to seek support. Rather, the text is a factual report about the conservation efforts that are already taking place.

18. A: This can be inferred from the second paragraph, which says that it was thought that the California populations originated from "nearby" beaches. There is no mention in the text of a preference for warm waters and, if anything, the text implies that they swim extremely well. Finally, the text tells us that the various populations of leatherbacks are genetically identical.

19. D: At the end of the fifth paragraph, the author states: "Early results have inspired a cautious optimism: leatherback turtle populations seem to be recovering." This does not describe a rapid recovery, so choice A is incorrect.

20. C: According to the author, "success of these conservation efforts will require a more complete understanding of the entire ecosystem in which the turtles live." The article goes on to state that this will necessitate "a broad approach that includes the restoration of feeding grounds, nesting beaches, and the migratory routes that connect them."

21. C: The article provides guidance for parents and guardians about educating children on the subject of money. After providing some background in the initial paragraphs, it ends with five paragraphs that suggest specific steps that can be taken for this purpose.

22. A: This is an example of a "hook", an introductory paragraph designed to intrigue the reader and encourage him to read further. Since most parents have experienced occasions when their child throws a tantrum in order to be given something he or she desires, they may wish to read on. The last sentence in this paragraph suggests that the relationship between money and a child's happiness is not so simple, and will be explored further in the text.

23. B: The article tells parents to take the time to explain the basics of money to their children. It tells us that children learn about money by observing their parents using it, and that parents should explain the reasons for their actions to children from an early age.

24. C: The author says that giving a child an allowance tied to the performance of certain family chores is an excellent way to teach the concept that money must be earned.

25. D: The author advises that, as children grow up and learn more, they should be allowed to make their own decisions about money and personal finances. Their decision-making should be supported with parental advice, but gradually the final decisions should be ceded to them.

26. A: The article provides information about a scheme to defraud internet users of money. It describes the mechanics of the fraud scheme and explains how the perpetrators intend to make money.

27. B: A *propensity* is a tendency to do something. Proclivity is a synonym for this. *Larceny* is a synonym for theft. Note that *pilferage* and *robbery* are also synonyms for theft, but that *talent,* which is a latent ability, does not mean the same thing as propensity, while *disinclination* has the opposite meaning.

28. B: According to the paragraph, the perpetrators cite many reasons for the need to send them money, among them payment of taxes, bribes to government officials, and legal fees.

29. D: Despite what might seem the unlikely nature of the come-on, according to the text the Nigerian letter scheme succeeds in bilking people out of millions of dollars annually.

30. C: The text indicates that all such information should be restricted to the resume, and that photocopies of book pages, for example, from which publication information could be deduced, are not acceptable.

31. D: The instructions state that applicants submitting excerpts must include a one-page statement in the manuscript about where it fits into the whole to orient the reviewers.

32. C: The professor argues that small, woody material is left on the tops of trees and is less likely to be reached by fire.

33. B: Plot A was salvage logged and burned worse than the unmanaged plot (Plot B). This study supports the professor's view that salvage logging increases the risk and severity of fire.

34. A: The question asks which option is the chief argument regarding fire prevention. Choices B and D are not helpful for fire prevention. Choice C is incorrect because logging decreases soil temperature. Choice B is a supporting detail from the passage but is not the main idea. Choice C contradicts the passage. Choice D is not mentioned in the passage.

35. D: The professor says the larger trees in old growth forests are more resistant to fire than smaller, younger trees. Choices A, B, and C all agree with the professor.

36. D: Choice D is not a supporting detail because it is a definition of salvage logging. The other choices are supporting details of the forest manager's argument.

37. B: In the first paragraph of the essay, the author characterizes amateurs as "an elite group within the music scene" and states that there are several "technological, demographic, and economic factors" that account for them doing better than professionals. The tone of the essay is documentary—the author doesn't make any judgments about whether this is a good development or a bad one. He simply states that amateurs are more successful relative to professionals than they have been before and goes on to examine the reasons for this. Therefore, choice B is correct.

38. D: The key is the phrase *directly support.* The essay needs to come right out and say the correct answer, not imply that it is true. Paragraph 3 says that digital file sharing "robs the professionals of what has traditionally been one of their biggest sources of revenue." Paragraph 2 provides less direct evidence, saying that many clubs that were once able to pay professionals now can't. Professionals have lost most of their income from both small clubs and recordings. Therefore, choice D is correct.

39. B: The second sentence in the final paragraph is a giveaway. If the "amateurs are the only ones who can afford to buy new gear and fix broken equipment, keep their cars in working order to get to shows, and pay to promote their shows," then the professionals must not be able to do any of those things, as stated in choice B.

40. C: The essay as a whole discusses how the current musical scene negatively affects professional musicians while leaving amateurs unharmed. The second paragraph, for example, discusses how professionals are no longer able to make a living playing small venues and must "fight more desperately than ever for those few lucrative gigs." The final paragraph states that, because of the effect on their finances, professionals are unable to maintain the gear and transportation they need to "keep the higher-paying gigs." It goes on to say that "a fairly skilled amateur . . . will be able to fake his way through most of what a professional does . . . to play professional shows." Therefore, professionals are falling behind amateurs at small venues (which professionals can't afford to play because of the lack of pay) and at professional gigs (where professionals can't play because they can't afford professional gear). Therefore, choice C is correct.

Language

1. D: A comma is not used to separate two clauses in a sentence if one of the clauses is dependent. In this sentence, the clause following the conjunction *but* lacks a subject and therefore depends upon the subject of the first clause.

2. D: *Exemplifies* is the correct choice because it means to serve as a typical or model example of something, which aligns perfectly with the passage's description of the collaboration between the Navajo Nation and the University of Arizona as a shining model demonstrating the principles of community-based participatory research. In contrast, Choice A (*circumvents*) implies avoidance or bypassing, directly contradicting the portrayal of the successful partnership in the passage. Choice B (*eclipses*) suggests complete overshadowing, which does not capture the collaborative essence intended by *exemplifies*. Choice C (*fabricates*) denotes a false creation, a concept that contradicts the genuine nature of the collaboration portrayed in the passage.

3. B: The word in place of the blank must modify the verb *did*. An adverb must be used to modify a verb, not an adjective. Of the choices presented, only *well* is an adverb. All the others are adjectives.

4. C: The passage suggests that the impact of climate change on coral reefs has been challenging to understand due to intricate relationships. However, Dr. Olivia Chang's recent findings offer hope for preservation, indicating a more definitive, or *conclusive*, explanation. The other options do not fit as well: *an intricate* implies complexity; *an elusive* suggests difficulty in understanding; and *a clear* does not capture the idea of a definitive explanation.

5. D: The transition "On the other hand" is appropriate because it clearly signals a contrast between the famous authors and the lesser-recognized ones, highlighting a shift in perspective. It effectively conveys the intended message that there are two different sides to the literary world in terms of recognition.

6. C: In the passage, it's mentioned that chameleons have the remarkable ability to change the color of their skin. The word *synchronization* is the most appropriate word in this context because it implies that chameleons synchronize, or match, their skin color with the environment, making them virtually invisible to predators or prey. The other choices, *prediction*, *moderation*, and *hibernation*, do not convey the same sense of matching or alignment with the surroundings and are not logical in this context.

7. B: In choice A, the question mark should be outside of the quotation marks, since it is not part of the title. In choice C, the title of the poem should be in quotation marks. Choice D should not use quotation marks since it is an indirect question.

8. A, D: Choice B lacks a verb and is not a complete sentence. Choice C should not have a question mark.

9. C: This is a compound sentence with one subject and two verbs. Choice A lacks a subject. The country name in Choice B requires no quotation marks. A comma should be used to set off the subordinate clause at the beginning of Choice D.

10. C: This choice makes explicit that the center fielder was rewarded because he broke the season record. Choice B suggests that breaking the record was itself a reward. Choice D suggests that he was being well rewarded (i.e., well paid) even before breaking the record.

11. B, D: These choices make it clear that the mechanic used the computer in order to perform the tests. Choice A makes the use of the computer appear incidental, while choice C suggests that the mechanic was obliged to perform the tests because he used a computer.

12. C: This paragraph describes checking accounts and their related services. Choice C continues that description by discussing ATM services and the charges that may accompany them. The other choices are also about banking, but they do not continue the description of checking account services.

13. A: This sentence, which suggests a visit in winter, leads naturally into the last sentence, which describes the weather conditions and wildlife activity at that time of year. The other choices are also about the Everglades, but bring up points that have nothing to do with the time of year.

14. A, D: This paragraph describes the law and the effects that it has had on the organic food market. Choices A and D follow the first sentence by beginning a description of the content of the law and leads naturally into the third sentence, which continues that description in more detail.

15. C: This sentence gives more information about the accident that led to the sinking of the ferry. The other choices give information about the area, but they do not continue the theme of the ferry sinking that is introduced in the topic sentence.

16. B: This paragraph describes the use of vegetable oil as a diesel fuel, the problems involved in using it, and how to solve those problems with an engine conversion. The fact that there are many automobiles in the U.S. is not integral to this topic and does not belong in this paragraph.

17. A: The singular pronoun *her* and singular noun *degree* are grammatically correct. The subjects, "Tracy" and "Vanessa," are connected by "or" and refer to two women, each of whom has her own degree. Choices B and D use "their degree," which would suggest the women share one degree (also eliminating the need for "each of" in B). B also uses "was" rather than "would be," which disagrees with "future employers." Choice C is awkward and unclear.

18. C: The original sentence is redundant and wordy.

19. A: This sentence contains an appositive that gives extra information and is set off with commas. Therefore, the subject ("Mr. King,") and the predicate (beginning with "created") should be a complete sentence that makes sense without the portion set off by commas. Choice B adds "he," which is not grammatically correct because "Mr. King" is already the subject. Choice C omits the second comma, not setting off the nonessential phrase "an individual of considerable influence." Choice D changes the meaning by saying that Mr. King literally gave his fortune to the community, but "give back" in the original simply means he contributed to the community in some way.

20. C: Choice C is the best answer because *while* indicates a side-by-side comparison, so it fits in this case, and it is a subordinating conjunction, so it is grammatically correct.

21. B: It is necessary to use the adverb *heavily* rather than the adjective *heavy* to modify the verb. Also, the possessive form *Norway's* is called for, since *Norways* would be plural and incorrect.

22. D: When separating the items of a list of 3 or more items with commas, use a comma after each item in the list. Note that choice A changes the meaning of the sentence and indicates that the ships are made of metal.

23. C: Since the livestock comprises a portion of the diversified agriculture described by the sentence, the word *includes* provides the most precise meaning. The phrasings in the other choices are incorrect or awkward.

24. A, C: It is not the needs that are imported, but rather the foods to fill the needs. Also, choice B uses the plural *countries* instead of the possessive *country's*.

25. A, D: Answer choices A and D correctly arrange the ideas to reflect the most effective meaning of the sentence. All other answer choices place the ideas in ways that are confusing or have incorrect punctuation.

26. A: Semicolons are used to separate items in a series when those items contain internal commas, such as in a listing of cities and states. Answer choice A correctly demonstrates this. Answer choice B places the semicolon between the city and its state, instead of between each city and state pair, and this is incorrect. A comma is always used to separate a single instance of a city and a state. Answer choice C separates the items in the series with commas, but this creates confusion for the reader since there are already commas between each city and its state. Answer choice D places commas between each item in the series but fails to include the necessary comma between each city and its state.

27. B: Choice B, *perspective*, is the most appropriate selection, as it accurately conveys how Jane Austen's novels provide readers with a distinctive and insightful lens through which to view the society and manners of her time. Choice A, *endorsement*, doesn't align with the context of the sentence, as it suggests approval or support rather than the insightful perspective on society and manners that Austen's novels offer. Likewise, Choice C, *commentary*, pertains to providing opinions or explanations but doesn't quite capture the essence of offering a unique viewpoint or deep insight into the subject at hand, which is the primary focus of the sentence. Lastly, Choice D, *refusal*, is entirely unrelated to the context of the sentence and lacks relevance.

28. A: *Additionally* is the appropriate choice, as it smoothly introduces the idea of providing extra information about the cave's ecosystem, particularly the bats. It maintains a logical flow in the text, highlighting the connection between the geological features and the biological significance of the cave system.

29. B: Choice B aligns best with the passage's emphasis on Shakespeare's beautiful representation of human life, making it the most logical and precise word. Choice A contradicts the passage by suggesting it *avoids* depth. Choice C, while similar to *captures*, implies direct copying, not creative representation. Choice D, *diminishes*, contradicts the passage's praise for enhancing human life's depth.

30. D: In the context of the sentence, it appears that Finlay's parents are attempting to *coax* him by promising a trip to his favorite toy store. Answer choice A makes little sense, as the sentence indicates Finlay's parents want him to participate in the recital. Answer choice B might work, but the promise of a trip to the toy store seems more like a reward than a punishment. Answer choice C makes no sense when added to the sentence in place of the word *cajole*.

31. A: *Complex* is the most fitting word to complete the sentence. The sentence describes critics debating the nature of the protagonist in a novel, with some seeing the character as a symbol of hope and others as a representation of despair. This suggests that there is a diversity of opinions regarding the character's attributes. The other choices, *one-dimensional*, *unambiguous*, and *predictable*, do not align with the sentence's context.

32. C: *Acrimonious* means "bitter" or "vitriolic" and is very similar in meaning to *rancorous*.

33. B: Answer choice B combines the sentences in the best way. The sentences are combined into a single sentence, and all of the details are still included. Answer choices A and D do a good job of combining the sentences, but they still consist of more than one sentence. Answer choice C combines the sentences, but it leaves out the part about how she "tried to find a way to attend both." There is no clear reason to leave this out, so answer choice C is not the best choice.

Mathematics

1. A, B, D: The cost for plan A is 1,200 × \$0.10 = \$120; for plan B it is \$48 + (600 × \$0.12) = \$120; for plan C it is \$75 + (300 × \$0.16) = \$123; for plan D it is \$100 + (200 × \$0.10) = \$120. So plans A, B, and D are each \$120, which is less expensive than plan C.

2. B, D: Note that ∠n and ∠p are corresponding angles for the transversal line L2 intersecting lines L3 and L4. If the corresponding angles are congruent, the lines must be parallel. And since ∠m and ∠o are complementary angles of ∠n and ∠p, respectively, ∠m and ∠o must be congruent.

3. A: To solve this problem, work backwards. Since there are 6,400 yeast cells present at 3 hours and the culture doubles every half hour, there were $6{,}400 \times \frac{1}{2} = 3{,}200$ cells present at 2.5 hours. At time $t = 0$, there were $6400 \times \frac{1}{2} \times \frac{1}{2} \times \frac{1}{2} \times \frac{1}{2} \times \frac{1}{2} \times \frac{1}{2} = 6400 \times \frac{1}{64} = 100$ cells in the culture.

4. C: Write two equations to express the problem. Since the entertainment portion (E) lasted 15 minutes less than 4 times the advertising portion (A), the first equation is $E = 4A - 15$. Since both sections add up to the total show length, 60 minutes, the second equation is $E + A = 60$. Substituting the first equation into the second yields:

$$\begin{aligned} 4A - 15 + A &= 60 \\ 5A &= 75 \\ A &= 15 \end{aligned}$$

Now, since $E + A = 60$, it follows that $E = 60 - 15 = 45$ minutes.

5. A: In order for two figures to be congruent, they must have the same size and shape. The two triangles in choice A have the same size and shape, even though the second triangle is rotated counterclockwise compared to the first triangle. The rectangles in choice B are the same shape, but they are not the same size. In choice C, the second circle has been vertically stretched, so the figures are not the same shape or size. In choice D, the second trapezoid has been horizontally stretched so it is not the same size as the first trapezoid.

6. C: When two parallel lines are intersected by a third straight line (called a transversal), the angles in matching corners are called corresponding angles and are congruent to one another. Lines L1 and L2 are parallel and are intersected by the transversal L3 to form corresponding angles ∠a and ∠i. Therefore, since ∠a = 70°, ∠i = 70°.

7. C: We first need to find the volume of water that Kasie is putting in each glass. The volume of a cylinder is $V = \pi r^2 h$. Since we know the radius is 1.25 and the height is 5 (ignore the actual height of the glass since it is not filled to the brim), we can write the following equation.

$$\begin{aligned} V &= (3.14)(1.25)^2(5) \\ V &\approx 24.53 \text{ in}^3 \end{aligned}$$

Now we need to find the number of cubic inches in 3 quarts.

$$\left(\frac{3 \text{ qt}}{1}\right)\left(\frac{1 \text{ gal}}{4 \text{ qt}}\right)\left(\frac{231 \text{ in}^3}{1 \text{ gal}}\right) = 173.25 \text{ in}^3$$

Finally, we divide 173.25 by 24.53 to find that Kasie could fill 7.06 glasses. In other words, she could completely fill 7 glasses.

8. B: Since $\frac{4}{5}$ of $\frac{5}{7}$ of 35 boys were at the practice, this is $35 \times \frac{5}{7} \times \frac{4}{5} = 35 \times \frac{4}{7} = 5 \times 4 = 20$.

9. A: From the definition of the PE ratio, $\frac{Price}{Earnings\ per\ share} = 12$. Therefore, earnings per share must be equal to $\frac{Price}{12} = \frac{\$6.00}{12} = \$0.50$. Since there are 3 million shares issued, the total earnings must be $\$0.50 \times 3{,}000{,}000 =$ \$1.5 million.

10. D: If Bob buys the paper every day for $1.50, in 7 days he will spend $7 \times \$1.50 = \$10.50$. If he subscribes, he spends only $3.50. Therefore, his savings is the difference $\$10.50 - \$3.50 = \$7.00$.

11. D: The cost per ounce can be calculated by dividing the cost of the bag by the number of ounces the bag contains. Thus, the cost per ounce can be calculated by writing $\$9.85 \div 16$, which equals approximately $0.62 per ounce.

12. A, B: You can see from the table that as a planet's orbital period grows shorter, its orbital speed increases. And the shorter the distance from a planet to the Sun, the greater its orbital speed. To see that choice C is incorrect, note that Saturn's diameter is less than that of Jupiter, and its orbital speed is less. To see that choice D is incorrect, note that Saturn's mass is greater than that of Earth, but its orbital speed is less.

13. B: The rational numbers for choice B can be compared by either converting all of them to decimals or finding common denominators and comparing the newly written fractions. Using the first approach, the rational numbers shown for choice B in order from left to right can be written as 6.4, 2.25, and 0.80. These numbers are indeed written in order from greatest to least. Also, the integer -2 is greater than -5. Thus, the numbers, $\frac{32}{5}, 2\frac{1}{4}, \frac{4}{5}, -2, -5$, are listed in order from greatest to least.

14. C: Alfredo's weekly base is $40 \times \$20 = \$800$. This week he made $\$950 - \$800 = \$150$ from overtime. At $30 per hour, this corresponds to $\frac{150}{30} = 5$ hours of overtime. Added to his normal workweek, he worked $40 + 5 = 45$ hours in all.

15. C, D: Tamara can pull any sock out the first time, since the color does not matter. For the second time, there is only one remaining sock out of 5 that matches the color of the sock she drew the first time, so the probability of drawing that one is $\frac{1}{5}$. This can also be written as 0.2 or 20%.

16. B: The average is the total number of seconds (T) divided by the total number of swimmers. If there are four swimmers, the average can be expressed as $\frac{T}{4} = 22$ seconds. So, $T = 88$ seconds. The total time for the first three swimmers is $(22.4 + 23.8 + 21.9)$ seconds $= 68.1$ seconds. Therefore, the last swimmer must swim his lap in $(88.0 - 68.1)$ seconds $= 19.9$ seconds.

17. A: According to the table, the mass of Venus is 0.815 times that of Earth. Since $0.815 \times 6 \times 10^{24} = 4.9 \times 10^{24}$, choice A is correct.

18. A, D: The mode is the value that occurs most often. In this case, there are two modes, because 23 and 127 each appear twice.

19. C, D: To see that choice A is incorrect, note that Saturn's mass is less than that of Jupiter, but its orbital period is longer. To see that choice B is incorrect, note that Saturn's diameter is greater than that of Earth, but its gravity is less. You can see that as the distance a planet is from the Sun grows, the length of the orbital period also grows. And as the length of the orbital period grows, the average orbital speed lessens.

20. B, C: There are 200 possible outcomes to this experiment, one for each of the marbles in the jar. Each outcome is equally likely. Thirty of the possible outcomes are for a blue marble to be drawn. Therefore, the probability of this outcome is $\frac{30}{200} = 0.15 = 15\%$, which is choice C. This can also be written as 0.15 or $\frac{3}{20}$, so choice B is also correct.

21. B: To answer this question, we first determine the total cost of the onions and carrots, since these prices are given. This will equal $2 \times \$3.69 + 3 \times \$4.29 = \$20.25$. Next, this sum is subtracted from the total cost of the produce to determine the cost of the mushrooms: $\$24.15 - \$20.25 = \$3.90$. Finally, the cost of the mushrooms is divided by the quantity in pounds to determine the cost per pound:

$$\text{Cost per lb} = \frac{\$3.90}{1.5} = \$2.60$$

Therefore, the mushrooms cost $2.60 per pound.

22. B: In scientific notation, the distance 149,600,000 km is written as 1.496×10^8 km. According to the table, Mercury is 0.39 times as far from the Sun as is Earth. Since $0.39 \times 1.496 \times 10^8 \text{ km} = 5.8 \times 10^7$ km, choice B is correct.

23. C: Since an 18% tip was added, the amount paid was equal to 118% of the total before the tip was added. Therefore, that total is calculated as $\$1{,}128.08 \times \frac{100}{118} = \$956.00$.

24. A: Note that ∠a and ∠c are corresponding angles and must be congruent and that ∠c and ∠k are corresponding angles and must be congruent. Therefore, ∠a and ∠k must be congruent. Furthermore, ∠k and ∠p are vertical angles (formed by two intersecting straight lines), so that ∠k is congruent to ∠p. Similarly, ∠a is congruent to ∠f. Therefore, all four angles are congruent to one another and statement A is true.

25. A: Since 12 inches equals 1 foot, each tile is 1 square foot in area. The area of the bedroom floor is $15 \times 18 = 270$ square feet. Therefore, the number of tiles that must be laid is 270. Since Morgan can lay 9 tiles per hour, the time required will be $\frac{270}{9} = 30$ hours.

26. A: Let d represent the distance between the two towns. Then $\frac{d}{90}$ is the time it takes Mischa to drive the distance, and $\frac{d}{60}$ is the time it takes Brenda to drive the same distance. Since this is 3 hours longer than Mischa's time, $\frac{d}{90} + 3 = \frac{d}{60}$. To solve this equation for d, first gather the terms with the variable on one side: $\frac{d}{60} - \frac{d}{90} = 3$. Isolate the variable to yield $d\left(\frac{1}{60} - \frac{1}{90}\right) = 3$. The least common multiple for the denominators is 180, so this is equivalent to $d\left(\frac{3-2}{180}\right) = \frac{d}{180} = 3$. This yields:

$$d = 3 \times 180 = 540 \text{ km}$$

27. A, D: The constant amount Kevin pays is $12.95; this amount represents the y-intercept. The variable amount is represented by the expression $\$0.07x$, where x represents the number of text messages sent and $0.07 represents the constant rate of change or slope. Thus, his total cost can be represented by the equation $y = \$0.07x + \$12.95$. The $12.95 can be subtracted from each side to yield $y - \$12.95 = \$0.07x$.

28. B: Substitute each of the given values for x and y into the equation, and simplify using the order of operations.

$$\begin{aligned}&(4)^2 - (2(3) - 3)\\ &= 16 - (6 - 3)\\ &= 16 - 3\\ &= 13\end{aligned}$$

29. C: Hiking due west at 3 mph, the first hiker will have gone 6 miles after 2 hours. Hiking due north at 4 mph, the second hiker will have gone 8 miles after 2 hours. Since one hiker headed west and the other headed north, their distance from each other can be drawn as:

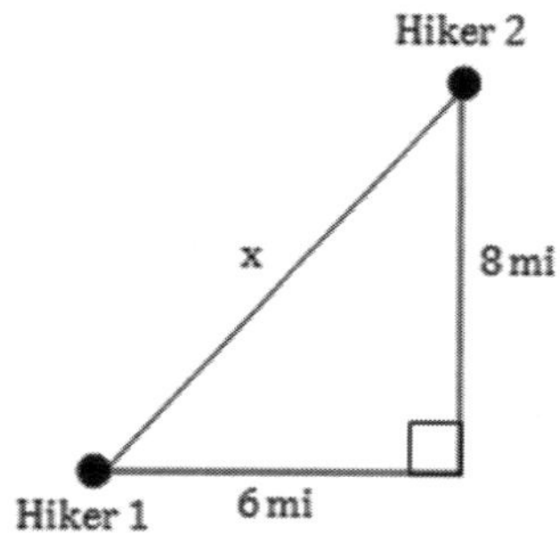

Since the distance between the two hikers is the hypotenuse of a right triangle, and since we know the lengths of the two legs of the right triangle, we can use the Pythagorean theorem ($a^2 + b^2 = c^2$) to find the value of x.

$$6^2 + 8^2 = x^2$$
$$36 + 64 = x^2$$
$$100 = x^2$$
$$10 = x$$

Therefore, the hikers are 10 miles apart after 2 hours of hiking.

30. D: This is a geometric series, in which a constant ratio is maintained between each term and the next. From the first two terms, for example, it can be seen that the ratio is $\frac{6}{3} = 2$. This holds for all other sequential terms. To calculate the next term in the series, multiply the preceding term by this ratio. This yields $24 \times 2 = 48$.

31. B: At 25 miles per gallon, Rouenna will need $\frac{500 \text{ mi}}{25\frac{\text{mi}}{\text{gal}}} = 20$ gal. At \$3 per gallon, this will cost:

$$\frac{\$3}{\text{gal}} \times 20 \text{ gal} = \$60$$

32. D: Substitute the given values into the expression, yielding $\frac{1}{3}(3)^2 + \frac{3\times4}{4} = 3 + 3 = 6$.

33. B: Out of a total of 55 men, 36 received a grade of 75 or higher (24 + 12). The percentage of men with passing grades is calculated as $\frac{36}{55} \times 100 \approx 0.65$, or approximately 65%.

34. B: Since clothing expenses are 8% of the total, on average, according to the chart, then household spending on clothes would comprise $0.08 \times \$40{,}000 = \$3{,}200$.

35. B: Two women scored in the range 95 and above. None of the men did. So, at least these two women scored higher than any of the men. It is possible that some of the women who scored in the range 84–95 also scored higher than any of the men (if none of the men had scores at the top of this range), but it is not possible to show this from the data in the table.

36. D: Solve by setting up the cross product: $2x = (-3) \times 8 = -24$. Divide both sides of this equation by 2 to isolate the variable: $x = -12$.

37. D: Two adjacent angles that form a straight line are called supplementary angles. In order to form a straight line, the sums of their measures must be 180°. Therefore, since $\angle a = 70°$, it follows that $\angle b = 180° - 70° = 110°$.

38. C: To calculate the mean, or average, add the stock prices and divide by the number of stocks. This yields:

$$\frac{127 + 23 + 23 + 127 + 30}{5} = 66$$

39. D: To determine the number of questions Joshua must answer correctly, consider the number of points he must earn. Joshua will receive 4 points for each question he answers correctly, and x represents the number of questions. Therefore, Joshua will receive a total of $4x$ points for all the questions he answers correctly. Joshua must earn more than 92 points. Therefore, to determine the number of questions he must answer correctly, solve the inequality $4x > 92$.

40. C: In order for figures to be similar, all sets of corresponding sides need to be proportional. All corresponding sides in answer C are at a 2:1 ratio. In answer A, the corresponding sides are 2 more for the second figure, instead of being 2 times larger. In answer B, one set of corresponding sides is at a 1:2 ratio, while the other set of corresponding sides is at a 2:1 ratio. In answer D, the corresponding sides are 3 more for the second figure, instead of being 3 times larger.

TABE Practice Test #2

Reading

Refer to the following for questions 1–11:

The Story of My Life

by Helen Keller

Have you ever been at sea in a dense fog, when it seemed as if a tangible white darkness shut you in, and the great ship, tense and anxious, groped her way toward the shore with plummet and sounding-line, and you waited with beating heart for something to happen? I was like that ship before my education began...

I felt approaching footsteps. I stretched out my hand as I supposed to my mother. Someone took it, and I was caught up and held close in the arms of her who had come to reveal all things to me, and, more than all things else, to love me.

[One afternoon] we walked down the path to the well-house, attracted by the fragrance of the honeysuckle with which it was covered. Someone was drawing water and my teacher placed my hand under the spout. As the cool stream gushed over one hand she spelled into the other the word *water*, first slowly, then rapidly. I stood still, my whole attention fixed upon the motions of her fingers. Suddenly I felt a misty consciousness as of something forgotten—a thrill of returning thought; and somehow the mystery of language was revealed to me. I knew then that "w-a-t-e-r" meant the wonderful cool something that was flowing over my hand. That living word awakened my soul, gave it light, hope, joy, set it free! There were barriers still, it is true, but barriers that could in time be swept away. I left the well-house eager to learn. Everything had a name, and each name gave birth to a new thought.

I recall many incidents of the summer of 1887 that followed my soul's sudden awakening. I did nothing but explore with my hands and learn the name of every object that I touched; and the more I handled things and learned their names and uses, the more joyous and confident grew my sense of kinship with the rest of the world.

I had my first lessons in the beneficence of nature. I learned how the sun and the rain make to grow out of the ground every tree that is pleasant to the sight and good for food, how birds build their nests and live and thrive from land to land, how the squirrel, the deer, the lion and every other creature finds food and shelter. As my knowledge of things grew I felt more and more the delight of the world I was in. Long before I learned to do a sum in arithmetic or describe the shape of the earth, Miss Sullivan had taught me to find beauty in the fragrant woods, in every blade of grass, and in the curves and dimples of my baby sister's hand. She linked my earliest thoughts with nature, and made me feel that "birds and flowers and I were happy peers."

But about this time I had an experience which taught me that nature is not always kind. One day my teacher and I were returning from a long ramble. The morning had been fine, but it was growing warm and sultry when at last we turned our faces homeward. Two or three times we stopped to rest under a tree by the wayside. Our last halt was under a wild cherry tree a short distance from the house. The shade was grateful, and the tree was so easy to climb that with my teacher's assistance I was able to scramble to a seat in the branches. It was so cool up in the tree that Miss Sullivan proposed that we have our luncheon there. I promised to keep still while she went to the house to fetch it.

Suddenly a change passed over the tree. All the sun's warmth left the air. I knew the sky was black, because all the heat, which meant light to me, had died out of the atmosphere. A strange odour came up from the earth. I knew it, it was the odour that always precedes a thunderstorm, and a nameless fear clutched at my heart. I felt absolutely alone, cut off from my friends and the firm earth. The immense, the unknown, enfolded me. I remained still and expectant; a chilling terror crept over me. I longed for my teacher's return; but above all things I wanted to get down from that tree.

There was a moment of sinister silence, then a multitudinous stirring of the leaves. A shiver ran through the tree, and the wind sent forth a blast that would have knocked me off had I not clung to the branch with might and main. The tree swayed and strained. The small twigs snapped and fell about me in showers. A wild impulse to jump seized me, but terror held me fast. I crouched down in the fork of the tree. The branches lashed about me. I felt the intermittent jarring that came now and then, as if something heavy had fallen and the shock had traveled up till it reached the limb I sat on. It worked my suspense up to the highest point, and just as I was thinking the tree and I should fall together, my teacher seized my hand and helped me down. I clung to her, trembling with joy to feel the earth under my feet once more. I had learned a new lesson—that nature "wages open war against her children, and under softest touch hides treacherous claws."

1. What is the meaning of the word *beneficence*?

a. Duties
b. Generosity
c. Stinginess
d. Danger

2. Paragraph 3 is mainly about the narrator...

a. Learning to write words with a pencil
b. Learning the difference between cold and hot water
c. Learning the location of the well-house
d. Learning that words have meaning

3. Why did Helen hold out her hand in paragraph 2?

a. She thought the visitor was her mother
b. She wanted to greet the visitor
c. She wanted to please her mother
d. She loved the approaching person

4. In paragraphs 7 and 8, Helen felt nervous because...

a. she was lost.
b. she was alone.
c. it was raining.
d. it was windy.

5. Which sentence best explains what Helen learned from Miss Sullivan?

a. "I learned how the sun and the rain make to grow out of the ground every tree that is pleasant to the sight..."
b. "There were barriers still, it is true, but barriers that could in time be swept away."
c. "Everything had a name, and each name gave birth to a new thought."
d. "...nature 'wages open war against her children, and under softest touch hides treacherous claws.'"

6. Which aspect of the selection best shows the close bond between Helen and Miss Sullivan?

a. The moment when Miss Sullivan spelled "w-a-t-e-r" into Helen's hand
b. When Helen learned to find beauty in nature
c. When Miss Sullivan proposed eating lunch by the cherry tree
d. The moment when Miss Sullivan pulled Helen from the tree

7. What is a major theme of the passage?

a. Family ties
b. Discovery
c. Disappointment
d. Youth

8. In paragraph 8, the narrator uses the phrase "hides treacherous claws" to explain that...

a. Miss Sullivan, beneath her kind exterior, is very mean
b. Helen continues to have violent temper tantrums
c. Climbing trees can be very dangerous.
d. Nature can be cruel.

9. By telling the story in the order that events occur, the author helps you understand...

a. The change that Helen went through after meeting Miss Sullivan
b. The way in which Helen learned to be brave
c. The strategies Miss Sullivan used to teach Helen
d. The confusion that Helen felt when she was with Miss Sullivan

10. Based on the passage, you can conclude that Helen...

a. Disliked Miss Sullivan
b. Is scared of nature
c. Didn't understand words before Miss Sullivan arrived
d. Never learned how to read or write

11. What tool of figurative language is used in the phrase: "...each name gave birth to a new thought."?

a. Metaphor
b. Hyperbole
c. Simile
d. Personification

Refer to the following for questions 12–15:

Adapted from "Roughing It"

by Mark Twain

After fifteen days of hiking along the Humboldt River, we reached Unionville. People who are used to the Mississippi grow accustomed to associating the term "river" with a great deal of watery grandeur. Consequently, such a person may feel rather disappointed to find that he can jump across the Humboldt until he is overheated, then drink it dry.

Unionville consists of eleven cabins built in a deep crevice on a bleak mountainside. The mountain walls rise so steeply around it that the sun only touches the rooftops for an hour out of each day. We built a small, rude cabin in the side of the crevice and roofed it with canvas, leaving a corner open to serve as a chimney, through which the cattle used to tumble occasionally, at night, and mash our furniture and interrupt our sleep. It was very cold weather and fuel for the fire was scarce. We shivered and bore it.

I confess that I had expected to see the mountains glittering with gold. I expected it to litter the ground, waiting to be picked up. Some suspicion that this might be an exaggerated notion kept me from sharing my expectation with my friends, yet I was perfectly satisfied in my own mind that, within a few days at the most, I would gather up gold enough to make me satisfactorily wealthy. And so, at the first opportunity, I sauntered nonchalantly away from the cabin, keeping an eye on the boys and stopping to contemplate the sky when they seemed to look at me. As soon as the coast was clear, I fled away as guiltily as a thief might have done and never halted until I was far beyond sight and call. Then, I began my feverish search for the riches of the mountains.

By and by, in the bed of a shallow rivulet, I found a deposit of shining yellow scales, and my breath almost forsook me. A gold mine! Picking up a bright fragment, I hid behind a boulder and polished it and scrutinized it with a nervous eagerness. It shone brightly in the light of the sun. I set about scooping out more, and for an hour I toiled down the windings of the stream and robbed its bed. But at last the descending sun warned me to give up the quest, and I turned homeward laden with wealth.

The boys were as hungry as usual, but I could eat nothing. Neither could I talk. I was full of dreams and far away. Their conversation kept interrupting my thoughts, annoying me at first, but presently I became amused.

Here they were, talking of privations and small economies that must be made, when our very own gold mine lay but a mile away. I decided to break the news to them calmly and to watch the play of emotions on their faces. I said:

"Where have you all been?"

"Prospecting."

"What did you find?"

"Nothing."

"Nothing? What do you think of the country?"

"Can't tell, yet," said Mr. Ballou, who was an experienced gold-miner. "It's fair enough here, maybe, but overrated. We won't starve, but we aren't going to get rich, here, either."

"So you think the prospects are pretty poor, eh?"

"I guess that's so, but we'll try it for a bit."

"Suppose, now," I put forth, "suppose you could find a ledge that would yield, say, a hundred and fifty dollars a ton—would that satisfy you?"

"Try us once!" from the whole party.

"Or suppose—merely a supposition, of course— suppose you were to find a ledge that would yield two thousand dollars a ton—would that satisfy you?"

"Here—what do you mean? What are you coming at? Is there some mystery behind all this?"

"Gentlemen," said I, "I am but a mere novice, of course, and don't know anything—but all I ask of you is to cast your eye on this and tell me what you think of it!" and I tossed my treasure before them.

There was an eager scrabble for it, and a closing of heads together over it under the candle-light. Then old Ballou said:

"Think of it? I think it is nothing but a lot of granite rubbish and nasty glittering mica that isn't worth ten cents an acre!"

So vanished my dream. So melted my wealth away. So toppled my airy castle to the earth and left me stricken and forlorn.

Moralizing, I observed, then, that "all that glitters is not gold."

So I learned then that gold in its native state is but dull, un-ornamental stuff, and that only low-born metals excite the admiration of the ignorant with an ostentatious glitter. However, like the rest of the world, I still go on underrating men of gold and glorifying men of mica.

12. Which of the following best describes the nature and tone of the passage?

a. Adventure
b. History
c. Drama
d. Caricature

13. In the second paragraph, the author describes cattle falling through the chimney of the cabin from the steep hillside above. This is an example of which of the following?

a. Burlesque
b. Illustrative detail
c. Character development
d. Denouement

14. How is Mr. Ballou able to recognize that the author's find has no value?

a. He is a mineralogist.
b. He has mined gold before.
c. He compares it to a gold watch.
d. He bites down on it to see if it is hard.

15. Which of the following BEST describes the ending of the passage?

a. A lament about lost riches
b. A comparison of minerals and men
c. An angry denunciation of mica
d. An expression of hope that he will find gold the next day

Refer to the following for questions 16–21:

In 1906, Elinore Pruitt Stewart moved to Denver for housework to support her daughter, Jerrine. Her employer in Denver was Mrs. Juliet Coney. A few years later, she moved to Wyoming to be a housekeeper for a rancher. The following passage is one of many letters that Stewart wrote to Mrs. Coney on life as a homesteader in Wyoming.

A Letter of Elinore Pruitt Stewart

January 23, 1913

When I read of the hard times among the Denver poor, I feel like urging them every one to get out and file on land. I am very enthusiastic about women homesteading. It really requires less strength and labor to raise plenty to satisfy a large family than it does to go out to wash, with the added satisfaction of knowing that their job will not be lost to them if they care to keep it. Even if improving the place does go slowly, it is that much done to stay done. Whatever is raised is the homesteader's own, and there is no house-rent to pay. This year Jerrine cut and dropped enough potatoes to raise a ton of fine potatoes. She wanted to try, so we let her, and you will remember that she is but six years old.... Any woman strong enough to go out by the day could have done every bit of the work and put in two or three times that much, and it would have been so much more pleasant than to work so hard in the city and be on starvation rations all winter.

To me, homesteading is the solution of all poverty's problems, but I realize that temperament has much to do with success in any undertaking, and persons afraid of coyotes and work and loneliness had better let ranching alone. At the same time, any woman who can stand her own company, can see the beauty of the sunset, loves growing things, and is willing to put in as much time at careful labor as she does over the washtub, will certainly succeed; will have independence, plenty to eat all the time, and a home of her own in the end.

Experimenting need cost the homesteader no more than the work, because by applying to the Department of Agriculture at Washington he can get enough of any seed and as many kinds as he wants to make a thorough trial, and it doesn't even cost postage. Also one can always get bulletins from there and from the Experiment Station of one's own State concerning any problem or as many problems as may come up. I would not, for anything, allow Mr. Stewart to do anything toward improving my place, for I want the fun and the experience myself. And I want to be able to speak from experience when I tell others what they can do. Theories are very beautiful, but facts are what must be had, and what I intend to give some time.

16. The writer of this letter is suggesting that women should own land and farm rather than:

a. Cook in a restaurant.
b. Open a bed and breakfast.
c. Do laundry for others.
d. Teach in a one-room schoolhouse.

17. Stewart mentions her daughter's potato crop. She does this to show:

a. That child labor is acceptable
b. That there are no schools in the area
c. That women work just as hard as men do
d. How easy it is to raise crops

18. What do you think Mrs. Coney's reaction to the letter might have been?

a. She was probably glad to be rid of such a lazy worker.
b. She may be glad to know that Mrs. Stewart is enjoying her time with homesteading.
c. She may have been sorry that she too did not homestead.
d. She was likely angry that Mrs. Stewart had written.

19. Which of the following does Stewart NOT give as an advantage of homesteading?

a. It takes less strength and work than doing laundry for others.
b. The worker cannot lose her job if she wants to keep it.
c. No one has to pay rent.
d. One can always find good company.

20. Which of the following is a risk for the poor in Denver?

a. The possibility of losing their jobs
b. The likelihood of a strike
c. The probability of a landslide
d. Losing their homes to fire

21. Which of the following describes the tone of the letter?

a. Complaining and bitter
b. Sad and lonely
c. Positive and encouraging
d. Hopeless and despairing

Refer to the following for questions 22–24:

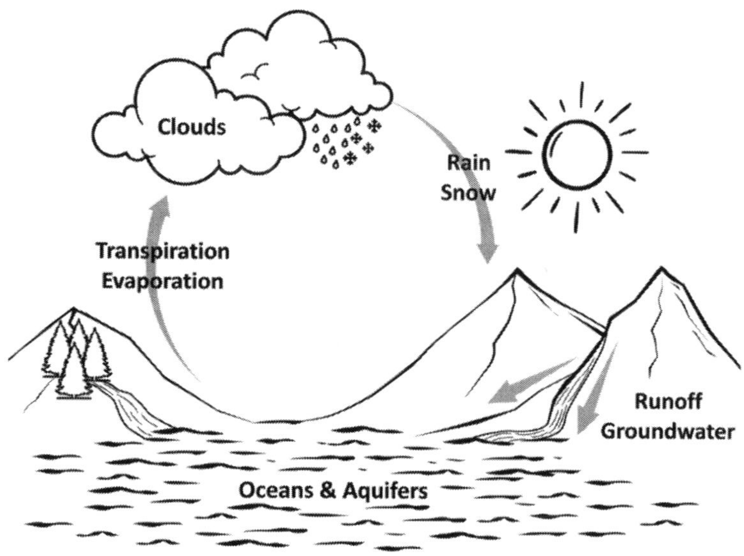

Energy from the Sun heats the water in the oceans and causes it to evaporate. This makes water vapor that rises through the atmosphere. Cooler temperatures at high altitudes cause this vapor to condense and form clouds. Water droplets in the clouds condense and grow, eventually falling to the ground as precipitation. This continuous movement of water above and below ground is called the hydrologic cycle, or water cycle, and it is essential for life on our planet. All the Earth's stores of water, including that found in clouds, oceans, underground, etc., are known as the *hydrosphere*.

Water can be stored in several locations as part of the water cycle. The largest reservoirs are the oceans, which hold about 95% of the world's water, more than 300,000,000 cubic miles. Water is also stored in polar ice caps, mountain snowcaps, lakes and streams, plants, and aquifers below ground. Each of these reservoirs has a characteristic *residence time*, which is the average amount of time a water molecule will spend there before moving on. Some typical residence times are shown in the table.

Average Reservoir Residence Times of Water

Reservoir	Residence Time
Atmosphere	9 days
Oceans	3,000 years
Glaciers and ice caps	100 years
Soil moisture	2 months
Underground aquifers	10,000 years

The water cycle can change over time. During cold climatic periods, more water is stored as ice and snow, and the rate of evaporation is lower. This affects the level of the Earth's oceans. During the last ice age, for instance, oceans were 400 feet lower than today. Human activities that affect the water cycle are agriculture, dam construction, deforestation, and industrial activities.

22. Which of the following is another name for the water cycle?

a. The hydrosphere
b. The atmosphere
c. The residence cycle
d. The hydrologic cycle

23. Other than atmospheric water, where do water molecules spend the least time?

a. Aquifers
b. Oceans
c. Glaciers
d. Soil

24. Which of the following statements is NOT true?

a. Cutting down trees affects the water cycle.
b. Ocean levels rise in an ice age.
c. Oceans hold most of the world's water.
d. Clouds are formed because of cold temperatures.

Refer to the following for questions 25–30:

History of England

by Charles Dickens

If you look at a Map of the World, you will see, in the left-hand upper corner of the Eastern Hemisphere, two Islands lying in the sea. They are England and Scotland, and Ireland. England and Scotland form the greater part of these Islands. Ireland is the next in size. The little neighbouring islands, which are so small upon the Map as to be mere dots, are chiefly little bits of Scotland, —broken off, I dare say, in the course of a great length of time, by the power of the restless water.

In the old days, a long, long while ago..., these Islands were in the same place, and the stormy sea roared round them, just as it roars now. But the sea was not alive, then, with great ships and brave sailors, sailing to and from all parts of the world. It was very lonely. The Islands lay solitary, in the great expanse of water. The foaming waves dashed against their cliffs, and the bleak winds blew over their forests; but the winds and waves brought no adventurers to land upon the Islands, and the savage Islanders knew nothing of the rest of the world, and the rest of the world knew nothing of them.

It is supposed that the Phoenicians, who were an ancient people, famous for carrying on trade, came in ships to these Islands, and found that they produced tin and lead; both very useful things, as you know, and both produced to this very hour upon the sea-coast. The most celebrated tin mines in Cornwall are, still, close to the sea. One of them, which I have seen, is so close to it that it is hollowed out underneath the ocean; and the miners say, that in stormy weather, when they are at work down in that deep place, they can hear the noise of the waves thundering above their heads. So, the Phœnicians, coasting about the Islands, would come, without much difficulty, to where the tin and lead were.

The Phœnicians traded with the Islanders for these metals, and gave the Islanders some other useful things in exchange. The Islanders were, at first, poor savages, going almost naked, or only dressed in the rough skins of beasts, and staining their bodies, as other savages do, with coloured earths and the juices of plants. But the Phœnicians, sailing over to the opposite coasts of France and Belgium, and saying to the people there, 'We have been to those white cliffs across the water, which you can see in fine weather, and from that country, which is called Britain, we bring this tin and lead,' tempted some of the French and Belgians to come over also. These people settled themselves on the south coast of England, which is now called Kent; and, although they were a rough people too, they taught the savage Britons some useful arts, and improved that part of the Islands. It is probable that other people came over from Spain to Ireland, and settled there.

Thus, by little and little, strangers became mixed with the Islanders, and the savage Britons grew into a wild, bold people; almost savage, still, especially in the interior of the country away from the sea where the foreign settlers seldom went; but hardy, brave, and strong.

The whole country was covered with forests, and swamps. The greater part of it was very misty and cold. There were no roads, no bridges, no streets, no houses that you would think deserving of the name. A town was nothing but a collection of straw-covered huts, hidden in a thick wood, with a ditch all round, and a low wall, made of mud, or the trunks of trees placed one upon another. The people planted little or no corn, but lived upon the flesh of their flocks and cattle. They made no coins, but used metal rings for money. They were clever in basket-work, as savage people often are; and they could make a coarse kind of cloth, and some very bad earthenware. But in building fortresses they were much more clever.

They made boats of basket-work, covered with the skins of animals, but seldom, if ever, ventured far from the shore. They made swords, of copper mixed with tin; but, these swords were of an awkward shape, and so soft that a heavy blow would bend one. They made light shields, short pointed daggers, and spears—which they jerked back after they had thrown them at an enemy, by a long strip of leather fastened to the stem. The butt-end was a rattle, to frighten an enemy's horse. The ancient Britons, being divided into as many as thirty or forty tribes, each commanded by its own little king, were constantly fighting with one another, as savage people usually do; and they always fought with these weapons.

25. According to the author, why did the ancient Britons regularly fight with each other?

a. They had many weapons.
b. They disliked the Phoenicians.
c. There were no roads or bridges.
d. They were divided into many tribes.

26. Which phrase best shows the change Dickens believes the Phœnicians caused in the ancient Britons?

a. "The Phoenicians traded with the Islanders..."
b. "They were clever in basket-work..."
c. "These people settled themselves on the south coast of England..."
d. "...the savage Britons grew into a wild, bold people..."

27. Which sentence or phrase best expresses the isolation of the islands of England and Scotland and Ireland?

a. "...which are so small upon the Map as to be mere dots"
b. "The Islands lay solitary, in the great expanse of water."
c. "they can hear the noise of the waves thundering above their heads."
d. "Thus, by little and little, strangers became mixed with the Islanders..."

28. Read this phrase from paragraph 7:

But seldom, if ever, ventured far from the shore.

Why does the author include this phrase?

a. To show the ways in which the people used boats
b. To highlight the irony of making boats
c. To show where the people used weapons
d. To explain why the people built fortresses

29. Why does the author begin the passage by describing a map?

a. To explain the location of the islands
b. To show the roads that run through England, Scotland, and Ireland
c. To show how the little bits of Scotland broke away from the main island
d. To show the size of the islands in relation to France and Belgium

30. What sentence or phrase best describes the lands in the interior of the islands? In other words, these lands are the parts away from the coast.

a. "These people settled themselves on the south coast of England, which is now called Kent..."
b. "Especially in the interior of the country away from the sea where the foreign settlers seldom went..."
c. The whole country was covered with forests and swamps.
d. "The ancient Britons, being divided into as many as thirty or forty tribes, each commanded by its own little king..."

Refer to the following for questions 31–35:

Section 1: Improving Diets

A healthier diet is something that many people want for themselves. However, this can be a struggle to put into practice for many people. This does not mean that just because it's hard and frustrating doesn't mean that people should stop trying.

A powerful and easy approach to improving diets is to know that some foods are so good for us that we can almost think of them as medicine. Some foods help to fight heart disease, cancer, or depression. Other foods help to lower cholesterol or blood pressure. Broccoli is high in vitamin K and vitamin C which help build strong bones and fight off cancers. Avocadoes can lower cholesterol and help reduce the risk of heart disease. Sweet potatoes are full of cancer-fighting and immune system-boosting vitamin A. Garlic can slow down the growth of bacteria and has been shown to lower cholesterol and blood pressure. Spinach is a great cancer fighter and has immune-boosting antioxidants important for eye health. Beans help lower risk of heart disease and breast cancer.

At some point, people want to give themselves the full treatment: diet, exercise, and general health overhaul. In the meantime, they can take the baby step of adding in one or more healthy food a week. This step is quick, easy, and painless. It couldn't be simpler to implement. Also, it will make their switch to healthy eating much easier to accomplish when they finally get there.

Section 2: Dietary Guidelines for Americans

The Dietary Guidelines for Americans is put together by the US Department of Health and Human Services and the US Department of Agriculture. The guidelines offer advice to people about food choices that advance good health and lower the risk of certain diseases (e.g., hypertension, anemia, and osteoporosis). In addition, this form offers a detailed outline on the kinds of foods that people should have in their diets. The outline is given so that additional supplements or vitamins may not be necessary. The form also has information on the types of exercise that are necessary for someone to stay healthy. Also, there is information on to handle and prepare certain foods to lower the risk of foodborne illness.

The Food Pyramid gave recommendations for the number of daily servings from each group. The USDA's Food Pyramid was heavily criticized for being unclear and confusing. In 2011, MyPlate replaced the Food Pyramid. MyPlate is much easier to understand because it has a picture of a dinner plate that is divided into four sections. So, this shows how our daily diet should be spread out among the different food groups. Vegetables and grains each take up 30% of the plate. Fruits and proteins each make up 20% of the plate. In the corner of the image is a cup that is marked as Dairy.

Most experts consider MyPlate to be a great improvement over the Food Pyramid. However, some it has still come under criticism from some quarters. Many believe too much emphasis is placed on protein, and some say the dairy recommendation should be eliminated altogether. The Harvard School of Public Health created its own Healthy Eating Plate to address what it sees as shortcomings in MyPlate. Harvard's guide adds healthy plant-based oils to the mix, stresses whole grains instead of merely grains, recommends drinking water or unsweetened coffee or tea instead of milk, and adds a reminder that physical activity is important.

Section 3: Preparing Better Meals in the Food Industry

People in the food industry that want to prepare a healthy meal for their customers should first decide on the nutritional goals of their menu. Once these goals have been set up, you should continue to plan by researching foods. These foods need to meet your goals without going beyond the available time and resource limits. Then, you can put together a meal plan that list several details. These details should have what foods will be included, the average time it takes to prepare and cook each of these meals, and the cost of preparing these meals. The next step is to decide on the best way of preparing the food for these meals. Think about which foods should be prepared first and the best ways to handle or prepare your food to lower the risk of illness. Also, think about methods that can be used to lower the cooking time. Finally, you can prepare the meal according to your plans.

When you need to decide on what foods to prepare, you need to think about several things. You should consider the food's nutritional value, the time it takes to prepare each food, the number of people to be served, and the cost of preparing each food. Each food has its own cooking time and has different nutrients. So, it is important to prepare foods that meet people's nutritional goals without using too much time for cooking the meal. Since you will likely have a budget for the meal, you need to review the number of people to be served and the cost of preparing each food. If the cost is too high, some meals may not be good choices to serve to large groups. For example, you are interested in serving a good source of protein for a meal. So, steak may be a good option for a small group of people. However, that would probably be too expensive for a larger group.

31. What is the main idea of Section 1?

a. Preparing a menu requires thorough research.
b. Some foods are healthier than others.
c. Positive diet changes can be simple.
d. Some people can make dietary changes and some cannot.

32. What is the purpose of including Section 2 in this passage?

a. To explain how the Food Pyramid was poorly designed
b. To cover the government's influence on the dietary recommendations for Americans
c. To show that there is no perfect system for coming up with dietary recommendations
d. To share information on generally accepted nutrition guidelines

33. What is the purpose of including Harvard's Healthy Eating Plate in Section 2?

a. To support the assertion MyPlate has received criticism
b. To suggest Healthy Eating Plate may replace current USDA dietary guidelines
c. It shows another option as a dietary guideline
d. To highlight the influence of an Ivy League school

34. According to the text, when preparing food for customers, all of the following are important EXCEPT which?

a. Foodborne illness
b. Nutritional value
c. Layering the flavors in a dish
d. Cooking time

35. What is the tone of the three sections?

a. Condemning
b. Informative
c. Serious
d. Pretentious

Refer to the following for questions 36–40:

"The Gift of the Magi"

by O. Henry

[Jim and Della are a young husband and wife. They are very poor, and it is Christmas Eve. Della has been able to save $1.87 for a Christmas present. To buy a better gift for her husband, she decides to sell her beautiful hair to buy a fob for Jim. The fob will be for Jim's watch which is his most prized possession.]

When Della reached home her intoxication gave way a little to prudence and reason. She got out her curling irons and lighted the gas and went to work repairing the ravages made by generosity added to love. Which is always a tremendous task, dear friends--a mammoth task.

Within forty minutes her head was covered with tiny, close-lying curls that made her look wonderfully like a truant schoolboy. She looked at her reflection in the mirror long, carefully, and critically.

"If Jim doesn't kill me," she said to herself, "before he takes a second look at me, he'll say I look like a Coney Island chorus girl. But what could I do—oh! What could I do with a dollar and eighty-seven cents?"

At seven o'clock the coffee was made and the frying pan was on the back of the stove hot and ready to cook the chops.

Jim was never late. Della doubled the fob chain in her hand and sat on the corner of the table near the door that he always entered. Then she heard his step on the stairway down on the first flight, and she turned white for just a moment. She had a habit of saying little silent prayers about the simplest everyday things and now she whispered: "Please God, make him think I am still pretty."

* * *

Jim stopped inside the door, as immovable as a setter at the scent of quail. His eyes were fixed upon Della, and there was an expression in them that she could not read, and it terrified her. It was not anger, nor surprise, nor disapproval, nor horror, nor any of the sentiments that she had been prepared for. He simply stared at her fixedly with that peculiar expression on his face.

Della wriggled off the table and went for him.

"Jim, darling," she cried, "don't look at me that way. I had my hair cut off and sold it because I couldn't have lived through Christmas without giving you a present. It'll grow out again—you won't mind, will you? I just had to do it. My hair grows awfully fast. Say 'Merry Christmas!' Jim, and let's be happy. You don't know what a nice—what a beautiful, nice gift I've got for you."

"You've cut off your hair?" asked Jim, laboriously, as if he had not arrived at that patent fact yet even after the hardest mental labor.

"Cut it off and sold it," said Della. "Don't you like me just as well, anyhow? I'm me without my hair, ain't I?"

Jim looked about the room curiously.

"You say your hair is gone?" he said, with an air almost of idiocy.

"You needn't look for it," said Della. "It's sold, I tell you—sold and gone, too. It's Christmas Eve, boy. Be good to me, for it went for you. Maybe the hairs of my head were numbered," she went on with a sudden serious sweetness, "but nobody could ever count my love for you. Shall I put the chops on, Jim?"

Out of his trance Jim seemed quickly to wake. He enfolded his Della.

* * *

Jim drew a package from his overcoat pocket and threw it upon the table.

"Don't make any mistake, Dell," he said, "about me. I don't think there's anything in the way of a haircut or a shave or a shampoo that could make me like my girl any less. But if you'll unwrap that package you may see why you had me going a while at first." White fingers and nimble tore at the string and paper. And then an ecstatic scream of joy; and then, alas! a quick, feminine change to hysterical tears and wails, necessitating the immediate employment of all the comforting powers of the lord of the flat.

For there lay the Combs—the set of combs, side and back, that Della had worshipped for long in a Broadway window. Beautiful combs, pure tortoise shell, with jeweled rims—just the shade to wear in the beautiful vanished hair. They were expensive combs, she knew, and her heart had simply craved and yearned over them without the least hope of possession. And now, they were hers, but the tresses that should have adorned the coveted adornments were gone. But she hugged them to her bosom, and at length she was able to look up with dim eyes and a smile and say: "My hair grows so fast, Jim!"

And then Della leaped up like a little singed cat and cried, "Oh, oh!"

Jim had not yet seen his beautiful present. She held it out to him eagerly upon her open palm. The dull precious metal seemed to flash with a reflection of her bright and ardent spirit.

"Isn't it a dandy, Jim? I hunted all over town to find it. You'll have to look at the time a hundred times a day now. Give me your watch. I want to see how it looks on it."

Instead of obeying, Jim tumbled down on the couch and put his hands under the back of his head and smiled.

"Della," said he, "let's put our Christmas presents away and keep 'em a while. They're too nice to use just at present. I sold the watch to get the money to buy your combs. And now suppose you put the chops on."

36. What is the meaning of the word *ardent*?

a. procrastinate
b. passionate
c. lukewarm
d. uncaring

37. What is the chronological order of these events?

(1) Jim gives Della's present to her | (2) Della prepares dinner | (3) Jim assures Della that he is not upset | (4) Della prepares her hair | (5) Della prays for Jim's reaction | (6) Jim receives his present from Della

a. 4, 3, 2, 1, 5, 6
b. 6, 1, 4, 3, 2, 5
c. 4, 2, 1, 5, 3, 6
d. 4, 2, 5, 3, 1, 6

38. In the passage, O. Henry uses several similes. Which of the following is not an example of a simile?

a. "her head was covered with tiny, close-lying curls that made her look wonderfully like a truant schoolboy."
b. "Jim stopped inside the door, as immovable as a setter at the scent of quail."
c. "'I hunted all over town to find it.'"
d. "And then Della leaped up like a little singed cat and cried, 'Oh, oh!'."

39. Which of the following best shows how O. Henry builds tension in the story?

a. "It was even worthy of The Watch. As soon as she saw it she knew that it must be Jim's."
b. "The door opened and Jim stepped in and closed it. He looked very thin and very serious."
c. "Jim looked about the room curiously. 'You say your hair is gone?' he said, with an air almost of idiocy."
d. "Jim was never late. Della doubled the fob chain in her hand and sat on the corner of the table near the door that he always entered."

40. What is the theme of this passage?

a. True love leads to the sacrifice of one's most precious possessions.
b. Christmas is the representation of the love and sacrifice needed by all.
c. The love between two people eventually leads to frustration.
d. People should not try to surprise each other gifts.

Language

1. Which of the following sentences is written correctly?

a. I knew the price of housing was going to increase; but I had no idea it would go up so much!
b. I knew the price of housing was going to increase: I had no idea it would go up so much!
c. I knew the price of housing was going to increase, but I had no idea it would go up so much!
d. I knew the price of housing was going to increase but I had no idea it would go up so much!

2. Which of the following sentences is written correctly?

a. As a matter of fact everything she said was; true.
b. As a matter of fact everything she said was—true.
c. As a matter of fact, everything she said was true.
d. As a matter of fact everything she said was true.

3. Which choice completes the text with the most logical and precise word or phrase?

Literature, as a cornerstone of the humanities, often serves as a reflection of society's values, beliefs, and cultural norms. Classic works of literature like George Orwell's *1984* or Harper Lee's *To Kill a Mockingbird* delve into complex social and moral issues. These novels not only entertain but also challenge readers to _________ ethical dilemmas, justice, and human nature. The humanities, through the study of literature and other artistic forms, provide us with a deeper understanding of the human experience and the complexities of the world around us.

a. obfuscate
b. contemplate
c. elude
d. resolve

4. Which choice completes the text with the most logical transition?

The study of genetics has revolutionized our understanding of heredity and inheritance. Prior to the discovery of DNA's structure, scientists had limited knowledge of how traits were passed from one generation to the next. ________ the elucidation of the DNA's double helix structure by James Watson and Francis Crick in 1953, genetics research advanced significantly, as this breakthrough enabled scientists to delve into the molecular underpinnings of genetics and explore the mechanisms behind trait inheritance.

a. In contrast to
b. Before
c. As a result of
d. Despite

5. Which of the following sentences is written correctly?

a. Me and her are going to the theater.
b. She and her mother went to church.
c. The sheriff were waiting for them.
d. Not, another word out of you.

6. Which choice completes the text with the most logical transition?

Science fiction authors have consistently pushed the boundaries of human imagination. ________, they craft intricate worlds filled with advanced technology, parallel universes, and extraterrestrial life. These writers transport readers to distant galaxies and offer thought-provoking insights into the potential futures that await us. Whether it's the dystopian visions of authors like George Orwell or the space-faring adventures dreamed up by Arthur C. Clarke, science fiction authors have an unparalleled ability to inspire us with their boundless creativity.

a. Nonetheless
b. Additionally
c. Moreover
d. As a result

7. Which TWO of the following sentences are written correctly?

a. The fluffy, Siamese cat slept in the shade.
b. Her native language, French, was easier for her to speak than English.
c. In a challenging environment, she found the best in herself.
d. We went shopping for a new camera, most were digital models.

8. Which of the following sentences is written correctly?

a. Here today gone tomorrow.
b. I can live anyway I want to.
c. I except the consequences.
d. This car is too big.

9. Select the TWO best answers that combine the following two sentences into one.

I spent $25,000 on a new car.
I don't have enough money left for maintenance.

a. After spending $25,000 on a new car, I don't have enough money left for maintenance.
b. I spent $25,000 on a new car because I don't have enough money left for maintenance.
c. I spent $25,000 on a new car, and I don't have enough money left for maintenance now.
d. When I spent $25,000 on a new car I don't have enough money left for maintenance.

10. Select the answer that best combines the following two sentences into one.

She was the first female president of the company.
Her success was met with derision from many people in the community.

a. When her success was met with derision from many people in the community, she became the first female president of the company.
b. She was the first female president of the company, but her success was met with derision from many people in the community.
c. She was the first female president of the company, whenever her success was met with derision from many people in the community.
d. She was the first female president of the company whose success was met with derision from many people in the community.

11. Choose the best sentence to fill in the blank in the following paragraph.

_________________________ This letter tells the employer why you are qualified for the job you are applying for. Effective application letters explain the reasons for your interest in their organization and identify your most relevant skills or experiences.

a. A letter of application should be sent with your resume to provide additional information.
b. It is not enough merely to send a resume in with your job application.
c. The resume and letter of application demonstrate your qualifications to prospective employers.
d. When applying for a job, always request a personal interview.

12. Choose the TWO best sentences to fill in the blank in the following paragraph.

_________________________ Books may be thrown from shelving. Roofs, rooms, and buildings may collapse, burying collections under furniture, beams, dirt, and debris or leaving collections exposed and vulnerable to wind, rain, and snow. Structural collapse may cause broken gas and power lines, leading to fire damage to collections as well as water damage from fire hoses and sprinklers.

a. Even if a library is well built, an earthquake may destroy the delicate books within.
b. The Loma Prieta earthquake did a lot of damage to libraries and their collections.
c. Earthquakes can damage library collections in many ways.
d. Never go into a library during an earthquake.

13. Choose the best sentence to fill in the blank in the following paragraph.

Sunscreens are lotions that help prevent the sun's ultraviolet rays from reaching the skin. _________________________ UVB is the main cause of sunburn, whereas the more penetrating UVA rays are the cause of wrinkling and sagging of the skin. They also add to the carcinogenic effects of UVB rays. Sunscreens vary in their ability to protect against UVA and UVB.

a. You can get a sunburn on cloudy days as well as on sunny ones.
b. The two types of ultraviolet radiation, UVA and UVB, damage skin and increase the risk of skin cancer.
c. The sun is particularly damaging at high altitudes.
d. A day without coffee is like a day without sunshine.

14. Choose the best sentence to follow and develop this topic sentence.

Tooth enamel is the hardest part of the human body.

a. Most people have 32 teeth.
b. It is made almost entirely of minerals with a small amount of organic material.
c. Dentures, bridges, and fillings are common dental appliances.
d. You should visit your dentist regularly to take care of your teeth.

15. Select the sentence that does not belong in the following paragraph.

In 1957 Fortune magazine ran an article about Jean Paul Getty. (1) <u>It suggested that Getty was the richest man in the world.</u> (2) <u>A museum is built on his estate today.</u> (3) <u>An interviewer asked Getty how much he thought he could really get in cash if he were to sell his oil, realty, art, and other holdings.</u> (4) <u>A note of gone-are-the-better-days crept into his response.</u> "I would hope to realize several billions," he said. "But, remember, a billion dollars isn't worth what it used to be."

a. 1
b. 2
c. 3
d. 4

16. **Of the two, <u>the oldest brother</u> had a much more difficult time in school.**

a. the oldest brother
b. the older brother
c. the earliest brother
d. the best brother

17. **We will begin with painting <u>first, and then secondly</u> we will start the decoupage process.**

a. first, and then secondly
b. firstly, and then secondly
c. first, and then second
d. first, then second

18. **Consider the following sentence:**

While speed is a measure of how fast an object is moving, velocity measures how fast an object is moving <u>and also indicates in what direction</u> it is traveling.

Select the best version of the underlined portion.

a. NO CHANGE
b. and only indicates in which direction
c. and also indicate in which directions
d. and only indicated in what direction

19. **Consider the following sentence:**

<u>A key factor taken into account during city planning is</u> where major services and amenities will be located.

Select the best version of the underlined portion.

a. NO CHANGE
b. Key factors taken into account during city planning is
c. A key factor taking into account during city planning is
d. Key factors, taken into accounting during city planning are

20. **Of the options below, which uses correct punctuation?**

a. Grady asked Abe, 'Did you know that an earthquake and a tsunami hit Messina, Italy, in 1908?'
b. Grady asked Abe, "Did you know that an earthquake and a tsunami hit Messina, Italy, in 1908"?
c. Grady asked Abe, "Did you know that an earthquake and a tsunami hit Messina, Italy, in 1908?"
d. Grady asked Abe, " 'Did you know that an earthquake and a tsunami hit Messina, Italy, in 1908'?"

21. **Which choice completes the text with the most logical and precise word or phrase?**

Tattoos have a long and colorful history, often with profound cultural meanings. Across the ages, people have used tattoos to show who they are, where they come from, and what they believe in. Whether it's the intricate Māori facial tattoos or the elaborate Japanese Irezumi, these designs tell captivating stories of cultures and traditions. Today, tattoos are like personal canvases where we paint our own tales, share our values, and honor our experiences. Their history reminds us of their timeless _____, as they bring together different cultures and showcase diversity and creativity.

a. monotony
b. stagnation
c. semblance
d. magnetism

22. Which TWO answer choices best combine the following four sentences into two sentences?

I'm usually good about keeping track of my keys. I lost them. I spent hours looking for them. I found them in the freezer.

a. I lost my keys even though I'm usually good about keeping track of them. I found them in the freezer after spending hours looking for them.
b. I spent hours looking for my keys and found them in the freezer. I had lost them, even though I'm usually good about keeping track of them.
c. I'm usually good about keeping track of my keys, but I lost them. After spending hours looking for them, I found them in the freezer.
d. Though I'm usually good about keeping track of my keys, I lost them. I had to spend hours looking for them and finally found them in the freezer.

23. Which of the answer choices is the closest in meaning to the underlined word in the following sentence?

The warning against smoking may have been tacit, but Beryl instinctively knew that her mother wanted her to avoid picking up the habit.

a. Complicated
b. Empty
c. Wordy
d. Unstated

24. What transition should be added to the beginning of sentence 2 below?

(1) I zoned out in class, turned work in late, talked during lectures, and handed in assignments after the due date. (2) Mr. Shanbourne just nodded.

a. Surprisingly
b. Actually
c. Furthermore
d. Instead

25. Of the options, which TWO are more effective ways to rewrite the following sentence?

She is saying that some of what the students are wearing to school is being distracting and inappropriate.

a. Some of the outfits students wear to school, she says, are distracting and inappropriate.
b. The outfits are distracting and not appropriate, she says, that students wear to school.
c. She says some of the outfits that students wear to school are distracting and inappropriate.
d. She says that it is distracting and inappropriate that students wear outfits to school.

26. Which choice completes the text with the most logical transition?

Lighthouses, with their towering structures and guiding beacons, hold profound symbolism in the maritime world. Serving as literal beacons, these iconic structures guide ships safely through treacherous waters. The significance of lighthouses extends beyond the maritime realm. ___________, lighthouses are often used in poetry as a metaphor for safety and comfort. They convey a timeless message of resilience and human ingenuity, offering a broader representation of strength and reliability and guiding the way to safety in challenging circumstances.

a. Therefore
b. Nonetheless
c. In contrast
d. For example

27. Identify the sentence that contains an error in usage, punctuation, or grammar. If no errors are found, choose the last option.

a. The metric system uses a "base-ten" system of measurement, which means its prefixes indicate multiples of ten.
b. If you ever need to measure something but do not have access to a ruler, these facts can help: The average credit card is $3\frac{3}{8}$ inches by $2\frac{1}{8}$ inches, the diameter of a quarter is around one inch, and the diameter of a penny is about $\frac{3}{4}$ inch.
c. Carbon monoxide Poisoning can cause disorientation and delirium, and it can induce a coma.
d. No mistake.

28. What is the most likely meaning of the underlined phrase in the sentence below?

The Western perspective expects moral actions to be quid pro quo; to put it another way, a Westerner assumes that if he or she does something considered "good," then he or she should, and will, be rewarded.

a. Something for nothing
b. Good merits money
c. To each his own
d. This for that

29. Which choice completes the text with the most logical and precise word or phrase?

Esports, or professional video gaming, has skyrocketed in popularity, becoming a global industry. Professional gamers showcase their skills in popular games like League of Legends and Dota 2, competing in major tournaments with large audiences and substantial prizes. Esports involves people in various roles, from players to coaches and broadcasters, and has ______ geographical boundaries, offering opportunities for recognition and financial success. This fast-growing industry is reshaping the entertainment landscape.

a. transcended
b. eluded
c. reprieved
d. precluded

30. Which of the answer choices is the closest in meaning to the underlined word in the following sentence?

The experience of being a plane crash survivor left an indelible impression on Johanna, and she suffered from nightmares for years afterwards.

a. Candid
b. Permanent
c. Inexpressible
d. Indirect

31. Which choice completes the text with the most logical transition?

Geckos, known for their remarkable climbing abilities, possess tiny, adhesive hairs on their toes called spatulae. These spatulae create attractive forces that allow geckos to cling to various surfaces, even upside down. ______, geckos are known for their remarkable agility, making them adept hunters and climbers in their natural habitats.

a. Similarly
b. However
c. Moreover
d. To illustrate

32. Which of the following sentences represents the best style and clarity of expression?

a. Without adequate preparation, the test was likely to be a failure for Zara.
b. The test was likely to be a failure for Zara without adequate preparation.
c. Without adequate preparation, Zara expected to fail the test.
d. Zara expected to fail the test without adequate preparation.

33. Which of the answer choices is the closest in meaning to the underlined word in the following sentence?

Despite the election of our first African American president being a huge achievement, education about African American history is still unmet to a substantial degree.

a. Base
b. Considerable
c. Minor
d. Trivial

Mathematics

1. A circle is inscribed within a square, as shown. What is the difference between the area of the square and that of the circle, where r is the radius of the circle?

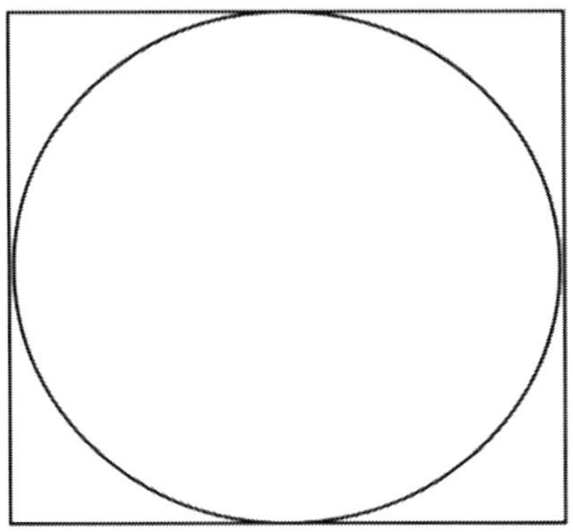

a. 2π
b. $\frac{4}{3}\pi r^3$
c. $r^2(4-\pi)$
d. $2\pi r$

2. For the number set $\{7, 12, 5, 16, 23, 44, 18, 9, Z\}$, which TWO of the following values could be equal to Z if Z is the median of the set?

a. 10
b. 13
c. 14
d. 17

3. Which of the following is true about the relationship between the two triangles shown below? Select the three that apply.

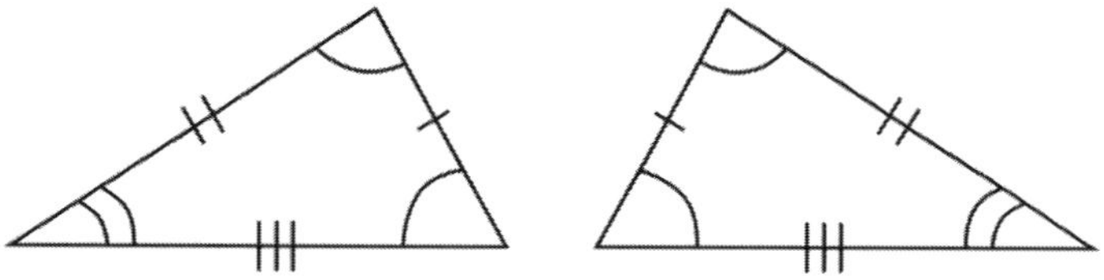

a. The triangles are similar.
b. The triangles are congruent.
c. The triangles are equilateral.
d. The triangles are scalene.

4. Herbert plans to use the earnings from his lemonade stand, according to the table below, for the first month of operations. If he buys $70 worth of lemons, how much profit does he take home?

Cash Flow Item	Percentage of Total Earning Used on Item
Lemons	35%
Sugar	20%
Cups	25%
Stand improvements	5%
Profits	15%

a. $15
b. $20
c. $30
d. $35

5. If $a \neq 0$, then $12a^2b \div 3a = ?$

a. $4b$
b. $4ab$
c. $9b^2$
d. $9ab$

6. Consider the number set $\{-1, 19, -5, 0, 15.3, 15.05, -3\}$. Which of the following choices shows the number set in order from least to greatest?

a. −1, −3, −5, 0, 15.05, 15.3, 19
b. −5, −3, −1, 0, 15.3, 15.05, 19
c. −5, −3, −1, 0, 15.05, 15.3, 19
d. 0, −5, −3, −1, 15.05, 15.3, 19

7. Hector's car holds 12 gallons of gasoline. He filled his tank for $22.44. Assuming Hector's tank was completely empty when he filled up, how much money did Hector pay per gallon of gasoline?

a. $1.87
b. $2.05
c. $18.70
d. $269.28

8. If $x = 2y - 3$ and $2x + \frac{1}{2}y = 3$, then what is the value of y?

a. $-\frac{2}{3}$
b. 1
c. 2
d. $\frac{18}{7}$

9. A business made 15% greater profit this year than last and expects to increase profit margins by 20% next year. If their profit was $30,000 last year, what is their projected profit for next year?

a. $34,500
b. $36,000
c. $39,675
d. $41,400

10. Which TWO of the following functions have the same y-intercept as the function graphed below?

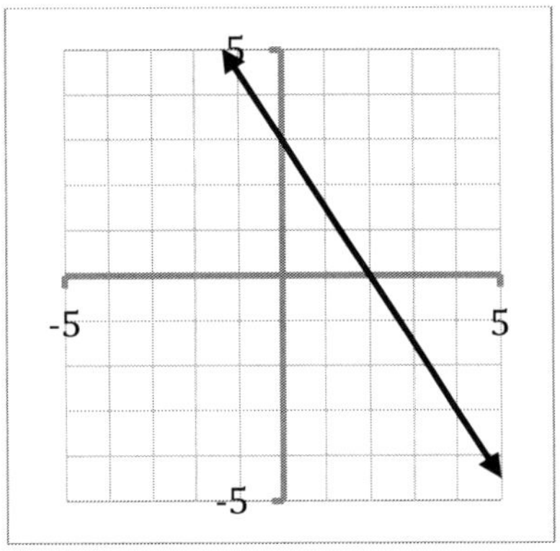

a. $g(x) = 2x - 4$
b. $g(x) = x^2 - 5x + 4$
c. $g(x) = x^3 + 3x^2 + x + 3$
d. $g(x) = \frac{3x+6}{2}$

11. The expression $-2i \times 7i$ is equal to

a. -14
b. 14
c. $14\sqrt{-1}$
d. $-14\sqrt{-1}$

12. If Nick can run 3 miles in 24 minutes, how many miles can he run in 3 hours?

a. 11.25 miles
b. 17.6 miles
c. 21.8 miles
d. 22.5 miles

13. Put the following numbers in order from the least to greatest: $2^3, 4^2, 6^0, 9, 10^1$.

a. $2^3, 4^2, 6^0, 9, 10^1$
b. $6^0, 9, 10^1, 2^3, 4^2$
c. $10^1, 2^3, 6^0, 9, 4^2$
d. $6^0, 2^3, 9, 10^1, 4^2$

14. It rained every day last week except Friday. If it rained twice as much on Monday as it did on Thursday, which of the following graphs could model the week's rainfall in inches?

a. 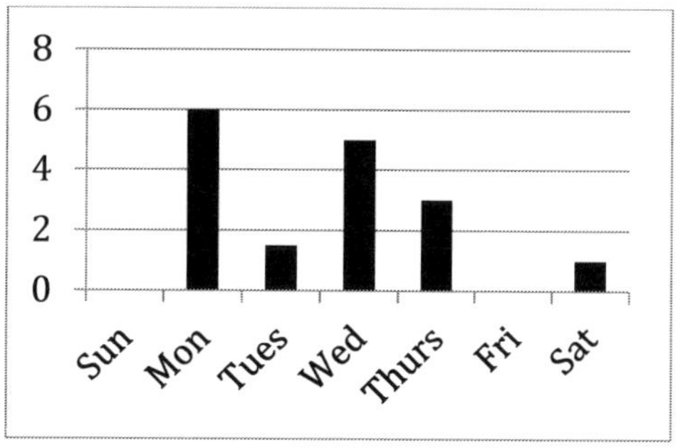

b. 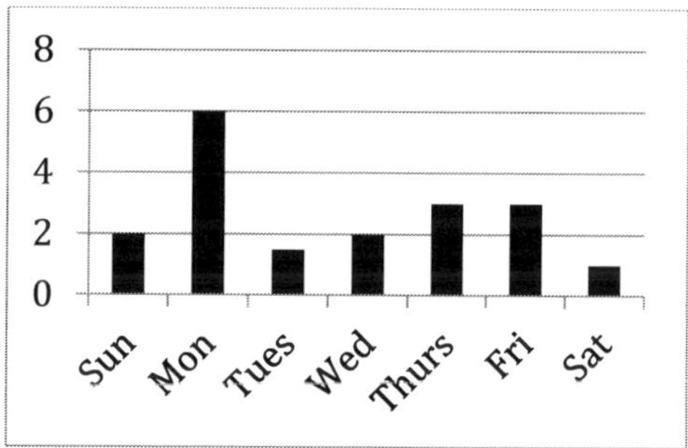

c. 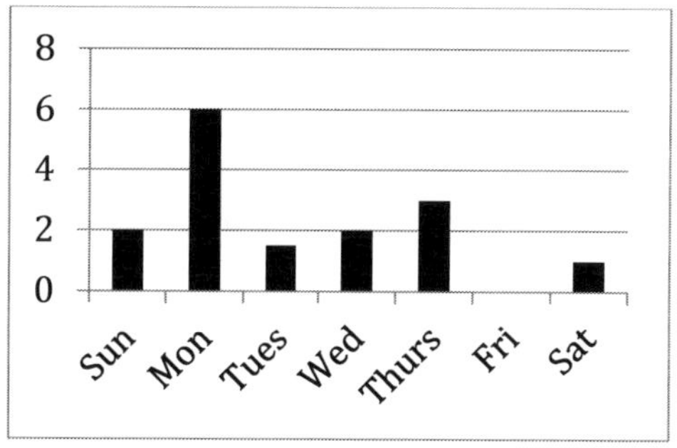

d. 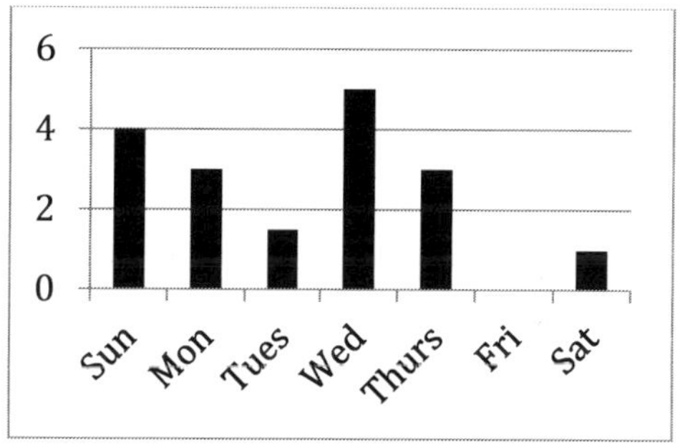

15. John buys 100 shares of stock at $100 per share. The price goes up by 10%, and he sells 50 shares. Then, prices drop by 10%, and he sells his remaining 50 shares. How much did he get for the last 50 shares?

a. $4,900
b. $4,950
c. $5,000
d. $5,500

16. Solve $(3x + 1)(7x + 10)$

a. $12x^2 + 17x + 10$
b. $21x^2 + 37x + 10$
c. $21x^2 + 23x + 10$
d. $21x^2 + 37x + 9$

17. The linear function $g(x)$ is graphed below.

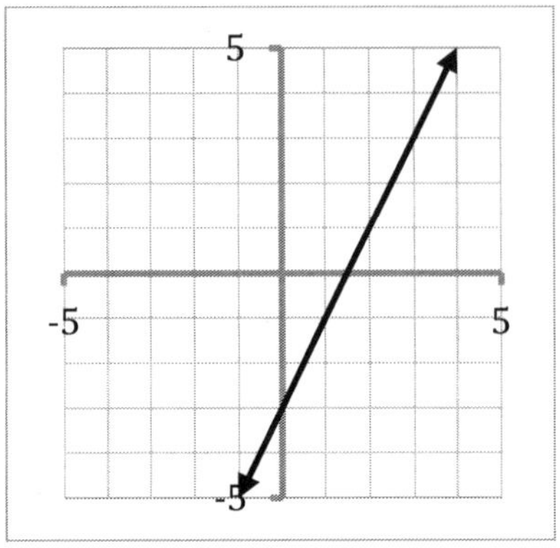

Which of the following is an explicit formula for $g(x)$.

a. $g(x) = -2x - 3$
b. $g(x) = -5x + 2$
c. $g(x) = 2x - 3$
d. $g(x) = 5x + 2$

18. Mr. Foster wants to put new carpet on the floor of his rectangular playroom. The playroom is 27 feet long and 18 feet wide. He has found an inexpensive carpet that is priced $14 per square yard. What would be a reasonable price for enough carpet to cover the floor of his playroom?

a. $486
b. $756
c. $1,260
d. $2,268

19. The scientific notation for the diameter of a red blood cell is approximately 7.4×10^{-4} centimeters. What is that amount in standard form?

a. 0.00074 cm
b. 0.0074 cm
c. 740 cm
d. 74,000 cm

20. Which of the following expressions is equivalent to $(a + b)(a - b)$?

a. $a^2 - b^2$
b. $(a + b)^2$
c. $(a - b)^2$
d. $ab(a - b)$

21. A blouse normally sells for $138, but is on sale for 25% off. What is the cost of the blouse?

a. $34.50
b. $67
c. $103.50
d. $113

22. In a game of chance, 3 dice are thrown at the same time. What is the probability that all three will land on a 6?

a. $\frac{1}{6}$
b. $\frac{1}{18}$
c. $\frac{1}{30}$
d. $\frac{1}{216}$

23. Two even integers and one odd integer are multiplied together. Which of the following could be their product?

a. 3.75
b. 9
c. 16.2
d. 24

24. Which of the following numbers would fit in the numerical sequence 24, ___, 6? Select the TWO that apply.

a. 12
b. 14
c. 15
d. 8

25. XYZ Industries made 20% greater profit this year than last, and expects to increase profit margins by another 20% next year. If their profit was $55,000 last year, what is their projected profit for next year?

a. $66,000
b. $73,920
c. $77,000
d. $79,200

26. Which TWO of the following statements are true?

a. Parallel lines have opposite slopes
b. Parallel lines have the same slopes
c. Perpendicular lines have reciprocal slopes
d. Perpendicular lines have opposite reciprocal slopes

27. A company has been asked to design a building for an athletic event. The building is in the shape of a square pyramid. The pyramid has a height of 481 feet, and the length of each side of the base is 756 feet. What is the approximate volume of the pyramid?

a. 1.21×10^5 ft^3
b. 4.85×10^5 ft^3
c. 9.16×10^7 ft^3
d. 2.75×10^8 ft^3

28. One method for calculating the area of a circle is to dissect it into a number of wedges. The circle below has a radius *r* and has been evenly dissected into 16 wedges.

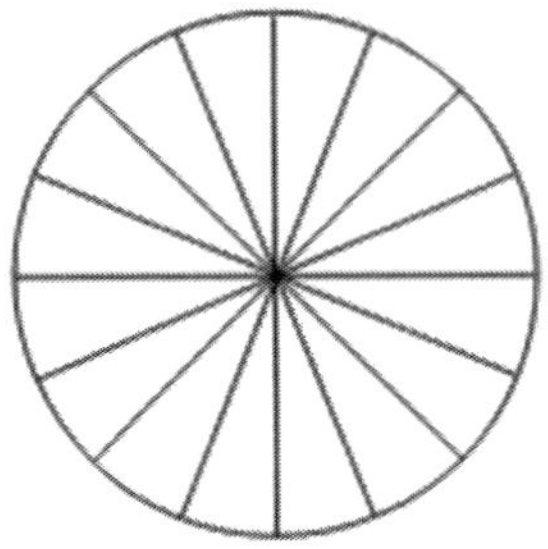

If the wedges are rearranged alternately to create a shape resembling a rectangle, as shown below, what is the approximate length of the rectangle?

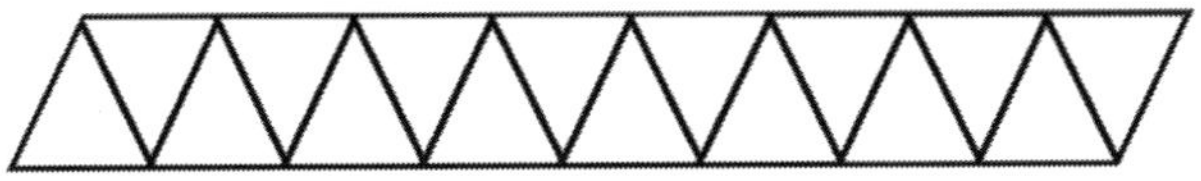

a. π
b. πr
c. r
d. πr^2

29. A bag contains 14 blue, 6 red, 12 green, and 8 purple buttons. 25 buttons are removed from the bag randomly. How many of the removed buttons were red if the chance of drawing a red button from the bag is now $\frac{1}{3}$?

a. 0 buttons
b. 1 button
c. 3 buttons
d. 5 buttons

30. A taxi ride costs \$4.25 for the first mile and \$0.70 for each mile after the first. Which of the following functions $c(d)$ gives the total cost (in dollars) of traveling d miles ($d \geq 1$)?

a. $c(d) = 3.55 + 0.70(d + 1)$
b. $c(d) = 3.55 + 0.70(d - 1)$
c. $c(d) = 4.25 + 0.70d$
d. $c(d) = 4.25 + 0.70(d - 1)$

31. A bag contains 8 red marbles, 3 blue marbles, and 4 green marbles. What is the probability Carlos draws a red marble, does not replace it, and then draws another red marble?

a. $\frac{2}{15}$
b. $\frac{4}{15}$
c. $\frac{32}{105}$
d. $\frac{64}{225}$

Refer to the following for question 32:

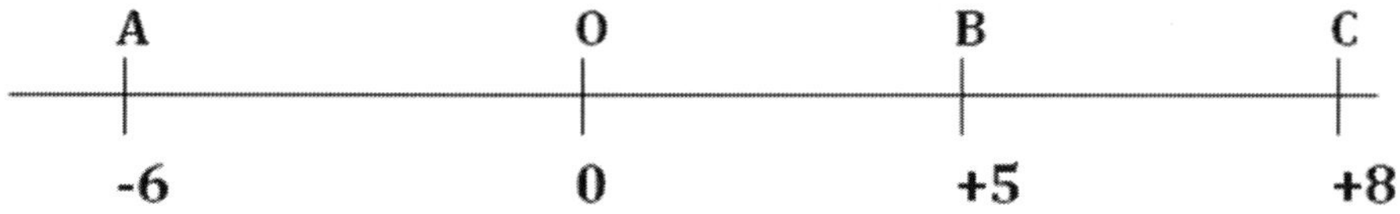

32. In the figure, *A*, *B*, and *C* are points on the number line, and *O* is the origin. What is the ratio of the distance *BC* to distance *AB*?

a. 3 : 5
b. 8 : 5
c. 8 : 11
d. 3 : 11

33. How many solutions does the equation $6x + 1 = 4x + 9$ have?

a. None
b. One
c. Two
d. Infinitely many solutions

34. The table below shows the breakdown of orders at a frozen yogurt shop. There were two flavors of yogurt (strawberry and lemon) and two sizes (small and large). If a person among those who ordered frozen yogurt is chosen at random, what is the probability that this person ordered a small serving of lemon yogurt?

	Strawberry	Lemon	Total
Small	12	9	21
Large	20	16	36
Total	32	25	57

a. $\frac{9}{25}$
b. $\frac{3}{7}$
c. $\frac{7}{19}$
d. $\frac{3}{19}$

35. Gitta brings $2,082 on a business trip. The trip will last 7 days. Which of the following is the best estimate for the amount of money she has to spend per day?

a. $200
b. $320
c. $240
d. $300

36. How many gallon jugs of water should Julia buy to completely fill a container in the shape of a rectangular prism if the length is 8 feet, the width is 4 feet, and the height is 3 feet (1 gallon = 231 cubic inches)?

a. 5
b. 718
c. 719
d. 165,888

37. A lotion bottle is in the shape of a square pyramid. If the base has a side length of 3.5 inches and the height of the container is 6 inches, how many cubic inches of lotion can the bottle hold?

a. 18.6 cubic inches
b. 24.5 cubic inches
c. 28.9 cubic inches
d. 32.5 cubic inches

Refer to the following for question 38:

The table below represents the test scores on a chemistry final, as well as the lab grades for the semester.

Final Exam	78	85	91	77	94	83	87
Lab Grade	84	86	98	90	97	85	90

38. What is the difference of the mean and median of the lab grades?

a. 0
b. 1.5
c. 3
d. 4.5

39. The table below shows the cost of renting a bicycle for 1, 2, or 3 hours. Which answer choice shows the equation that best represents the data? Let C represent the cost of the rental and h stand for the number of hours of rental time.

Hours	1	2	3
Cost	\$3.60	\$7.20	\$10.80

a. $C = 3.60h$
b. $C = h + 3.60$
c. $C = 3.60h + 10.80$
d. $C = \frac{10.80}{h}$

40. Use factoring to identify the zeroes of the function $f(x) = x^2 + 5x - 24$. Select the TWO that apply.

a. −8
b. −6
c. 3
d. 24

Answer Key and Explanations for Test #2

Reading

1. B: The word *beneficence* is used to show how nature helps the plants and animals on Earth. For example, nature provides sunlight and rain to help trees grow. Choice A is incorrect because *duties* and *beneficence* are not synonymous. Choice C is incorrect because nature gives the sunlight and the rain. This makes it the opposite of *stingy*. Later, Keller experiences the dangers of nature. However, choice D is incorrect because paragraph 5 is about the generosity of nature.

2. D: The paragraph shows the narrator's discovery that words have meaning. Choice A is incorrect because the narrator and Miss Sullivan do not use a pencil. Instead, Miss Sullivan uses her fingers to spell words into the narrator's hand. Choice B is incorrect because the narrator does not focus on the distinction between hot and cold water. Choice C is incorrect because the focus of the paragraph is not on learning the locations of places.

3. A: Helen says in the second sentence that she stretches out her hand to who she thinks is her mother. Choice B is incorrect because Helen is not aware that a visitor is coming. Choice C is incorrect because there is no mention that she wants to please her mother. Choice D is incorrect. Helen assumes the person approaching is her mother, but she does not mention loving her mother in the passage.

4. B: Helen is alone and defenseless as the storm approaches. Choice A is incorrect because Helen is not lost. She knows where she is, but she is unable to get out of the tree to go home. The wind and approaching rain make Helen uncomfortable, however, choices C and D are incorrect. We know Helen is upset about being alone because of the relief she expresses in Miss Sullivan's presence later.

5. C: Miss Sullivan opens up Helen's world by showing her that words have meaning and every object has a name. Choice A is incorrect because Helen is only able to learn about nature through the words taught by Miss Sullivan. Choice B is incorrect because the observation about barriers is not what she learned from Miss Sullivan. Choice D is incorrect because the sentence is not about what Helen learned. Instead, it is about the idea of learning.

6. D: Helen describes "[longing]" for Miss Sullivan's return and clings to her upon being rescued. Choice A is incorrect because Miss Sullivan teaches Helen water early in their relationship before they had developed a bond. Choice B is incorrect because that is a personal growth in Helen, not a growth in the relationship of Helen and Miss Sullivan. Choice C is incorrect because it does not show the bond between Helen and Miss Sullivan. Instead, this moment simply shows something Helen and Miss Sullivan are doing together.

7. B: The passage shows Helen's discoveries about language and nature. While Helen develops a close tie with Miss Sullivan, Miss Sullivan is not Helen's family. So, Choice A is incorrect. Choice C is incorrect because the passage never mentions or implies disappointment. Choice D is incorrect because the text does not emphasize Helen's youth.

8. D: This phrase is used to explain how nature, although generous and peaceful, can be violent and dangerous. Choice A is incorrect because Miss Sullivan does not show any cruelty towards Helen. Choice B is incorrect because this paragraph shows Helen feeling nervous but does not show her having a temper tantrum. Choice C is incorrect because Helen was in danger from being alone in the tree as the storm approached. The phrase "treacherous claws" is about the danger of being alone in the tree rather than the danger of climbing the tree.

9. A: The narrator describes her life before the arrival of Miss Sullivan, then she explains her life after and all the changes she experiences. Helen may have become braver with Miss Sullivan, but this is not the focal point of the story. This makes choice B incorrect. Choice C is incorrect because only part of the passage shows the strategies that Miss Sullivan uses to teach Helen. Choice D is incorrect because Helen feels security rather than confusion when she is with Miss Sullivan.

10. C: The passage is about how Miss Sullivan teaches Helen words have meaning. Choice A is incorrect because Helen expresses a clear fondness for Miss Sullivan. Choice B is incorrect because Helen is not scared of nature; rather, she realizes that nature can be generous and dangerous. The passage does not clearly say that Helen learns to read or write. Instead, it shows the beginning of her relationship with words and implies that Helen will continue to learn.

11. D: A non-human thing (e.g., a name) is described with a human quality or action (e.g., birth). Choice A is not correct because there is not a comparison being made. Choice B is not correct because there is no exaggeration in the sentence. Choice C is not correct because there is not a comparison being made with the words *like* or *as*.

12. D: A caricature is a representation that ludicrously exaggerates the defects of a thing or person. The author first mocks the Humboldt River for being so small, suggesting that it might be possible to drink the whole thing dry. He goes on to mock his own greed, with his exaggerated stalking of gold minerals.

13. A: Burlesque is a form of humor that makes use of ludicrous exaggeration. The description is obviously absurd and meant to exaggerate the inconveniences presented by the steep hillsides surrounding the town.

14. B: Mr. Ballou is described as "an experienced gold miner". His role in the passage is to provide a grounding in reality and to puncture the author's illusions about the ease of getting rich by finding gold.

15. B: In the final paragraph, the narrator compares minerals to men. He suggests men of a lower quality are overrated like mica, and men of a higher quality are underrated and harder to identify like gold.

16. C: The question asks which job is less desirable than homesteading according to the writer. Choice C is correct because Stewart speaks of going out to wash as less preferable than homesteading. Choices A, B, and D are incorrect because the letter does not mention cooking in restaurants, opening a bed and breakfast, or teaching.

17. D: Growing potatoes is so simple that her six-year-old can do so with little help. The issue is not child labor. So, choice A is incorrect. Stewart does not mention schooling. So, this makes choice B incorrect. Stewart's point has nothing to do with whether women work as hard as men. So, choice C is not the correct response.

18. B: Stewart mentions the hard work of laundry, but she does not speak of any enjoyment of it as she does about homesteading. Choice A cannot be correct because Stewart does not seem to be lazy. Choice C is possible, but there is no evidence to support that idea. Choice D cannot be correct because no reason for anger is given.

19. D: Stewart says that homesteading is a lonely task. For example, she mentions that "persons afraid of ...loneliness had better let ranching alone." Stewart explains in the letter that her work uses less strength than washing. So, choice A is wrong. Choice B is also incorrect because it is addressed in the first paragraph of the letter. Choice C is incorrect because it is mentioned as an advantage in the first paragraph.

20. A: Stewart directly states that women would have "the added satisfaction of knowing that their job will not be lost to them if they care to keep it." Although going on strike was common at the time, Stewart does not mention it. So, choice B is incorrect. Denver is in the Rocky Mountains, but landslides are not mentioned as a risk. So, choice C cannot be the correct answer. Fire is always a risk, but Stewart does not bring it up in the letter. So, choice D is not the correct answer.

21. C: The letter is positive and full of reasons homesteading is a good choice. Choice A is incorrect because the narrator expresses enthusiasm for homesteading without criticizing others. She even suggests homesteading might not fit everyone. Choice B is incorrect because the narrator mentions loneliness, but does not indicate she is sad in any way. Choice D is incorrect because Stewart never expresses hopelessness.

22. D: The term *hydrologic cycle* is defined in the first paragraph, where it is described as being equivalent to the *water cycle*. It is derived from the Greek root *hydros*, which means "water."

23. D: According to the table, the average residence time of water in soil is only two months. Only its residence time in the atmosphere (9 days) is shorter. Residence time is the average amount of time a water molecule spends in a reservoir before it moves on to another reservoir in the water cycle.

24. B: According to the final paragraph, ocean levels actually fall during an ice age. More water is stored in ice caps and glaciers when the temperatures are very cold, so less water stays in the oceans as liquid.

25. D: The correct answer is D because the author says that the ancient Britons were divided into many tribes and each had a king. The passage does say Choice A is incorrect because the passage says the ancient Britons had weapons, however, it doesn't say the weapons were the reason they fought. Choice B is incorrect because the text says the ancient Britons fought each other. It does not mention them fighting the Phoenicians. Choice C is incorrect because paragraph 6 says that there were no roads or bridges. The author gives this detail in order to describe the land. This detail does not support paragraph 7 which says that the ancient Britons regularly fought.

26. D: The correct answer is D because the word *grew* shows that the ancient Britons changed after the Phoenicians arrived. Choice A is incorrect because the answer choice only shows something that the Phoenicians did with the Britons; however, it does not describe how the Britons changed. Choice B is incorrect because basket-work is something the ancient Britons did before the Phœnicians interacted with them. Choice C is incorrect because it refers to the French and Belgians who moved to England.

27. B: The word *solitary* refers to isolation or being alone. Also, the sentence says that the islands are alone in a great expanse of water. So, this shows that other lands do not surround the islands. Choice A is incorrect because the sentence only talks about the size of the small islands around Scotland. It does not talk about where the islands are in relation to larger lands. Choice C is incorrect because it refers to people on the island, not the island in relation to the rest of the world. Choice D is incorrect because it shows the opposite of isolation; the sentence shows how the people who came to the islands (e.g., the French, Belgians, and Spanish) mixed with the ancient Britons.

28. B: The phrase "But seldom, if ever, ventured far from the shore" means that the boats didn't go far from shore. This implies that the boats may not have had much use in spite of the effort to build them. Choice A is incorrect because the text does not explain specifically how the boats were used. The author does describe weapons in the same paragraph. However, the phrase in the question focuses on the boats that the people made. The paragraph only moves onto weapons in the second sentence. Choice D is incorrect because the author does not connect the boats (discussed in paragraph 7) to the fortresses (discussed at the end of paragraph 6).

29. A: Choice A is the best answer because the first paragraph describes the location of the islands on the map. Choice B is incorrect because there were no roads that ran through England, Scotland, or Ireland during the time period that the passage is describing. Choice C is incorrect because the details about the small islands are only a small part of the first paragraph. Most of the paragraph describes how the islands appear on the map. Choice D is incorrect because the paragraph does not mention the size of the main islands. Also, the paragraph does not mention France or Belgium. Those countries are first mentioned in paragraph 4.

30. C: Choice C is the correct answer because this answer choice describes the lands by mentioning swamps and forests. Choice A is incorrect because it describes the coast, not the interior land of the island. Choice B is incorrect. It is about the interior of the island, but does not describe the land. Choice D is incorrect because it discusses the tribes and the people rather than the features of the lands (e.g., the swamps and forests).

31. C: The first section covers how people want to change and the options that are available to them. As people move towards a healthier lifestyle, they can work at small steps on their way to better health. Choice A is incorrect because the first section does not mention menus. Choice B is incorrect because the paragraph lists benefits of certain foods but does not suggest any are better than others. Choice D is incorrect because the passage mentions that the process is a struggle for many, not an impossible task.

32. D: The overall passage is information for someone who is interested in the food industry. So, choice A is not correct. The reason is that there is not much of a comparison or contrast between the Food Pyramid and MyPlate. Choice B is incorrect because the focus of the passage is not on government involvement. Choice C is incorrect because the text says some groups disagree about certain dietary suggestions but does not make recommendations.

33. A: Choice B is wrong because there is no mention of Harvard's guidelines replacing MyPlate. Choice C is also incorrect. It is another approach to dietary guidelines, but it was included to support a claim, not provide diet options. Choice D is wrong because Harvard is included for their material, not their Ivy League status.

34. C: Layering flavors is important in cooking but is not mentioned in the text. The text clearly discusses foodborne illness, nutritional value, and cooking time as a matter of efficiency.

35. B: Each section of the passage has the tone of educating readers. So, choice A is wrong because the tone is not blaming readers. Choice C is close, but it is not the best answer choice. Choice D is wrong because the tone of the material is not snobbish or cocky.

36. B: The word *ardent* means passionate or devoted. Look at the word in the context of the sentence: "The dull precious metal seemed to flash with a reflection of her bright and ardent spirit," and think about Della's actions. Choice A is not correct because Della has planned and saved to buy her husband a Christmas present. So, she has not procrastinated (i.e., waited too long to start on something). Choices C and D are synonyms. They are wrong because Della shows over and over again that she cares very much for her husband.

37. D: The first event in the story is Della preparing her hair (4). The next event in the story is Della preparing a meal for the night (2). Then, Della prays about the reaction that Jim will have to her hair (5). The next event is Jim assuring Della that he is not upset about her decision to cut her hair (3). Then, Jim gives the combs to Della (1). Finally, Della gives the fob chain to Jim (6).

38. C: The sentence "'I hunted all over town to find it.'" is an exaggeration or hyperbole. The other answer choices have similes.

39. C: In the beginning of the story, Della has her hair cut off. She does this so she can get money for Jim's gift. However, she is worried about how she will appear to her husband and is concerned that he will be very angry or worse. When Jim keeps asking about Della's hair, it almost seems as if he is angry about it.

40. A: The entire story is about how Della and Jim are deeply in love. They sell a prized possession to buy a present for the other. Choice B is wrong because the overall meaning of this passage is not about a holiday. Choice C is wrong because it fails to recognize how Della and Jim overcome difficulty and have a deeper love for each other after giving their gifts. Choice D is wrong because the focus of the passage is not on buying the right gift for a loved one. Instead, the focus is on giving up a thing that you care about to show how much you love someone.

Language

1. C: Both clauses in this sentence are independent, having both a subject and a verb, so it is appropriate to separate them with a comma.

2. C: The comma in option C is used to separate the introductory statement from the main clause in the sentence.

3. B: To *contemplate* means to think deeply or consider something carefully. In the context of the passage, the word *contemplate* fits because it conveys the idea that literature encourages readers to think deeply and critically about complex issues. It aligns with the passage's message that literature serves as a reflection of society's values and beliefs and encourages readers to engage with these topics on a thoughtful level.

4. C: "As a result of" is the most appropriate choice here because it indicates a cause-and-effect relationship. The discovery of the double helix structure of DNA is presented as a cause of the significant advancement in genetics research. This transition logically connects the two sentences by explaining that the groundbreaking discovery led to the subsequent advancement of genetics research.

5. B: Choice A is incorrect because *me* and *her* are object pronouns. The sentence requires subject pronouns (e.g., *I* and *she*). Choice C is incorrect because the subject *sheriff* and verb *were* do not agree. Choice D is incorrect because of the unnecessary comma.

6. C: *Moreover* is used to indicate that something is adding to or reinforcing the point made in the previous sentence. In this passage, the previous sentence talks about science fiction authors pushing the boundaries of human imagination. It emphasizes that the authors not only push the boundaries of human imagination but also craft intricate worlds, transport readers to distant galaxies, and inspire with their creativity.

7. B, C: Choice A is incorrect because *Siamese* is considered part of the noun and should not be listed like an adjective with *fluffy*. Choice B correctly sets off "French" in commas. In choice C, an introductory clause is correctly set off by a comma. Choice D is incorrect because it combines two separate ideas and leaves the second part of the sentence without a subject.

8. D: Choice D is a simple sentence. Choice A lacks a comma, choice C incorrectly uses the word "except" in place of "accept," and choice B incorrectly uses "anyway," when it should say "any way".

9. A, C: The two sentences imply a cause and effect: spending $25,000 on the car has left the writer with insufficient funds for maintenance. Choice B implies the opposite causality. Choice D is incorrect because it does not use consistent tense.

10. B: Choices A and C are incorrect because they reverse the order of events. Choice D incorrectly says the company had multiple female presidents.

11. A: Choice B does not provide adequate context for the following sentences. Choice C provides too much information and makes the later sentences redundant. Choice D is not relevant to the rest of the paragraph.

12. A, C: Choice B is incorrect because it talks about a specific earthquake that happened while the text discusses a hypothetical earthquake. Choice D is not an appropriate answer choice because the text is about damage to books, not humans.

13. B: The sentences following the blank describe the differences between UVA and UVB rays. Choice B introduces this idea.

14. B: Choice B provides more information about tooth enamel and explains why it is hard. Choices A, C, and D are about teeth, but do not continue the discussion of tooth enamel.

15. B: This paragraph is about Fortune's article on Getty and his answer to a question about his wealth. The information about the museum is unrelated to the other information presented in the paragraph and does not belong here.

16. B: When comparing two people or things, the correct comparative word would be *older* rather than *oldest*. If there were more than two, you would use the comparative word *oldest*. The other choices change the intended original meaning of the sentence.

17. C: When putting things or people in order, the words must agree in the series. You can use *first, second, third,* and so forth, or you may use *firstly, secondly, thirdly*, and so forth. In this sentence, answer choice C is the best choice because the two words *first* and *second* agree in the series, and in this case it sounds better. *Firstly* and *secondly* sound awkward. Also, it is correct to use *and then* in the sentence rather than answer choice D which uses only the word *then*.

18. A: The sentence implies that *velocity* is used to indicate more than one value, which eliminates B and D. The phrase includes a verb whose subject is "velocity," which is singular, but "indicate" (not "indicates") in choice C would agree with a plural noun. The original version of the sentence (choice A) agrees with the singular noun, and the *and* reflects that velocity is used to indicate more than one value.

19. A: Answer choice B is incorrect because the plural "key factors" and the singular "is" do not agree. The "taking" in choice C makes it incorrect. Choice D has a misplaced comma. The original sentence (choice A) makes sense as the singular "A key factor" and "is" agree with each other.

20. C: Choices A, B, and D are incorrect. Double quotes are the default quotation marks. Single quotes belong inside double quotes when one quote is quoting another quote. In this case, the quote is asking a question, so the question mark belongs inside the quotation marks.

21. D: *Magnetism* is the word that best aligns with this context, as it suggests that tattoos have an attractive, captivating, and compelling quality. This word conveys the idea that tattoos draw people in, unite diverse cultures, and showcase diversity and creativity, reminding us of their timeless appeal and their ability to bring people together through their stories and cultural significance.

22. A, C: Answer choices A and C offer the most effective combination of the sentences. The other answer choices result in choppy or unclear combinations of the four sentences.

23. D: If Beryl knew instinctively, it is safe to say that her mother's warning was not stated outright. Therefore, answer choice D is the best option.

24. A: *Surprisingly* indicates the reaction was unexpected. Answers B and D are incorrect because *actually* and *instead* imply an alternative reaction was mentioned. Choice C does not work because the second sentence does not further support the first sentence; it is a new idea.

25. A, C: Choice B is incorrect because the phrase "that students wear to school" is a dangling modifier. It should come after the word it modifies, *outfits*. Also, *not appropriate* should be *inappropriate*. Choice D is incorrect because the word order changes the meaning of the sentence by stating that any outfits are distracting and inappropriate.

26. D: *For example* is the most suitable choice because the sentence describes one use of lighthouses as a symbol rather than their real-world use to guide ships.

27. C: Carbon monoxide Poisoning can cause disorientation and delirium, and it can induce a coma.

> Error: Capitalization
>
> The word "poisoning" does not need to be capitalized because it is not a proper noun.

28. D: The sentence says Westerners believe people who do good things will be rewarded. The phrases for options A, B, and C would not make sense if they replaced *quid pro quo* in the sentence.

29. A: *Transcended* fits the context, as it suggests that esports has gone beyond, or risen above, geographical boundaries, which is in line with the passage's description of its global growth and influence. This word choice conveys that esports has expanded and reached a level that surpasses geographic limitations, allowing opportunities for recognition and financial success across the world.

30. B: The context of the sentence suggests that the trauma of surviving the plane crash left long-term memories that haunted Johanna for many years. As a result, *permanent* is the best synonym for *indelible*. The other options make little sense in the context of the sentence.

31. C: *Moreover* is the appropriate choice because it signals that additional information or a related point is about to be presented. In this case, it introduces the fact that geckos are known for their agility and proficiency as hunters and climbers, expanding on their remarkable climbing abilities discussed in the first sentence.

32. C: Answer choice C summarizes the ideas within the sentence simply and clearly. Choice A phrases the second clause poorly. Choices B and D contain a dangling modifier where the modifier, "without adequate preparation", is separated from the noun it modifies.

33. B: The use of *substantial* in this sentence has a meaning that is closest to *considerable*. The other choices are antonyms of *substantial*.

Mathematics

1. C: The side of the square is equal to the diameter of the circle, or twice the radius, $2r$. The area of the square is this quantity squared, or $4r^2$. The area of the circle is πr^2. Subtracting the area of the circle from the area of the square gives the difference between the two areas.

$$4r^2 - \pi r^2$$

A common r^2 can be factored out of each term to get the expression $r^2(4 - \pi)$.

2. B, C: The median of a set of numbers is one for which the set contains an equal number of greater and lesser values. Besides *Z*, there are 8 numbers in the set, so that 4 must be greater and 4 lesser than *Z*. The 4 smallest values are 5, 7, 9, and 12. The 4 largest are 16, 18, 23, and 44. So *Z* must fall between 12 and 16.

3. A, B, D: Since the two triangles have all three corresponding pairs of sides and corresponding pairs of angles marked congruent, then the two triangles are congruent. Similar triangles are the same shape but not necessarily the same size; they have congruent angles. All congruent triangles are similar triangles, so the two triangles are similar as well as congruent. Equilateral triangles are triangles that have sides with all the same measure within the same triangle, not in relation to another triangle. These triangles are not equilateral but scalene: all three sides are different lengths.

4. C: If \$70, the amount used to buy more lemons, represents 35% of Herbert's earnings, then 1% corresponds to $\frac{\$70}{35} = \$2$. To determine how much profit he takes home, multiply the dollar amount that represents 1%, which is \$2, by 15 to get $\$2 \times 15 = \$30$. Therefore, Herbert takes home \$30 in profit.

5. B: To divide expressions that contain variables, divide pairs of like variables (or constants) that appear in both the numerator and denominator. For this problem, first divide the constants: $12 \div 3$, then divide the a's: $a^2 \div a$. Since $a^2 \div a$ is equivalent to $\frac{a^2}{a^1}$, use the quotient rule, $\frac{x^a}{x^b} = x^{a-b}$, to simplify it. There is no change to b, since the divisor does not contain the variable b:

$$\frac{12a^2b}{3a} = \frac{4a^{2-1}b}{1}$$
$$= 4ab$$

6. C: When ordering negative numbers, it helps to remember that the largest digit has the smallest value. That makes –5 our smallest value, followed by –3, and finally –1. Next comes 0 because 0 separates our negative numbers from our positive numbers. To compare decimals, we can insert zeros at the end of each number so that each value has the same number of digits. Here, that would look like 15.05 and 15.30. When we start comparing digits from left to right, we see that the first place value that differs is the tenths place. Because 3 is greater than 0, we know that 15.3 is greater than 15.05. Finally, our greatest number of the set is 19 because positive 19 is greater than all the other numbers in the set. That makes our ordered list –5, –3, –1, 0, 15.05, 15.3, 19.

7. A: To find Hector's price per gallon we must divide the total amount of money Hector paid, \$22.44, by the number of gallons he received, 12. $\$22.44 \div 12 = \$1.87$, so Hector paid \$1.87 per gallon of gasoline.

8. C: The given equations form a system of linear equations. Since the first equation is already given in terms of x, it will be easier to solve it using the substitution method. Start by substituting $2y - 3$ for x in the second equation.

$$2x + \frac{1}{2}y = 3$$
$$2(2y - 3) + \frac{1}{2}y = 3$$

Next, solve the resulting equation for y. Distribute the 2 and then combine like y-terms in the result.

$$4y - 6 + \frac{1}{2}y = 3$$
$$\frac{9}{2}y - 6 = 3$$

Finally, isolate the variable y by adding 6 to both sides and then dividing both sides by the coefficient of y, which is $\frac{9}{2}$.

$$\frac{9}{2}y = 9$$
$$y = 2$$

Therefore, the value of y is 2.

9. D: Last year's profit was \$30,000, and this year's profit was 15% greater than that. We add 15% by multiplying by 0.15 and adding to the original number, or simply multiplying by 1.15. This gives us a current year profit of $\$30{,}000 \times 1.15 = \$34{,}500$. To project next year's profit of an additional 20%, we multiply this year's profit by 1.2: $\$34{,}500 \times 1.2 = \$41{,}400$. Choice A is incorrect because it is equal to this year's projected profit. Choice B is incorrect because it calculates 20% more than \$30,000, skipping a year. Choice C is incorrect because it calculates 15% profit for both years rather than 15% and then 20%.

10. C, D: The y-intercept of a function is the point where the line passes through the y-axis; it therefore has an x-coordinate of zero. Since the graphed function passes through the y-axis at (0,3), its y-intercept is 3. To determine which function has the same y-intercept, substitute 0 for x into each function and see if the result is 3. Start with the choice A, which is $g(x) = 2x - 4$.

$$2(0) - 4 = 0 - 4 = -4$$

Since the result is not 3, the y-intercept is not 3. Next try choice B, $g(x) = x^2 - 5x + 4$.

$$(0)^2 - 5(0) + 4 = 0 - 0 + 4 = 4$$

The y-intercept of the second function is not 3 either. Try choice C, $g(x) = x^3 + 3x^2 + x + 3$.

$$(0)^3 + 3(0)^2 + (0) + 3 = 0 + 0 + 0 + 3 = 3$$

When each equation is simplified, both C and D have a y-intercept of 3.

11. B: The product is equal to $-14i^2$. Since $i^2 = -1$, the product can be written as $(-14)(-1) = 14$.

12. D: If Nick runs 3 miles in 24 minutes, his rate is $\frac{24}{3} = 8$ minutes per mile. Now we need to find how many miles he can run in 3 hours, or $3 \times 60 = 180$ minutes. We can set up a ratio.

$$\frac{8 \text{ min}}{1 \text{ mi}} = \frac{180 \text{ min}}{x \text{ mi}}$$

Now we cross-multiply.

$$8x = 180(1)$$

Dividing each side by 8 yields $x = 22.5$ miles.

13. D: When a number is raised to a power, you multiply the number by itself the number of times indicated by the power. For example, $2^3 = 2 \times 2 \times 2 = 8$. A number raised to the power of 0 is always equal to 1. So, 6^0 is the smallest number shown. Similarly, for the other numbers:

$$9 = 9;\ 10^1 = 10;\ 4^2 = 4 \times 4 = 16$$

Since $1 < 8 < 9 < 10 < 16$, we can write the order as $6^0, 2^3, 9, 10^1, 4^2$.

14. C: We are looking for a graph with two key pieces of information: rainfall every day except Friday, and an amount of rain on Monday double the rain on Thursday. Answer choice A is incorrect because it shows no rain on Sunday. Answer choice B is incorrect because it shows rain on Friday. Answer choice D is incorrect because the amount of rain on Monday is equal to the amount of rain on Thursday. Only answer choice C is correct because it shows no rain on Friday, 6 inches on Monday, and 3 inches on Thursday.

15. B: The stock first increased by 10%, or \$10 (10% of \$100), to \$110 per share. Then, the price decreased by \$11 (10% of \$110) so that the sell price was $\$110 - \$11 = \$99$ per share, and the sell price for 50 shares was $\$99 \times \$50 = \$4{,}950$.

16. B: Use the FOIL method (First, Outer, Inner, Last) to solve this equation:

$$\begin{aligned}&(3x + 1)(7x + 10)\\ &= (3x)(7x) + (3x)(10) + (1)(7x) + (1)(10)\\ &= 21x^2 + 30x + 7x + 10\end{aligned}$$

Combine like terms to get the answer:

$$21x^2 + 37x + 10$$

17. C: Linear functions can be written in the form $g(x) = ax + b$. To determine the value of a, notice that $g(x)$ increases by 2 every time x increases by 1. For instance, when x goes from 0 to 1, the value of y goes from -3 to -1; and when x goes from 1 to 2, the value of y increases from -1 to 1. Since $g(x)$ increases by 2, the value of a is 2, so the function is $g(x) = 2x + b$. Next calculate the value of b. From the graph, you can tell that $g(0) = -3$. Use this to calculate b:

$$\begin{aligned} g(0) &= -3 \\ 2(0) + b &= -3 \\ 0 + b &= -3 \\ b &= -3 \end{aligned}$$

Thus, the function is $g(x) = 2x - 3$.

18. B: It is necessary to find the area of the floor by multiplying the dimensions together. However, since the dimensions are given in feet and we only know the price of carpeting per square yard, converting the dimensions from feet to yards first is helpful. Since there are 3 feet in a yard, dividing each of the dimensions by 3 will give us the measurements in yards.

$$18 \div 3 = 6$$

$$27 \div 3 = 9$$

So, the floor is 6 yards by 9 yards, which is an area of 54 square yards. Last, we multiply 54 by 14, since each square yard costs $14 and there are 54 square yards.

$$54 \times 14 = 756$$

So, the price of the carpet should be $756.

19. A: To solve, you will need to move the decimal 4 places. Since the scientific notation has a negative power of 10, move the decimal left. If the power of 10 is positive, you need to move it to the right.

$$7.4 \times 10^{-4} = 7.4 \times 0.0001 = 0.00074$$

Therefore, the standard form of the diameter of a red blood cell is 0.00074 centimeters.

20. A: Compute the product using the FOIL method, in which the first terms, the outer terms, the inner terms, and finally the last terms are figured in sequence of multiplication. As a result, $(a + b)(a - b) = a^2 + ba - ab - b^2$. The middle terms, ba and $-ab$, cancel each other out, which leaves $a^2 - b^2$.

21. C: 25% off is equivalent to $\frac{25}{100} \times \$138 = \$34.50$, so the sale price becomes $\$138 - \$34.50 = \$103.50$.

22. D: For each die there is a $\frac{1}{6}$ chance that a 6 will be on top because a die has 6 sides. The probability that a 6 will show for each die is not affected by the results from another roll of the die. In other words, these probabilities are independent. So, the overall probability of throwing 3 sixes is the product of the individual probabilities: $P = \frac{1}{6} \times \frac{1}{6} \times \frac{1}{6} = \frac{1}{6^3} = \frac{1}{216}$. Therefore, the probability that all three dice will land on a 6 is $\frac{1}{216}$.

23. D: Integers consist of all positive and negative whole numbers and the number zero. The product of three integers must be an integer, so you can eliminate any answer choice that is not an integer. The product of two even integers is even. The product of an even and odd integer is even. The only even choice is 24, and we can see that $2 \times 4 \times 3 = 24$.

24. A, C: There are multiple possible types of sequences that could be formed from these numbers. One possibility is to divide each term by 2 to get the next term: 24, 12, 6. Another is to subtract 9 from each term to obtain the next: 24, 15, 6. So the two correct answers are 12 and 15.

25. D: Last year's profit was \$55,000, and this year's was 20% greater than that. We add 20% by multiplying by 0.2 and adding to the original number, or simply multiplying by 1.2. This gives us a current year profit of $55{,}000 \times 1.2 = \$66{,}000$. We multiply by 1.2 again to project next year's profit: $66{,}000 \times 1.2 = \$79{,}200$.

26. B, D: Parallel lines have the same slopes. The slopes of perpendicular lines, on the other, are reciprocals and have the opposite sign. In the figure below, line A has a slope of $-\frac{1}{2}$, and line B has a slope of 2.

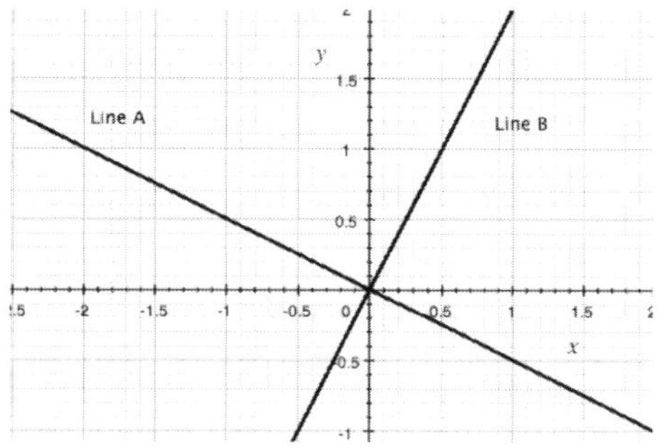

27. C: The formula for the volume of a pyramid is $V = \frac{1}{3}Bh$, where B is the area of the base and h is the height of the pyramid. The base is a square with a length of 756 feet on each side. So, the area of the base is $A = s^2 = (756 \text{ ft})^2 = 571{,}536 \text{ ft}^2$. With a base of $571{,}536 \text{ ft}^2$ and a height of 481 ft, the volume of the pyramid is $V = \frac{1}{3}(571{,}536 \text{ ft}^2)(481 \text{ ft}) \approx 9.16 \times 10^7 \text{ ft}^3$.

28. B: When the wedges are rearranged into the rectangle, half of the wedge arcs form the top length of the rectangle and the other half of the wedge arcs form the bottom length of the rectangle. Since all of the wedge arcs combine to form the entire circumference of the circle, the length of the rectangle is half of the circumference of the circle. The formula for the circumference of a circle with radius r is $C = 2\pi r$. Half of that circumference is $\left(\frac{1}{2}\right) 2\pi r = \pi r$. Answer C is the width of the rectangle. Answer D is the area of the rectangle.

29. B: Add the 14 blue, 6 red, 12 green and 8 purple buttons together to get a total of 40 buttons. If 25 buttons are removed, there are 15 buttons remaining in the bag. The chance of drawing a red button is now $\frac{1}{3}$. So, you divide 15 into thirds to get 5 red buttons remaining in the bag. The original total of red buttons was 6; so $6 - 5 = 1$. One red button was removed, so choice B is correct.

30. D: The function for the cost of a taxi ride is a combination of a constant function for the first mile and a linear function for the rest of the ride. The constant function is $c_1(d) = 4.25$ since the cost of the first mile is \$4.25. For the linear part, subtract 1 from d to exclude the first mile, and then multiply the result by 0.70 since it costs \$0.70 per mile. The result is $c_2(d) = 0.70(d - 1)$. Finally, write the function for the total cost of the taxi ride by adding the two functions.

$$c(d) = 4.25 + 0.70(d - 1)$$

31. B: The events are dependent since the first marble was not replaced. The sample space of the second draw will decrease by 1 because there will be one fewer marble to choose from. The number of possible red marbles for the second draw will also decrease by 1. Thus, the probability may be written as $P(A \text{ and } B) = \frac{8}{15} \times \frac{7}{14} = \frac{8}{15} \times \frac{1}{2} = \frac{8}{30} = \frac{4}{15}$. The probability he draws a red marble, does not replace it, and draws another red marble is $\frac{4}{15}$.

32. D: The figure is a number line. So, the distance from point A to point B will be the difference of $B - A$. This is $5 - (-6) = 5 + 6 = 11$. Also, the distance from point B to point C will be the difference of $C - B$, which is $8 - 5 = 3$. So, the ratio $BC : AB$ will be $3 : 11$.

33. B: The equation is solved below:

$6x + 1 = 4x + 9$	Subtract $4x$ from both sides of the equation
$2x + 1 = 9$	Subtract 1 from both sides of the equation
$2x = 8$	Divide by 2 on both sides of the equation
$x = 4$	

Therefore, the equation has only one solution.

34. D: We can see from the table that 9 people ordered a small serving of lemon yogurt and that a total of 57 orders were placed. So, the probability is 9 out of 57, or $\frac{9}{57}$. We can divide both the numerator and denominator by 3 to reduce the fraction to $\frac{3}{19}$. Choice A is the probability of choosing a small serving given that lemon yogurt was selected (not the overall probability). Choice B is the probability of choosing lemon given that a small serving was selected ($\frac{9}{21}$ reduces to $\frac{3}{7}$). Choice C is the probability of choosing a small serving ($\frac{21}{57}$ reduces to $\frac{7}{19}$).

35. D: The total amount she brought on the trip should be rounded to a reasonable (and compatible) amount; \$2,082 can be reasonably rounded to \$2,100. \$2,100 can easily be divided by 7 days, which gives \$300 per day.

36. C: We first need to find the volume of the container. Since we will need to know the volume in cubic inches to convert to gallons, we convert each measurement from feet to inches by multiplying each by 12. Thus, the length is $8 \times 12 = 96$ inches, the width is $4 \times 12 = 48$ inches, and the height is $3 \times 12 = 36$ inches. The volume of a rectangular prism is $V = lwh$, so we can calculate the container's volume.

$$V = 96 \times 48 \times 36 = 165{,}888 \text{ in}^3$$

Now we need to find the number of gallons needed to fill this container.

$$\left(\frac{165{,}888 \text{ in}^3}{1}\right)\left(\frac{1 \text{ gal}}{231 \text{ in}^3}\right) = 718.13 \text{ gallons}$$

Since the problem is asking for the number of gallon jugs to completely fill the container, we need to round up. Buying 718 jugs will almost completely fill the container, but a little water will be needed from jug 719.

Choice A is incorrect because it only multiplies the volume in feet by 12 to convert to inches, rather than multiplying each dimension. Choice B is incorrect because it rounds down instead of up. Choice D is incorrect because it is the volume in cubic inches rather than gallons.

37. B: The volume of a pyramid may be calculated using the formula $V = \frac{1}{3}Bh$, where B represents the area of the base and h represents the height of the pyramid. Since the base is a square, the area of the base is equal to 3.5^2, or 12.25 square inches. Substituting 12.25 for B and 6 for h gives $V = \frac{1}{3}(12.25)(6)$, which simplifies to $V = 24.5$. Therefore, the bottle can hold 24.5 cubic inches of lotion.

38. A: We first find the mean, or average, of the lab grades by adding them and dividing by the number of grades.

$$\frac{84 + 86 + 98 + 90 + 97 + 85 + 90}{7} = \frac{630}{7} = 90$$

Then we find the median by arranging the grades in increasing order and finding the middle value: 84, 85, 86, 90, 90, 97, 98. The middle number is 90. So, the difference of the mean and median is $90 - 90 = 0$.

39. A: This equation is a linear relationship that has a slope of 3.60 and passes through the origin. The table shows that for each hour of rental, the cost increases by $3.60. This matches with the slope of the equation. Of course, if the bicycle is not rented at all (0 hours), there will be no charge ($0). If plotted on the Cartesian plane, the line would have a y-intercept of 0. The first choice is the only one that meets these requirements.

40. A, C: The zeroes of a function are the domain values where the function equals 0. So, in this case, the zeroes are the values of x for which $f(x) = 0$. To find the zeroes of the function, set up an equation and then solve it for x. The first step is to factor the quadratic expression.

$$f(x) = 0$$
$$x^2 + 5x - 24 = 0$$
$$(x + 8)(x - 3) = 0$$

When the coefficient of x^2 is 1, factor the quadratic into a product of binomials $(x + a)(x + b)$, where a and b are chosen so their product is the constant term in the quadratic (including sign), and their sum is the coefficient of the linear term in the quadratic (the x-term). Then use the zero-product rule to solve the result. Using the factorization of f, write two equations and solve them both for x.

$$x + 8 = 0 \quad \text{or} \quad x - 3 = 0$$
$$x = -8 \qquad\qquad x = 3$$

TABE Practice Test #3

To take this additional TABE practice test, visit our online resources page:
mometrix.com/resources719/tabe1314

How to Overcome Test Anxiety

Just the thought of taking a test is enough to make most people a little nervous. A test is an important event that can have a long-term impact on your future, so it's important to take it seriously and it's natural to feel anxious about performing well. But just because anxiety is normal, that doesn't mean that it's helpful in test taking, or that you should simply accept it as part of your life. Anxiety can have a variety of effects. These effects can be mild, like making you feel slightly nervous, or severe, like blocking your ability to focus or remember even a simple detail.

If you experience test anxiety—whether severe or mild—it's important to know how to beat it. To discover this, first you need to understand what causes test anxiety.

Causes of Test Anxiety

While we often think of anxiety as an uncontrollable emotional state, it can actually be caused by simple, practical things. One of the most common causes of test anxiety is that a person does not feel adequately prepared for their test. This feeling can be the result of many different issues such as poor study habits or lack of organization, but the most common culprit is time management. Starting to study too late, failing to organize your study time to cover all of the material, or being distracted while you study will mean that you're not well prepared for the test. This may lead to cramming the night before, which will cause you to be physically and mentally exhausted for the test. Poor time management also contributes to feelings of stress, fear, and hopelessness as you realize you are not well prepared but don't know what to do about it.

Other times, test anxiety is not related to your preparation for the test but comes from unresolved fear. This may be a past failure on a test, or poor performance on tests in general. It may come from comparing yourself to others who seem to be performing better or from the stress of living up to expectations. Anxiety may be driven by fears of the future—how failure on this test would affect your educational and career goals. These fears are often completely irrational, but they can still negatively impact your test performance.

Elements of Test Anxiety

As mentioned earlier, test anxiety is considered to be an emotional state, but it has physical and mental components as well. Sometimes you may not even realize that you are suffering from test anxiety until you notice the physical symptoms. These can include trembling hands, rapid heartbeat, sweating, nausea, and tense muscles. Extreme anxiety may lead to fainting or vomiting. Obviously, any of these symptoms can have a negative impact on testing. It is important to recognize them as soon as they begin to occur so that you can address the problem before it damages your performance.

The mental components of test anxiety include trouble focusing and inability to remember learned information. During a test, your mind is on high alert, which can help you recall information and stay focused for an extended period of time. However, anxiety interferes with your mind's natural processes, causing you to blank out, even on the questions you know well. The strain of testing during anxiety makes it difficult to stay focused, especially on a test that may take several hours. Extreme anxiety can take a huge mental toll, making it difficult not only to recall test information but even to understand the test questions or pull your thoughts together.

Effects of Test Anxiety

Test anxiety is like a disease—if left untreated, it will get progressively worse. Anxiety leads to poor performance, and this reinforces the feelings of fear and failure, which in turn lead to poor performances on subsequent tests. It can grow from a mild nervousness to a crippling condition. If allowed to progress, test anxiety can have a big impact on your schooling, and consequently on your future.

Test anxiety can spread to other parts of your life. Anxiety on tests can become anxiety in any stressful situation, and blanking on a test can turn into panicking in a job situation. But fortunately, you don't have to let anxiety rule your testing and determine your grades. There are a number of relatively simple steps you can take to move past anxiety and function normally on a test and in the rest of life.

Physical Steps for Beating Test Anxiety

While test anxiety is a serious problem, the good news is that it can be overcome. It doesn't have to control your ability to think and remember information. While it may take time, you can begin taking steps today to beat anxiety.

Just as your first hint that you may be struggling with anxiety comes from the physical symptoms, the first step to treating it is also physical. Rest is crucial for having a clear, strong mind. If you are tired, it is much easier to give in to anxiety. But if you establish good sleep habits, your body and mind will be ready to perform optimally, without the strain of exhaustion. Additionally, sleeping well helps you to retain information better, so you're more likely to recall the answers when you see the test questions.

Getting good sleep means more than going to bed on time. It's important to allow your brain time to relax. Take study breaks from time to time so it doesn't get overworked, and don't study right before bed. Take time to rest your mind before trying to rest your body, or you may find it difficult to fall asleep.

Along with sleep, other aspects of physical health are important in preparing for a test. Good nutrition is vital for good brain function. Sugary foods and drinks may give a burst of energy but this burst is followed by a crash, both physically and emotionally. Instead, fuel your body with protein and vitamin-rich foods.

Also, drink plenty of water. Dehydration can lead to headaches and exhaustion, especially if your brain is already under stress from the rigors of the test. Particularly if your test is a long one, drink water during the breaks. And if possible, take an energy-boosting snack to eat between sections.

Along with sleep and diet, a third important part of physical health is exercise. Maintaining a steady workout schedule is helpful, but even taking 5-minute study breaks to walk can help get your blood pumping faster and clear your head. Exercise also releases endorphins, which contribute to a positive feeling and can help combat test anxiety.

When you nurture your physical health, you are also contributing to your mental health. If your body is healthy, your mind is much more likely to be healthy as well. So take time to rest, nourish your body with healthy food and water, and get moving as much as possible. Taking these physical steps will make you stronger and more able to take the mental steps necessary to overcome test anxiety.

Mental Steps for Beating Test Anxiety

Working on the mental side of test anxiety can be more challenging, but as with the physical side, there are clear steps you can take to overcome it. As mentioned earlier, test anxiety often stems from lack of preparation, so the obvious solution is to prepare for the test. Effective studying may be the most important weapon you have for beating test anxiety, but you can and should employ several other mental tools to combat fear.

First, boost your confidence by reminding yourself of past success—tests or projects that you aced. If you're putting as much effort into preparing for this test as you did for those, there's no reason you should expect to fail here. Work hard to prepare; then trust your preparation.

Second, surround yourself with encouraging people. It can be helpful to find a study group, but be sure that the people you're around will encourage a positive attitude. If you spend time with others who are anxious or cynical, this will only contribute to your own anxiety. Look for others who are motivated to study hard from a desire to succeed, not from a fear of failure.

Third, reward yourself. A test is physically and mentally tiring, even without anxiety, and it can be helpful to have something to look forward to. Plan an activity following the test, regardless of the outcome, such as going to a movie or getting ice cream.

When you are taking the test, if you find yourself beginning to feel anxious, remind yourself that you know the material. Visualize successfully completing the test. Then take a few deep, relaxing breaths and return to it. Work through the questions carefully but with confidence, knowing that you are capable of succeeding.

Developing a healthy mental approach to test taking will also aid in other areas of life. Test anxiety affects more than just the actual test—it can be damaging to your mental health and even contribute to depression. It's important to beat test anxiety before it becomes a problem for more than testing.

Study Strategy

Being prepared for the test is necessary to combat anxiety, but what does being prepared look like? You may study for hours on end and still not feel prepared. What you need is a strategy for test prep. The next few pages outline our recommended steps to help you plan out and conquer the challenge of preparation.

Step 1: Scope Out the Test

Learn everything you can about the format (multiple choice, essay, etc.) and what will be on the test. Gather any study materials, course outlines, or sample exams that may be available. Not only will this help you to prepare, but knowing what to expect can help to alleviate test anxiety.

Step 2: Map Out the Material

Look through the textbook or study guide and make note of how many chapters or sections it has. Then divide these over the time you have. For example, if a book has 15 chapters and you have five days to study, you need to cover three chapters each day. Even better, if you have the time, leave an extra day at the end for overall review after you have gone through the material in depth.

If time is limited, you may need to prioritize the material. Look through it and make note of which sections you think you already have a good grasp on, and which need review. While you are studying, skim quickly through the familiar sections and take more time on the challenging parts. Write out your plan so you don't get lost as you go. Having a written plan also helps you feel more in control of the study, so anxiety is less likely to arise from feeling overwhelmed at the amount to cover.

Step 3: Gather Your Tools

Decide what study method works best for you. Do you prefer to highlight in the book as you study and then go back over the highlighted portions? Or do you type out notes of the important information? Or is it helpful to make flashcards that you can carry with you? Assemble the pens, index cards, highlighters, post-it notes, and any other materials you may need so you won't be distracted by getting up to find things while you study.

If you're having a hard time retaining the information or organizing your notes, experiment with different methods. For example, try color-coding by subject with colored pens, highlighters, or post-it notes. If you learn better by hearing, try recording yourself reading your notes so you can listen while in the car, working out, or simply sitting at your desk. Ask a friend to quiz you from your flashcards, or try teaching someone the material to solidify it in your mind.

Step 4: Create Your Environment

It's important to avoid distractions while you study. This includes both the obvious distractions like visitors and the subtle distractions like an uncomfortable chair (or a too-comfortable couch that makes you want to fall asleep). Set up the best study environment possible: good lighting and a comfortable work area. If background music helps you focus, you may want to turn it on, but otherwise keep the room quiet. If you are using a computer to take notes, be sure you don't have any other windows open, especially applications like social media, games, or anything else that could distract you. Silence your phone and turn off notifications. Be sure to keep water close by so you stay hydrated while you study (but avoid unhealthy drinks and snacks).

Also, take into account the best time of day to study. Are you freshest first thing in the morning? Try to set aside some time then to work through the material. Is your mind clearer in the afternoon or evening? Schedule your study session then. Another method is to study at the same time of day that you will take the test, so that your brain gets used to working on the material at that time and will be ready to focus at test time.

Step 5: Study!

Once you have done all the study preparation, it's time to settle into the actual studying. Sit down, take a few moments to settle your mind so you can focus, and begin to follow your study plan. Don't give in to distractions or let yourself procrastinate. This is your time to prepare so you'll be ready to fearlessly approach the test. Make the most of the time and stay focused.

Of course, you don't want to burn out. If you study too long you may find that you're not retaining the information very well. Take regular study breaks. For example, taking five minutes out of every hour to walk briskly, breathing deeply and swinging your arms, can help your mind stay fresh.

As you get to the end of each chapter or section, it's a good idea to do a quick review. Remind yourself of what you learned and work on any difficult parts. When you feel that you've mastered the material, move on to the next part. At the end of your study session, briefly skim through your notes again.

But while review is helpful, cramming last minute is NOT. If at all possible, work ahead so that you won't need to fit all your study into the last day. Cramming overloads your brain with more information than it can process and retain, and your tired mind may struggle to recall even previously learned information when it is overwhelmed with last-minute study. Also, the urgent nature of cramming and the stress placed on your brain contribute to anxiety. You'll be more likely to go to the test feeling unprepared and having trouble thinking clearly.

So don't cram, and don't stay up late before the test, even just to review your notes at a leisurely pace. Your brain needs rest more than it needs to go over the information again. In fact, plan to finish your studies by noon or early afternoon the day before the test. Give your brain the rest of the day to relax or focus on other things, and get a good night's sleep. Then you will be fresh for the test and better able to recall what you've studied.

STEP 6: TAKE A PRACTICE TEST

Many courses offer sample tests, either online or in the study materials. This is an excellent resource to check whether you have mastered the material, as well as to prepare for the test format and environment.

Check the test format ahead of time: the number of questions, the type (multiple choice, free response, etc.), and the time limit. Then create a plan for working through them. For example, if you have 30 minutes to take a 60-question test, your limit is 30 seconds per question. Spend less time on the questions you know well so that you can take more time on the difficult ones.

If you have time to take several practice tests, take the first one open book, with no time limit. Work through the questions at your own pace and make sure you fully understand them. Gradually work up to taking a test under test conditions: sit at a desk with all study materials put away and set a timer. Pace yourself to make sure you finish the test with time to spare and go back to check your answers if you have time.

After each test, check your answers. On the questions you missed, be sure you understand why you missed them. Did you misread the question (tests can use tricky wording)? Did you forget the information? Or was it something you hadn't learned? Go back and study any shaky areas that the practice tests reveal.

Taking these tests not only helps with your grade, but also aids in combating test anxiety. If you're already used to the test conditions, you're less likely to worry about it, and working through tests until you're scoring well gives you a confidence boost. Go through the practice tests until you feel comfortable, and then you can go into the test knowing that you're ready for it.

Test Tips

On test day, you should be confident, knowing that you've prepared well and are ready to answer the questions. But aside from preparation, there are several test day strategies you can employ to maximize your performance.

First, as stated before, get a good night's sleep the night before the test (and for several nights before that, if possible). Go into the test with a fresh, alert mind rather than staying up late to study.

Try not to change too much about your normal routine on the day of the test. It's important to eat a nutritious breakfast, but if you normally don't eat breakfast at all, consider eating just a protein bar. If you're a coffee drinker, go ahead and have your normal coffee. Just make sure you time it so that the caffeine doesn't wear off right in the middle of your test. Avoid sugary beverages, and drink enough water to stay hydrated but not so much that you need a restroom break 10 minutes into the test. If your test isn't first thing in the morning, consider going for a walk or doing a light workout before the test to get your blood flowing.

Allow yourself enough time to get ready, and leave for the test with plenty of time to spare so you won't have the anxiety of scrambling to arrive in time. Another reason to be early is to select a good seat. It's helpful to sit away from doors and windows, which can be distracting. Find a good seat, get out your supplies, and settle your mind before the test begins.

When the test begins, start by going over the instructions carefully, even if you already know what to expect. Make sure you avoid any careless mistakes by following the directions.

Then begin working through the questions, pacing yourself as you've practiced. If you're not sure on an answer, don't spend too much time on it, and don't let it shake your confidence. Either skip it and come back later, or eliminate as many wrong answers as possible and guess among the remaining ones. Don't dwell on these questions as you continue—put them out of your mind and focus on what lies ahead.

Be sure to read all of the answer choices, even if you're sure the first one is the right answer. Sometimes you'll find a better one if you keep reading. But don't second-guess yourself if you do immediately know the answer. Your gut instinct is usually right. Don't let test anxiety rob you of the information you know.

If you have time at the end of the test (and if the test format allows), go back and review your answers. Be cautious about changing any, since your first instinct tends to be correct, but make sure you didn't misread any of the questions or accidentally mark the wrong answer choice. Look over any you skipped and make an educated guess.

At the end, leave the test feeling confident. You've done your best, so don't waste time worrying about your performance or wishing you could change anything. Instead, celebrate the successful completion of this test. And finally, use this test to learn how to deal with anxiety even better next time.

Review Video: Test Anxiety
Visit mometrix.com/academy and enter code: 100340

Important Qualification

Not all anxiety is created equal. If your test anxiety is causing major issues in your life beyond the classroom or testing center, or if you are experiencing troubling physical symptoms related to your anxiety, it may be a sign of a serious physiological or psychological condition. If this sounds like your situation, we strongly encourage you to seek professional help.

Online Resources

Due to our efforts to try to keep this book to a manageable length, we've created a link that will give you access to all of your online resources:

mometrix.com/resources719/tabe1314

It's Your Moment, Let's Celebrate It!

Share your story @mometrixtestpreparation